A
REVOLUTION
IN
ARMS

A
REVOLUTION
IN
ARMS

A HISTORY OF THE
FIRST REPEATING RIFLES

Joseph G. Bilby

WESTHOLME
Yardley

First Westholme Paperback 2015

Copyright © 2006 Joseph G. Bilby

Original photographs by John Hubbard © 2006 Westholme Publishing

Westholme Publishing, LLC
904 Edgewood Road
Yardley, Pennsylvania 19067
Visit our Web site at www.westholmepublishing.com

ISBN: 978-1-59416-206-0
Also available as an eBook.

Printed in the United States of America.

This book is dedicated, with love, to my wife, Patricia, without whose encouragement, support, suggestions, proof reading and, most of all, tolerance and forbearance, it would not have been possible.

Contents

PREFACE

HISTORIANS HAVE OFTEN CALLED THE AMERICAN CIVIL WAR THE "first modern war," pointing to the use of observation balloons, the telegraph, trains, land mines, ironclad warships, rifled small arms, prototype machine guns, and other innovations. More recent scholarship has, however, challenged some of these "firsts." Although the first combat honors for ironclad naval warfare still go to the 1862 clash between the *Monitor* and *Virginia*, by 1860 Britain, France, and Russia all had more sophisticated armor plated ships in service. Other American Civil War "firsts," including rifled artillery, had already been tested or used in combat in Europe. No one can deny, however, that the Civil War witnessed the introduction of the first repeating rifles firing self-contained metallic cartridges—an indisputable American first. The introduction of rapid fire repeating small arms would create new and more deadly tactical possibilities, and no other innovation of the turbulent 1860s would have a greater effect on the future of combat. This book details the story of how that "first" came to be.

ONE

Past is Prologue

IN LATE MAY 1864, LIEUTENANT COLONEL THOMAS W. HYDE, A STAFF officer in the Army of the Potomac's VI Army Corps, found himself leading a catch-all command of a few hundred cavalrymen, most of them armed with repeating carbines. While on a foraging expedition, Hyde's force was shot at by a small enemy patrol.

As the Yankees responded with a fusillade of fire, the Rebels scooted away. Hyde's attempts to stop the shooting were futile, and the Yanks didn't cease firing until they emptied their guns. The din startled Major General Horatio Wright, who, believing Hyde's men were seriously engaged, rushed an infantry brigade to their support. When it was over, Lieutenant Colonel Hyde found two dead enemy horses, and ruefully concluded that he had had "quite a lesson in the improper use of rapid-firing arms."[1]

What Hyde learned, by its absence, was the importance of discipline, fire control, and proper application of force in modern combat. He was dealing with the dawn of a new age in warfare, standing at the beginning of a long road, but at the end of an even longer one, a road that stretched backward over the ages.

At the outset there was man the scavenger, who didn't have much to work with. He had neither the strength nor the speed nor the teeth to bring down game. What he had, however, was manual dexterity and the capacity to think. So man thought. And then he moved up the food chain from scavenger to sometime predator by picking up a rock and ambushing passing herbivores and birds. Although he could obtain dinner by smacking a beast on the head, man's work exposed him to kicking and pecking and goring, and grievous wounds and broken bones leading to an early death. So he thought some more. And then it may have dawned on him: "I can throw this thing!"

Some say man is a thinking animal, others that he is a risible animal, and that these attributes make him human. One could just as easily posit that man is a throwing animal—or at least a projectile-oriented animal. Most sports involve chucking one thing or another accurately over varying distances—and man, intentionally or not, settled on this ability as the best of all possible physical characteristics defining him as a food gatherer, or defender or, eventually, sportsman. As one historian of the subject has pointed out, "The best stone for all purposes is about the size of a cricket-ball, or baseball, perhaps a bit heavier." No doubt early men engaged in stone throwing.[2]

Stone throwing as a method of primitive warfare has endured over the ages, as evidenced by the reported stoning skill of Swiss soldiers at the Battle of Kappel during a religious civil war in 1531. The short-range stone throwing accuracy and speed of Australian aborigines were compared to that of "a magazine rifle" by nineteenth-century observers. The French and British allegedly stoned each other in Egypt in 1801, and Confederate infantrymen defending an unfinished railroad cut at Second Manassas in 1862 ran out of ammunition and effectively used stones in a last-ditch defense.[3]

An early missile weapon of note was the stone-throwing sling, which, according to some sources, dates to 30,000 B.C. in its most primitive form, a notched stag antler. This projector was soon replaced by a more efficient model, with two pieces of cord attached to either side of a woven or leather pocket. The longer the sling's cords, the longer its potential range.[4]

We have ancient written testimony regarding the use of slingers in military action, the most famous, of course, the oft-told tale of David and Goliath. The sling, which requires constant practice from childhood in order for most people to achieve even a modicum of accuracy in its use, is most commonly associated with ancient people from rocky, mountainous areas, like the Israelites and the Greeks. The weapon was also used extensively by native Americans in the Andes, and examples have been found in Indian burials in the southwestern United States. In more recent years the classic sling, along with the more modern "slingshot" or "catapult," saw use in the ranks of Palestinian *Intifada* fighters. Although slingers can achieve a high degree of short-range accuracy, it is likely that the biblical reference to seven hundred sling experts who "could hit a single hair" is a tad hyperbolic.[5]

Although shepherds like David no doubt picked up rounded river stones of the right shape and heft as projectiles, Bronze Age military stone sling ammunition was tooled into spherical shape, ranging from golf to tennis ball size. The sling continued in use as a weapon into the classical Greek and Roman eras, usually with military issue cast-lead ammunition, often inscribed with unit identifications or insults to the enemy.[6]

Slingers were traditionally recruited from certain, presumably sling-oriented, ethnic groups and/or geographical areas, including the Israelite tribe of Benjamin or the natives of the Balearic Islands, but it is not clear that such precision as that demonstrated by David was necessary for a military slinger. Although accuracy is often possible in the hands of an expert at short range, the sling appears to have been used as an "area fire" weapon at ranges up to several hundred yards. A sling stone barrage was often used either to soften an enemy mass formation up for a cavalry or heavy infantry assault or, conversely, to cover a retreat.

There were other stutter-steps along the way to perfecting muscle-powered projectile distance and accuracy. Then, as now, stone-tossing ability, whether by hand or mechanically assisted, must have varied from individual to individual. For many, no doubt, fire-hardened wooden sticks, which scholars of the subject believe came along after stone throwing but before the perfected sling, provided a somewhat safe standoff hunting capability. When eventually mated with a sharpened stone for a point, they also proved a more effective killing machine—and self-defense device when man himself was on the menu. Spear-length, however, provided minimal safety range when poking at a creature the size and temperament of a wooly mammoth, and depended on close ambush of a wary animal, a task easier contemplated than performed. Thrown primitive spears often did not have the energy to penetrate thick animal skin.

There had to be a better way, and man, thinking again, would find it eventually. There were other detours, however. One example of a transitional projectile is the throwing stick, in its various configurations. Some of these devices were merely stones affixed to sticks, the stick serving as a handle to gain leverage and distance. In its pure form, this projectile weapon survived into the twentieth century in more out of the way spots in the world. A tribute to the continuing efficiency of such a seemingly crude device is that its basic principle was used in the famous German "potato masher" hand grenade of World Wars I and II.[7]

Perhaps the best known throwing-stick-style projectile is the boomerang. Although similar weapons may have been used in ancient India and Egypt, this angled flat stick with a sharpened edge is, along with its name, an Australian aborigine invention. Contrary to popular belief, most boomerangs are not designed to return to their thrower, but to spin through the air and accurately take down small to medium game. A smaller, lighter version, designed for bird hunting, can be made to return by a skillful operator, providing that it misses its target. Modern returning boomerangs are specifically designed for sport throwing, not hunting, and vary in aerodynamic design from the original object.[8]

Primitive man, no doubt, threw spears a short distance at his quarry with increased success once he hafted a razor-sharp chipped flint point to the wooden shaft, and the modern sport of javelin throwing recalls those efforts. The Masai ceremonial spear is the most prominent example of such a weapon still extant. The double-edged three-foot steel blade of the Masai spear, or the Zulu *Assegai*, both of which can be used for stabbing as well as throwing, is, however, a far more effective weapon than anything Stone Age hunters could hope to own.

The most significant advance in the development of true projectile weapons was the *atlatl*, a launching platform that dramatically increased projectile range, penetration and accuracy. The name is a relatively modern one derived from the Aztec term for a device used by native Americans to effectively hurl short flint bladed spears at sixteenth-century Spanish conquistadors, who rendered it from the unpronounceable to European tongues *xuiatlati*.[9]

The atlatl, a very basic energy storage and release tool, is a grooved stick, piece of bone, or antler between two and three feet long. It is loaded by resting a spear-like projectile called a dart, feathered at the rear for stability, in the groove and engaging it in a nub fitted to the rear of the device. When whipped forward in a rapid pitching motion to discharge its dart, the atlatl dramatically increases the leverage of the human throwing arm, as well as acting on the harmonics of the dart itself to add velocity and range. Some more sophisticated versions of this spear thrower were equipped with retention thongs to wrap around a thrower's thumb as well as adjustable stone stabilizing weights. When "fired," the atlatl can be rapidly "reloaded" with a spare dart.

Atlatls came in various sizes, for hunting various fish and game as well as, in the case of the Aztecs for sure and other groups by implication, use in war. It is impossible to determine exactly when this projectile heaving device came into man's armory, but archeologists claim evidence of its use 25,000 years ago in North Africa and at least 17,000 years ago in Europe. It certainly crossed over into North America from Siberia with the first migrations to the New World and was also used in Australia, where it was known as the woomera.[10]

Modern tests have revealed that atlatls are capable of throwing darts one hundred yards, although it seems likely they were probably used as killing devices in the twenty- to thirty-yard range. With groups of hunters showering an animal or small herd with razor sharp flint pointed darts at relatively close range, success ratios were no doubt fairly good.

"All previous projectile weapons pale as human muscle energy storage and transfer devices before the bow. The atlatl might have placed man at the pinnacle of the food chain, but the bow assured his position atop it. The archaeological discovery of what appear to be arrowheads in North Africa suggest that the bow and its arrow projectile may well have been an integral part of man's hunting and defensive armament for at least 30,000 and as much as 50,000 years. These projectile points, however, may have been used in a type of atlatl dart.[11]

Although slingers from the Balearic Islands were prized as mercenaries in the ancient world, and thrown javelins like the Roman *pilum* were important infantry arms on occasion, the bow was the ultimate long-range projectile military arm of the pre-gunpowder days, and was used on every continent except Australia. In laminated composite form it made the nomadic "horse archer" feared from the Great Wall of China to the plains of Eastern Europe. Laminated bows could be shorter and still retain the power of a longer "self" bow, an important feature to mounted warriors. Lamination was achieved by using layers of bone, sinew, and wood glued together. Although there were variations in the genre, Turkish recurved bows have been noted at pull strengths up to 160 pounds. One expert notes that the Oriental "recurved composite bow had an extraordinary strong strength-length ratio," but this did not necessarily mean it was capable of long range fire. One such bow analyzed by Major B. H. Pope, brother of Dr. Saxton Pope (the "father" of modern sport hunting archery), had a "cast" of only a hundred yards. Some Turkish bows, however, made by world-class bowyers at the top of their game, have been reported as being capable of casting an arrow almost a thousand yards.[12]

The simple wooden bow, also known as a "self" bow, evolved where there was suitable wood to construct it—and people didn't ride horses to war. The closest analysis we have of a primitive "self" bow and its arrows is of the one constructed of juniper wood by Ishi, the last survivor of the California Yana Indians, in 1911. Ishi, who had lived his whole life until that time isolated from white settlers, made a bow and arrows that were intensively studied by Dr. Saxton Pope. Another Native American, Seminole Charlie Snow, was a very accurate instinctive game and target archer at ranges up to 50 yards. Beyond that, Charlie's accuracy was poor, and he missed a puma with several shots at 60 yards. Plain wooden bows, some, like Ishi's, backed with sinew, endured into the modern era in many areas of the world.[13]

Another type of wooden bow, more powerful than Ishi's, survived among the Liangulu people of Kenya into the 1960s. Liangulu bowmen were enthusiastic and remarkably successful elephant poachers until disarmed by Kenyan authorities. Although the Liangulu killed elephants with poisoned arrowheads, their bows had to be powerful to enable an arrow to penetrate thick pachyderm skin. Surviving examples average over 100 pounds of draw weight, and one example is known with a 131-pound draw weight.[14]

Liangulu bow ballistics are almost identical to those of the legendary English longbow, a key weapon in late Middle Ages battles like Crecy and Agincourt and arm of the legendary Robin Hood. The origins of the longbow are disputed, but similar bows may have existed among German tribesmen in the third century A.D. as well as Anglo-Saxon invaders of Britain and Norsemen raiding the British Isles six hundred years later.[15]

Although Norman archery is often credited with contributing to William the Conqueror's victory at Hastings in 1066, the bows employed by his archers were not classic longbows. Though self bows, they were shorter and much less powerful than their successors. True longbow development in Britain has generally been credited to the Welsh, who defended their mountain fastnesses against both Anglo-Saxon and Norman penetration for generations before gradually succumbing to English domination in the centuries following the conquest.[16]

By the thirteenth century, archers, many of them Welsh, were a standard component of English armies. The true origins of the longbow, which is distinguished by being constructed of yew with sapwood on the back and heartwood on the front providing a natural flex, still remain murky, however, as similar examples have been found in Germanic burial sites dating to the eighth century. Some scholars now believe the longbow came to British shores in the hands of Saxon invaders.[17]

Whatever its origins, the long bow became perhaps the most renowned bow of all time. Its fearsome reputation originated in the reign of Edward I, the infamous "Longshanks," who preferred the revealing nickname "Hammer of the Scots." Edward's bowmen hammered William Wallace's Scots at Falkirk in 1298. The archers shot the dense Scottish formations of spearmen, called schilltrons, to pieces, beginning the longbow era.

In the hands of a well-trained man, the longbow was an accurate and powerful short-range weapon. As a long-range instrument, up to and beyond 200 yards, it was at its best as an area fire war machine against a relatively immobile force packed into a small area. Such situations usually, but not always, occurred when archers were part of a defensive force, as at the most famous English victories in France, Crecy, Poitiers, and Agincourt, or could maneuver against a static defensive force, such as Wallace's at Falkirk.

The fearsome success of the longbow in fourteenth- and fifteenth-century combat was largely due to the happy coincidence of advanced English tactical thought (brought on, some might argue, by desperation) coupled with the abysmal tactical skills displayed by their French opponents. At 200 to 300 yards, longbow archers rained successive volleys of "flight" arrows fired at a high trajectory on a deep, slow moving, often mud-bound enemy formation, injuring and killing lightly armored horses and foot soldiers. At close range, the enemy was showered with heavier "sheaf" arrows, which provided better penetration, especially against chain mail armor. Both techniques were often used in the same battle, perhaps most notably at Agincourt. After enemy troops were driven to distraction by blizzards of close-range arrows, men at arms, including archers armed with mallets and daggers, waded in to finish them off.[18]

French defeats in the Hundred Years War were largely a result of the fact that the French allowed the English to set the parameters for major engagements, hindering French efforts to exercise the numerical advantage they usually possessed. Given a dry battlefield, a long-range crossbow bolt barrage followed by the charge of a well-armored mounted force deployed in a widely spaced series of lines, while other forces maneuvered against the English flanks and rear, would probably have resulted in French victories, regardless of the presence of archers.

By the mid-fifteenth century, French mastery of artillery and new, more open field tactics, coupled with heavier arrow-proof armor, royal patronage of both longbow and crossbow marksmanship and a national patriotic revival inspired by Joan of Arc turned the tide. Beginning at Patay in 1429 and ending at Castillon in 1453, the French counteroffensive drove both English knights and English archers from their country.[19]

With the loss of France, the role of the longbow archer as the supreme arbiter of battle began to ebb. Although bowmen were still a significant segment of the rival death-dealing machines in the internecine Wars of the Roses, hints of change were in the air. In 1485, at Bosworth Field, the last battle in that series of family conflicts for the crown of England, the victor, Henry Tudor employed 2,000 French mercenaries with *handgonnes,* or hand-held firearms.[20]

The victory song of the longbow last echoed in 1513, ending as it began, against the Scots, when an invading Scottish force was decisively defeated by an English army including archers—and artillery—at Flodden. Although the English won the battle, archery shared the decisive role with the big guns, as heavy armor worn by some of the Scots proved a successful defense against English arrows.[21]

The early French failure to effectively use their own archers, mostly armed with the crossbow, was largely a function of class arrogance, not the technical attributes of the weapon. The crossbow, a simple wooden bow turned sideways and mounted on the front of a wooden stock, was easier to master and more powerful than standard self-bows. It fired bolts, which were thicker and heavier than the self-bow's arrow. The origins of the crossbow appear to lie in China, where fairly sophisticated versions of the weapon, including a repeating variety with a magazine of bolts attached, were in use by the second century A.D., and there are references to its use by the Romans a century later.[22]

Some sources claim that crossbows were used, along with self-bows, by William the Conqueror's expeditionary force in 1066. They were certainly in widespread use at the close of that century during the First Crusade. The early crossbow was manually cocked by pulling the bowstring back with both hands until it engaged a catch. To release the catch and fire the weapon, the crossbow archer pulled a trigger like device on the underside of his bow. As the centuries progressed, the simple crossbow became more technologically advanced and powerful. Manual cocking gave way to a pulley device cocking aid which was, in its turn, superseded in the early fourteenth century by a "goat's foot" cocking lever. The latter years of the fourteenth century saw the introduction of a very powerful steel crossbow, which was cocked by a geared wheel known as a "crannikin." Later crossbows had excellent penetration power, but were slow to load.[23]

Although it had a significantly slower rate of fire than the longbow, the crossbow's power, accuracy, flat trajectory and shorter user training period made it a popular military weapon by the end of the fifteenth century. Longbows could be and were used for hunting, but the crossbow seems to have been the preferred arm for the chase, even in Britain, home of the long-bow. Finnish hunters used a light crossbow for squirrel hunting as late as the turn of the nineteenth century.

The king's deer fell prey to stealthy hunters equipped with both longbows and crossbows, but due to the European tradition of royal game ownership, such use by common folk, although apparently fairly common, was decidedly illegal and severely punished, provided the poachers could be caught. Most privately owned projectile tossing sporting arms were, officially at least, legally limited to target practice.[24]

Target shooting with crossbows became a favorite pastime of German burghers, countering the jousting tournaments of the knightly class. In the early fourteenth century, archery societies were founded in a number of different German cities that were conducting yearly shooting festivals. By 1387, a great archery tournament was held in Magdeburg, with shooters from "Brunswick, Halberstadt, Quedlinburg, Aschersleben, Blackenberg, Kalbe, Salza and Halle" in attendance. These tournaments reached their height of popularity around 1500 and declined thereafter, in the turmoil of the Reformation and subsequent bitter internecine Christian religious wars.[25]

Because of its inherent military value, archery practice was often widely encouraged by the authorities. The German target shooting tournaments were promoted in the Hapsburg Empire as a preparedness measure against the rising Ottoman Turkish tide in the Balkans. In 1369, King Charles V of France, locked in the Hundred Years War with the English, ordered his subjects to "grow skillful in the arts of bow and crossbow in pleasant sites and appropriate places in the provinces," and recommended "rewards be given to the best shots."[26]

Due to the importance of the longbow to the English military, practice with that weapon was not only encouraged, but also mandated. In 1470, Edward IV of England decreed that "every Englishman, or Irishman living in England must have of his own a bow of his own height, made of yew, wyche or hazel, ash, auburne or any other reasonable timber." As in France, local authorities established target ranges, and failure to practice could result in a fine.[27]

Even with the blessing of kings, however, the days of longbow and crossbow as major implements of war and sport were numbered, as gunpowder came into use across Europe. Although its origins are obscure, most scholars agree that the basic formula for the mixture originated in China as a pyrotechnic and made a slow progress westward. A variety of original prescriptions called for the addition of spices, coloring agents, and even, according to one source, human sperm. By the early thirteenth century, at least one version of the recipe, apparently sans sperm, arrived in Western Europe, where British alchemist Roger Bacon recorded it in his cryptic notes.

Popular legend has it that a fourteenth-century German monk, Berthold Schwartz, took Bacon's formula a step further by preparing and exploding it. Although there is no provenance for that story, available evidence suggests that gunpowder was used as a propellant in Moorish Spain in the late thirteenth century. By then, the formula had been standardized into a mixture of 75 percent potassium nitrate, 10 percent sulfur, and 15 percent charcoal. Early on, gunpowder was, quite literally, a powder. By the fifteenth century, however, the ingredients were mixed, wet down with water, or, preferably urine, that of a wine-drinking bishop being the most desirable, molded into cake form, dried, and then ground into a more efficient burning granular configuration. Gunpowder was initially used in cannon manned by mercenary artillerists. Due to their wall demolition ability, these guns proved highly popular with European kings determined to extend their power by subduing recalcitrant vassals and Ottoman Turkish sultans obsessed with capturing Constantinople.[28]

With the increased quality of gunpowder by the early fifteenth century, "handgonnes," which could be carried, loaded, and fired by one or two men, began to appear. A handgonne was simply a small cannon barrel, initially mounted on a wooden pole or "tiller" and later on a piece of lumber vaguely resembling a modern gunstock. Like its wall-battering big brother, the handgonne was loaded from the muzzle with powder and used a lead or stone ball as a projectile. Inserting a red-hot iron wire through its "touch hole" to ignite the charge fired the gun. More sophisticated handgonnes had a concave spot surrounding the "touch hole" to hold a priming charge ignited with a slow-burning, saltpeter-soaked cord called a "match." Bore diameters varied, ranging from .50 (half-inch) caliber to one inch.[29]

Europeans, especially the English, readily gave up the bow for the gun, although an old guard, most notably scholar Roger Ascham in his work *Toxophilus*, resisted the change. Training an archer to shoot effectively with a longbow having a pull strength of well over 100 pounds was a long and arduous process, and successive plague epidemics had eroded the population base from which a pool of archers was recruited and maintained. While it took years to train an effective combat archer, a man could be trained to use a firearm fairly effectively in less than a day. In addition, the bow itself had become a less effective weapon. Since Crecy, where armor proved susceptible to arrow penetration, armor strength had increased to the point where, by the early sixteenth century, it was largely arrow-proof, although vulnerable to firearms projectiles.[30]

Albeit crude by later standards, the handgonne rapidly wrought a revolution in the projectile-tossing business. The short training time necessary for a man to achieve proficiency made gunners particularly attractive to monarchs and generals. Soldiers armed with handgonnes were in the field as early as 1381, when the German town of Augsburg supplied thirty of them to a military expedition. There were shooting contests in Augsburg as early as 1429. By 1476, a Swiss army deployed 6,000 handgonne men. As powder quality improved, the plate armor penetration power of a stiffly loaded handgonne outclassed the strongest bow, effectively ending the days of chivalry.[31]

The handgonne evolved into the matchlock, which came into use in the early sixteenth century. The earliest matchlock was fired by using a simple S-shaped piece of iron called a "serpentine" tacked to the side of the stock, with which the shooter could guide the match cord to the touch hole. Later matchlocks used a true lock or simple plate with a trigger lever connected to a separate serpentine. Pulling the trigger lowered the match into a pan of priming powder affixed to the side of the barrel near the breech. Powder ignition in the pan caused flame to enter a side-drilled touch hole and explode the main charge in the gun's barrel. In its final incarnation, the matchlock lock used a spring which, when released by the trigger, quickly dropped the match into the pan, speeding ignition.[32]

There were two basic styles of matchlock. The large, heavy musket (from the Spanish *mosquete*) required a forked rest to hold the barrel and was used by musketeers in a battle formation including a large number of pikemen, who kept mounted knights from overrunning the gunners while they reloaded. A lighter, handier gun was called an *arquebus*, or *caliver*, and was favored by light troops and explorers. A matchlock gunner carried his powder charges in wooden bottles slung across his breast (often twelve in number and nicknamed "the twelve apostles") on a bandoleer, his finer grained priming powder in a flask, and his round balls in a separate bullet pouch, both also attached to the bandoleer.[33]

The matchlock was simple, inexpensive, and quite effective when compared to the handgonne. It rapidly became a standard weapon in the progressive armies of Europe and Asia. Matchlocks, most of them more sophisticated than the sixteenth-century European models, were still in use in India hundreds of years after they became obsolete in the western world. Early nineteenth-century British East India Company soldiers complained that Indian matchlocks were superior in range and accuracy to their own muskets, carbines, and pistols.[34]

Matchlocks were the first firearms capable of being used in hunting, albeit awkwardly, and several ornate examples intended for use by wealthy sportsmen exist, although these may be target arms. Laws forbidding the ownership and use of firearms (passed to encourage archery) were eased in England in 1542, when guns were allowed to target shooters, and a European drawing of 1566 shows hunters stalking sitting ducks with matchlock muskets, no doubt loaded with small shot. Although English law forbade the issuance of a hunting license to those who could not afford a hundred-pound security deposit, bird poaching with military surplus matchlocks was not unheard of, especially in remote coastal marshes.[35]

The matchlock had obvious disadvantages as a military and sporting arm. Its match had to be continually advanced in the serpentine jaws, or else it would extinguish. If it did go out, it was re-lit with its other end, which also smoldered, creating an obvious hazard around black powder. For safety's sake the whole match was often removed from the gun while reloading, slowing the rate of fire. Musketeers involved in night movements were easy to spot as their matches glowed in the dark, and wind and rainfall spelled disaster to soldier and sportsman alike.[36]

Initially, it appeared the answer to the problems posed by the matchlock might lie in the wheel lock, an invention sometimes attributed to Leonardo Da Vinci, and also to Nuremberg clockmaker Johann Kiefuss. The wheel lock, which made its appearance around 1515, featured a new, elegant ignition system employing a serrated wheel that entered the gun's priming pan from below. The wheel, affixed to the lockplate, was connected to a heavy mainspring by a short chain, which was wound tight by a "spanner" which the shooter usually wore suspended from his neck. Once the wheel-lock's barrel was loaded, pan filled, and wheel wound, a "dog" or hammer, with pyrites in its jaws, was lowered into the pan. Pulling the gun's trigger released the wheel, which spun against the pyrites, creating a shower of sparks, igniting the priming and firing the gun.[37]

As might be suspected, wheel locks, often a production sideline of clockmakers, were expensive guns, and the matchlock musket remained king of the battlefield through the late seventeenth century. The wheel lock did, however, make the first real pistols possible. With no worries of glowing matches, cavalrymen could carry a brace of wheel-lock handguns in pommel holsters, and pistol drill soon became a part of every mounted force's repertoire. Most wheel-lock long guns were made for sporting purposes, and King Henry VIII acquired a collection of German target rifles, which he and his friends used for "shooting at marks."[38]

Although matchlocks were the predominant arms of early European explorers and settlers in America, wheel locks were in use in this country early on. They were expensive compared to matchlocks, but provided state-of-the-art hunting and self-defense capability, a high priority with colonists. The wheel lock never replaced the matchlock. Both systems existed side by side, each with its own role, until both were supplanted by the next step in the ladder of firearm evolution—the flintlock.[39]

Rudyard Kipling, that peerless poet of empire, once wrote, "If we as Britons have reason to bless any arms—save our Mothers'—those arms are Brown Bess." The "Bess" that Kipling praised was the .75 caliber flintlock smoothbore musket, which faithfully served British infantrymen from the 1730s through the end of the Napoleonic era and beyond.

The flintlock, which first appeared on the scene in the early seventeenth century, was the longest used mainstream ignition system in firearms history. Although Kipling praised the sturdy but plain soldier's Bess, by 1800, British and Italian sport shooters shouldered exquisite flintlock fowlers and double-barreled "sporting guns" by makers like Joseph Manton, their balance rivaling the finest products of the modern era. Germans and Americans had much to be proud of in their accurate Jaeger and Pennsylvania rifles, and the gun barrels turned out by Spanish makers were acknowledged to be the best in the world. At the turn of the nineteenth century, the flintlock in all its forms had reached the apogee of the European and American gun maker's art. It seemed to many soldiers and sportsmen that guns could simply get no better—perfection had been reached.

The origins of this seemingly perfect system, also known as a "firelock," are, like many of the great inventions of the early modern era, hazy. Inspired by the wheel-lock gun's ability to produce ignition via a shower of sparks, gun tinkerers in several European countries attempted to find a firing mechanism with a similar degree of reliability but a cheaper production cost.

The first flintlock was the "snaphaunce," allegedly a period Dutch term for "pecking hen." Attached to the snaphaunce lockplate were a cock with a piece of flint secured in its jaws, a covered pan for priming powder, and a separate hammer. The hammer was a piece of steel manually lowered over the pan, which was uncovered manually prior to firing. Control and power for the lock mechanism were supplied by a sear, mainspring, and tumbler located inside the lockplate. Pulling the trigger released the mainspring, propelling the cock forward. When flint scraped hammer, sparks (actually tiny bits of shaved hot metal) showered into the pan, ignited the priming, and fired the gun.[40]

Legend has it that the poultry metaphor for the snaphaunce was derived from Dutch chicken thieves who invented the lock because the glowing matches of their matchlock arms made them visible in the dark. That story is unlikely. When the cock of a snaphaunce flies forward and "pecks" at the hammer, the rationale for the terminology seems obvious. The true geographic origin of the snaphaunce is debated, with some scholars citing Scandinavia, although production was common in the gun making centers of Italy and Germany by the late sixteenth century.[41]

More animal imagery appears in the first English version of the flintlock. The "dog lock," developed in the early seventeenth century, was so called because an external "dog," or catch, engaged the rear of the cock as a half-cock safety. Otherwise, since the internal tumbler engaging the sear had only one notch, the cock could be positioned only at a full cock ready to fire mode. The dog lock's hammer, also called a "frizzen," doubled as a pan cover. When the flint struck the frizzen, which was held under tension by pressure of an external spring, it kicked open the pan automatically and created a spark shower at the same time.[42]

Yet another style of flintlock was the Spanish *miquelet*, which featured an external mainspring. The miquelet became a popular design across North Africa and even spread as far as Turkey and Russia. This style of lock

remained popular well into the
nineteenth century, and travelers
observed miquelet lock pistols stuck
in the sashes of Balkan bandits as
late as 1908. Turkish miquelets
were much favored in Albania. The
design did not catch on in northern
Europe or America, however,
except in the Spanish colonies.[43]

By the late seventeenth century
most European flintlocks were pat-
terned on a style attributed to the
French gunsmith Marin le
Bourgeoys, who developed it
around 1610. The "French lock"
was similar to the English dog lock,
but had an internal half-cock notch
on the tumbler rather than a dog for
a safety. For the purposes of this
discussion all of the above variant
systems will be considered flintlocks, which were, by the early eighteenth century, the predominant

Close up of the lock area of a British
smooth bore "Brown Bess" musket with
the pan open for depositing a priming
charge. After priming, the frizzen was
closed over the pan and the hammer,
which had a piece of flint in its jaws,
cocked. Pulling the trigger released the
hammer, which flew forward, scraping
the flint on the frizzen while knocking it
forward to expose the priming charge.
The spark ignited the priming and,
almost simultaneously, the main charge
in the barrel. (*AntiqueFirearms.com*)

military and sporting firearms in the western world.

The flintlock's greatest influence was felt on the battlefield. When King
William landed in Britain from Holland in 1688 as successor to the deposed
James II, he brought with him an aggregation of foreign troops and weapons.
William's battles with James' Irish loyalists at the Boyne, Aughrim, and the
siege of Limerick were fought with a mix of arms. Flintlock muskets, however, outnumbered matchlocks in the Anglo-Dutch Williamite army, and gave
it an initial tactical advantage over Irish Jacobites mostly armed with
matchlocks.[44]

The few flintlocks in the Irish ranks were issued to "fusileers" guarding
the artillery, where a glowing match was deemed imprudent around large
powder charges. To redress the arms imbalance, the Jacobites ordered 3,000
flintlock "fusils" from their French patrons. The English and Irish were
among the last combatants in Europe to bow to the inevitable and discard
the matchlock musket in place of the superior flintlock.[45]

Imported Continental flintlocks predominated in British military service
until the reign of King George I. In 1715, George's government created the
Board of Ordnance, which established the ordnance system of manufacture.

The system created standards of government acceptance for weapons and developed a network of domestic contractors who supplied the government with musket parts, which were delivered to approved gun builders, who assembled them into finished muskets.[46]

The "Brown Bess," although the best known personal firearm of its age, was, along with its Continental counterparts, quite crude in comparison to the fine sporting arms developed during the flintlock era. Until the development of a significant gun making industry in the middle to late seventeenth century, the British imported most of their sporting flintlocks as well as military weapons. Even with domestic flintlocks available, however, there was still a demand for fancy foreign arms, and the diarist Samuel Pepys detailed flashing a gaudy French gun before the lads hanging around the Bull Head Tavern in 1667.[47]

The increasing availability of the graceful smoothbore flintlock "fowler" in the seventeenth century gave birth to the beginnings of wing shooting. Although Gervase Markham advocated every possible manner of taking birds, including making them drunk, in his 1621 tome on bird hunting, *Hunger's Prevention, or the Whole Art of Fowling by Water and Land*, he gave some consideration to firearms as well. Markham recommended a 16 bore fowling piece, medium size shot, and a stealthy approach using all possible cover, including the "stalking horse" used by bird hunters in the days of the matchlock. Hiding behind a trained, docile "stalking horse," gunners could gradually approach their feathered quarry without detection. Lacking a live "stalking horse," Markham advised hunters to carry a stuffed equine along with them—the first portable blind.[48]

In Markham's day, shooting sitting ducks was still considered respectable. By 1686, however, gentlemen who had taken up the new sport of "shooting flying" frowned upon the practice. Richard Blome's *The Gentleman's Recreation* advocated shooting flushed quarry on the wing while astride a halted horse, with attendants on foot to reload guns and dogs to retrieve downed game. Blome also addressed the qualities of a good flintlock in detail, including how to determine the proper fit and function of lock parts as well as cleaning and maintenance.[49]

By the early eighteenth century, wing shooting had evolved into a sport familiar to the modern shotgunner, and the proper equipment and practice for going afield were thoroughly spelled out in "Mr. Markland's" *Pteryplegia: or, the Art of Shooting Flying*. Couched in the unlikely format of a poem, *Pteryplegia* thoroughly covers the state of the bird shooting art in 1727, including detailed instructions on loading and caring for the flintlock fowling piece and an admonition to the shooter to limit his intake of brandy while in the field.[50]

In America, the smoothbore was more in use in settled communities, where it could double as bird gun with shot and a militia weapon with ball. The American rifle, favored on the frontier, had its genesis in the arms produced by immigrant German gun makers in Pennsylvania, although many were made in other colonies, particularly Maryland and Virginia. The spiral grooves cut in the rifle's barrel stabilized the undersized round ball projectile, which was loaded encased in a greased patch, making it more accurate than a ball fired from a smoothbore fowling piece or musket. In the New World, the short, heavy caliber German rifle metamorphosed into the slim, graceful, smaller bored "long rifle." In the hands of the frontier "long hunter," usually a farmer who, when the harvest was in, trekked into the wilderness for hunting trips lasting weeks or even months, the rifle acquired legendary status.[51]

Their accuracy made rifles not only useful for hunting, but also for certain military missions, although most colonial era soldiers preferred the smoothbore musket. The musket was much less accurate than the rifle, but could be loaded and fired with prepared paper cartridges up to three times a minute, compared with once a minute for the rifle. It was effective on mass formations up to 100 yards or so, and was made with provision to mount a bayonet, which the American rifle was not.

Popular legend to the contrary, the American rifle did not win the Revolution, and George Washington at one point requested more men with smoothbore muskets and fewer riflemen. The deadly accuracy of rifles carried by tough frontiersmen made the difference on several battlefields, however, including Saratoga, New York, where, in October 1777, Pennsylvania rifleman Timothy Murphy sniped British General Simon Fraser out of the saddle at a range exceeding 200 yards to turn the tide of battle. At King's Mountain, South Carolina, three years later, British Major Patrick Ferguson, inventor of an innovative breech-loading flintlock rifle, was killed and his entire force destroyed by rifle-armed frontiersmen.[52]

The rifle was not unknown to the British, and some were produced in Britain well before the Revolution. General Edward Braddock ordered a dozen English made rifles for his ill-fated expedition to Fort Duquesne in 1755, although it appears that they were intended for hunting rather than combat use. The British hired German mercenary riflemen to fight the Americans during the Revolution, which led to the odd situation of a brigade of smoothbore musket armed Americans fighting a British force with German riflemen in the ranks at Hubbardton, Vermont, in 1777.[53]

Their unpleasant American experience taught the British army a number of lessons, one of which was that, although the majority of soldiers in an army should carry relatively rapid-fire muskets, it was good to have some riflemen around for special tasks. In August 1800 the British army created the 95th regiment, also known as "The Rifle Brigade." The 95th was armed with the flintlock Baker rifle. Continental European and American armies had rifle armed detachments for special service as well. The predominant arm in the British and other armies into the early 1840s remained, however, the flintlock smoothbore musket.

The flintlock was the most significant development in firearm history to date, but it was far from perfect. Although much more efficient than the matchlock, it retained a certain susceptibility to wind, rain, and even excessively damp weather, especially for that microsecond when the flint scraped the frizzen and kicked open the pan. It also required some skill to "fix" a flint in the proper position in cock's jaws, which was critical to performance and flint life. One of the main duties of British army junior officers in an era when the ability to think was seldom a requirement for a commission was to check their men's flints to make sure that they were set to make initial contact with the frizzen no more than one third of the way down its face, showering the maximum amount of sparks into the pan. Not all did, as extensive tests conducted by the British East India Company reveal a 15 percent misfire rate with flintlock muskets. The civilian misfire rate was no doubt considerably less.[54]

Military arms could never compare in style and reliability with the single- and double-barreled fowling pieces turned out by elite British gun makers in the early nineteenth century. These guns, with precisely tuned locks, lined touchholes, and "waterproof" pans designed to channel moisture away from the priming charge, were the most reliable firearms produced to that time.

As with any mechanical product, there is always room for improvement in firearms. But no one could come up with a significant one until Alexander Forsyth, a Scottish parson and wildfowl hunter, began to experiment with fulminates. It was a dangerous business with which some Frenchmen had already blown themselves sky-high. Forsyth persisted, however, and his work made possible the next chapter—and the one after that.

As the story goes, Forsyth, a simple Scottish country parson and avid wildfowler, grew frustrated with the performance of his flintlock shotgun while abroad in the moors. According to Forsyth, in addition to not being completely waterproof, the flintlock's pan flash gave ducks the millisecond of warning they needed to escape his shot pattern.

There is truth in that tale, but the whole story is, as most stories are, a tad more complex. Forsyth, an honors graduate of King's College, Aberdeen, was a man of science as well as religion, and his interest in developing a new priming system was based on the failed experiments of others with fulminates, or metallic salts, in Germany and France in the seventeenth and eighteenth centuries. Scientists had attempted to harness the power potential of fulminates for industrial purposes, particularly as a replacement for gunpowder, but after a number of people were killed in laboratory explosions, scientific enthusiasm declined.[55]

Forsyth realized that the unstable fulminates were too powerful for use as propellants. He believed, however, that they held promise as priming compounds that would speed up firearms ignition, and developed a gun lock that replaced the priming pan with an attached container of fulminate of mercury powder. The fulminate reservoir was popularly called a "scent bottle" because it resembled a perfume vial.

Once the Forsyth gun's barrel was loaded from the muzzle, the "scent bottle" was tipped manually to spill fulminate powder into an internal chamber, which also contained a piston. The gun's hammer was cocked, and when released by pulling the trigger, hit the piston, crushing and exploding the priming compound inside the chamber and firing the gun.

In 1805, Forsyth offered his system to the British government, then locked in a life-or-death struggle with Napoleon Bonaparte's France, and the Master General of the Ordnance agreed to install a laboratory for the Scottish parson at the Tower of London. A subsequent Master General, however, fearful the Tower would blow up, revoked the contract. Forsyth subsequently patented his invention and began to make sporting guns based on it.[56]

Although effective, Forsyth's system was still awkward and expensive. His invention, however, led others to further experimentation. The ultimate result was the percussion cap, featuring a fulminate mixture sealed in a small copper cup. The cap was placed over a hollow nipple threaded into a gun's breech and was detonated by its falling hammer. Several people, including upscale British shotgun makers Joseph Manton and Joseph Egg, claimed credit for inventing the percussion cap, but it was first patented in the United States in 1822 by Joshua Shaw, an expatriate British artist.[57]

Although some conservatives stuck to their flintlocks, "caplock" or "cap and ball" guns, including a number converted from the old flintlock system, quickly became popular in the sport shooting community. The superiority of the caplock's quick ignition was graphically demonstrated in the sport of live pigeon shooting, a combined test of shotgun marksmanship and wagering skill that swept Britain in the 1820s.

The percussion system coincided with an upsurge of British interest in the rifle, prompted by Prince Albert's enthusiasm for deer stalking in Scotland and the expansion of British colonial hunting grounds in Africa, India, and Ceylon. Colonial hunting rifles used on big and dangerous game were of large caliber and capable of handling a stiff powder charge. Patched round balls tended to "strip" the rifling when fired with heavy charges, resulting in inaccuracy. Two solutions evolved: the Forsyth system of shallow groove slow twist (rate of turn) rifling of one turn in 120 inches, and the two-groove rifle designed for a belted ball or bullet-style projectile.

Sir Samuel Baker, a prominent explorer who shot just about everything that moved, had a favorite four-bore (100 caliber) two-groove muzzle-loading caplock rifle which weighed 22 pounds. This massive gun fired a 3-ounce belted round ball or 4-ounce winged conical bullet over a 400-grain powder charge.[58]

As large game began to disappear in the Middle Atlantic and Mid-western United States in the

The Forsyth lock replaced the priming pan with an attached reservoir of fulminate of mercury powder. Because it resembled a perfume vial the reservoir was called a "scent bottle." Once the Forsyth gun's barrel was loaded from the muzzle, the "scent bottle" was tipped manually to spill fulminate powder into an internal chamber, which also contained a piston. The gun's hammer was cocked, and when released by pulling the trigger, hit the piston, crushing and exploding the priming compound inside the chamber and firing the gun. (*W. Keith Neal Collection*)

early nineteenth century, the Pennsylvania rifle of Revolutionary War days evolved into the small bore (.32 to .36 caliber) cap and ball full or half stock Squirrel rifle. Western hunters and explorers, who encountered hostile Indians and dangerous game like the grizzly bear, tended to favor heavier caliber firearms, with the generic Plains rifle, represented by the Hawken style gun, averaging over .50 caliber.

Although the round ball remained a favorite projectile in the South, New England target shooters and deer hunters increasingly used the flat based "picket ball," shaped like a modern bullet, in their caplock muzzleloaders. By the 1840s the picket bullet was being touted as the ideal hunting and target projectile, and rifles were showing up at ranges with aperture and telescopic sights mounted on them. By the time of the Civil War, this style of rifle had progressed as far west as St. Louis, where a number were purchased from gun shops to arm the Sixty-sixth Illinois Infantry, Birge's Western Sharpshooters, in 1861. Heavy benchrest muzzle-loading caplock rifles dominated the target shooting game in the Northeast, and, by the 1870s, splendid double-barreled picket ball rifles of around .45 caliber were the Yankee hunter's choice when afield for black bear or whitetail deer.[59]

The military was the last bastion of the flintlock. Throughout their research into new rifles and projectiles, French army Captain Claude Minié and his fellow Gallic small-arms reformers, including Captain Gustave Delvigne, had to buck older officers who believed that the smoothbore flintlock musket was the ultimate military weapon and the round ball the only fit projectile for a firearm. Despite the opposition of many senior commanders, however, new firearms and tactical ideas gained more of an audience in France than in Britain.[60]

The Duke of Wellington, who headed the British military, generally believed that the .75 caliber smoothbore Brown Bess would serve his old soldiers' grandsons was well as she had them. Eventually, however, the duke was forced to concede that the percussion system was the wave of the foreseeable future, and the British army adopted a caplock smoothbore musket in 1842, the same year the American army did. In his last years in office the victor of Waterloo reluctantly agreed to trials of Captain Minié's new underbore-size conical projectile, with its hollow base filled with an iron plug to aid in expansion into the rifling grooves on firing. Trials conducted in 1850 resulted in the adoption of the .70 caliber P51, which replaced both the model 1842 musket and the Brunswick rifle, a belted round ball gun, in British service. The Minié ball combined the musket's advantage of easy loading and the rifle's superior accuracy to give birth to a new type of small arm, the rifle musket, which would replace smoothbores in the world's armies by the mid-1850s.

The P51 was sighted to 900 yards, and the British were quick to take advantage of the gun's long-range capability in the rolling, open terrain they encountered in the Crimean War. At Alma, the British "Light Division" advanced firing at will on the enemy, wreaking havoc on Russian formations at ranges up to 400 yards. British infantrymen continued to use their rifled arms to good effect during the subsequent siege of Sevastopol. An Irishman in the Rifle Brigade took 600-yard pot shots at enemy soldiers running to the latrine, averring that, even if he missed, it "would be as good as a dose of opening medicine" for the terrified Russians.[61]

The soldiers who used their new arms so effectively in the Crimea were pretty much self-taught marksmen. This was not to be the case in the future, however, at least in the British service. In 1853, the British army adopted the P53 .577 caliber Enfield rifle musket, which became as ubiquitous in the nineteenth century as the AK-47 is in modern times. That same year, following the lead of the French reformers, who had been the first to use the new conical projectiles and had established a marksmanship institute, the Ecole de Tir, Britain's increasingly professional army established its own School of

The .577 caliber P53 British Enfield rifle musket, left, and the .58 caliber US 1855 Springfield rifle musket, in the hands of the soldier above, and their later variants, were the most common shoulder arms of the American Civil War. Both weapons were muzzle loaders, combining the ease of loading, barrel length and bayonet reach of the old smoothbore musket with the accuracy of the rifle, hence the name "rifle musket." Unlike previous rifles and muskets, which fired a round ball, the rifle musket projectile was a hollow based conical bullet which was under bore diameter for ease in loading. This conical bullet, popularly called a Minié ball after the French captain who first advocated it, was expanded by powder gases on firing to engage the gun's rifling, which imparted a stabilizing spin conducive to relatively long range accuracy. Even with these advantages, however, the rifle musket was still a muzzle loader; its cartridges, containing power and ball, were made of paper and the gun had to be externally primed with a percussion cap after loading. With fragile ammunition and no real increase in loading speed over the smoothbore, the rifle musket was but a temporary way-station on the long march to an effective repeating rifle. (*Top, USAMHI; left, private collection, photograph by John Hubbard*)

Minié balls from the Civil War. Minié balls were cast of lead and weighed on average 500 grains, or 14 to the pound. The three on the left are Union examples identified with three rings. The third from the right is an English made ball and the one to its right is a Confederate ball identified by its two rings. On the far right is the result of a Minié ball hitting a hard surface such as a rock or bone. This example is a Confederate ball and its appearance demonstrates how these balls, once deformed, were able to inflict such deadly wounds. (*Private collection, photograph by John Hubbard*)

Musketry. The school was located at Hythe, on the Kent coast, where miles of beaches provided space for ranges, allowing study of the effect and accuracy of long-distance small-arms fire.[62]

The United States adopted the Springfield .58 caliber rifle musket, firing the American version of the Minié ball, in 1855. Unfortunately, American soldiers paid little attention to French and British marksmanship training methods, and this neglect became evident during the Civil War. There was no official firearm training doctrine in either the Union or Confederate armies. Although this mattered little with the smoothbore muskets largely used by both sides in 1861 and 1862, increasing numbers of rifle muskets in the ranks, including American made Springfields and imported British Enfield and Austrian Lorenz guns could have made a difference if used properly.

Mere familiarity with weapons was not enough to guarantee effectiveness with the new rifled arms. The key to long-range accuracy with the rifle musket was correctly estimating range and setting sights to compensate for the gun's rainbow trajectory, a skill that was, however, largely ignored in America.

As the war progressed, Irish-born Confederate General Patrick Cleburne, who had served in the British army as an enlisted man, used a British manual to train his men in proper marksmanship and range estimation techniques. Cleburne's men quickly became the most deadly shots in either army.

Although Cleburne's adjutant, Major Calhoun Benham, modified the British manual for Confederate use, and federal authorities had a French manual translated, weapons training for most Civil War soldiers remained very haphazard, and largely limited to loading and firing drill without live ammunition and occasional "familiarization firing." The men of the Thirteenth New Jersey Infantry entered their first fight at the battle of Antietam in September 1862 without ever having fired their Enfield rifle muskets. Officers usually had their men hold fire until the enemy was quite close, negating the rifle musket's range potential of 500 to 900 yards. The result of all this was that, in its only big war, the gun never lived up to its potential.[63]

From the time the first shot was fired from the first muzzle loading hand cannon, firearms makers dedicated themselves to making guns fire faster. Early on, they realized this was best achieved by loading from the breech rather than the muzzle. Rapidity of fire would be a convenience for sportsmen, but promised a vital battle-winning edge for military men. Soldiers armed with fast firing breechloaders could concentrate a heavy volume of fire on an enemy force armed only with muzzleloaders, resulting, many believed, in rapid victories at little cost for the nation that first adopted a perfected breech-loading system. European museums are filled with ingenious and bizarre examples of early attempts at perfecting breechloaders using matchlock, wheel lock and flintlock ignition systems. They were curious, complex, and delicate, and some of them were as dangerous to the operator as the target. None, however, worked well enough to supplant muzzle loading small arms.

Repeating firearms were offered as early as the mid-seventeenth century. The most efficient of these early repeaters used cylinders to revolve loaded chambers into place behind the barrel for firing. Once cylinder reloading time was computed into the mix, however, many of these guns actually had an overall rate of fire no greater than muzzleloaders, and it was not a practical system as long as flint and steel were necessary for ignition. But percussion priming made reliable repeating guns possible. Within a few years the revolver, with its five or six chambers rotating around an axis pin with a percussion nipple on the rear of each one, was an established firearm. Samuel Colt patented his revolver in 1836. Colt also made repeating rifles on the same principle. When Colt's patent rights expired in the late 1850s, a number of competitors of varying quality entered the market, both in America and abroad. Guerrilla fighters, usually armed with multiple handguns, made very effective use of cap and ball revolvers during the Civil War.

The era of percussion ignition would not last long. The caplock was hardly in general use when gun designers were working on a successor system. Forsyth's fulminate compound made a number of things possible, including practical breech loading, the logical next step.

TWO

BREECHLOADER TO REPEATER

B REECH LOADING IS AN IDEA AS OLD AS FIREARMS. SOME FOURTEENTH-century light artillery pieces were loaded using separate breech chambers containing powder charge and ball, held firm in the gun by a wedge when firing. This type of cannon endured into the early seventeenth century, when it was generally abandoned due to excessive powder gas escape and the tendency of breeches to crack.[1]

Breech-loading small arms were available at a surprisingly early date, and Henry VIII had a matchlock breechloader dated 1537 in his arsenal of hunting guns. According to British gun maker and historian W. W. Greener, the king's breech-loading arquebus had a swiveling breech block "similar to the [1865] Snider breech-action" but hinged on the left side. The gun was loaded with a removable metal chamber that had a "false flash-pan and touch-hole on one side that fits into the flash-pan upon being placed in the chamber." Whether or not the gun was provided with additional chambers, which could be classified as an early form of cartridge holding both powder charge and ball, for rapid reloading, is unknown. According to another source, Henry had several varieties of breech-loading matchlocks in his personal gun collection.[2]

Greener believed that Henry's gun was of French manufacture, but similar firearms of German make are also known and have been described as "fairly common" in the sixteenth century. One surviving specimen has its chamber held in place with a cotter pin after loading. Interestingly, breech-loading wheel-lock guns were apparently rare, although one is in the collection of a Prague museum.[3]

Interest in breech loading, however, persisted into the flintlock era, and included hinge breech designs similar to Henry's matchlock, barrels that screwed off to load, and an Italian-made pistol which operated in a strikingly similar manner to the American Civil War era Smith carbine patented in

1857. Like the Smith, the pistol's breech was opened by a spring in the gun's trigger guard. When pressed, the spring released a latch holding the breech and barrel together at a hinged joint and the gun broke open at a ninety-degree angle, muzzle pointing down, for loading with a cartridge of some sort. Other designs appeared elsewhere in Europe, including Britain. Some flintlock breechloaders were operated by twisting the breech to the right of the gun, exposing a chamber for loading with loose powder and ball.[4]

Like their matchlock predecessors, most of these early flintlock breech-loading firearms leaked gas at the breech joint to a greater or lesser degree on firing, and gunpowder residue corroded the necessarily close-fitting parts, hindering whatever breech-sealing properties they had. This defect was less noticeable with a hunting arm that was not subjected to rough handling and fired repeatedly and was thoroughly cleaned more often than a military musket. In addition, of course, breechloaders, which required precision hand-work to create, were much more expensive than muzzle-loading military arms. For both of these reasons, the military stuck with the simple, reliable, durable musket, which, in its own right, was fairly easy to load and maintain.

Since breech loading, should it ever be perfected, did promise significant advantages to both sportsman and soldier, however, assiduous inventors continued to apply themselves to solving systemic problems. The use of a threaded breech block of some sort seemed the most likely solution to excessive gas escape, and Isaac de la Chaumette, a Frenchman residing in England, designed one of the best early breech-loading guns around such a system in 1721.

To operate the Chaumette gun, which used a vertical screw breech plug to limit gas escape, the operator swiveled its trigger guard in one direction to open the breech for loading, and in the other direction to close it prior to firing. Once loaded, the gun's pan was primed and it was cocked and fired in the same manner as a muzzle-loading flintlock. Several prominent British gun makers made Chaumette system breech-loading rifles, including one for King George I.

The Chaumette-style action was advocated for trial use in cavalry carbines by the French Marshal Maurice de Saxe. Despite de Saxe's endorsement, there is no evidence that the French army ever formally adopted the weapon, although one source states Chaumette breech carbines were issued to a regiment of dragoons and in a limited number to the navy. Greener maintained that the "Amusette du Marechal de Saxe" was "soon discarded, on account of the great danger in manipulating the weapon, for the friction was so great that the gun frequently went off before the breech-plug was returned to its place."[5]

Nor did the British military adopt the Chaumette, although a wall gun with the Frenchman's action was used to fire an eight-ounce ball 800 yards in Dublin in 1761. The Chaumette's major drawback as a military arm was that its action screw threads began to fill with powder fouling after a few shots, making it difficult to operate and drastically reducing its rate of fire. Efforts to muscle close fouled breeches may be responsible for the story about friction producing premature ignition in the Chaumette. This defect was not as important in hunting guns, but rendered the Chaumette action unsatisfactory for military applications.[6]

Fascinated by the idea, however, Patrick "Pattie" Ferguson, a young British light infantry officer, set about improving the Chaumette. His solution to the fouling problem was to cut transverse channels across the screw threads, which reduced fouling accumulation and improved the overall rate of fire. While Ferguson was working on his gun, the Revolutionary War broke out in America. British officers soon encountered American riflemen in the sieges of Boston and Quebec and were impressed by their effectiveness. Their reports led the British government to order muzzle-loading rifles for special use by some soldiers of their own light infantry from both English and German gun makers, as well as contract for German mercenary riflemen.

In the spring of 1776, Ferguson demonstrated his new breechloader for a number of important government officials and army officers, including Lord Viscount Townshend and Lord Amherst. In "a heavy rain and a high wind" Ferguson fired his rifle for five straight minutes, maintaining an aimed fire rate of four rounds a minute, and, at one point, firing six rounds in a minute. The performance was notable, including hitting a bull's-eye of unreported size at 100 yards from the prone position. A subsequent demonstration before the British royal family at Windsor Castle, in which he told the king he could fire seven shots a minute, gained his invention even more favorable publicity.[7]

While the Ferguson rifle's standard rate of fire was not significantly higher than the British army issue smoothbore Brown Bess musket, the gun was much more accurate than the musket. It was also faster to load than the usual muzzle-loading rifle, which used a patched ball to properly engage the rifling. A Ferguson shooter merely dropped a naked ball into the open breech, followed by a powder charge, then swiveled the breech closed and primed the gun's pan. More significantly, the Ferguson was easier for a prone soldier to load.

Ferguson and his gun impressed their lordships, and in June they cancelled muzzle-loading rifle orders in progress, instructing the gun makers to fill the balance of the contracts with Ferguson breechloaders. Four British

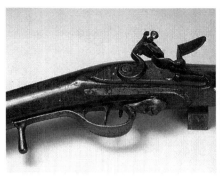 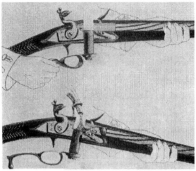

The Ferguson rifle was loaded by turning the trigger guard to open the breech, pressing a ball into the breech, filling the chamber with powder, and then turning the guard back to close the breech. The firing mechanism was the same as a standard flintlock. The Ferguson mechanism opened the breech with a single twist which enabled rapid reloading, an advance over earlier breechloaders. Fouling caused by black powder after a few shots—which plagued all firearms of the period—tended to reduce the potential advantages of rapid breechloading. (*National Park Service*)

makers—William Grice, Benjamin Willetts, Mathias Barker, and Galton & Son, produced a total of 670 muzzle-loading rifles for the British army in 1776. In addition, each produced twenty-five Fergusons.[8]

The Ferguson rifle was the first breechloading arm to be sent into a combat zone with a major military force. As a result of his demonstration, Captain Ferguson was authorized to raise a 100-man company of green-clad light infantry for American service. These men were not selected due to any civilian marksmanship background (minimal to nonexistent in Britain among the common folk) but drawn from a detachment of recruits and noncommissioned officers of the Sixth and Fourteenth Regiments of Foot stationed at Chatham Barracks. Ferguson assumed command of this company on March 6, 1777, and personally conducted a brief but intensive training regimen in tactics and shooting. At the end of the month the detachment took ship for America to join General Sir William Howe's army in New York City.[9]

On July 23, 1777, Howe initiated a leisurely campaign to capture Philadelphia, leaving New York by sea with a 15,000-man force, including Ferguson and his riflemen. After landing at Head of Elk, Maryland, the British commander slowly led his army north, skirmishing with Rebel forces until he encountered General George Washington's army of Continental troops reinforced by militia at Brandywine Creek on September 11.

Washington concentrated his best troops to contest a British crossing of the Brandywine in the vicinity of Chadd's Ford, covering his right flank with a light cavalry screen. By 8:00 A.M. the British advance, commanded by General Wilhelm Baron Von Knyphausen, including Ferguson's riflemen and the Tory light infantry Queen's Rangers, engaged Brigadier General • William Maxwell's light infantry brigade, an elite force of picked troops from various Continental regiments, most likely including a contingent of riflemen. Maxwell conducted a fighting withdrawal across the Brandywine. On reaching the creek, the British halted, but continued to exchange fire with the main American force on the other side.[10]

It might have been about this time, when Washington was directing the overall fight, that the American commander shared the historical timeline for a brief instant with Pattie Ferguson and his rifle. The captain, who was busy skirmishing with and directing his company, later recalled that a mounted senior American officer, accompanied by another rider who he described as an elaborately garbed "French Hussar" rode into rifle range. Ferguson raised his breechloader, aimed and then declined to fire, thinking it an ungentlemanly act to shoot a fellow officer nobly going about his business. Pattie later stated his belief that the officer was Washington, who was then present across the creek. The "French Hussar" may have been Count Casimir Pulaski, who was serving as a volunteer aide-de-camp to Washington at the time.

The American general soon had urgent business elsewhere. After successfully drawing Washington's attention to the Chadd's Ford line, Howe sent 5,000 men under General Charles Cornwallis to cross the Brandywine upstream while Von Knyphausen's forces continued their desultory skirmishing with Washington's main force. By late afternoon the flanking column was across the creek and in the American rear. As volleys crashed to the north, Von Knyphausen attacked across the creek, his offense spearheaded by Ferguson's company and the Queen's Rangers. The Americans were driven from the field in heavy fighting, opening the way to the fall of Philadelphia.

Howe lost 583 men killed, wounded, and missing at Brandywine, among them Pattie Ferguson. Shortly after he declined a shot at the American officer, Ferguson was hit in the right elbow by a rifle ball, which shattered the joint. He gamely refused amputation and painfully convalesced in British-occupied Philadelphia for the next eight months, undergoing several operations without anesthetic to remove bone fragments from his now permanently disabled arm and teaching himself to write left-handed. During his long period of disability Ferguson's experimental rifle company was disbanded and its men returned to their original units, most likely due to the fact that he was no longer physically fit to command it, and no one else had the skill or inclination to do so. The rifles were apparently placed in storage.[11]

Following his recovery, although his arm remained relatively useless, Ferguson received other assignments, including cleaning out privateers along the New Jersey coast and then commanding Loyalist regular troops and local loyal militiamen in the southern Campaign of 1779. He was killed on the afternoon of October 7, 1780, near King's Mountain, South Carolina. Although he was allegedly buried under a cairn of rocks on the battlefield, evidence suggests that Ferguson's bones were scattered hither and yon by wolves and other scavengers.

Perhaps as mysterious as Pattie Ferguson's final resting-place is what happened to his rifles—and why? Only one or two of the original 100 rifles made for Pattie's company still survives, one in the collection of the Morristown, New Jersey, National Military Park and the other in the Tower of London. Another Ferguson, which some think is the rifle the inventor used in the 1776 trials and later presented to Captain Abraham De Peyster, his second-in-command in the South, is in the collections of the Smithsonian Institution.[12]

Other rifles were made on Ferguson's patent, but most still extant arms appear to be high quality sporting rifles. According to one source, six such specimens, varying in detail, were listed in 1928 as being in collections in America and Britain. The British East India Company sent sixty Ferguson military rifles to India for field trials in 1776-1777, where they were considered, along with an assortment of muzzle-loading rifles, valuable assets, although some were lost in action in Madras. As far as is known none was ever returned to Britain.[13]

Why did Ferguson's rifle go out of production even before he died? Evidence is sketchy. Howard L. Blackmore, a British arms expert, suggests that the gun's stock was inherently weak due to the cutouts necessary to fit the plug housing, as evidenced by cracks in surviving specimens. Blackmore also notes that the Ferguson was loaded with a loose ball and charged from a powder flask, not the standard musket or carbine paper cartridge, and was deemed by some conservative British military leaders as too complicated for their troops to manage or keep clean and in good firing order. Blackmore's conclusions are educated guesses, and we can do no better, for the only published contemporary account of what may have happened is an enigmatic comment on the Ferguson in a 1785 British history of the Revolution: "It is not certain that these improvements [breech loading] produced all the effect in real service which had been expected, from those astonishing specimens of them that were displayed in England."[14]

Were there inherent defects in the Ferguson that made it less desirable in actual service? If not, would it have been possible to manufacture the

Ferguson in large numbers given the technology of the day? Could wide-spread use of Pattie Ferguson's breechloader have turned the tide of the Revolution for the British? Although many romantics think so, that possibility, dispensed with at the time by all concerned, including apparently Ferguson himself, was never in play.

Other breech-loading flintlocks, of different design, were invented around the same time as the Ferguson improvement on the Chaumette. Sometime in the 1760s locksmith Giuseppi Crespi of Milan devised a rear-hinged breech that lifted for loading at its front. During the early 1770s Crespi breechloaders were issued on a trial basis to selected units of the Austrian army and thus actually pre-date the introduction of the Ferguson in service, although the Ferguson was most likely the first breechloader used in battle.[15]

The Crespi showed promise, and an additional number of Austrian muzzle-loading muskets and carbines were converted to the Crespi system at Ferlach and issued to troops in the field for more extended trials. They were withdrawn from service after "certain drawbacks" were discovered, however, and placed in storage. Despite their drawbacks the Crespi guns were temporarily issued to volunteer troops on at least two emergency occasions when the Hapsburgs fought the French following the French Revolution.[16]

In the years after the American War for Independence, British gun maker Durs Egg, one of the Ferguson makers, also produced a rear hinged-breech breechloader based on the Crespi system. Although apparently issued to several dragoon regiments in 1784-1785, the Egg gun was withdrawn from service due to reports of excessive gas leakage on firing, which may well have been the Austrian rationale for retiring the Crespis.[17]

Another breech-loading flintlock that may have had at least limited troop trial issue is the Fusil de Vincennes M/1778. In this innovative French gun the barrel was slid forward and twisted 180 degrees to expose the breech for loading, then returned to a locked position after loading. How many of these guns actually were manufactured and issued is unknown, but they were later produced commercially by a Dutch gunsmith named J. G. Ertel.[18]

Still other breech-loading flintlock designs were invented in the late eighteenth and early nineteenth centuries. The production of most of these devices was extremely limited, perhaps to the inventor's model, and included one example with a unique sliding barrel gas seal now in the Prague Military Museum. French General René de Montalembert's screw secured breech block appeared to have more promise than most, but, although tested by the French military, it was abandoned as impractical.[19]

The most successful breech-loading flintlock, if numbers manufactured and issued are considered, was the American Hall rifle, patented by John H.

Hall of Portland, Maine. Although reminiscent of the Crespi and Egg systems, with its breech designed to rise for loading, Hall's rifle, with a distinct centrally hung hammer and flash pan, was simpler and easier to manufacture than either of the European guns. It was also inherently more accurate, since it was a rifle, rather than a smoothbore.

Hall, born to a relatively prosperous New England middle-class family, opened a woodworking shop in Portland in 1808. In 1813 he married Statira Preble, niece of Captain William Preble, a hero of the war against the Tripoli pirates. Although Hall had no prior interest in or experience with firearms, he had an abiding love for things mechanical, and this led him to the invention of his breech-loading rifle.[20]

Hall filed a patent application for the gun in the spring of 1811, but was advised by then Superintendent of Patents Dr. William Thornton, that he, Thornton, had actually invented the same system prior to Hall. Puzzled by this response, Hall subsequently traveled to Washington, where Thornton, unable to show the New Englander any drawings or other evidence, apparently produced a Ferguson rifle and claimed it to be his model. That gun, of course, was the invention of someone else and was an entirely different approach to the problem of breech loading.[21]

Still claiming the tilt breech rifle was his invention, Thornton refused to grant a patent to Hall. When Hall appealed to Secretary of State James Monroe to mediate the dispute, Monroe was reluctant to intervene and advised the inventor to come to some agreement with the superintendent. Although one authority states that Thornton improved the Hall patent by "adding a slant cut to the breech section . . . so that its upper end was on a tangent and thus made a slightly closer fit to the breech of the barrel," more recent scholarship contests that assertion. The result of discussions between Hall and Thornton, however, was a shared patent, with Thornton to receive half of all royalties received from patent rights leased to other manufacturers. Hall and Thornton's patent was not only the first for an American breech-loading design, but also the first for an American-designed firearm.[22]

The agreement, which Hall soon regretted, resulted in Thornton opposing Hall's efforts to manufacture and sell rifles to the government on his own, since Thornton would not share in the profits of such sales. Thornton's role and business tactics in this sorry affair casts considerable doubt on his reputation as a prolific early American inventor.[23]

Determined to both thwart Thornton and maintain control of his own production process, Hall raised and spent $20,000 on facilities, machinery, and raw materials, a significant sum in those days, by 1817. Although a few Hall sporting rifles had been manufactured and sold, the inventor had to secure government contracts to prosper as an arms maker. He hoped to follow in the footsteps of fellow New England gun maker Eli Whitney, who, despite fudging his promise to produce muzzle-loading muskets with interchangeable parts, was heavily subsidized by the government in his armsmaking efforts.[24]

In late 1813, the War Department ordered Hall guns for testing, and in succeeding months the inventor delivered five rifles and three smoothbore muskets using his system to Lieutenant Colonel George Bomford, an ordnance officer based at Albany, New York. Bomford was impressed with the Hall guns and recommended ordering several hundred more for further testing under field conditions. Unfortunately for Hall, his manufacturing facility, a small shop in Portland, could not produce enough arms in the time allotted to meet the terms of the contract.

Hall spent the War of 1812 years training workmen and perfecting his gun and, more important, promising to produce rifles that were made of completely interchangeable parts. In 1816 he wrote Bomford that he could produce a gun with parts "so much alike that . . . if a thousand guns were taken apart & the limbs thrown promiscuously together in one heap they may be taken promiscuously from the heap & will all come right."[25]

Although Hall did not get the contract for 1,000 guns that he anticipated, his promise of parts interchangeability, an important government goal promised but not achieved by Eli Whitney, garnered enough interest for a trial order of 100 rifles at $25 each in January 1817. Satisfied with the results, and responding to requests from the Maine Congressional delegation, which Hall enlisted on his behalf, on March 19, 1819, the government ordered another 1,000 rifles. As part of the deal, Hall was hired at Harper's Ferry Arsenal in Virginia at $60 a month and was to receive a dollar for every one of his rifles manufactured.

Although Hall assumed the title of assistant armorer at Harper's Ferry in 1819, he had to supervise the building of a special shop and all of the tooling necessary to produce his breechloader before he could make a single rifle. He did not complete his first thousand guns until 1825, and significant numbers of Halls did not get into the hands of troops until 1826.

Intensive testing proved the Hall, the first breech-loading firearm put into mass production, to be quite satisfactory for military use. One gun was fired 7,186 times without any serious malfunctions. In an 1826 rapid-fire test, thirty-seven Hall breechloaders were pitted against thirty-seven smoothbore muskets. The Halls outshot the muskets, 955 shots to 626.[26]

Despite the rapidity advantage, there was no initial intention for Hall rifles to replace the muzzle-loading smoothbore musket in the army's line

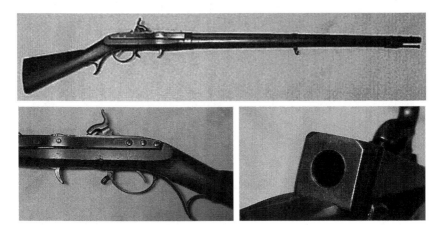

An M1819 Hall rifle with a Harper's Ferry alteration—a percussion cap lock—dated 1832 on the breech. The breech was broken and tilted open by pulling the lever forward of the trigger guard. The exposed chamber was then loaded with shot and powder. (*Sharpsburg Arsenal*)

units, but to supplement and possibly replace the muzzle-loading service rifles already issued. Infantrymen in line of battle firing .69 caliber muskets loaded with buck and ball ammunition composed of a heavy round ball and three buckshot provided devastating close-range firepower. Rifles were useful special purpose tools, however, and in 1824 two companies of the Fortress Monroe, Virginia, garrison were issued Halls. By 1832 the Sixth United States Infantry regiment, stationed at Fort Leavenworth, Kansas, was almost entirely armed with Hall rifles.[27]

Halls were issued to the militia as well, since these part-time soldiers were not disciplined enough to fight in line of battle like the regulars, and would assume a role as skirmishers and sharpshooters, harassing the enemy rather than dealing the *coup de main* in time of war. In order to supplement the Halls coming off government assembly lines at Harper's Ferry, the government contracted with Simeon North of Middletown, Connecticut, for an additional 5,000 Hall rifles. Total production of Hall flintlock rifles between 1824 and 1840 was 19,680, with another 3,190 produced in percussion ignition through the end of production in 1844.[28]

By the early 1830s Halls, while still relegated to a second place, along with muzzle-loading rifles, behind smoothbore muskets, were in evidence on the frontier. An 1834 ordnance survey reveals 334 Halls and 554 Model 1803 muzzle-loading rifles in storage at the St. Louis and Baton Rouge arsenals, most in for repairs, indicating hard usage in service.[29]

Hall rifles served well in a supplementary role in the Black Hawk, Seminole, and Mexican Wars, but were never destined to become the standard United States issue arm. John Hall died in 1841, although his breech design would survive him for a number of years. In a major sense the Hall rifle was a revolutionary gun that bridged the transition and revealed the future, a role the Ferguson failed to fill. The first truly successful flintlock breechloader, John Hall's gun was also the first flintlock arm produced in quantity with interchangeable parts and the last breechloader to use flintlock ignition. Flintlock breechloaders suffered the same problems as flintlock muzzleloaders—sensitivity to wind, rain, and other causes of misfires, including dull flints and clogged vents.

Alexander Forsyth's successful use of fulminate priming, followed by Joshua Shaw and other inventors' convenient encapsulation of fulminates in copper, started the flintlock down the road to obsolescence as a sporting gun, and the perfection of the percussion system made it obsolete as a military weapon. By the early 1840s the percussion system was rapidly replacing flint and steel in the armies of the world.

In addition to its obvious advantages in a muzzle-loading arm, the percussion ignition system made practical breech loading a much more promising proposition—and creative gun makers were quick to take advantage. As early as 1812, Samuel Pauly, a Swiss gunsmith residing in Paris, developed a breech-loading gun firing a self-contained cartridge using fulminate priming. In 1832, another Frenchman named Robert invented an experimental percussion ignition breech-loading infantry rifle, which was followed a year later by the Hall carbine. The Hall carbine, a short-barreled percussion variant of John Hall's system, intended for cavalry use, became the chief long arm of the United States mounted forces for over twenty years. It was produced in several calibers with several varying breech opening devices through 1852 and was, from its inception in 1833, always manufactured with percussion ignition. It was the first percussion weapon adopted by the United States army.[30]

The breech loading idea was particularly attractive to mounted men. As infantry armament became more potent with the arrival of the rifle musket in the 1850s, cavalrymen looked to breech-loading carbines to help fill the firepower gap. Although dragoons usually employed their carbines in dismounted combat, breechloaders were also far easier to reload on horseback. Rapid reloading was an obvious plus to often-outnumbered American frontier soldiers. At least as important, a projectile would not roll out of the barrel of a breechloader when slung muzzle down over a dragoon's shoulder on a horse jouncing across the prairie.

With these desirable attributes in mind, the United States dragoons were issued the first Hall carbines, with an improved lever designed by contractor

Simeon North to raise the breech for loading with a paper cartridge. Like its parent flintlock rifle, the Hall carbine did leak some gas at the breech, a situation exacerbated after considerable use, especially on the frontier. In addition, if the ball was not securely positioned atop the powder, or slid forward, the charge moved away from the ignition point, resulting in misfires. On occasion, powder spilled in loading migrated under the breech block, which, as the breech/barrel joint widened with wear, occasionally led to unpleasant and unexpected explosions. Last, like the common infantry musket, the Hall carbine did not have a rifled barrel, but was made as a smoothbore in order to shoot buckshot effectively when needed. The general opinion of the Hall carbine was that it was less durable than a muzzle-loading carbine, and that its advantage of more rapid reloading was to some degree offset by its inaccuracy and limited effective range.[31]

The Hall carbine possessed another characteristic that endeared it to dragoons on the frontier. The breech block included the hammer and trigger mechanisms. It could be removed from the gun easily by troops going off duty and carried as a pocket pistol for self-defense. Since soldiers did not always frequent the most respectable establishments, these easily concealed hideout guns came in handy in "social" situations. Dragoon Sam Chamberlain recalled that when off duty in Mexico in 1847 he habitually carried a Bowie knife and loaded Hall carbine chamber for self-defense. On one occasion he "sprang behind a large table used as a bar, drew the chamber of my Hall's Carbine (that I always carried in my pocket), said a short prayer and stood cool and collected, at bay before those human Tigers, guerillars." Although tackled, Chamberlain redeemed himself in a knife duel, had his loaded Hall chamber restored and went on his way. At least that was his story.[32]

As the Hall was beginning to become obsolete as other designs came on the market, a limited issue of the innovative Jenks breechloaders was field-tested. Invented by South Carolinian William Jenks in 1838, with a view to replacing the Halls in service, these guns proved disappointing. Originally designed as a flintlock, the Jenks was operated by raising a lever inletted into the small of the stock to withdraw a piston and open the breech for loading with loose powder and ball. The piston was intended to provide a better breech seal than the Hall barrel-breech interface.[33]

Although the flintlock version was found wanting by the military, a later percussion Jenks with a sidehammer, sometimes called a "mule ear," ignition passed its initial tests with flying colors. A sample gun was fired a total of 14,800 times, and the only problem encountered by a board of officers considering its adoption was that one nipple split. Field tests proved less than satisfactory, however, and Captain Enoch Steen of the First Dragoons reported that the Jenks was difficult to load and cap, fouled excessively, and was, in summation, "totally useless in the hands of a dragoon." The inventor protested, stating that his gun had been used with the 100-grain powder charge of the Hall rather than the 65-grain charge it was designed for. Nonetheless, the Jenks was not selected as the army's new breechloader, although a number were ordered by the Navy, and apparently met that service's different requirements.[34]

In 1858, most of the Navy Jenks were updated with James Merrill's patents to ease loading and improve the breech seal. These arms were found to be satisfactory in service, albeit certainly not the ultimate answer to the breech-loading problem. Merrill's carbines and rifles were the final development of the Jenks design. Though never popular, over 15,000 were purchased during the Civil War.

In the years leading up to the Civil War, horse soldiers like Captain Steen's company provided the American army's primary firearm field testing service, and the dragoons and cavalry were where new breechloaders made their first service appearance. By the late 1850s the weapons mix in the mounted arm, the First and Second Dragoons, First and Second Cavalry and the Mounted Rifle Regiment, included, in addition to handguns and sabers, a bewildering array of long arms, all now with percussion ignition. Even though the Hall, despite its drawbacks, seemed to prove that breech loading was indeed the future of firearms, some troopers were issued older smooth-bore muzzleloaders, and others the United States 1855 series of long range .58 caliber muzzle-loading rifles, carbines, and pistol-carbines firing the conical Minié ball. Still others carried old Hall or new Sharps breech-loading carbines.

Small arms technology was advancing rapidly, however, and in 1857 the army tested twenty breechloaders for possible adoption. All of these guns were "capping breechloaders," using unprimed semi-fixed ammunition with a cartridge containing powder and bullet that required an external percussion cap for ignition, and all had rifled barrels. Some, like the Sharps and the Hall, used a somewhat fragile paper or linen cartridge, which was fast becoming old technology.

Although the Sharps was on the verge of obsolescence by 1857, it was the most popular breechloader of the time. Invented by Christian Sharps in 1848, the gun was originally produced in an evolving series of models through 1851 equipped with a tape primer invented by Dr. Edward Maynard. The tape primer, which became popular on a number of firearms in the 1850s, including the Springfield Model 1855 family of muzzle-loading small arms, was similar to the modern caps used in a modern toy cap gun. Explosive pellets encased in a paper roll were serially mechanically advanced under the hammer each time the gun was cocked, eliminating the need to manually place a percussion cap on a cone or nipple and thus increasing the gun's rate of fire.

The 1852 model Sharps replaced the Maynard primer with a patented pellet priming system that propelled wafer-like primers from a magazine under the hammer as it descended on the nipple. In a pinch, the Sharps could also use a manually affixed percussion cap. This version in its Model 1855 configuration was the gun tested in the trials. The Sharps was easily loaded by a working a lever to drop its breech block and expose its breech for inserting a combustible linen cartridge, and was sealed against gas escape on firing with a moveable breech face, platinum ring, and sliding chamber bushing.[35]

Although the Sharps had the usual black powder breechloader problems with powder fouling, which accumulated in the chamber and hindered inserting cartridges and on the breech block and slowed lowering and closing it, the gun was the most popular breechloader ever issued to the pre-Civil War U.S. military. After one Indian fight in 1853, Captain Richard Ewell of the First Dragoons, later a Confederate general, summed up the Sharps as "superior to any firearm yet furnished the dragoons."[36]

Newer designs, including the Smith, used disposable cartridge cases of various materials, including foil and rubber, to seal gas leakage far better than any previous breechloaders, but were still dependent on exterior ignition by a percussion cap affixed to a nipple. All of the newer ammunition was, however, more robust than the paper cartridge.

The Smith was opened for loading by pushing a small lever inside the trigger guard, which released the hinged barrel to drop for insertion of a rubber cartridge containing powder and bullet. After the breech was closed, the gun's nipple was capped with a conventional percussion cap before firing. Although the Smith ranks fourth in Civil War Federal carbine purchases, it apparently had some durability problems due to wear at the breech hinge joint and extraction problems due to the use of a wartime expedient paper and foil cartridge.[37]

New Jersey-born Washington, D.C., dentist Edward Maynard, who had invented the tape primer that bore his name, also invented the Maynard rifle. The breech of his gun opened for loading by lowering a lever that also served as a trigger guard. Maynard used a revolutionary reloadable copper cartridge case with a wide rim to facilitate extraction by the shooter's fingers after firing.

The Burnside carbine, designed in 1853 and patented in 1856 by Ambrose Everett Burnside, a young army officer who was destined to become a famous, if luckless, Civil War general, was the first arm using a separately primed metallic cartridge ordered and issued by the United States government. The Burnside evolved through a series of design changes to become one of the most common Civil War era breech-loading carbines, third in numbers behind the Spencer and the Sharps. Since Burnside ammunition consisted of a tapered copper case containing both powder charge and bullet, it was very water-resistant.

In the trials the Sharps, with its primer magazine, and from which the shooter did not have to remove an expended cartridge case since it consumed the cartridge entirely, proved the fastest firing gun (eighteen shots in fifty-five seconds). The Colt five-shot revolving rifle (which loaded at the front of its cylinder using a combustible cartridge) was the most accurate arm tested. The Burnside, however, was chosen the best overall weapon for cavalry use and a number were ordered for field testing.[38]

At the outbreak of the Civil War, Federal ordnance chief Brigadier General James W. Ripley was besieged by inventors of "patent breechloaders" seeking lucrative contracts. Although Ripley is often castigated for not showing enough interest in new arms technology, much of this criticism fails to appreciate the realities of his position. The general was committed to getting the largest quantity of proven muzzle-loading Springfield .58 caliber rifle muskets into the hands of hundreds of thousands of infantrymen in the shortest possible time—all else was secondary.

Ripley was committed to breechloaders for the cavalry, but most inventors were in no position to rapidly manufacture a significant quantity of arms. In addition, the field durability of many of these guns was unknown, with ammunition resupply a potential logistic nightmare. The Sharps was a proven product, had a factory already dedicated to its manufacture, and was the understandable first choice of the ordnance department.

Early in the war, it appeared that guns in storage and those rolling off an expanded Sharps production line would provide more than enough carbines to uniformly arm the Federal cavalry, initially limited to the five regular regiments. When large numbers of volunteer cavalry regiments were authorized in the wake of Bull Run, however, the need for carbines increased exponentially. General Ripley opposed ordering Sharps rifles for elite infantry use because the factory could not produce both rifles and carbines at the same time and had to be retooled to make rifles, losing valuable carbine production time. When he finally caved in to political pressure to order Sharps rifles for Colonel Hiram Berdan's sharpshooter regiments, carbine production fell significantly behind.

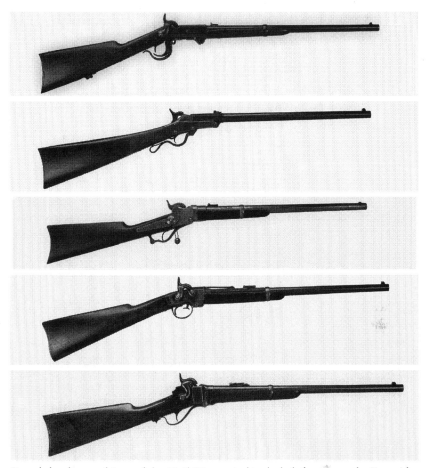

Breech-loading carbines of the Civil War period included, from top, the Burnside, the Maynard, the Starr, the Smith, and the Sharps. These carbines were all significant steps on the road to self contained ammunition, but had brief careers as combat weapons. They used semi-self contained cartridges consisting of powder and ball that were inserted in the gun's breech in their entirety but were fired by separate priming—a percussion cap fitted to a nipple just like the rifle musket. The Sharps was the best known and liked of these guns, but its somewhat fragile linen cartridge represented the oldest technology. The Starr was a disliked inferior knockoff of the Sharps' system. The Smith used a rubber or composition cartridge, and the Burnside and Maynard, the most technologically advanced, used copper cartridges. Ironically, despite its "old technology" the Sharps had a decided advantage in rapid fire situations, since its cartridge was entirely consumed on firing, whereas with the Burnside, Maynard, and Smith, empty cartridge cases had to be removed by hand before the gun could be reloaded. Later Burnsides had a "bump" ejector that was supposed to loosen the fired case from the breechblock, but none used the fully self-contained internally-primed metallic case ammunition and effective extraction/ejection systems of the repeating Henry and Spencer.(*Private collection; photographs by John Hubbard*)

The shortage of carbines inevitably led to contracts with inventors and entrepreneurs for a variety of guns of varying quality, which began to trickle into service in the spring of 1862. The best of these—the Burnside, Smith, and Gallager—were purchased in fairly large quantities, as were lesser numbers of more dubious designs like the Cosmopolitan and the Gibbs. Each of these guns required a unique cartridge and spare parts supply, however, complicating the work of ordnance officers.

In Europe, events had moved faster. The 1842 percussion ignition Norwegian Kammerlader, which appears to have been inspired by the Hall, was the first breech-loading gun in general issue to a military force. Others would shortly follow.

The perfect military breech-loading system, however, required a cartridge that was not only easy to load, but sturdy and self-contained, with powder, primer, and bullet all in one package. Such a cartridge could also make successful repeating arms a real possibility.

Interestingly, the idea of an internally primed cartridge was strongly opposed by some ordnance officers. The thought of wagonloads of highly explosive black powder cartridges and percussion caps packed with them traveling with armies was bad enough. The thought of wagons full of primed cartridges that could be detonated by a sharp blow was worse. Whenever possible, armies physically separated primers and powder. Artillery fuses, for example, were kept separate from their shells. Percussion caps for muskets were packed with cartridges, but separately wrapped.

Perfect cartridges or not, even early on in the development of firearms, some inventors, not content with developing breechloaders, were advancing the concept of repeating arms loaded with a number of charges that could be fired in succession or at one time. As early as 1662, Samuel Pepys recorded in his diary that he witnessed "a gun to discharge seven times, the best of all devices I ever saw." Two years later he recorded that "there were several people by, trying a new fashion gun to shoot often, one after another, without trouble or danger, very pretty."[39]

Some early repeating flintlocks were made with dual magazines, one for powder, another for bullets, in their buttstocks, while others used a revolving magazine to position charges for firing charges into the barrel. Still others, like the invention of Joseph Belton, loaded a number of charges on top of one another in the gun's breech. A sliding lock fired each charge in turn, and the shooter hoped that the ball of the unfired charge behind created a seal against the flame of the one being fired in front. Although several of his guns were made, Belton's idea, floated before the U.S. government in 1777 and the British in 1784, failed to capture the military imagination. Perhaps

surprisingly, repeaters of this type were popular
to a degree in Russia in the late seventeenth and
early eighteenth centuries. Tricky to load and
somewhat dangerous due to the possibility of
simultaneous explosions, these guns were a
developmental dead end.[40]

In 1698 the British Gunmakers' Company
reported "a gun with four chambers" made by
one James Gorgo. Other early revolving flintlock
makers included gunsmiths John Shaw and John
Dafte, who produced revolving handguns and
muskets in the early eighteenth century. James
Puckle is probably the best known of the early
repeating arms inventors, for his proto-machine
gun, a hand-cranked revolving cannon mounted
on a tripod and designed to fire "round bullets"
against Christians and "square bullets" against
Turks. A 1722 test of the Puckle gun left British

An unidentified Union cavalry soldier with a Smith
carbine. (*USAMHI*)

military authorities unimpressed, although two of them were apparently purchased for a 1727 expedition to the islands of St. Lucia and St. Vincent.[41]

Most early revolving and magazine guns were limited to a few prototype
models. Multiple barrel repeaters, side by side or one above the other, were
far more common. One four-barreled gun is reported in the fifteenth century and a number of six- and seven-barreled guns from the sixteenth and
seventeenth centuries survive in European collections. These guns were
usually either fired by multiple independent locks (in the case of double
barrels) for separate repeat shots, or one lock for guns intended to fire all
charges at once or, with rotating barrels, usually accomplished manually, in
succession.[42]

Multi-barreled guns, however, except for the fine British double-barreled
shotguns produced by the shop of Joseph Manton beginning in the 1790s,
were heavy, expensive to make, and difficult to "zero" so that the barrels shot
to the same point of aim at a given distance. For these reasons, they were, in
general, impractical military arms, although occasionally issued in limited
numbers to special purpose troops. From 1768 through 1798, Austrian
sharpshooters were issued double-barreled flintlock over and under guns,
with the top barrel rifled and the bottom barrel smooth, a combination rifle
and musket, increasing versatility and obviating the need for precise zeroing
of both barrels. Some thought was given to equipping the entire Austrian
infantry with this arm, which, unfortunately, weighed more than sixteen
pounds, a fact that left the idea stillborn.[43]

The Nock "volley gun" is probably the best example of the multi-barreled arm that discharged all of its charges at one time. Designed by James Wilson, 655 of these .46 caliber, seven-barreled volley guns were made by London gunsmith Henry Nock, one of the great British military gun makers of the late eighteenth century. British military authorities decided that the volley gun was not practical for army use, but might have a role in naval warfare. In the event, however, naval officers were not enthusiastic about volley guns either, mostly due to the danger of the muzzle flash from the multiple discharge setting fire to sails. Although some of the Nock arms were issued to a fleet that sailed to Gibraltar in 1782, no information about their actual use, if any, has come to light.[44]

A more sophisticated and lighter early repeating arm, a flintlock which used the principle of a cylinder bored to accept several charges revolving around a central arbor to provide successive shots, was patented by American Elisha H. Collier in the United States in 1816 and in Britain in 1818. The Collier's cylinder moved each chamber into firing position by use of a spring, while another spring moved the cylinder forward to provide a gas seal at the breech and a small powder magazine automatically refilled the gun's priming pan each time it was cocked.[45]

Although everyone agreed that the Collier was an ingenious design, when the inventor demonstrated it before a British military board in 1819, the board members decided it was "too complicated and expensive." Collier redesigned his gun for percussion cap ignition and simplified it further by eliminating the complex cylinder rotation method, returning to Britain for another field trial in 1824. Manually rotating the cylinder, and reloading the gun, Collier managed only 100 shots in twenty-nine minutes, and hit a target of unspecified size at 100 yards seventy-one times. As one authority points out, the performance was "little better than the performance of a musket" for a comparable length of firing time.[46]

Although in the event the percussion Collier turned out to be an ingenious failure, it inspired less complex and more effective revolving arms. The first significant one would be the invention of Samuel Colt. Born in 1814, Colt, who some historians believe got a good look at a Collier revolving rifle on a trip to London as a young man, had gunsmiths making prototypes of his invention as early as 1832 and patented a revolving firearm in February, 1836. In that year he founded, with family financial support, the Patent Arms Manufacturing Company in Paterson, New Jersey.

Although Colt is historically better known for handguns, rifles were part of the Colt line from the beginning. The Colt Model 1837 "lever ring" revolving rifle, an eight- to ten-shot arm chambered in a series of calibers from .34 to .44, used a ring in front of the trigger to cock the gun and revolve its cylinder into firing position. Sam Colt succeeded in convincing the Federal government to purchase fifty of these guns for trial by troops fighting Seminole Indians in Florida, where they were "well received."[47]

By 1839 Colt was offering a revolving shotgun and a six-shot carbine in .52 caliber, which replaced the lever ring system with an external hammer that, when manually cocked, engaged a pawl that moved the chamber into battery. Unlike his earlier guns, which had to be disassembled to reload, the new arm could be reloaded with paper cartridges or loose powder and ball pressed into the front of the cylinder chambers by a loading lever that rested alongside its barrel. Sam managed to sell the Texas navy 180 of these carbines and arranged a United States government trial between his carbine and the single-shot breech-loading Hall. Although accuracy results from both guns were virtually identical, the Colt, as might be expected, won the rate of fire competition hands down.[48]

Through skillful promotion and exploitation of the trial results, Sam Colt was able to sell his new carbines to both the Army and Navy for use against the persistent Seminoles. A field evaluation filed in 1842 by Lieutenant John McLaughlin, an early enthusiast for repeating arms, proved favorable in some aspects. McLaughlin attested to the fact that Colt's guns, despite fears to the contrary, were rugged and stood up to the rigors of campaigning by his Marines. They were "constantly employed in the field & in canoes from the 9th Oct. until the 22 Decr. 1841" and stood the test better than ordinary muskets.[49]

Unfortunately, however, serious problems beyond durability also arose, to include occasional multiple chamber ignition and cylinder explosions. These safety issues, coupled with a failure of parts interchangeability, halted government procurement of Colt carbines and hastened the end of the Patent Firearms Company, which went bankrupt in 1841. Although remaining guns, including revolving long arms, continued to be sold though the early 1840s, Sam Colt was personally out of the gun business until 1847. The advent of the Mexican war, however, reawakened memories of the effectiveness of Colt guns in Texas service. United States Army Captain Samuel Walker, a former Texas Ranger, collaborated with Sam Colt in the design of a massive new .44 caliber handgun, known today among collectors today as the "Walker Colt," and large government orders ensued.

The new contracts put Colt back in the gun business for good. Although production was largely confined to handguns for several years, drawings and sample copies of new revolving rifle designs exist from the 1846-1847 period and there was apparently a limited production revival of a modified version of the 1839 carbine made for the state of Rhode Island.[50]

With his Paterson works long gone, Colt went to the well-established industrial firm of Eli Whitney to produce the Walker design. Profits from this venture were used to establish the Colt Patent Fire Arms Company in Hartford, Connecticut. The 1849 discovery of gold in California ensured Colt's success, as the civilian handgun market expanded dramatically. The Model 1849 "Baby Dragoon" .31 caliber pocket revolver quickly became an arm of choice for men headed for the gold fields.[51]

The major problems of multiple chamber ignition and exploding cylinders apparent in Florida were easily addressed. The defective cylinders appear to have been the result of manufacturing errors, while the multiple ignitions were caused by poorly fitting percussion caps that exposed a chamber to ignition by flame generated when another chamber was fired. Although remedied in later years, these Florida defects would dog the Colt for generations, earning later revolving rifle designs, including his, an undeserved reputation well into the twentieth century.[52]

The Colt Company did not offer a standard long gun again until its "New Model" of 1855. This sidehammer design, resulting from development work by Sam Colt and his factory manager Elisha K. Root, was applied to pocket pistols, rifles, and shotguns. The New Model rifle entered production in 1857 in .36 and .44 calibers, and the army purchased over 400 for field-testing. Colt subsequently increased the frame size of the Model 1855 rifle to accommodate a five shot .56 caliber cylinder, which he hoped would be more acceptable for military use and, just before the Civil War, developed a .65 caliber revolving rifle for consideration by the Navy. These larger calibers were designed to use standard .58 and .69 caliber ammunition in a pinch.[53]

Although they appeared on the frontier shortly after their introduction, Colt repeating rifles appear to have first entered large-scale combat in the Italian Risorgimento war of 1860. One account of the Colt in action noted: "It appears that from our correspondent of the *London News*, that this rifle is used by Garibaldi's sharp shooters to some extent, and with much favor. It possesses breech-loading advantages and dis-advantages; and admits of great rapidity of fire at a given moment. The difficulties are first, that the instrument requires care to keep it in order, and may at times clog; a common trouble of all breech-loaders; it offers peculiar temptation to too rapid and careless firing."[54]

Colt revolving rifles, some in .44 but most in .56 caliber, proved to be the first repeating rifles used in a major conflict, the American Civil War. Although disregarded and demeaned in postwar literature, the Colt Model 1855, especially in the war's first two years, was usually praised for its effectiveness and considered a desirable arm.

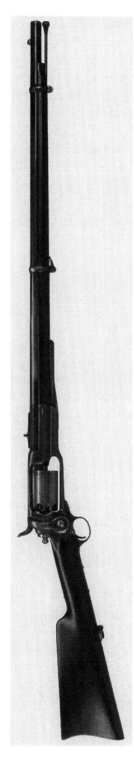

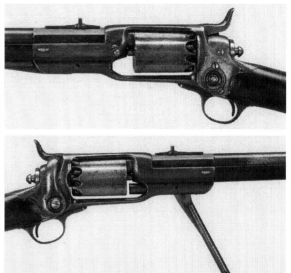

The Colt "New Model" 1855 sidehammer revolving rifle. At the beginning of the Civil War, the five-shot .56 caliber (shown here) and six-shot .44 caliber Colts were the only effective repeating rifles on the market. The .56 caliber was a wartime procurement and as such they were in great demand in certain quarters, especially in the western theater, where General Rosecrans was impressed by the military sense of using repeating firearms for fast moving special operations. Berdan's Sharpshooters used Colts until their Sharps rifles were available, and, despite early misgivings, considered them good arms. Although Colt rifles acquired a latter day reputation for multiple charge ignition, there is no real evidence that this was a significant problem. Before firing, each chamber was individually charged using a paper cartridge, in which the paper was discarded after powder and bullet were loaded, or a faster loading combustible cartridge, which was inserted in its entirety in the chamber. As each chamber was loaded, the bullet was rammed home with the rammer attached to the rifle in front of the chamber (above) and then the nipple at the rear of each chamber was fitted with a percussion cap. Although useful early in the war, the Colt became "old technology" rapidly after the introduction of the self contained cartridge and the Spencer and Henry arms that fired such ammunition. Still, the Colt persisted in service into early 1865 in some units. (*Private collection; photographs by John Hubbard*)

Not only was the 1855 an effective repeater, it was accurate as well. In an 1859 United States Navy test, a .56 caliber Colt was fired 250 times at a target of unspecified size at a range of 500 yards, and only seven shots missed. The officer in charge of the tests reported that the Colt rifles "were not cleaned, and sufficient time only allowed for them to cool when hot. They worked smoothly and easy. None failed to go off, and the cylinders showed less [fouling] deposit than usual."[55]

Despite this, the men of Berdan's Sharpshooters, initially issued Colts, "thought at first that these Colts would not shoot true, but this proved not exactly the case, as they were pretty good line shooters." Charles A. Stevens, the unit historian, recalled that sharpshooter "Andrew J. Pierce . . . while on the way down the Potomac made a trial shot of the five chambers . . . at a buoy bobbing up in the river some 400 yards distant" and hit it twice.[56]

Some Colt Model 1855s, already in government storage or purchased on the open market, were in the hands of troops as early as the fall of 1861. Between November 1861 and February 1863 the Federal government purchased 4,613 Model 1855s directly from Colt. Major General William S. Rosecrans thought highly of the Colt and called for as many as he could get.[57]

When a limited number of Colts were available to a unit, they were usually issued to soldiers who were engaged as "skirmishers" deployed as individuals or in small groups between main lines of battle. During the Civil War the terms "sharpshooter" and "skirmisher" were often used interchangeably. The Thirty-seventh Illinois Infantry equipped its "two flanking companies and all non-commissioned officers with Colt's repeating rifle." One soldier declared the outfit's Colts "the prettiest guns I ever saw." They were effective as well. After a year of use the regiment reported that "the Colt's revolving rifles . . . are of the best quality." A significant number of Colts were still in use by the Thirty-seventh during the final quarter of 1864. Arms historian John D. MacAulay lists twenty-six Union cavalry and twenty-nine Federal infantry units armed, in whole or in part, at one time or another, during the war, with Colt revolving rifles. The overwhelming majority of these units served in the west.[58]

The men of the Second Michigan Cavalry, Major General Philip Sheridan's original command, were issued Colt revolving rifles, perhaps the ones turned in by Berdan's men when they finally received their long-awaited Sharps single-shot breechloaders. The Second used its Colts quite effectively in a number of actions, and the Colt armed Twenty-first Ohio Infantry added its firepower to the Spencer repeating rifles of Brigadier General John T. Wilder's "Lightning Brigade" at Chickamauga. Although ultimately in a losing cause, the Twenty-first fired over 43,000 rounds of ammunition before being overrun by Rebels armed with rifle muskets.

Privately owned Colt rifles were on the frontier soon after their introduction. U.S. Army Assistant Surgeon Albert J. Myer, left, displays his around 1857. During the Civil War Myer became the army's chief signal officer. Right, unknown enlisted man with a Colt. (*USAMHI*)

Many of the 765 Colt revolving carbines and rifles purchased by the Federal government in the years leading up to the Civil War were stored in arsenals in the South and subsequently issued to Rebel units, along with Model 1855s captured from Yankee forces. North Carolina began the war with sixty Colt carbines and 120 Colt rifles, which were issued to state troops. Among other Rebel units armed with at least some Colt repeating long arms were the First Virginia, Third Texas, and Thirteenth Tennessee Cavalry, as well as the Eighth Virginia and Eleventh Mississippi Infantry.[59]

There were some drawbacks to the Colt revolving rifles, however. The historian of the Ninth Illinois Cavalry remembered that "the Colt's revolving rifle was an excellent arm, and had served us well on many an occasion; but there was one serious objection to them; when being discharged they would shoot splinters of lead into the wrist and hand of the man firing." This problem, characteristic of all revolvers, even modern ones, occurs when they "go out of time," creating a slight misalignment between chamber mouth and barrel, causing lead to shave from a bullet making the jump between the two. It is seldom noticed in handguns, where the shooter's left hand and arm are behind the cylinder-barrel gap. A captain in the Second Michigan Cavalry reported that his men's Colts were "liable to get out of order and can't easily be repaired." Other officers complained that the stocks and locks of the Colts were liable to break.[60]

Colonel Berdan's men "feared the danger of all the chambers exploding at once," or "chainfire," no doubt recalling the unfortunate Florida field tests of the first Colt revolving carbines, although this fear seems to have been greatly exaggerated. Sam Colt always maintained that one of his guns, *properly loaded*, would not chainfire. To test the likelihood of this possibility, arms historian William B. Edwards tested Colt's premise and reported on it in his classic work *Civil War Guns*. Edwards loaded a .56-caliber Colt revolving rifle cylinder with powder charges and unlubricated snug-fitting Minié balls. Without applying any grease to the chamber mouths, he covered the cylinder's face with loose powder which he touched off with "a long match." Although the powder "whooshed up," none of the chambers went off. Edwards deduced that: "A Colt's [percussion] revolver, loaded with proper bullets rammed home, is as safe from accidental discharge as is an ordinary metallic cartridge .38 Police Positive Special."[61]

One veteran, who thought there was "but little to choose between" the Sharps and the Spencer repeater, and considered the Henry repeater a "magnificent weapon" and "very accurate," believed the Colt revolving rifle "as good or better than any, in the hands of men who are cool and know how to use it." He also noted, however, that the Colt's "loading must be done without flurrying" and it was "a poor weapon to give to green troops on this account."[62]

The Model 1855 Colt New Model rifle would prove to be the apogee of the combustible cartridge separately primed repeating firearm. The next step toward modernization would require a sturdy self-contained cartridge, with priming, propellant charge, and projectile all in the same package. Such a cartridge would feed an effective repeating rifle that would work smoothly, without concern about "flurrying" while loading, an asset to veteran as well as green troops.

  # THREE

THE SEARCH FOR THE PERFECT CARTRIDGE

B Y THE MID-1850S, EVEN CONSERVATIVE OFFICERS KNEW THAT THE future of military small arms lay in breech loading of some sort, and the number of inventors offering such systems began to proliferate. It was also clear, however, that a self-contained cartridge, with bullet, propellant, and priming in one neat package that sealed the bore from gas escape on firing and was waterproof and sturdy enough to survive abuse in the field, was as important as a gun to shoot it. As with many other technical advances, work on both problems had begun many years before.

The first steps toward perfecting the breech-loading system through development of a self-contained cartridge were taken in Europe. On September 29, 1812, Samuel Pauly, a Swiss gunsmith residing in Paris, was granted French patent number 843 for a breech-loading firearms system. By that date, the Chaumette-Ferguson twisting trigger guard breech access was an idea whose time had come and gone, replaced by variants of a rising breech, separate from the barrel itself and loaded from its front, like the Crespi and Hall. Pauly's design differed dramatically from those contemporary efforts, and opened for loading by lifting a lever extending down the wrist of the stock, superficially resembling the later Westley Richards "monkey tail" design. As the lever, which to some resembled a monkey's tail, rose, the gun's breech block swung upward, exposing a loading chamber that was integral with the rear of the barrel.[1]

As important an innovation as Pauly's breech design was, however, his ignition system and ammunition were also a radical departure from previous efforts. Unlike every other breech-loading design of the era, the Pauly was not a flintlock. Its external hammer served only to cock an internal striker, or firing pin. The Pauly was loaded with a paper cartridge containing bullet and powder inserted in a rimmed, metallic base primed with fulminate, which, when hit by the striker, detonated, exploding the powder to fire the gun.

Paper wadding was included in the cartridge to seal the breech against excessive gas escape.[2]

Although it would seem the potential military advantages of such a system were self-evident, Pauly's early efforts to gain an audience with the French army were frustrated. He finally succeeded in demonstrating his gun before a General Savary who, on January 2, 1813, wrote Emperor Napoleon Bonaparte that he was "astonished" when "in my presence in my garden he [Pauly] fired 22 rounds in two minutes." The following day Napoleon, recently returned to France from his Russian disaster and perhaps eager for some military *deus ex machina* to save his imperial bacon, ordered a formal trial of the gun. The emperor was soon preoccupied trying to stave off his many enemies, who were closing in for the kill from all over Europe, however, and failed to follow up on his order. It was not until the summer of 1814, with Bonaparte simmering in his first exile on Elba, that the Société d'Encouragment pour l'Industrie conducted a thorough test of Pauly's invention. Pauly was apparently a pragmatist, and also demonstrated his invention for Russian officers in Paris with the allied army of occupation, who reportedly purchased a number of guns from him.[3]

Although representatives of two major powers thus evaluated the Pauly system, neither country adopted it. Unfortunately, details on the actual test results of Pauly's breechloader are lost to history, so we can only speculate as to the cause of its apparent failure to impress enough for military adoption. One drawback might well have been suspicions of its durability in the field, and another the cost and manufacturing difficulty, not only of the guns themselves but also of their unique ammunition. Pauly cartridge bases were reloadable and reusable, but individually machined. It is quite possible that since the capacity of manufacturers to mass produce identical objects with the same dimensions was still in the future, the bases would fit well only into a specific gun, a limitation that would cause a supply nightmare.

Whatever the cause for its rejection, the Pauly breechloader design enjoyed a limited but steady popularity among French sportsmen, with improvements patented in 1816 and 1818 and apparent production by a number of small custom gunsmiths. Pauly himself went on to patent a high-powered air gun in Britain, and several pistols made on this design still survive.[4]

Muzzle-loading guns, smoothbore and then rifled, remained the mainstay of the infantry forces of the major powers for more than fifty years after Pauly patented his breech-loading system. Although military muzzleloaders were sturdy and, to use a modern term, idiot proof in the hands of the average recruit, the paper cartridges that they and all early breechloaders, including the Pauly, used remained comparatively fragile items.

As late as the American Civil War, when more durable semi-fixed and fixed metallic ammunition was making a widespread appearance, the rifle musket cartridge used by most infantrymen was still made from paper. Assessments of the paper cartridge's durability in the field were not optimistic. A correspondent of the *Army & Navy Journal* wrote that "any soldier can tell you that after a long march many of his cartridges are useless, the powder having sifted out, and that in tearing cartridges more or less powder is wasted, even at target practice, much more in the heat of the battle." Powder spillage during the loading process affecting ballistic consistency was one reason the Springfield .58 caliber musket powder charge was raised from sixty to sixty-five grains by the middle of the Civil War.[5]

In the first half of the nineteenth century, most American inventors of military breech-loading guns applied themselves to developing a firearm and ammunition that addressed the military requirements of durability, rapid reloading, and sealing the breech from gas escape. The ammunition used in these designs was invariably fired by external ignition, initially, as in the case of the Hall, flint and steel, and subsequently, with designs like the Sharps, Smith, and Maynard, by percussion cap.

Europeans went a step further, attempting to develop a firearms system that achieved the American goals and also adhered to the Pauly concept of internal priming to create a complete cartridge package. Johann Nicholas Von Dreyse, a former Pauly employee who set up shop in Erfurt in 1827, improved on the Swiss inventor's design for both gun and ammunition with his "needle gun," a weapon that appeared in prototype form in 1835.[6]

Dreyse's invention involved a stiff paper or cardboard cartridge that was self-contained, but had a unique internal structure, with a .52 caliber bullet glued into a paper sabot which took up the "windage" between the bullet and the gun's .60 caliber bore. The sabot's base wad held fulminate priming and was followed by a powder charge. Sabot and wad were supposed to eliminate gas blowby to the front and escape to the rear, but this apparently did not always occur.

The Dreyse gun's breech was opened to receive the cartridge by operating a bolt encased in a tubular receiver. A "needle" or firing pin projected from the front of the bolt and was separately cocked and held by a sear which was lowered, releasing the needle, when the gun's trigger was pulled. The needle then penetrated the rear of the cartridge, and drove through the powder charge into a hole in the sabot to detonate the fulminate and fire the round.[7]

The Prussian army bought its first needle guns, the direct ancestors of all breech-loading bolt-action military rifles, in 1841, although it referred to them as "percussion rifles" in documents for security purposes and did not issue them in any significant numbers for several years. This initial purchase was followed by Prussian acquisition of a series of other models and variants on the basic Dreyse, including a huge rampart or wall gun used by the Prussians in their 1864 war against the Danes.[8]

Although the Prussian army intended to keep the needle gun secret, word got out pretty quickly, and copies began to appear around Europe in the early 1850s. As early as the summer of 1849 a British ordnance representative traveled to Prussia and examined some needle guns. On his return he was instructed to make several examples for testing by the British military.[9]

Formal trials of the British-made needle guns versus standard rifles and muskets were conducted in 1850, and, while the needle rifle "had the highest rate of fire and was reasonably accurate," there were problems closing the bolt as the gun heated and fouled from continued firing. Although George Lovell, the British maker, conceded that perhaps he had not made his needle guns as well as the Prussian arms, the British government soon lost interest in the breechloaders, opting for a variant of the muzzle-loading French Minié rifle, with its relatively fast loading and effective long-range capability, the latter distinctly superior to that of the needle gun.[10]

First used by the Prussians against street rioters in 1849, and then in the Danish war of 1864, the needle gun gained its greatest reputation in the Austro-Prussian War of 1866. Although it was already obsolescent due to the introduction of metallic cartridge military weapons in America, the Prussian breechloader proved its dominance over the Austrian Lorenz muzzleloader. Some critics, however, ascribe the Prussian success in 1866 more to good tactical disposition on the part of the Prussians and the lack of same on the part of their opponents as much as to the firepower superiority of the breech loading system. The Austrian muzzleloaders were more accurate and had greater effective range than the Prussian breechloaders. Austrian commanders failed to exploit the range advantage of their small arms, however, and maneuvered their men in dense formations, making them better and closer targets for the Prussians.[11]

Variants of needle-fire guns using self-contained paper cartridges with various types of gas sealing schemes proliferated for a brief period in the late 1860s, with Russia, France, and Italy adopting different versions. The French Chassepot was the most significant, as it moved the priming compound to the rear of the cartridge and prevented the escape of gas on firing with a rubber breech seal. Although a better design, the Chassepot lost the Franco-Prussian War of 1870 to the Dreyse needle gun, the last major conflict for either arm, again due to tactical rather than technological inferiority. The self-contained

The Dreyse Model 1841 "needle gun." The gun's breech was opened to receive the cartridge by operating a bolt encased in a tubular receiver. A "needle," or firing pin, projected from the front of the bolt and was separately cocked and held by a sear which when the gun's trigger was pulled, lowered and released the needle The needle then penetrated the rear of the paper cartridge, drove through the powder charge into a hole in the sabot, detonated the charge and fired the round. (*AntiqueFirearms.com*)

metallic cartridge, used in combat during the American Civil War, with priming compound in the cartridge base, subsequently became the standard for all military weapons.[12]

The use of metal as a cartridge material was not new. Some successful American breech-loading designs introduced in the pre-Civil War period, like the Burnside and Maynard, used semi-fixed copper ammunition to provide a successful breech seal. The French, however, as they had with self-contained paper ammunition, again took the lead in the initial development of self-contained metallic cartridges.

Another Pauly successor was Casimir Lefaucheux, who, as early as the 1830s was producing guns designed to fire his pinfire cartridge. Like the needle gun round, the pinfire cartridge contained powder, shot, and priming all in one neat package. It was fired when the gun's hammer hit a pin projecting from the side of the base and drove it into an internal fulminate primer. Guns chambered for pinfire ammunition had a notch atop the barrel from which the "pin" extended. Pinfire shotgun ammunition, with metal base and paper or cardboard body, was perfected by a French gun maker named Houllier in 1846 when he patented a wad that provided the best gas seal to date on firing.

Pinfire revolvers in small calibers firing completely copper-cased ammunition became popular on the European continent, and the new pinfire shotgun shell made significant inroads with French target shooters and hunters by the early 1850s. The 1851 Great Exhibition in Hyde Park brought LeFaucheux's invention to the attention to the British shooting public and sporting gun makers as well. Some Continental pinfire shotguns were less than safe, as the concept of pressure curves was not completely understood by gun makers of the day, many of whom produced breech actions not sturdy enough and barrels too thin to withstand the pressure of the new ammunition. The nature of pinfire ammunition in and of itself was problematic as well, since, although it was water resistant and self-contained, it could on occasion detonate if dropped, stepped on, or otherwise roughly handled. In addition, the pinfire cartridge had to be loaded with its pin protruding from the breech under the hammer. Although a slot was provided for the pin, fumbling around with such ammunition, along with its low power potential for long range shooting, proved a combat disadvantage.[13]

Because of the above liabilities, the pinfire system proved a dead end for military, and, eventually, sporting use, although heavier caliber LeFaucheux pinfire revolvers were developed in France for military use, and some of these guns and ammunition were purchased by the Federal government during the Civil War. The system did prosper for a considerable time in small- to medium-bore sporting rifles, revolvers, and shotguns, and hung on for generations in cheap handguns made in Belgium.

Aside from double-barreled guns and those with revolving cylinders, the pinfire round was unusable in a repeating arm due to the need for its cartridge "pin" to fit in exactly the same position under the hammer for every shot and poor potential for feeding through a magazine into the action. A slicker, more streamlined cartridge was needed before such an arm could be successfully introduced.

American Walter Hunt thought he had one. Hunt was a prolific polymath of an inventor, not untypical of the early nineteenth century, when technology bloomed and formal education was rare. Hunt invented "the safety pin, lockstitch needle, fountain pen and various new and novel innovations." Among the latter was the "rocket ball," which he patented in 1848. Hunt's "ball" was a self-contained cartridge in which a hollowed out conical bullet actually served as a cartridge case holding the powder charge capped in the rear with a cork or paper wad. Priming was separately supplied by a fulminate "pill" that fed into the action automatically as the cartridge was chambered.[14]

Shortly afterward, Hunt patented a repeating rifle to shoot his rocket ball. His "Volition Repeater" sported a trigger that did double duty by acting as a lever, in conjunction with a second lever, to feed cartridges from a tubular magazine attached to the underside of the gun's barrel up and into its chamber.[15]

Only one Volition Repeater is known to survive today, and it appears none may have ever been manufactured save the patent model. Shortly after Hunt patented the gun, however, New York City manufacturer George A. Arrowsmith acquired the patent and hired gunsmith Lewis Jennings to turn the idea into a viable firearm. Jennings modified the gun by reducing its two loading levers to one, patented that idea on December 25, 1849, and assigned the patent to his employer. He could not, however, work out other internal bugs that kept the Hunt rifle from functioning reliably.[16]

Arrowsmith promoted the gun, however, with hopes of peddling the patents, and was able to sell the refined design to another speculative manufacturer, one Courtland C. Palmer, for the then very substantial sum of $100,000. Palmer attempted to have 5,000 Jennings repeaters in .54 caliber made by the prominent Vermont contract firearms manufacturer, Robbins and Lawrence. Unfortunately the Jennings rifle proved too complex, even with improvements, to produce as a functioning marketable gun. The primer feed proved particularly difficult to perfect. Some Jennings guns were finished as single-shot breechloaders, and some even as muzzleloaders between 1848 and 1852, but there is no information as to how many, if any, were ever sold as repeaters.[17]

Despite the failure of his repeater, Jennings had made some real improvements on the basic Hunt design, including a rack and pinion gear for the lever and the feeding system for the "rocket balls." But he could go no further. Palmer made one more attempt to save the failed repeating rifle system and hired gunsmith Horace Smith in 1851 in a last effort to perfect it. In the resultant "Smith-Jennings" rifle, patented by him in 1851, with assignment of the patent to Palmer, Smith retained the pill priming system of the earlier models, but returned to the ring trigger design of the original Hunt, but used it as both loading lever and trigger. Pushing the lever forward loaded the gun from its under-barrel magazine and retrieving it fired it. Robbins and Lawrence were able to produce over 1,000 of three variants of the Smith-Jennings, all in .54 caliber. Distribution of the gun was not wide, but several are reported as being in use in California in 1851.[18]

There was a better way on the horizon. And once again, its origins were French. Enter Gustave Flobert. At the age of sixteen, Flobert was apprenticed to a Paris gun and sword maker named Sattler. During the 1840s, while the pinfire was still in the process of becoming the gold standard in Gallic breech-loading technology, Flobert, aided by his younger brother Ernest, developed a new type of cartridge. Flobert ammunition used a bigger percussion cap as both detonating device and, aided by a bit of black powder, propulsive charge for a small bullet fitted into its open end. The space between priming compound and bullet was not entirely filled with powder, according to Flobert, to "confine the burning inside the cartridge" rather than in the barrel. The Flobert cartridge, developed in 1846 and patented in 1849, was intended for indoor target shooting, and far too anemic to attract the attention of military men.[19]

Flobert's patent also covered, along with his ammunition, "a new firing mechanism able to produce with great economy new guns." His low-powered rifle dispensed with a breech block and used the hammer and a double-jawed cartridge case extractor to contain the pressure of the fired round. The gun was improved in 1855 with a hinged breech block, which permitted chambering for larger six- and nine-millimeter cartridges useful for pest control and gave Flobert the idea of expanding to the profitable military market. Although most of his guns were of the "salon" or indoor target variety, Flobert did eventually develop a method of converting a muzzle-loading musket into a single shot breechloader and, presumably, a cartridge to go with it, by the early 1860s. The French government, then rearming with the new Chassepot breechloader, was not interested, however.[20]

In the United States, meanwhile, Horace Smith, who had improved the Hunt-Jennings rifle as much as it could be given its ammunition, made the acquaintance of Connecticut gunsmith Daniel Wesson. Some have speculated that this fateful meeting happened during the production of the Smith Jennings repeater at Robbins & Lawrence, or shortly thereafter, when they both were employed by Allen, Brown & Luther, makers of "pepperbox" handguns. Whenever it occurred, Smith & Wesson historian Roy Jinks surmises that both men discussed the Jennings rifle and came to the conclusion that in order for a magazine repeating rifle to work, its ammunition had to be entirely self-contained, and that the Flobert cartridge represented the wave of the future.[21]

Daniel Wesson, who had learned his craft in the shop of his late brother, the noted target rifle maker Edwin, began to make a few experimental single-shot Flobert-type pistols in 1851. He crafted ammunition out of percussion caps and buckshot purchased from independent ammunition maker Crittenden and Tibbals. Once Wesson had the process of making small-caliber single-shot cartridge pistols down, he and Horace Smith began to tackle the idea of larger caliber, more powerful ammunition, and a repeating rifle to fire it in.[22]

On May 10, 1853, Smith and Wesson applied together for a patent on an improvement in the Flobert cartridge, with priming compound spread across the base of the cartridge and tallow lubricant behind the ball. The patent was issued on August 8, 1854. Almost simultaneously, the partners filed a patent on a new gun, which used a finger lever acting as a trigger guard to cock the gun's hammer and feed their new cartridge from a magazine into the weapon's firing chamber while an extractor removed the fired cartridge case. Although the Smith & Wesson metallic cartridge rifle represents a quantum leap in firearms design, it never entered production, most likely, according to Jinks, because it is "doubtful . . . that the system was made to function successfully due to a lack of proper cartridges or failure of the system to ignite the cartridges reliably."[23]

Whatever the reason, none of the guns are known to have been sold to the public, although one, a .50 caliber rimfire rifle made in 1852, prior to the patent application, survives in the Winchester collection. Smith and Wesson, impatient at the fact that ammunition technology had not kept pace with their fertile inventiveness, abandoned the idea of producing a rimfire magazine repeater and modified the parts already in production for use in an arm firing an improved version of the old Hunt rocket ball. The advance was significant in concept. Even though the new rocket ball still suffered from a lack of power, it became a true self-contained round with the addition of an internal cup holding a fulminate primer centered by a cork wad. The rocket ball was fired when the gun's trigger was pulled, releasing its hammer to strike a firing pin that then hit the primer.

The original Smith & Wesson "Volcanic" arms were .31 and .41 caliber handguns, but unsatisfactory and erratic results with the rocket ball ammunition led the inventors to sell their ammunition idea, along with its sophisticated repeating rifle design, to a group of investors including Oliver Winchester in 1855. Although they had been frustrated in their attempt to find a suitable cartridge, Smith and Wesson had perfected the mechanical aspect of a repeating rifle using an under the barrel magazine and a toggle link feeding system to move cartridges from the magazine to the chamber.

In their new enterprise, Smith and Wesson returned to the idea of perfecting their metallic cartridge and a gun that could fire it effectively. In 1857, in conjunction with a young inventor named Rollin White, they developed a small seven-shot breech-loading revolver that fired their advanced version of the Flobert cartridge. The advent of the Smith and Wesson "Number 1" handgun was made possible due to the White's surprisingly simple patent. White's idea of revolver chambers (bored completely through as opposed to being closed at one end by a nipple to hold a percussion cap) heralded the beginnings of one of America's most notable firearm manufacturers.

Prior to the White patent, most revolvers, save pinfires, were loaded by inserting loose powder and ball or a combustible cartridge into each chamber from the front of the cylinder. Once the charges were rammed home, usually by a rammer attached to the gun's frame, a percussion cap was affixed to the nipple on the rear of each chamber.

Dispensing with that, the new .22 rimfire round was simply inserted in the rear of each chamber. The .22 was made by taking a copper case and mechanically spinning priming compound into its rim, which extended beyond the base of the case. Once the copper case was primed, it was loaded with a small four-grain powder charge under a twenty-nine-grain conical bullet. This somewhat anemic cartridge, detonated when the gun's hammer hit the cartridge rim, was the first serious self-contained ammunition put into mass production. It still exists in a more powerful form today as the .22 Short, and although unimpressive by modern standards, provided a dramatic breakthrough in ammunition technology in its day.

The new rimfire cartridge was not perfect, however. The copper cartridge case had to be soft in order that the revolver hammer could detonate the priming compound, but if it was too soft it could rupture on firing, which often occurred. Smith and Wesson devised a recoil plate to bolster the case base and prevent rupturing, but later abandoned it as ammunition quality improved. In 1857, however, rimfire ammunition larger than .22 was not available—nor was a rifle to fire it and take advantage of its greatest potential—use in a rapid-fire repeater.[24]

With the mechanical creativity present in the New England manufacturing community in the 1850s, both cartridge and rifle would not be long in coming. New England's thriving pre-Civil War firearms industry, in fact all of New England's industrial base, had its origins in the United States military's desire for weapons with interchangeable parts and a private arms industry sufficient to meet the needs of the military in time of war. In order to foster both of these concepts, the Federal government established two National Armories, at Springfield, Massachusetts, and Harper's Ferry, Virginia, in the 1790s. While the government had persistent production and consistency problems with the Harper's Ferry Armory early on, Springfield flourished. According to one historian, the Massachusetts location "coincided with a cultural and economic predisposition towards adaptability and change."[25]

Ironically, although the concept of interchangeable parts, so important to establishing the "American System" of manufacturing, had its birth in Federal government policy which inspired New England's private arms manufacturers to strive to meet the government standard, Harper's Ferry produced the first small arms with complete interchangeability. It took a Yankee to do it, however.

Although his name is often cited in connection with the principle of interchangeability, Eli Whitney was not that Yankee. Whitney, the most prominent private American gun maker of his era, was, as a historian of industrialization characterized him, a bit of a "song and dance man" in his presentations to the government. Whitney promised much more than he could produce in the way of muskets with interchangeable parts as specified in a contract he signed in 1798. Failing to satisfy the government's requirements,

Whitney was, however, responsible for significant progress on the way to perfecting the American System. Unlike prior arms contractors, Whitney was determined to reduce gun making from an artisan-based business to a mass production one, training essentially unskilled labor to perform one vital task among many. Using machinery and untrained labor, he made significant progress in the direction of true industrialization.[26]

The gun maker who finally solved the interchangeable parts problem and made true mass pro-

Smith and Wesson Number 1, first manufactured in 1857, represents a key advancement in cartridge and firearm technology. The six-shot pistol had bored-through cylinder chambers that allowed .22 rimfire metallic cartridges to be quickly and easily loaded from behind, dispensing the need for percussion caps. (*Smith and Wesson*)

duction possible was John Hall (who we met in the last chapter). After contracting with the government to produce breech-loading guns in 1819, Hall designed machine tools, patterns, and gauges to produce his rifle at Harper's Ferry. Disdainful of the artisan production culture of the main Harper's Ferry armory, Hall built his rifle shop at a separate location. The cranky Yankee had numerous philosophical, personal, and mechanical problems with the Harper's Ferry management, and did not produce any guns until 1823. Once the Hall factory was in a production mode, however, it delivered the first guns, or for that matter mechanical products produced anywhere, with fully interchangeable parts.[27]

Meanwhile, the government subsidized Yankee "mechanician" culture that developed as a result of planting Springfield Armory in the heart of New England spawned a number of trained men who subsequently worked at private factories throughout the region, including Horace Smith. One of the most significant developments at Springfield Armory, which affected the private manufacturing sector was Thomas Blanchard's 1819 invention of the Blanchard lathe. Blanchard's innovation, using a metal pilot to guide carving blades to replicate the pilot on several other objects simultaneously, was capable of making the unique cuts in a piece of wood necessary to create a musket stock. Within four years Springfield had fourteen Blanchard lathes in use. The applicability of this invention to the manufacture of numerous civilian products, including furniture, provided a major industrial breakthrough.[28]

Innovation was not completely lacking at Harper's Ferry or among Southerners, however. The armory there was not only the first Hall factory, but also the industrial home of an innovative attempt to create a single-shot rifle firing a large caliber self-contained center fire cartridge. In 1856 and 1858, George W. Morse patented such a gun, using a breech block that pivoted to the rear and housed an internal hammer for cartridge ignition. Morse sold 100 sample arms to the U.S. War Department in 1858, and was given time and money to convert muzzle-loading muskets to his system. He chose Springfield Armory for the site of the conversions, but the Secretary of War moved the experiment to Harper's Ferry in the summer of 1860 and ordered all tools and gauges, as well as sample arms, shipped there from Massachusetts. Before large-scale production could begin, however, the Civil War broke out. Shortly afterward, the Confederates captured Harper's Ferry and Morse went south, where he made approximately 1,000 breech-loading carbines for the South Carolina militia. A total of fifty-four muskets were converted at Springfield and another 600 or so at Harper's Ferry. How many of the latter survived the Armory fire of 1861 is unknown, and the idea was not pursued.[29]

It was out of this culture of industrial progress, based in the firearms industry, that Benjamin Tyler Henry emerged as a pivotal figure in the quest for a self-contained cartridge usable in a repeating firearm. Daniel Wesson left the Volcanic Repeating Arms Company in 1856 to resume partnership with Horace Smith to make their new .22 caliber rimfire revolver under the Rollin White patent. Volcanic had been undercapitalized, due to a large amount of money invested in machinery since its inception, and by 1856 was dependent on loans from its investors not only to make current expenses, but to pay off previous loans. In December 1856, Volcanic president and creditor Nelson B. Gaston died, and the company became insolvent, failing in February 1857. The company's other investor and director, Oliver Winchester, assumed Gaston's position and purchased the bankrupt company's assets and patents to become sole owner of what he now called the New Haven Arms Company. Although an astute businessman, Winchester was not a firearms designer and hired Hollis Smith as works superintendent. Smith was succeeded by former employee B. Tyler Henry as works superintendent on May 1, 1858. Henry had worked for the large private arms contractor Robbins and Lawrence, as well as Smith & Wesson. As with many of the principal firearms manufacturing technicians of the 1850s, however, Henry, born in 1821 in Claremont, New Hampshire, had begun his career at Springfield Armory.[30]

New Haven Arms continued to produce the expensive Volcanic guns chambered for the less than satisfactory "rocket ball" ammunition. Although New Haven sold a number of Volcanic guns by the end of 1857, allowing

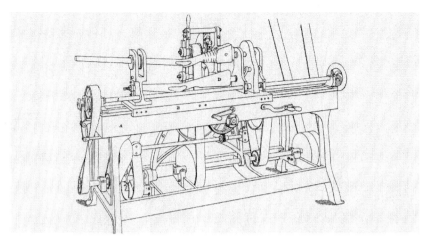

Thomas Blanchard's 1819 invention, a lathe that used a metal pilot and former to guide carving blades to replicate the former on several other objects simultaneously, made it possible to mass produce wooden musket stocks. The invention was adapted to the manufacture of civilian products, including furniture, providing a major industrial breakthrough. A. Frame. B. Carriage. C. Gun Stock. D. Former. E. Cutter Head. F. Guide Wheel. G. Swinging Frame. H. Feed Motion. I. Shaft for revolving the stock and former. (*Ordnance Memoranda Number 22*)

Winchester to retire much of the debt he had incurred when purchasing the company, profits were not overwhelming. Henry, encouraged by Winchester and perhaps inspired by Smith and Wesson's work with .22 rimfire ammunition and their early flawed attempt to create a sort of super Flobert .50 caliber rimfire round, determined to develop a copper-cased rimfire round to replace the rocket ball and then modify the Volcanic rifle to shoot it.

Since the ammunition for his new gun would have rimfire priming, Henry modified the Volcanic design by drilling a hole in the breech bolt so that a firing pin might be used to detonate self-contained cartridges. His firing pin was double-pronged, hitting the cartridge case at two points opposite each other, thus helping to insure ignition of rimfire ammunition which might not have priming compound spread evenly around the case rim. Henry also developed an ejector that threw the fired cartridge case clear of the gun when the lever was worked to reload the chamber from the magazine after firing.[31]

The heart of the Henry rifle's success, however, was in the ammunition itself. Oliver Winchester instructed Henry to come up with a larger cartridge than Smith and Wesson's .22. In 1860, Henry not only modified the Volcanic rifle to fire self-contained cartridges, but developed a .44 caliber rimfire round with a charge of 26 grains of powder loaded behind a 216-grain bullet to shoot in it. The Henry rifle's under the barrel magazine held fifteen of these rimfire rounds: an additional cartridge loaded in the gun's chamber made it a "sixteen shooter."[32]

Henry's patent of October 16, 1860, combined generations of cartridge and rifle development technology and made the concept of a reliable rapid-fire repeating rifle a reality. The timing of the patent appeared apt, as war clouds gathered on the horizon. On November 6, Abraham Lincoln was elected as the sixteenth president of the United States. On December 20, South Carolina seceded from the Union in response. By the spring of 1861, seven states had seceded and had created the Confederate States of America. War between the sections was in the offing.

It would seem that Oliver Winchester, with Henry's patent for a truly revolutionary firearm assigned to his New Haven Arms Company, was in an excellent position to help save his country and make a good deal of money at the same time. Unfortunately, due to debt incurred in expanding his shirt manufacturing company, Winchester was not in a financial position to purchase the needed tooling to produce the new rifle. In an attempt to remedy that situation and acquire development capital, Winchester contracted to produce 3,000 Walch ten-shot percussion revolvers at his New Haven Arms plant. Unfortunately, the Walch was another one of those ideas whose time never came. There were no sales of the cumbersome handgun until 1863, and more than half of those guns were subsequently returned as defective.[33]

The actual outbreak of war on April 12, 1861, seemed to provide an opportunity for New Haven arms. Following the Confederate attack on Fort Sumter in Charleston Harbor and Lincoln's subsequent call for 75,000 volunteers to restore the Union two days later, Virginia, North Carolina, Tennessee, and Arkansas seceded and joined the Confederacy.

In the wake of the Fort Sumter attack and Lincoln's call for troops, Oliver Winchester, approaching solvency again, quickly ordered machinery he had been hesitant about acquiring a mere few months before. He then began contracting with outside firms, including Colt, for component parts of his rifle, including iron frames and buttplates. Although other pioneers in the rimfire firearms business tended to buy their ammunition from established ammunition makers like Crittenden and Tibbals, Winchester purchased the tooling to make his own cartridges.[34]

Oliver Winchester may not have been a great technical expert or "mechanician," but he was an astute businessman. Born in 1810, he was the type of entrepreneur capitalist who made the production of new and novel manufactured goods a reality in mid-nineteenth century America. Winchester, like most of the new men of business and industry of his era, began life a farm boy, rising to become a building contractor and then menswear merchant.

Patent drawings of the Henry rifle breechloading mechanism as reproduced in the company's catalogue in 1865. When the lever that doubles as a trigger guard is pulled down, the empty cartridge case (if a round had already been fired) was ejected and the hammer was cocked. As the lever was returned, the next round in the magazine was pushed up and into the firing chamber.

He had enough technical ability to design a cloth-cutting machine to speed up the production of shirts, an invention which produced enough surplus wealth for him to invest in other areas, and the savvy to sell the products of those other areas. Firearms became his most important products.[35]

As early as 1858 Winchester had a story planted in *Frank Leslie's Illustrated Weekly* describing the trouble-prone Volcanic gun as combining "every quality requisite in such a weapon, with many advantages which no similar invention has yet succeeded in attaining." One Volcanic handgun purchaser provided a testimonial statement that few other shooters of the day would have endorsed, calling the Volcanic "the *ne plus ultra* of Repeating or Revolving Arms, and far superior in many respects to Colt's much extolled revolver." One particular piece of New Haven Arms' advertising hyperbole had portrayed the Volcanic as "the most powerful, and effective weapon of defense ever invented." Now, with a much better rifle in the Henry, Winchester made plans early on to sell his truly revolutionary gun to both the military and commercial markets.[36]

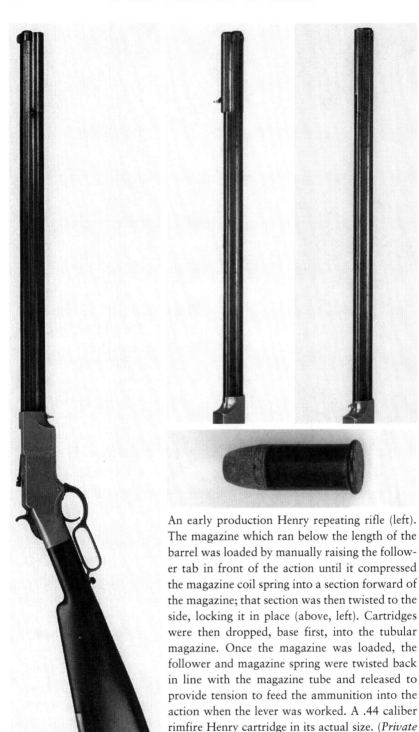

An early production Henry repeating rifle (left). The magazine which ran below the length of the barrel was loaded by manually raising the follower tab in front of the action until it compressed the magazine coil spring into a section forward of the magazine; that section was then twisted to the side, locking it in place (above, left). Cartridges were then dropped, base first, into the tubular magazine. Once the magazine was loaded, the follower and magazine spring were twisted back in line with the magazine tube and released to provide tension to feed the ammunition into the action when the lever was worked. A .44 caliber rimfire Henry cartridge in its actual size. (*Private collection; photographs by John Hubbard*)

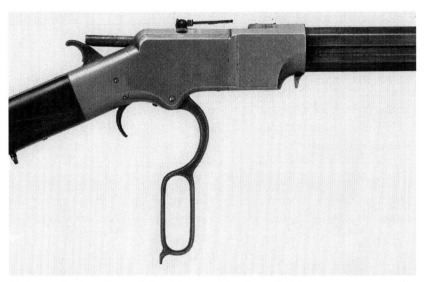

Early production Henry rifle with rear sight dovetailed into a groove atop the action. Later guns had the sight set in a dovetailed slot in the barrel. Note the cocking piston that automatically pushed the hammer back when the lever was operated. (*Private collection; photograph by John Hubbard*)

Despite his marketing skills, it would be a tough sell. Despite the need for firearms, Union Army Chief of Ordnance Brigadier General James W. Ripley was not interested in experimenting with new guns when he had hundreds of thousands of new recruits to arm with the basic muzzle-loading rifle musket, which was in short supply.

In the weeks following April 12, 1861, Ripley was besieged by inventors, crackpot and otherwise, touting their patent firearms as the solution to suppressing the rebellion in short order. The general was not impressed by these untried weapons systems and was particularly leery of repeating arms, which had, up through and including the Volcanic, a reputation for unreliability and fragility. Although Oliver Winchester's Henry would indeed prove to be a quantum leap forward in repeating arms technology, what is obvious in retrospect would prove surprising at the time. The Henry, from Ripley's viewpoint, was expensive, used ammunition that was available only from its manufacturer, and was probably wasteful of that. Neither the gun nor its cartridges was in production, had been exposed to any service field trials, or had any track record in the civilian market, so there was no way of telling how reliable and durable they might or might not be. In brief, the head of ordnance had other more important fish to fry, and he disregarded the Connecticut arms maker and his gun. It was not an unreasonable stance in the spring of 1861.

Ripley was not alone in that attitude, and one astute prewar commentator noted that "up to this time, [1859] . . . so many contrivances of great ingenuity have been found to fall short, more or less. . . . And it would seem the greatest difficulty is getting over the difference between a weapon that is unobjectionable as a gentleman's rifle or sporting gun, and one that will remain serviceable in the hands of common soldiers in the field—I might almost say, one that will not in his hands become wholly useless as a firearm in a few weeks."[37]

Oliver Winchester, however, like other arms makers, did not hesitate to go over Ripley's head, and handmade presentation guns were soon on the way to prominent politicians, including Navy Secretary Gideon Welles. He got the attention of Welles, a fellow Connecticut man. In May 1862, Navy Lieutenant William Mitchell tested the Henry for accuracy, rapidity of fire, and endurance at the Washington Navy Yard and reported his results to Captain John A. Dahlgren. The rifle performed well in endurance and accuracy tests, firing 1,040 rounds without cleaning and hitting an eighteen-inch-square target with fourteen of fifteen shots at a range of 348 feet. Turning to rapid fire, Mitchell was able to shoot "187 shots . . . in 3 min. 36 sec. These [shots] were fired in rounds of 15 shots each, the actual time of firing only counted. One round (15 shots) were [sic] fired in 10.8s; 120 shots were loaded and fired in 5 min. 45 sec. This includes the whole time from first shot to last."[38]

Following an earlier test of a Henry prototype, Captain Gustavus A. De Russy of the Fourth U.S. Artillery commented that the Henry would be "a most useful addition to the weapons we now have in service." The Ordnance Chief of the Army of the Potomac believed the "Henry rifle appears to be quite equal to any in service, in the compactness of its machinery and the accuracy of its fire," and recommended that the government "purchase a number sufficient for one regiment." Despite the favorable reports, however, military contracts for the Henry were not forthcoming.[39]

Had they come, it is doubtful they could have been filled for some time. The actual date of the beginning of Henry rifle production is in dispute. Winchester historian Herbert C. Houze believes that some, if not all of the early iron-frame guns, 500 of which were made, may have been manufactured for New Haven Arms by Colt's Patent Firearms Manufacturing Company. As evidence, Houze cites correspondence that Oliver Winchester contracted a $4,200 debt to the Colt Company on a "Patent Arms Account" in May 1861. This money may have been for producing guns, but also may have been for parts or tooling, as Colt was a leading manufacturer of the machine tools used to produce firearms, as well as firearms themselves. The company was also known to take on jobs producing other than Colt arms. In the 1850s Colt remanufactured a large number of surplus U.S. smoothbore muskets into rifled muskets sold to both the Russian government and agents for Italian revolutionary Giuseppi Garibaldi. Houze notes that Colt production of Henry rifles in 1861 is, barring more evidence, however, merely "speculation."[40]

James W. Ripley (1794–1870) was Chief of Ordnance, United States Army from 1857 to 1863.

Although one historian has Abraham Lincoln test firing a Henry rifle against a muzzle-loading rifle musket in the summer of 1861, such a scenario, based on the apparently faulty memory of one William A. Stoddard, a secretary in the White House given to latter-day self-promotion, is unlikely. The first Henry rifles did not appear on the open market until the summer of 1862, but some early bronze-framed guns were certainly in existence by the end of April. On April 24, 1862, Winchester sent three complimentary rifles and three hundred cartridges to Colt Superintendent Elisha K. Root as gifts for Root himself and Colt executives John S. Jarvis and Horace Lord, perhaps as a return for manufacturing favors earlier extended. For various reasons, which we shall examine in later chapters, Henry production was never extensive. By October 1862 only 900 Henry rifles had been manufactured. In late 1864, Henry production peaked at 290 rifles a month, and a total of only 13,000 were manufactured through 1866.[41]

Although in the end the Henry would prove a fine combat arm, despite the lack of Federal purchases, another repeating rifle soon appeared on the scene, and that gun would, by the end of the war, become the favorite firearm of the Union army. Like the Henry, it was the product of a New England "mechanician" who had absorbed his technical education on the job in the Connecticut River Valley—Christopher Miner Spencer.

FOUR

CHRISTOPHER SPENCER INVENTS
A GUN

JOHN HAY, ABRAHAM LINCOLN'S SECRETARY, APTLY DESCRIBED
Christopher Miner Spencer, inventor, manufacturer, and salesman extra-
ordinaire, as a "quiet little Yankee who sold himself in relentless slavery to
his idea for six weary years before it was perfect." Historian Robert V. Bruce
has suggested that if Spencer was not, then he should have been the model
for Mark Twain's *Connecticut Yankee in King Arthur's Court*. Hay and Bruce
had it right, for Christopher Spencer was indeed a remarkable man. Born to
a farm family in Manchester, Connecticut, in 1833, he embodied all the best
aspects of that nineteenth-century New England mechanical aptitude and
entrepreneurial capitalism that changed the industrial culture of the world.[1]

Spencer's ninety-year-old maternal grandfather, Revolutionary War veteran and gunsmith Josiah Hollister, began to teach him the crafts of metal and
wood working at a very early age. When Christopher was fourteen, Hollister
made him a present of an old flintlock musket, which the precocious
Spencer immediately "sporterized" into a hunting gun, as many young lads
in the 1950s did, more or less effectively, with a World War II surplus
Mauser or Enfield rifle. In 1847 Spencer began working as an apprentice
machinist in a silk mill owned by brothers Charles and Rush Cheney in
South Manchester. After spending a year with the Cheneys, Spencer moved
on, no doubt with their blessing, to serve an advanced apprenticeship with
Manchester Center, Connecticut, machinist Samuel Loomis. While absorb-
ing the machinist's trade under Loomis' instruction, young Spencer used
information abstracted from the book *Comstock's Philosophy*, a popular
introduction to the science of the time, to build his own small steam engine.[2]

Although few would ever approach his genius, Christopher Spencer's
move from farm to factory was one of many similar stories lived by ambitious
young men in early nineteenth-century New England. Most of the first factory workers in the American Industrial Revolution began life as country

folk. For some the transition from the erratic labor of a semi-medieval agri-cultural life to the more structured and sustained demands of a formal indus-trial workplace was difficult. When newly appointed superintendent Lieutenant Colonel Roswell Lee arrived at Springfield Armory following the War of 1812, he found his recently rural workforce "working at their own pace." Historian David F. Hawke notes that the armory workforce, like many in the developing New England economy, "came to work with hard liquor in their lunchpails. When bored they left their work benches to gamble at cards, roughhouse or simply idle the time away in idle talk." Colonel Lee dis-charged over a dozen shiftless employees in his first hours at the armory, and then established the parameters of a more modern factory work structure.[3]

Other New England farm boys, like Christopher Spencer, adapted far more readily and, indeed, eagerly, to the new standards demanded by a pro-gressive industrial system. Spencer, however, was no doubt aware early on that he was not leaving the drudgery of rural life behind to become a mere cog in a new industrial world. His new world became one of infinite possi-bilities and his ultimate place in it a step far up the technological ladder, fit-ting cogs to the gears of mass production. In this new, still forming universe, native ability mattered far more than academic credentials. Over the winter of 1848 Spencer attended the only formal schooling of his life, a twelve-week stint at the Wilbraham Academy in Massachusetts. It was all he would need, and he returned to further his mechanical education at Loomis' shop in the spring of 1849.

In 1850, Spencer, now an accomplished mechanic, returned to work at the Cheney brothers' mill, where he demonstrated a genius not only for maintaining and repairing machinery but also for designing new tooling to perform complex manufacturing tasks. During the ensuing four-year period that Spencer worked for the Cheneys he formed a strong friendship with his employers. The brothers encouraged the talented young man to increase his skills and broaden his work experience. Following their advice, Spencer sub-sequently plied his trade as a machinist at several locations, including the New York Central Railroad locomotive repair shop in Rochester, New York.

Christopher Spencer's longtime interest in firearms and weaponry led to an employment stint with the Ames Manufacturing Company in Chicopee Falls, Massachusetts, a major maker of swords and other cutlery as well as machine tools for the arms making industry. After leaving Ames, Spencer broadened his hands on gun making experience by moving to the Colt Firearms factory in Hartford. By the early 1850s, when Spencer worked there, Colt had become the most prestigious private arms making firm in the world.

After a year at Colt, Spencer was persuaded by Charles Cheney to return to the brothers' employ in 1854. They appointed him superintendent of their new Hartford silk ribbon factory, where he put in an eleven-hour workday six days a week. While at the Hartford mill, Spencer designed new labor-saving labeling and thread-spooling machines, patenting them in 1859 and 1860, respectively. With the permission and encouragement of the Cheneys, in his spare time Spencer used the plant machine shop to work on his burgeoning innovative firearms ideas.[4]

Important as his silk ribbon processing machines were, Christopher Spencer's spare-time invention would prove vastly more important in the history of American industry and warfare. As early as 1857, Spencer's fertile brain had germinated an idea for a breech-loading repeating rifle. With Smith and Wesson's refinement of the viable self-contained rimfire cartridge initially developed by Flobert, it was clear to Spencer that the technology of ammunition development had arrived at the point at which a true repeating firearm of simple, practical, and durable design was possible.

Although his rough wooden model of 1857 is lost to history, Spencer's subsequent patent model, submitted with his application to the United States patent office at the end of 1859, revealed the basics of his gun. The proposed rifle featured a "movable breech" which, in conjunction with other parts, served "the purpose of withdrawing the cases of the exploded cartridges from the chamber of the barrel and for conducting new cartridges thereinto from a magazine." The Spencer magazine, like that of its contemporary, the Henry, was tubular, with one round resting directly behind the other. Unlike the Henry, however, which had its magazine and spring located under its barrel with an open slot for the follower to travel in, a potentially vulnerable design, the Spencer magazine was located in the gun's buttstock, to the rear of the action, and well protected from the elements. Although it used a rolling block rather than a carrier/lifter, the movable breech mechanism that transferred cartridges from the Spencer magazine to the gun's chamber was actuated, like that of the Henry, by a lever. Once a cartridge was in the chamber, the shooter cocked the external hammer and fired his Spencer by pulling the trigger, thus releasing the hammer to hit the firing pin which, in turn, hit the rim of the cartridge, exploding the priming and firing the round. Working the lever ejected the empty cartridge case and chambered another round from the magazine. Christopher Spencer's father, Ogden Spencer, in return for 50 percent of future profits, financed the patent model, which cost $293.67 to produce.[5]

Spencer initially foresaw the market for his invention in the sporting arms area, with distinct military possibilities if rimfire ammunition could be produced in heavier calibers than those avail-able in the late 1850s. The first handmade prototype Spencer rifles, created by Spencer and gunsmith Luke Wheelock in the Cheney Hartford plant's workshop, were chambered for a .36 caliber cartridge. By 1861 Spencer and Wheelock had pro-duced a larger .44 caliber gun, the ballistic equivalent of the Henry.

With the outbreak of the Civil War, Spencer and his friends the Cheney broth-ers concluded, as Samuel Colt had realized early on in his career, and firearms business neophyte Oliver Winchester was quick to perceive, that military contracts were the meat and potatoes of the gun making indus-try. This was especially true when the firearms product was technologically advanced and expensive to manufacture and thus had to be sold to the public at a high cost. The rapidly gathering war clouds of 1861 had convinced Spencer and his backers that a large market for innovative weaponry would soon materialize. That market, Spencer believed, demanded a more powerful cartridge than his proto-types had chambered.

Christopher Miner Spencer (1833–1922) was tutored in the gunsmith's art by his grandfa-ther, a Revolutionary War veter-an, shot targets with President Lincoln, and played perhaps as influential a role in industrial history as any single American; in addition to inventing his famous guns, he made a fortune from his automatic screw mak-ing machine, and built a steam-powered automobile in 1901. (*Windsor Connecticut Historical Society*)

Oliver Winchester already had a produc-tion staff and factory building producing Volcanic arms to put to work on the new Henry rifle, and, after purchasing new machine tools designed to make the Henry, also added a cartridge making production line to churn out .44 rimfire ammunition. Christopher Spencer, on the other hand, began with nothing, and had to outsource some of the production work on his design, including parts for his prototype arms, as well as all the ammunition they would fire. In 1861, Spencer approached an established ammunition maker, Crittenden & Tibbals of South Coventry, Connecticut, with a proposal to develop a large caliber rimfire round for his gun, the largest caliber yet attempted in that format. In the few years since Smith & Wesson had debuted their .22 rimfire cartridge, companies like Crittenden & Tibbals, large-scale makers of more conventional ammunition like combustible revolver cartridges, had expanded rimfire technology so that the manufacture of much larger calibers was feasible. For Spencer, the company developed a large copper-cased rimfire round that they labeled their "No. 56 Army" and that later became popularly known as the .56-.56 Spencer cartridge.[6]

The army expressed a desire for all of its new arms to be in the standard infantry .58 caliber bore diameter of the muzzle-loading Springfield rifle musket, with the implication that it should also use the rifle musket's sixty-grain powder charge. This was more than a bit beyond available rimfire capability of the time. Spencer, however, no doubt felt that guns chambered for the new Crittenden and Tibbals cartridge, which, although theoretically a .52 caliber, fired a bullet in the same nominal .54 caliber diameter as the Sharps rifle that had been found acceptable for special purpose infantry use, would pass military muster.

There has been much confusion over the years as to the actual caliber of the first Spencers, with some believing it was .56 caliber, a rational supposition at first glance. The double-digit identification in the caliber nomenclature actually refers, however, to the diameter of the copper cartridge case at base and top, indicating a straight-sided round. The Spencer bullet was "heeled," like a modern .22 caliber long rifle round, with a slightly smaller diameter base fitting in the case mouth and exposed lubricant filled grooves to reduce the fouling resulting from the explosion of its forty-five grain black musket powder propellant charge.

In reality, there is a great deal of variation in the bore diameters of .56-.56 guns, and the ammunition chambered for them, even though they are supposed to fire a nominally .52 caliber cartridge. In black powder days, neither bore nor bullet diameter tolerances were considered as critical for accuracy as they are today. The charcoal-based propellant "boosted" undersized bullets up to bore diameter, atoning for a multitude of machining sins. One surviving .56-.56 cartridge from an unknown maker has a bullet diameter measuring .536.[7]

The ultimate look of the Spencer rifle also owed a considerable debt to the Sharps, since the inventor, rushing in May 1861 to get a prototype gun together for military trials, prevailed upon his friendship with Richard Lawrence of the Sharps company for help. Lawrence sold Spencer a number of parts, and the first Spencer was built using them, leading to a parts interchangeability that existed as long as both guns were made. Spencer historian Roy M. Marcot notes a number of similar and identical parts between the Sharps New Model 1859 rifle and the Spencer prototype rifle of 1861, including the barrel, stock, rear sight, and some internal lock parts, and a

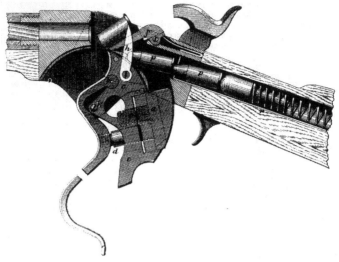

The Spencer mechanism, which was the same for both rifle and carbine, used the trigger guard as a lever that, when lowered and raised, automatically removed a fired cartridge case, picked up a new cartridge from the spring loaded buttstock magazine and chambered it for firing. Unlike the Henry rifle, the Spencer's lever did not cock the gun's hammer at the same time it ejected a fired case and chambered a new round, making for a slower overall rate of fire. At right are examples of Spencer cartridges. The one on the far left is the .56-.56, used in all

Model 1860 Spencer rifles and carbines, and the other the .56-.50, developed by the US government specifically for carbine use in late 1864. The Model 1865 Spencer was chambered for the latter round. (*Patent drawing; private collection, photograph by John Hubbard.*)

surviving early Spencer prototype arm has a sight marked "R. S. Lawrence / Patented / February 15, 1859." The acquisition of a Sharps barrel was likely responsible for the diameter of the bullet Crittenden and Tibbals loaded in their .56-.56 ammunition.[8]

The advent of Civil War in April 1861 created a huge potential firearms market, especially for innovative weapons that worked in the real world as well as they did in their inventors' fertile imaginations and patent applications. Like other "patent arms" purveyors, Spencer used any influence available to promote his repeater. He assigned all rights to the gun to his patrons, the Cheney Brothers, and they in turn agreed to pay him a $1 royalty on every gun produced. Charles Cheney was better connected than Spencer, and a neighbor and "intimate friend" of Navy Secretary Gideon Welles. On June 4, 1861, Welles wrote the Washington Navy Yard Commandant, Commander John A. Dahlgren, himself an ordnance designer of no mean ability, introducing the Cheney brothers, "gentlemen whom I am happy to number among my special friends and whom I commend to your very favorable regard." Welles requested that Dahlgren test "a newly invented breech-loading arm" they were bringing to the Navy Yard. What the Secretary wanted, the Secretary got, especially when he described his request as "a special favor."[9]

Charles Cheney and Spencer brought a handmade prototype rifle to Washington for the commander to test, but Dahlgren's report was not a "special favor." Dahlgren was genuinely impressed by the Spencer rifle, which, although he had a military officer of the era's aversion to what he considered excessively complicated machinery for issue to enlisted men, he termed "compact and strong." The Navy tests were not extensive, but "the piece was fired 500 times in succession partly between two mornings. There was but one failure to fire, supposed to be due to the absence of fulminate [priming]; in every other instance the operation was completed." Spencer later recalled that he fired twenty-one rounds in sixty-two seconds for Dahlgren. Dahlgren himself emptied the gun's seven-round magazine in ten seconds and, including reloading, ninety-one rounds were fired over a twenty-nine-minute period. In concluding his report, the commander recommended that "a number of these pieces be introduced for trial in service."[10]

Based on Dahlgren's recommendation, on June 22 the Navy's Bureau of Ordnance and Hydrography ordered 700 Spencer rifles with 30-inch barrels and sword bayonets at $43 each, along with 70,000 rounds of .56-.56 ammunition.

Shortly after the navy tests, Spencer and the Cheneys secured an army test of their gun. Captain Alexander Dyer of the ordnance corps gave the new rifle a more thorough wringing out than Dahlgren had, exposing it to an approximation of combat conditions, reporting that:

> I fired the Spencer Repeating Rifle some eighty times. The loaded piece was then laid upon the ground and covered with sand, to see what would be the effect of getting sand into the joints. No clogging or other injurious effect appeared to have been produced. The lock and lower parts of the barrel were then covered with salt water and left exposed for twenty-four hours. The Rifle was then loaded and fired without difficulty. It was not cleaned during the firing, and it appeared to work quite as well at the end as at the beginning.[11]

Spencer lever action repeating rifle (top) and Sharps Model 1859 breechloading single-shot rifle. Note the similarity of the lever and other parts between the two guns. Overall rates of fire of the Sharps and Spencer were not that different, considering the time needed to reload the Spencer magazine. In some cases, the Sharps rate of fire may well have exceeded that of the Spencer. The Sharps also fired a more powerful cartridge and was considered more accurate, especially at longer ranges. The Spencer held the advantage of being capable of a rapid fire "burst" of seven rounds (eight if one round had been loaded in the gun's chamber) which would significantly exceed the Sharps' rate of fire, as well as using ammunition that was impervious to the elements and rough handling. Sharps cartridges were often damaged in soldiers' cartridge boxes, especially those of cavalrymen, from the jouncing they received on the march. (*Private collection; photographs by John Hubbard*)

The Spencer's sturdiness, heavy caliber and apparent relative ease of manufacture impressed Dyer greatly, but failed to result in any army orders. Pressing their case, the Cheneys hired lobbyist R. S. Denny, who operated out of Willard's Hotel, the famed Washington watering hole, to press their case. In October 1861, Denny wrote ordnance chief General Ripley proposing a sale to the government of 5,000 Spencer rifles and 5,000 carbines at $35 each, with delivery at the rate of 1,000 guns a month to begin in January 1862. Ripley, besieged by hundreds of similar proposals and determined to get muzzle-loading rifle muskets, which were in short supply, in the hands of the men of the rapidly expanding Union army as soon as possible, ignored Denny.[12]

Spencer, unwilling to give up on the possibility of an army contract, traveled to Washington himself in early November and conducted a personal demonstration of his rifle for Major General George B. McClellan. General McClellan was at that time commander of all Union forces in the field, but made his headquarters with the Army of the Potomac. McClellan passed the sample gun on to Colonel C. P. Kingsbury for further evaluation. Kingsbury, a regular army ordnance captain who had been appointed as a colonel in the Volunteer service, was acting as the Army of the Potomac's chief of ordnance. The colonel had a lot on his plate, and Spencer's case was only one of a large number of tasks assigned to him in the creation and equipping of a great army from scratch. According to McClellan's report on the period, "Great difficulty existed in the proper organization of the [Army of the Potomac ordnance] department for the want of a sufficient number of suitable officers to perform the duties at the various headquarters and depots of supply. Far greater obstacles had to be surmounted, including the fact that the supply of small-arms was totally inadequate to the demands of a large army, and a vast proportion of those furnished were of such inferior quality as to be unsatisfactory to the troops and condemned by their officers."[13]

Despite his busy schedule, Kingsbury reported that the Spencer rifle, which he termed a "carbine," had "favorably impressed" him. Although he expressed the usual initial hesitancy that "the breech loading arrangement appears somewhat complicated," the colonel cited both the Dahlgren and Dyer tests in support of his final conclusion that "the mechanism is not easily deranged and is strong and compact." Kingsbury recommended the Spencer for "picket service and for cavalry and light infantry."[14]

In addition to requesting Kingsbury's opinion of the gun, General McClellan tasked a board of three officers—Captains Alfred Pleasonton and Alfred Sully and Lieutenant S. C. Bradford—to perform additional tests on the Spencer. Pleasonton and his fellow officers reported favorably on the

Spencer, preferring it to the Henry, noting that "the cartridges, being in copper tubes [as were the Henry's], are less liable to damage" and that the rifle was "simple and compact in construction, and less liable to get out of order than any other breech-loading arms now in use."[15]

Another Union officer, Colonel Hiram Berdan, tested the Spencer in December 1861, but with mixed results. Berdan was the commander of the First United States Sharpshooters. Although Berdan's men were offered Springfield muzzle-loading rifles by General Ripley, they clamored for breechloaders, most particularly the Sharps. Assistant Secretary of War Thomas A. Scott sent Berdan a

Unidentified Union infantrymen armed with Sharps Model 1859 rifles. (*USAMHI*)

Spencer to test, but while he was shooting it "the butt of one of the cartridges burst and some powder blew through the slot, in the gate, into my face and eye, destroying the entire sight for a moment." Although he recovered his sight, Berdan requested a meeting with Christopher Spencer "to see if it is not possible to guard against similar accidents." Though such accidents did occur occasionally with early rimfire ammunition, there is, unfortunately, no record of whether or not Berdan and Spencer ever met. The Sharpshooters went to war the following spring with Colt revolving rifles, however, and later traded them in for Sharps rifles. They were never issued Spencers.[16]

Since Ripley still appeared unmoved and did not respond with an army contract, Charles Cheney conducted a second political end run, appealing to Gideon Welles once more. Welles set up an interview for Spencer and Warren Fisher, a wealthy Boston financier now in partnership with the Cheney brothers and treasurer of the nascent Spencer arms making firm, with James G. Blaine. Blaine, the influential chairman of the Maine Republican Party, subsequently pressed Assistant Secretary of War Scott to lean on the reluctant Ripley. In response, Scott instructed Ripley to conduct extensive tests of not only the Spencer, but also the Henry repeating rifle, another Gideon Welles favorite.[17]

Bypassing Scott, Ripley responded rapidly and directly to Secretary of War Simon Cameron, noting that he had reviewed the previous tests, and had personally examined the guns. In his report of December 11, 1861, he asserted, quite correctly, that "it is impossible, except where arms are defective in principle, to decide with confidence, in advance of such practical trials, on their value or otherwise, as military weapons." The general went on to note that he found the weight of both Henry and Spencer with loaded magazines objectionable, and, more important, was concerned regarding their dependence on a distinctive ammunition, presently in limited supply and of which the durability under service conditions was yet to be determined. Last, in his weakest argument against technological progress, Ripley stated that he thought the Spencer and Henry had not established any superiority over existing single-shot breechloaders and that their additional cost was considerable. In conclusion, he recommended that he did not "consider it advisable to entertain or accept either of the propositions for furnishing these arms."[18]

No doubt Ripley thought he had stifled such nonsense once and for all, but he had not bargained on the persistence and persuasiveness of the Spencer Repeating Rifle Company and its agents. This time the response came in the form of a letter from Warren Fisher. A week after Ripley's report, Fisher wrote directly to Cameron, proposing to sell the government 10,000 Spencer rifles with bayonets and other "appendages" for $40 each. According to Fisher, deliveries would begin with a delivery of 500 guns in March, 1862, followed by 1,000 rifles a month in April though November, with the final 1,500 to be delivered in December.[19]

Simon Cameron was a very "reachable" politician, to say the least. Whatever went on between the Secretary of War and Fisher and the Cheneys is lost to the silent discretion of history. The Secretary was a powerful former Pennsylvania Senator and Republican presidential candidate, appointed to his position as a reward for assistance in the election campaign of 1860. Although his ethical reputation was less than sterling, he had considerable political clout when it came to awarding military contracts. In addition, Spencer historian Roy Marcot speculates that Blaine and possibly even Gideon Welles were "unpublished stockholders in the Spencer Repeating Rifle Company," which certainly did not hinder the Cheneys in seeking a contract. At any rate, after Fisher's letter to Cameron, Assistant Secretary Scott ordered Ripley to order 10,000 Spencer rifles, with the understanding that the first 500 would be in government hands by the end of March. On December 26, 1861, Ripley, now with no choice, caved in and ordered the guns. Unlike the Navy version of the Spencer, the army rifles were ordered with triangular bladed socket bayonets that slipped over the muzzle in a similar manner to those used on the standard rifle musket. By substituting the socket for the saber bayonet, army rifle cost was reduced to $40 per gun.[20]

So Spencer and the Cheneys had their order, the terms of which they accepted on December 31. The only things they lacked were a factory, machinery, and a workforce—with their first delivery date a mere three months away. The influential and efficient Cheneys went to work with a will to move their business from a mere paper agreement to a functioning entity. On January 23, 1862, after convincing other investors of the soundness of their young protégé's idea, the brothers formally incorporated the Spencer Repeating Rifle Company in Boston, Massachusetts. Spencer himself was not an officer in the company, but an employee whose assigned patent rights guaranteed him the per-gun royalty he had previously agreed upon with the Cheneys.

The Cheneys found factory space in the Chickering and Sons Piano-Forte company factory in Boston in January 1862, and they and their partners raised a large sum of money to purchase machinery, hire workmen, and sketch out a production plan. Christopher Spencer was installed as supervisor of the works. Spencer later recalled that "the installation of the machinery, building a forging shop, making of tools, fixtures, gauges, and many special machines, and finishing the first of the Navy guns, all within a year, was a Herculean task." Although the Cheneys and their partners were businessmen, not engineers or machinists, they realized in short order, if they had not already known, that there would be no delivery of 500 Spencer rifles in March 1862. It was simply an impossible task—which no doubt gave General Ripley a degree of smug satisfaction.[21]

It didn't take the Spencer Company principals long to begin trying to postpone the unrealistic delivery dates they had agreed to in their desperation to land a contract. When Simon Cameron was forced out of office after a Congressional censure and shipped off to Russia as ambassador, saving the contract by postponing delivery dates assumed primary importance. Edwin Stanton assumed the position of Secretary of War on January 20, and his office began to review the ordnance contracts Cameron had let out, willy-nilly, across the north. Fisher, the Spencer Company's contract representative, petitioned the War Department to postpone the initial delivery date until April.[22]

There was more to come than just risking Stanton's jaundiced eye. Fisher and his company would soon be scrutinized, along with over a hundred other arms contractors, by the Special Commission on Ordnance and Ordnance Stores, established in March 1862 to review and evaluate the status of the government arms contracts and contractors who had made their initial deals with Cameron. Although the Spencer Company principals had to be encouraged by the front-page article praising their gun that appeared in *Scientific American*, there was cause for worry.

The commission was comprised of several diverse and distinguished citizens, Joseph Holt, Robert Dale Owen, and Major Peter V. Hagner. Holt, a Kentuckian and a "War Democrat," had served as Postmaster General and Secretary of War in the James Buchanan administration. A well-known attorney, he would later become the U.S. Army's Judge Advocate General and prosecute the Lincoln assassination conspirators. Owen was the son of proto-socialist Robert Owen. A former member of the House of Representatives, he had also served as ambassador to Italy and was a prominent social reformer and abolitionist. Hagner provided the technical savvy the commission needed to accomplish its mission. He was an experienced army ordnance officer and West Point graduate who had served against the Seminoles in Florida and in the Mexican War and would eventually become commander of Watervliet Arsenal in New York and inventor of a postwar cartridge box.[23]

Apparently replying to an official inquiry from Stanton's office, on February 4 Fisher assured the dour Secretary of War that save for failing to meet the first month's delivery date, the rest of the Spencer contract would be faithfully fulfilled. Fisher took the initiative in contacting the commission on March 22, advising the commissioners that he had read "newspaper reports" of the coming investigation and was available to answer questions at their pleasure.[24]

There certainly would be questions, as there was no way that any Spencer rifles were going to be delivered to the government in the time period specified in the contract. Work was proceeding apace in the Chickering building, however, and Fisher's letter to the commissioners promised that a "pattern rifle" made at the factory would be arriving in Washington "in a few days," and included copies of correspondence with General Ripley on the subject. Fisher realized that the commission would be considering a diverse array of contracts, many of them dubious proposals from an assortment of flimflam men, ne'er-do-wells, and deadbeats approved by Cameron and his entourage, and wished to disassociate himself from the riffraff. The Spencer Company treasurer stated unequivocally that he would be at the commission's disposal, prepared to appear in person, given "a few days notice" to explain the status of Spencer production.[25]

On April 23 Fisher forwarded the pattern rifle, its extractor improved over the originally tested gun, to Ripley's office, along with assurances that explanations of the delay would be forthcoming and comprehensive. In return, Ripley, stalling once more, complained that the pattern gun, "although it appears to be well finished," had malleable rather than wrought iron hardware, which the general found "decidedly objectionable." Fisher countered that the pattern gun's furniture was indeed made of wrought iron.[26]

Fisher's problems with the commission, which had the power to cancel the entire Spencer contract, would be more serious than his exchanges with the prickly ordnance chief. On April 25 he personally appeared in Washington and testified under oath that the Spencer Company had no guns ready for delivery and would have none before July. According to Fisher, however, the company was not a fly-by-night entrepreneur of the type that proliferated in the war's early days, and had invested $135,000 to acquire the machinery and gauges necessary to produce its rifle. He further stated that the Spencer Company had 130 men already at work and that parts for the rifle were already actually being made. Although the navy contract for 700 guns was entered into prior to the army one, Fisher advised that he believed his company could complete that contract and deliver all 10,000 army rifles within the contract's initial parameters, which established a completion date of January 1863.[27]

The day after Fisher's appearance before the Commission, Major Hagner contacted Ripley and requested any reports in the Ordnance office relevant to the Spencer as well as Ripley's own opinion on the gun as a potential service arm be sent to him and his fellow commissioners. The commission was also interested in whether or not the quality of the sample arm forwarded by Fisher was "satisfactory." The general delayed his response until June 9, at which time he sniffed that if the gun parts he had contended were malleable iron were indeed wrought iron (which they were) then he had no objection in accepting the sample arm as the model for the rest of the contract run.[28]

On May 27, Fisher wrote a long and detailed letter to the commissioners. In it, he explained that the Spencer arms company was a serious player in the contracting game, with over $198,000 invested in machinery, subcontracts, and salaries, reiterated the successful army and navy tests of the gun and detailed the progress of the contract and the company's relationship with the government from its inception. Arguing desperately to keep the contact valid, he offered to change the terms from 10,000 rifles to 13,000 carbines, half in .56-.56 and half smaller versions in .44 rimfire at $30 each. Fisher concluded that cancellation of the contract would entail financial disaster for the partners in the company and their workforce as well, and that he was ready to return to Washington to confer with the commissioners at any time they wished.[29]

In the end, the commission decided to keep the army's contract with the Spencer Company, but to reduce it to 7,500 rifles, with initial deliveries to take place in June 1862. Fisher had saved his company, but still had a bit of fancy footwork to do with the government representatives, since June deliveries were still impossible. Stating that he could have delivered in June if

Ripley had not taken so long to approve the pattern arm, Fisher petitioned to postpone first delivery until July or August, conceding a $5 per rifle discount for tardiness.[30]

While this exchange was transpiring, Christopher Spencer, in addition to setting up the factory in the Chickering Piano-forte building in Boston, took the time to invent a single-shot carbine. Most likely, as Roy Marcot suggests, considering General Ripley's ready acceptance of breechloaders for cavalry and his preference for lighter single-shot arms for that service, the new lightweight Spencer design, patented on July 29, 1862, was a fallback option should the repeater contract be cancelled by the commissioners. It answered another chronic Ripley complaint in that it could be used with loose powder and ball as well as .44 rimfire cartridges. The gun had a swing out breech that could be converted to percussion ignition by the installation of a nipple. Only two prototype guns and the patent model are known to exist today, and it is doubtful any were ever manufactured. A .56-.56 caliber version of this single-shot gun, which was in development at this time, may well be the "smaller size, say six and half pounds" heavy caliber carbine offered by Fisher in his letter of May 27.[31]

Despite Fisher's promise to begin delivering Spencer rifles sometime in the summer of 1862, he was unable to keep his word. July and August came and went, and there were no Spencer rifles in government arsenals or in the hands of troops. And General Ripley, crankier than usual because of the political pressure brought on him to accept the Spencer, and probably miffed because the commission did not cancel the contract altogether, did not miss the opportunity to harass Fisher about his failure to live up to his promise. When Fisher petitioned the general to extend the initial delivery date yet again, Ripley replied that the commission's decision was "final."[32]

What may have saved the army contract and the company as well was the persistence of a Michigan officer, Lieutenant Colonel Joseph Tarr Copeland. In the summer of 1862, the thirty-nine-year-old Maine-born Copeland, who had moved to Michigan in the 1840s after studying law under Daniel Webster, was second in command of the First Michigan Cavalry. Copeland was slated for promotion to colonel and command of a newly raised regiment of Michigan cavalry, and wanted his future command to be more than mundane horse soldiers. The colonel envisioned a role for his new unit as heavily armed "mounted riflemen or sharpshooters," each trooper equipped with two revolvers and one of the most modern breech loading rifles available. Copeland's idea was actually a throwback to the old "dragoon" concept of mounted men capable of fighting effectively on foot as well as horseback. Although it contradicted the purpose of cavalry in battle perceived by many in the decade prior to the war, the role in the war of the dragoon or mounted infantryman was an idea whose time had come—once again. And Copeland was well aware of the existence of the Spencer rifle, which would meet his needs perfectly.[33]

Although he is obscure today, Copeland, a Michigan state senator and state Supreme Court justice before the war, was not without influence. His new unit was called the Fifth Michigan Cavalry, not "Mounted Rifles," but he would not give up on the idea of having his men equipped with breech-loading repeaters. Throughout the summer of 1862, while his regiment was recruiting, Copeland wrote and badgered every influential person he could, including Michigan governor Austin Blair and the state's Congressional delegation, to get Spencers for his regiment, even though they were not yet available from the manufacturer. Such a commitment would not only ensure that the Fifth would be an effective combat force, but would also provide an enlistment incentive to recruits.[34]

But no Spencers were forthcoming. In September, Ripley offered the Fifth a com-

Joseph Tarr Copeland (1813 –1893) was lieutenant colonel of the First Michigan cavalry, then colonel of the Fifth Michigan cavalry, and finally, as a brigadier general, commander of the Army of the Potomac's Michigan Cavalry Brigade, a position he relinquished to George A. Custer in June 1863. (*Library of Congress*)

bination of imported French muzzle loading rifles and Sharps breech loading carbines, which appalled the colonel. Michigan adjutant general John Robertson, a Copeland ally, sent a representative to plead the Fifth's case with Secretary of War Stanton, and Governor Blair wrote General in Chief Henry W. Halleck—all to no avail.[35]

General Ripley was not exactly doing his utmost to get Spencers to the Fifth Michigan Cavalry. Every delay made it more likely that the company's contract would be cancelled, which would no doubt suit the general fine. Production and assembly of rifle parts progressed at the Boston factory throughout 1862, however, and the ability of the company to deliver large numbers of rifles on a monthly basis came closer and closer to reality. In mid-August Warren Fisher informed Ripley that the factory was ready for government inspectors to do their work, but the general responded that he was the wrong person to advise, referring Fisher to Major Hagner, former Commissioner and now ordnance chief at the New York arsenal.[36]

Ripley finally caved to the political pressure, however, and contacted Fisher to arrange a delivery date for the first 1,000 rifles. In October he informed Copeland that the Fifth would indeed be armed with Spencer rifles and ordered Hagner to issue the regiment 1,200 Spencer rifles as rapidly as he could. Fortunately, there were finally rifles available to fill the order. On November 21, 1862, Hagner telegraphed Ripley that "the inspection of rifles will be finished tonight & forwarded by fast passenger train tomorrow."[37]

Most historians have assumed that the Navy's order was finished first, since it predated the army contract. This does not appear to be the case, although Spencer himself, in a handwritten early twentieth century account, asserted that "the navy guns were completed long before any orders were received from the War Department." The inventor's recollection, which buttresses the story of early navy delivery and is coupled with a swipe at the reactionary Ripley, is completely incorrect. Historian Wiley Sword has conclusively proved that the army rifles were indeed finished and shipped before the Navy's order. Sword speculates that the army shipment was hastened by a combination of fear on the part of the Spencer Company that further delays might result in the cancellation of the entire gun contract, on which they had already technically defaulted due to late delivery, and Ripley's bow to the political pressure brought to bear on him by Copeland.[38]

In the event, "fast passenger train" or not, the first 500 of Copeland's Spencers did not arrive in Detroit until December 5, the day after the Fifth, and its sister regiment the Sixth Michigan Cavalry, had departed for Washington. By December 23, one trooper from the Fifth was complaining that he had been issued "a saber and a revolver" but no carbine or rifle. Apparently less than half the regiment's men were armed at all at that date. On December 27, however, the Spencers finally caught up with the Fifth. After they were issued, one soldier wrote, quite accurately, "there is not a regiment in Washington as well equipped as we are."[39]

The fact that Secretary of the Navy Gideon Welles was a friend of the Cheneys whose service never threatened contract cancellation may also have played a role in briefly deferring delivery of the navy guns. By the end of the year, however, those 700 rifles with saber bayonets were ready for inspection by a Naval ordnance officer and, it was hoped, acceptance in fulfillment of the contract. Captain Jonathan S. Chauncy supervised a "rigid" inspection and test firing of the guns at the Spencer factory in Boston. Each rifle barrel was proof fired with massive charges of 280 and 250 grains of powder behind a bullet, with only one barrel failing. Once assembled, the rifles were function fired with standard cartridges. Of the 6,000 rounds of Crittenden &

Tibbals ammunition consumed in the testing, only four rounds failed to fire. Chauncey reported that the Spencer was "one of the most effective arms in use" and "very strongly and compactly made." He recommended the Spencers for Naval use "without hesitation."[40]

Although accepted in December 1862, the Navy rifles were not delivered until two months later, long after the men of the Fifth Michigan Cavalry received theirs. In the meantime, Brigadier General Alfred W. Ellet, commander of the Mississippi Marine Brigade, an army unit manning ships on the Mississippi River, contacted Oliver Winchester with an inquiry about ordering 1,000 Henry rifles. On February 3, 1863, the Navy took delivery of 703 Spencers, with one shipped to the Naval Academy, moved from Annapolis to Newport, Rhode Island for the duration of the war, and the rest to Boston and Philadelphia. Included in the order were more than 200,000 rounds of ammunition and 140 cartridge boxes, presumably specially designed for the Spencer.[41]

By January 1863, Spencer rifle production was up to fifty rifles a day, and by the middle of that month, the remainder of the 1,200 rifles requested by Copeland had been delivered. The Fifth Michigan Cavalry's actual strength at this time was around 900 men, and the overage of Spencers, initially stored in Washington, were issued to the Sixth Michigan Cavalry's "Companies A, C, D, E, H and possibly G."[42]

More Spencer rifles were soon on their way to the army. On January 19, Major Hagner shipped 1,000 rifles to Columbus, Ohio. Close to half of these guns were issued to the Fifth, Sixth, Seventh, and Eighth Companies of Ohio Sharpshooters. In all, Ohio raised ten independent companies of Sharpshooters during the war. The first three became part of the Fourteenth Missouri Infantry, which in turn became the Sixty-sixth Illinois Infantry, otherwise known as Birge's Western Sharpshooters. In the summer of 1862 Ohio raised another five companies of sharpshooters, the Fifth through the Eighth. Largely recruited in Cuyahoga County, the men of these companies were selected after shooting a five-shot "string" at a target. In order to qualify for the Sharpshooters, a candidate had to fire a shot group which was then measured by a string wound around pegs inserted in the bullet holes. Shooters could fire at either 100 yards offhand, or 200 yards while using a rest. Anyone whose "string" exceeded twenty-five inches in length was rejected. The Buckeyes were clothed in standard issue uniforms, but with green trim and facings, since green was the traditional color of sharpshooters and rifle regiments.[43]

The Fifth, Sixth, and Seventh Ohio Sharpshooter Companies were mustered in at Camp Cleveland, and organized as a battalion under the command of Captain Gershom M. Barber of the Fifth Company. Although armed with Spencers, these companies were not sent immediately to the front, remaining at Cleveland through March 1863.

While company officials no doubt breathed a sigh of relief when they saw their guns pass inspection and shipped off to the army, the limited military contracts in effect were not sufficient to keep the Spencer Company in business and pay off the debts incurred to build machinery and equip the Chickering factory. More orders were needed to keep the machinery running, make back its cost and eventually see a profit. Publicity helped. As early as late 1861, Spencer had apparently demonstrated his rifle at the Chickering factory for the public, or at least interested state officials and members of the press. Two years later the *Boston Journal* recalled that "we witnessed some experiments with the Spencer repeating Rifle, at their Armory grounds in Tremont street, in this city." The reporter stated that he had predicted at the time that "it would prove of rare and matchless value as a military weapon." The initial publicity no doubt did no harm when Massachusetts set about conducting trials to choose a breechloader for state service in May 1863. Of the twenty-five weapons submitted to the trials, the Spencer was judged most worthwhile, and Massachusetts ordered 2,000 rifles.[44]

In February 1863, with the hopes of generating additional orders, the company sent Christopher Spencer on a sales trip to Murfreesboro, Tennessee, to visit the Army of the Cumberland. Spencer left for the front with a sample rifle and a supply of ammunition. Not one to waste company money, the frugal young inventor kept a meticulous expense record, skipping breakfast, allotting fifty cents for dinner, twenty-five cents for supper and a dollar a night for pre-Pullman era sleeping cars. At one point Spencer apparently had dinner at the home of a Nashville woman whom he met through the auspices of a Pennsylvania officer and whose husband was in the Confederate army. Years later he recalled the dinner with his usual hazy memory as occurring "a few days after the battle of Stone's River [Murfreesboro], while the smoke had barely cleared away." Spencer (before a Southern audience) praised the woman, who fed him even though he "was the inventor of the rifle which was dealing death to the innocent boys of the south," and bore him no "animosity but the expressed wish that I had never been the cause of the invention." In fact, Spencer did not leave for Tennessee until more than two months after the battle, and his host probably had no idea of who he was, as no Spencers had yet been used in combat.[45]

Despite his faulty recall of the details, the Army of the Cumberland proved a good choice for Spencer's visit. It was commanded by Major General William Starke Rosecrans, an officer who had displayed an intense interest in acquiring new small arms technology for his men. Although a descendant on his mother's side of a signer of the Declaration of Independence, Rosecrans was born in 1819 on a hardscrabble farm in Delaware County, Ohio, and was a brilliant if largely self-educated young man when he won an appointment to West Point in 1838. He graduated fifth in his class at the military academy and was commissioned in the Engineer Corps, where he served an uneventful ten years as a second lieutenant. Promoted to first lieutenant in 1853, Rosecrans resigned from the army the following year to pursue a business career. Although the ex-officer fancied himself an inventor and patented several inventions, including kerosene lantern parts and a method to manufacture soap, private sector wealth and fame eluded him.

William S. Rosecrans (1819 –1898), commander of the Army of the Cumberland, suffered a defeat at Chickamauga against forces directed in part by his former West Point roommate, James Longstreet. (*Library of Congress*)

Seriously injured in an industrial accident in 1859, Rosecrans had barely recovered by the outbreak of the Civil War. He quickly rejoined the army, serving as an Engineer Corps colonel and then commander of the Twenty-third Ohio Infantry in General McClellan's West Virginia campaign in the summer of 1861. Rosecrans' abilities contributed to McClellan's victory over Confederate General Robert E. Lee at Rich Mountain on July 11, and from then on his rise was assured. As a brigadier general he later commanded troops in the west under Generals John Pope and Ulysses S. Grant, fighting at Corinth and Iuka. Rosecrans was promoted to major general of Volunteers in October 1862, with a date of rank of March 21, 1862, and assigned to command the newly created Army of the Cumberland, then in Kentucky. Although Grant was not enamored with Rosecrans' conduct as a subordinate, he thought him a capable officer who would do well with an independent command.[46]

Rosecrans advanced the Army of the Cumberland south and fought a brutal drawn battle against Confederate General Braxton Bragg's army at Murfreesboro on December 7, 1862. Following the fight, Bragg withdrew, allowing the Union to call the battle a victory, for which Rosecrans later received the "Thanks of Congress."

Early on in his Civil War career, General Rosecrans came to the conclusion that a mounted infantry force, equipped with the fastest firing weapons available, would be useful to both protect his lines of communication and serve as an offensive tool. By the summer of 1862, Colt revolving rifles, the only repeaters available, had proved their worth in the hands of Union soldiers. Among other reports, Colonel Philip Sheridan of the Second Michigan Cavalry noted that "the enemy attempted to drive Captain Campbell from his position by a charge through the open field. In this they did not succeed, but were gallantly repulsed with great loss, my men reserving their fire until they were within 25 or 30 yards, when they opened on them with their Colt's revolving rifles."[47] As early as June 15, Rosecrans had begun a campaign of "badgering and hounding everyone in authority from president on down for more cavalry and more horses, more weapons and more equipment for the cavalry he already had."[48]

The weapons "Old Rosey" was most interested in were Colt Model 1855 revolving rifles like those Colonel Sheridan's men used so effectively, with breech-loading single-shot carbines his second choice. In July, after assuming command of the Army of the Mississippi from the departing Major General John Pope, he informed the Ordnance Bureau office in St. Louis that "twelve hundred and fifty Colt's army revolvers and 1,100 carbines or revolving rifles are required for the cavalry division." Shortly afterward he wired Washington requesting General in Chief Halleck to "please give our cavalry repeating rifles," and then requested "one thousand breech-loading or revolving arms" from Secretary of War Stanton. The general was persistent, and historian of Civil War tactics Brent Nosworthy notes that over a nine-month period, he "directed no fewer than 19 missives to the secretary of war, his assistant, the commander-in-chief, and the chief of staff" arguing for more breech-loading and repeating rifles for his troops.[49]

As the months passed, Rosecrans' tactical ideas concerning mounted riflemen equipped with repeaters took on a more definitive form. On November 16 he wired Stanton that it was "a matter of great importance that we should arm some infantry with revolving rifles and use them as sharpshooters," and asked the secretary to "carry out this measure by furnishing 4,000 revolving rifles," adding that "prompt action . . . is called for." Rosecrans also saw a vital role for conventional cavalry and was an admirer of good saber work. At the same time he was campaigning for repeating rifles, he ordered 3,000 sabers.[50]

"Rosey" had a tactical soulmate in Colonel General John T. Wilder, a brigade commander in his Army of the Cumberland. The thirty-two-year-old New York-born and raised Wilder, descendant of Revolutionary and War of 1812 veterans, moved to Ohio at the age of nineteen, and was operating a foundry in Greensburg, Indiana, at the outbreak of the Civil War. Initially drawn to the artillery, Wilder ended up as colonel of the Seventeenth

Indiana Infantry in June 1861. By December 1862 he commanded a brigade including his own regiment, the Seventy-second and Seventy-fifth Indiana and Ninety-eighth Illinois Infantry regiments, and the Eighteenth Indiana Light Artillery Battery. Following a fruitless pursuit of mounted Confederate raiders with his foot soldiers that month, Wilder came to the conclusion that his brigade should be mounted and armed with the latest and best available weapons. Rosecrans quickly agreed, and the brigade, save the Seventy-fifth Indiana, which opted out of the mounted role, was soon provided with horses. Wilder, a creative commander, also supplied his men with long handled axes, for dual use as close quarter weapons and for building quick field fortifications. The brigade took on the nickname of "the Hatchet Brigade." It was still limited, due

John T. Wilder (1830–1917) was a nationally recognized expert on foundry techniques before the war. He received a brevet brigadier general's commission in August 1864 but was forced to retire two months later due to recurrent typhoid fever. (*Library of Congress*)

to arms availability, however, to muzzle-loading weapons.[51]

Although Colonel Wilder's thoughts on mounted infantry and its armament perfectly dovetailed with those of his commander, Wilder's vision extended beyond the obsolescent Colt rifle to newer technology. The colonel was initially interested in the Henry repeater, which had seen limited combat use in Kentucky since the summer of 1862. On March 20, 1863, Wilder wrote Oliver Winchester from Murfreesboro, "At what price will you furnish me *nine hundred* of your 'Henry's Rifles,' delivered at Cincinnati, Ohio, *without* ammunition, *with* gun slings attached? Two of my regiments, now mounted, have signified their willingness to purchase these arms, *at their own expense.*"[52]

Wilder's contacts with Oliver Winchester failed to pan out, however, due to the painfully slow 200 guns per month production rate at New Haven Arms Company. The eager young colonel did not have time to get on the Henry waiting list, so for him Christopher Spencer's visit to Tennessee was a welcome event.[53]

It made sense that Spencer and Wilder would hit if off, since both were self-made men of the new industrial age. Wilder had learned the trades of a draftsman, pattern maker, and millwright on the job and had invented a number of hydraulic machines, a field in which he accomplished enough to become a widely acknowledged expert by 1860.[54]

Popular history would have it that after witnessing Spencer's demonstrations, Wilder was so eager to get a shipment of the inventor's rifles that he proposed to his men that they purchase the guns directly from the factory themselves, using his personal line of credit as security. This was the case when the colonel and his men were considering Henrys, and the available evidence suggests that it was an unnecessary step to acquire Spencers, and actually not even possible at the time. While Henrys were available, albeit limited by production capability, in the open market, the entire production of the Spencer factory was committed to fulfilling the government contract for 7,500 army rifles in a timely manner, in hopes of securing even more contracts. The inventor's trip to the Army of the Cumberland was intended to spur requests of Spencers by commanders through the normal conduits of supply, exhausting the current government order and stimulating new ones. Spencer's own account seems to confirm this scenario. He noted that after meeting Wilder, the colonel "asked me to ride over to Headquarters with him and show the rifle to Gen. Rosecrans whom he thought would make a requisition for them for his [Wilder's] troops. The visit was successful."[55]

No doubt Wilder did talk with Spencer about requesting some of the rifles already contracted for, and this discussion has, over the years, been combined and confused with the attempted Henry order. As early as March 1863, bugler Henry Campbell of Eli Lilly's Indiana artillery battery was reporting camp scuttlebutt on the Henry/Spencer orders to his hometown newspaper, with a bit of a chauvinistic home state spin: "The Seventeenth Indiana, our most enterprising Regt. had all intended buying themselves the Henry 16 shot rifle and paying for them out of their wages . . . Gen. [Colonel] Wilder admiring the zeal manifested by this Regiment, to make themselves the most effective command in the service has just closed a contract with Mr. Spencer the inventor of the celebrated 'Spencer 7 shooting rifle' to furnish our entire Brigade with them at the expense of each man."[56]

An increasing number of Spencers entered the supply pipeline as production finally began to achieve its promise, and the guns became available for issue to some of the units now clamoring for them. On April 15, 1863, General Ripley ordered a thousand Spencers shipped to General Rosecrans, with another thousand promised in three weeks. There is no doubt that most of these guns went to Wilder's men. Serial numbers of surviving Spencer rifles with provenance to the 123rd Illinois include guns numbered 5794, 6404, and 6667, all within the range of the first 7,500 contract guns. Ironically, more than a month before, Ripley had made yet one more attempt to cancel the Spencer contract, allegedly due to failure of the company to deliver arms on schedule.[57]

Despite General Ripley, both Henry and Spencer repeating rifles were arriving at the front in increasing numbers by early 1863, albeit through radically different distribution methods. Henrys had already seen limited use in action and both guns would face their first significant field tests in the coming year. The needs of war fuel progress, and the world of weaponry was on the cusp of change.

FIVE

LOUISVILLE TO GETTYSBURG

WHILE FISHER, THE CHENEY BROTHERS, AND CHRISTOPHER Spencer were spending the summer and fall of 1862 desperately trying to meet government contract demands for their rifle and expand the numbers of guns contracted for, Oliver Winchester had other problems promoting his Henry rifle. Although Winchester, like Spencer, had secured a favorable Navy test of the Henry through the auspices of Navy Secretary Gideon Welles, unlike in the case of the Spencer, no contracts were forthcoming.

Winchester had a viable, modern repeating rifle design, however, and a factory to produce it as well as the ammunition to fire in it, and there was a war on. Since he had no Federal or state government contracts for his gun, he decided to market it the old-fashioned way, through the rough and tumble of the free enterprise system. He knew he had an excellent product and hoped that individual sales and the favorable word-of-mouth advertising he expected as his rifles got into the hands of people across the country would perhaps stimulate some state or Federal orders. Private sales would also help to balance the New Haven Arms ledger books and keep the Henry assembly line in production status while government contracts might be in the offing.

In order to sell a lot of guns, of course, Oliver Winchester first had to make them. Although startup time for Winchester was far shorter than it would be for Spencer, Fisher, and the Cheneys, Henry rifles were not available to the general public for some time after 1861. The earliest evidence of the existence of other than prototype Henrys is the shipment of three completed guns and ammunition to Elisha K. Root of Colt in April 1862. On May 2, Winchester shipped another Henry via Adams Express to General Carl Schurz, a distinguished and influential German American and former Minister to Spain. Schurz had been commissioned a brigadier general two weeks earlier and was in residence at Willard's Hotel in Washington while awaiting a command.[1]

Whether one considers these presentation guns as early production arms or pre-production samples, the Henry can still claim the honor of the first practical metallic cartridge repeating rifle offered for sale in the United States. With Henrys due to come off the line in reasonable numbers by summer, Winchester made efforts to get his sales force in place in the spring of 1862, hiring John Brown of Columbus, Ohio, as his general agent. As the first rifles became available, Winchester had William C. Stanton, his old salesman from the Volcanic Arms days, travel to Louisville, Kentucky, with some sample guns. Kentucky, a politically bifurcated border state rent by its own Civil War, would prove a fertile ground for private small arms sales.

Three days after the April 12, 1861, Confederate attack on Fort Sumter, President Lincoln's call for four regiments from Kentucky to assist in suppressing the rebellion was rejected by the state's governor, Beriah Magoffin. On May 28 Magoffin, reflecting the view of the Kentucky legislature, proclaimed his state's neutrality in the conflict. Subsequent elections in June and August, however, boycotted by many Southern sympathizers, resulted in a Unionist Federal congressional delegation and state legislature. Brigadier General Robert Anderson, the hero of Fort Sumter and a native Kentuckian, was placed in command of Union forces in the area but was careful not to provide a provocation that might initiate a pro-Confederate coup by the Southern-leaning Kentucky Militia.

As summer deepened, the naïve idea of neutrality in the national struggle slipped from Kentucky's consciousness. In August, U.S. Navy Lieutenant William "Bull" Nelson established Camp Dick Robinson in Garrard County to recruit Union soldiers. On September 3, Confederate General Leonidas Polk moved Confederate troops into Kentucky from Tennessee, occupying Columbus. In response, Brigadier General Ulysses Grant advanced a force to Paducah. Union and Confederate forces soon clashed in a series of skirmishes at Camp Wildcat, Saratoga Springs, and Ivy Mountain.

In a desperate attempt to salvage the situation for the South, pro-Confederate Kentuckians held a convention in Russelville that established a second state government with George W. Johnson as governor and proclaimed the state's secession from the Union. On December 10, the Confederate States Congress recognized this rump government as representing Kentucky and admitted the state to the Confederacy. Although the political maneuvering would prove too little and too late, the Confederacy was not willing to let Kentucky slip easily. Increasing violence, much of it in the form of Guerrilla warfare and raiding, would reawaken the old Kentucky nickname—a "dark and bloody ground."

Against a background of these rapidly unfolding events, William C. Stanton contacted *Louisville Journal* editor George Denison Prentice. The sixty-year-old Connecticut-born Prentice had been editor of the *Journal* since 1831 and was nationally known for his witty epigrams, poems, and a biography of Henry Clay. He was also a strong Union man. Prentice's Unionist sympathies were no doubt reinforced when Stanton made him a gift of a new Henry rifle. Oliver Winchester, following the example of Samuel Colt, advised one of his distributors that "presents, when judiciously made . . . are good investments." Prentice's certainly was. The editor waxed eloquent on his Henry, writing on June 26, 1862, that it was "the most beautiful and efficient rifle we ever saw" and, with reference to the gun's magazine capacity, averred that it was "equal to fifteen [men] armed with [an] ordinary gun." Prentice advised his readers that Stanton was in town and staying at the Louisville Hotel and that James Low & Company had Henrys for sale.[2]

Within a short period of time, Low was joined by two other Henry retailers, John M. Stokes and Son and A. B. Semple & Sons. All three advertised in Prentice's *Journal* and, despite the stiff $42 retail cost of the Henry, "the best rifle ever offered to the public" began to sell to home guardsmen and local citizens interested in personal self-defense in perilous times. Sales were fueled as Prentice set the scene in troubled Kentucky: "In these days, when rebel outlaws are becoming common in Kentucky, when guerrillas are scouring different counties nightly, and practicing the most atrocious outrages, when even the central positions of our State are openly threatened, and when it is understood in high quarters that secret companies are on foot for a sudden and general insurrection at some favorable moment, it behooves every loyal citizen to prepare himself upon his own responsibility with the best weapons of defense that can be obtained." And what better weapon was there than the Henry?[3]

Aside from his undoubted skills as a wordsmith, Prentice apparently knew a business opportunity when he saw it. By the end of August, the editor himself had secured the position of New Haven Arms Company sales agent for Louisville, and bought 280 Henry rifles at $25 each for resale at $42 apiece. Competitors' advertisements were dropped from the *Journal* and now one of Prentice's customers could pick up his newspaper, a Henry, and ammunition all at the same location. Other dealers in Indiana and Ohio were soon selling Henrys as well, and by October 1862, about 900 had been shipped to the Midwest.[4]

That summer, as George D. Prentice began his career as a gun dealer, forces were gathering that would be his undoing. Outflanked and driven from Kentucky and much of Tennessee, Confederate forces were gathering for a counteroffensive into the Bluegrass State. Confederate General

Braxton Bragg and Major General Edmund
Kirby Smith launched that attack in late
August.

On August 14, Kirby Smith's 9,000 man
force left Knoxville. In advance of Smith's
little army, Colonel John Hunt Morgan's
cavalry brigade marauded across Kentucky,
covering 1,000 miles in twenty-four days.
The fast moving Morgan captured 1,200
prisoners (which he paroled) and lost fewer
than 100 men on his rampage. Although
Smith did not capture the Union force
guarding the Cumberland Gap, as anticipated, on August 30 he defeated a force of
6,500 raw Union troops at Richmond,
Kentucky. Smith reached Lexington on
September 1, where Morgan's horsemen
rejoined him. When Covington proved too
tough a nut for Smith to capture, he joined
Bragg's command, which had been maneuvering against Union Major General Don
Carlos Buell. Buell fell back before the
Rebel advance until he was reinforced by

Oliver F. Winchester (1810
–1880) was a clothing manufacturer who invested in the
Volcanic Repeating Arms
Company in 1850. Over the
next three decades he worked to
make mass-produced repeating
rifles a reality. (*Buffalo Bill
Historical Center*)

the command of "Bull" Nelson, now an army major general. Buell than
advanced and fought an outnumbered Confederate army under Bragg in the
bloody and inconclusive battle of Perryville on October 8. Following
Perryville, Bragg withdrew into Tennessee.

Although the invasion of Kentucky failed to secure that state for the
Confederacy, it scared a number of Unionist Kentuckians severely. Among
the dispirited Federal loyalists was George D. Prentice. Many, including
Prentice, were fearful that Louisville would fall to the invading
Confederates, and a number of women and children left the state for Ohio.
Added to the editor's depressed state of mind about the future of Union
Kentucky was the fact that his son, a Confederate artillery officer serving in
the invasion force, was mortally wounded in a fight with Yankee soldiers and
died on September 29.[5]

It was all too much for Prentice, apparently. In September, when the
Rebels seemed in the ascendancy, the editor dumped his supply of Henrys
below wholesale cost. His rationale, expressed later, was that he wanted to
help arm the citizenry in the face of imminent danger, but the ultimate des-

tination of those 280 rifles, most sold by the end of September, could not be determined at the time of sale.

Some most certainly went South—or at least to Southern sympathizers. And some of these apparently saw use by Confederate soldiers while the Kentucky invasion was still in progress. On August 18, Colonel Rodney Mason of the Seventy-first Ohio Infantry, besieged by Rebels commanded by Lieutenant Colonel Thomas Woodward's First Kentucky Confederate Cavalry at Clarksville, Tennessee, was called upon to surrender. In order to assure that his defense would be hopeless, Mason dispatched "Lieutenant-Colonel Andrews to examine and count their force, which he did, and on his return stated that they were over 800 strong, one company armed with volcanic rifles (16-shooters)." With a force of less than 200 men at his disposal, Mason surrendered.[6]

There is little doubt that the "16-shooters" in Woodward's command were not "volcanic rifles" but brand-new Henrys. Wiley Sword reports several other low serial numbered Henrys in the "100-300" range with Confederate association, "including rifle no. 165, crudely inscribed '5th Tenn. Cav., July 27, 1862.'" While a Rebel horseman may have captured this gun from a Yankee Kentucky militiaman on that date, it might also have been purchased by him or presented to him by a Southern sympathizer after being snatched up at Prentice's fire sale. There is also an extant photo of Captain Lorenzo D. Fisher of the Tenth Kentucky Partisan Rangers holding a Henry rifle prior his death at the end of 1862. This gun could have come from Prentice's lot as well. Thus, ironically, the first Henrys fired in actual combat may well have been in the hands of Confederate soldiers.[7]

Were there Henrys in Confederate ranks outside Kentucky in 1862? Heros von Borcke, a Prussian officer and volunteer aide on General J. E. B. Stuart's staff, who joined the Confederate army on the Virginia peninsula on May 31, 1862, was described by Major Moxley Sorrel of General James Longstreet's staff as being "an ambulating arsenal." According to Sorrel's postwar memoir, von Borcke carried "a double barreled rifle . . . across his back, a Winchester carbine hung by his hip, heavy revolvers . . . in his belt, right and left side," among other arms. Sorrel's memoir, penned in a postwar world where "Winchester" had become a synonym for lever-action repeating rifle, did not, of course refer to a true Winchester, but would lead one to believe Von Borcke may have had a Henry. As arms historian Wayne R. Austerman points out, however, this is unlikely. Considering production and distribution records, if the Prussian was carrying a lever action, it was most likely the older Volcanic model.[8]

Although it threw a significant scare into the Federal government and local Unionists, the Confederate invasion of Kentucky in the late summer of

1862 should have created a sales bonanza for Oliver Winchester, since his product was represented at several retail outlets in the state. Seeing the potential market the Rebel threat created, and before he was aware Prentice had dumped his entire stock on the market at bargain prices, undercutting and angering other dealers, Winchester had instructed a St. Louis retailer with whom he was closing an account to send even more rifles to the Louisville gun dealing editor. On October 9, 1862, however, Prentice's account as a dealer for the New Haven Arms company was closed. By the end of that month the 900 Henry rifles known to have been shipped to the Midwest had been sold. Where many of them were was anyone's guess.[9]

Prentice would redeem himself somewhat shortly afterward, however. Apparently his disposal of Henrys had placed enough of them in public hands to do what Oliver Winchester had in mind—get word-of-mouth advertising and sales rolling. Unionist James M. Wilson purchased a Henry from Prentice. According to a widely repeated story, Wilson, who feared for his safety in Rebel Guerrilla-infested Kentucky, "had fitted up a log corn crib across the road from his front door as a sort of arsenal, where he had his Henry Rifle, Colt's Revolver, &c." Why Wilson did not store his weapons in the house where they would presumably be handier in an emergency was not noted. At some point seven Confederate irregulars "rode up, dismounted, and burst into his dining room and commenced firing upon him with revolvers." They all missed, and Wilson asked his captors to shoot him outside, so his family would not witness his demise. Once out the door, however, he broke loose, sprinted for the corn crib as shots zipped around him, secured his Henry, and dispatched all seven guerrillas. Wilson was in the process of raising Company M of the Twelfth Kentucky Cavalry, a new Union regiment then forming in the state. So impressive was his feat in laying low his seven assailants that "the state of Kentucky armed his [Wilson's] company with the Henry rifle." It was quite a story, although Oliver Winchester wrote that he had "heard some marvelous stories" concerning Wilson's fight with the guerrillas, "but not on such authority as to give us full confidence in their accuracy." The story was great press, however, and Winchester did eventually use an account of the affair in his catalog, but kept it in the second person, since Wilson apparently never confirmed it on his own.[10]

Whatever the actual details, Wilson was a good man with a rifle, and the state did indeed order 104 Henrys for Company M through George D. Prentice, now recovered from his panic. The Twelfth was mustered into active service in November 1862, and the guns were apparently ordered on October 12, 1862, and delivered in January 1863. Prentice actually ordered ninety-six more Henrys for Kentucky to arm another company of the Twelfth, but the state reneged on the second order. In all, Winchester shipped 120 rifles to Prentice, and he sold the overage to members of the general public.[11]

Although most officers armed themselves with revolvers and/or swords, Wilson took his personal Henry rifle to the war. Following a skirmish against guerrillas in the spring of 1863, his brigade commander, Colonel Richard T. Jacob, cited the captain's heroism and marksmanship. Jacob reported that "Captain Wilson, of the Twelfth Kentucky Cavalry, rushed into the midst of the enemy and laid many a man low with his Henry rifle."[12]

By January 1863, when regular shipments of Spencers were beginning to flow to the front, knowledge of the Henry's worth as a combat weapon had already begun to spread beyond Kentucky. Major Albert C. Ellithorpe of the Army of the Frontier's First Indian Home Guard Regiment wrote that he would "like to raise a battalion of sharpshooters and have the Henry rifle. I can make it equal to two regiments, and a terror to the enemy." Ellithorpe was a true fan of the Henry, and a surviving early specimen in "relic-dug" condition, bearing serial number 325, is reportedly inscribed "Col. N. P. Chipman / Maj. Gen. Curtis Staff / pres. by Maj. A. C. Ellithorpe / 1st Indiana Regt."[13]

By the end of December 1862, when the first Spencer rifles finally caught up with the Fifth Michigan Cavalry in that regiment's camp at Washington, the Henry rifle, although not an officially contracted arm, had seen limited but active service in both Union and Confederate armies for almost six months. When the first Spencer, in the combat soldier slang of the day, saw "the elephant," is rather vague. There is one indication that this may have occurred in late 1862. Colonel Benjamin Crowninshield of the First Massachusetts Cavalry, in his 1891 history of the regiment, reported that Sergeant Francis O. Lombard used a Spencer prototype during an October reconnaissance in force to Smithfield, Virginia. According to Crowninshield, in a skirmish on October 16, "the first Spencer rifle, a handmade one, was used effectively in the hands of Sergeant Lombard of Company F. He had formerly been employed at the Smith & Wesson factory at Springfield, and was an expert in guns. It became, afterward, a famous weapon—the first magazine gun."[14]

This tantalizing tidbit, recorded in a regimental history published twenty-nine years after the event, is the only record we have of a Spencer in combat prior to 1863. No other information, in the *Official Records*, soldier memoirs, letters, diaries, Spencer company literature, or the papers of Christopher M. Spencer confirms or even mentions Lombard's possession or use of a Spencer rifle in the fall of 1862. Lombard himself was later promoted to lieutenant, but did not survive the war. He was killed in action at New Hope Church, Virginia, on November 27, 1863, and was not around to con-

firm or deny the report when it was published in 1891. Nor does any rifle associated
with him survive.

Perhaps, as Roy Marcot surmises,
Spencer may have made Lombard's
acquaintance in the New England gun
trade and given him a rifle to test in combat
sometime in late 1862. It is equally possible
that Lombard, who had worked at Smith &
Wesson and was presumably acquainted
with the Volcanic and thus its lineal descendant, used a personally owned Henry in
that long-ago skirmish in Virginia, and that
Colonel Crowninshield's memory failed
him and he confused the two repeaters. If
so that would not be the sole example of
such error in Civil War memoir literature.
The story must remain, as Marcot aptly puts
it, "an enigma."[15]

The early distribution of Henry rifles
directly to the field served the purpose of
exhaustive military endurance field trials
that would have been held in the pre-war
world. The Henry stood up well overall,
although there were some unforeseen
problems, as with any new product, then
and now. Five guns were sent to General
Agent John W. Brown in October 1862 for
unspecified repairs and were quickly fixed
and returned to their owners. Captain
Wilson's troopers, the first unit armed
entirely with the Henry, provided a better
test of real and potential problems. In early

Lieutenant Colonel Allen L.
Fahnestock of the Eighty-sixth
Illinois holding his privately
purchased Henry rifle. During
the attack on Kennesaw
Mountain in June 1864, when
the Eighty-sixth was pinned
down, Alason P. Webber borrowed Fahnestock's Henry and
provided covering fire for hours
to allow his comrades a chance
to carry off their wounded, an
action that earned Webber a
Medal of Honor. (USAMHI)

1863 the captain reported a firing pin failure rate of 25 percent. Apparently
some of the double-pronged Henry firing pins were too short to make firm
contact with the cartridge case rim on firing. This may have been due to poor
tolerances of either firing pins or ammunition.[16]

Oliver Winchester himself specified two other function problems created
by use and abuse of his gun in the field. Releasing the Henry's magazine follower to slam home without any cartridges in the magazine battered the

gun's frame and hindered feeding, and excessive dry firing, or pulling the trigger without a round in the chamber damaged the rifle's bolt. New Haven Arms addressed these problems in existing guns returned for repair by enlarging the frame's feeding port and replacing the broken bolt with a new, stronger one. These changes were also introduced to all new production Henrys from March 1863 on.[17]

Occasional ammunition failures were also noted. Although Winchester angrily dismissed rumors that defective ammunition reportedly was loaded with tobacco rather than gunpowder, he did admit to some problems, apparently caused by tallow bullet lubricant melting in hot weather and leaking into and destroying cartridge powder charges. It probably seemed initially like a good idea to Winchester to produce both rifle and ammunition, giving New Haven Arms a monopoly. The possibility of an interruption of manufacture of the sole source of ammunition was not appealing to Ordnance Department officers, however, leading New Haven arms to contact Crittenden and Tibbals as potential alternative manufacturers of Henry ammunition. Perhaps due to the heavier caliber competition posed by the Spencer in early 1863, Winchester also touched base with Smith & Wesson, exploring the possibility of producing a more powerful .44 caliber load, with a longer cartridge case and heavier bullet and powder charge. Potential ammunition problem solutions were given an extra impetus with an explosion at New Haven's ammunition factory in May 1863, producing that very interruption in the supply that the army feared.[18]

Problems with parts breakage and ammunition supply were minor compared with the inability of New Haven Arms to increase production beyond 200 rifles a month. After the lull caused by Prentice dumping guns on the market below cost, business picked up and demand swelled, as word-of-mouth endorsement was abetted by retail advertising placed by Oliver Winchester. By May, Henry supply lagged one to two months behind demand, however, and Winchester admitted, "we are entirely out of rifles." Part of the production problem was the limited factory space available at the New Haven Arms Company plant, cost and availability of machinery, and a war time skilled labor supply diminished by the demands of military enlistment and competing arms makers.[19]

As Oliver Winchester pleaded with distributors and dealers to be patient as he attempted to increase production, the campaigning season of 1863 was about to open. Demand for both Henry and Spencer rifles would soon increase exponentially.

In the fall of 1862, Major General Ulysses S. Grant, commander of the Department of the Tennessee, moved his army against Vicksburg,

Mississippi, a critical Mississippi River port that, along with Port Hudson, Louisiana, were the only remaining roadblocks to Union control of the entire length of the river. An end-of-the-year assault led by Grant's subordinate, Major General William T. Sherman, against the Vicksburg defenses at Chickasaw Bluffs failed. The Union commander kept his men busy over the winter digging canals in an attempt to create a bypass route to move south along the west bank and avoid the big guns that dominated the river from Vicksburg, however. When these attempts failed, Grant actively explored other ways to achieve his goal by crossing the swamps, bayous, and numerous small waterways around the city. In April Commodore William David Porter ran his gunboats by the Vicksburg defenses and a Union force managed to cross the Mississippi south of the city soon after. In a series of fast-moving maneuvers and battles in mid-May, Grant defeated Confederate forces in the field decisively and bottled up the survivors in the city, which he proceeded to place under siege.

While Grant invested Vicksburg, General Rosecrans, still encamped at the scene of his drawn battle at Murfreesboro, was strongly urged by the Federal leadership in Washington, personified by Union General in Chief Major General Henry W. Halleck, to move on General Bragg's Confederate army, then screening Chattanooga. Keeping Bragg off balance would, it was hoped, prevent him from detaching troops to assist the Confederates battling to hold on to Vicksburg. A technologically open-minded and innovative soldier, Rosecrans was deliberative, perhaps to a fault, when planning a campaign, and did not get his three army corps (XIV, XX, and XXI), totaling 65,000 men, moving until the middle of June. When the army moved, though, it moved rapidly and deceptively on Bragg's 44,000-man force, deployed along the Duck River at Shelbyville and Wartrace north of Tullahoma, the rail junction town that would give the campaign its name.

In the tentative maneuvering prior to the onset of the campaign, Colonel Wilder's men would get a chance to try out their new Spencer repeaters, the first of which arrived on May 15. Deliveries apparently continued for the rest of the month, as the men of the Ninety-eighth Illinois received theirs on May 31. These guns were no doubt part of the 2,000 rifles ordered sent west by Ripley a month before. Although Wilder was a detail-oriented commander, he seems to have failed to give his men any more than a perfunctory introduction to their revolutionary new weapons. According to brigade historian Glenn Sunderland, "as soon as each man had drawn his weapon and ammunition, they scattered like schoolboys to the woods to try out their 'seven shooters' on rabbits, squirrels, turkeys and almost anything else that moved." There was apparently none of the formal marksmanship training of the day, which involved intensive drill in distance estimation to compensate for the looping trajectory of bullets and making sure guns shot to where their sights indicated they should. To be fair, marksmanship instruction was rare in either army in the American Civil War.[20]

Captain Gershom M. Barber's Ohio Sharpshooters received their Spencers in early May as well. As befitting their unit title, the Ohioans were a bit more organized in their training with the new guns. Barber wrote on May 19 that he had "been drilling my Battalion together with some companies of the 10th Ohio Infantry in target practice for sometime past and it has given me a fine opportunity to test your Rifle and compare it with the 'Enfield,' and the result is more than forty per cent in favor of the Spencer Rifle. It is admitted by all who have witnessed our practice that we have the best gun in the army."[21]

They may not have shot as well as the Buckeyes, but Wilder's men would have the honor of drawing first blood with their Spencers. On June 4 his brigade advanced on Liberty, Tennessee, and engaged in a brief firefight with a small Confederate force, capturing twenty men of the First Kentucky Confederate Cavalry, a regiment initially raised by President Lincoln's brother-in-law, Benjamin Hardin Helm. The following morning the men of Wilder's mounted infantry brigade, joined by a brigade of Federal cavalry, advanced once more, skirmishing with their Spencers and driving the First Kentucky, Eighth and Eleventh Texas, and Third Regular Confederate Cavalry before them. Almost a year after the first Henry rifles were used in combat, the Spencer finally received its baptism of fire. One officer engaged wrote the Spencer Company that a captured Confederate lieutenant asked "what kind of *Hell-fired* guns have your men got?" He added that "Col. Wilder is highly delighted with the rifles, and says that his first appreciation of them has been more than realized."[22]

A more notable test was soon to come. A ridge ran along the front of Bragg's army, channeling any advancing Union forces to four passes or "gaps." Although this geographical feature apparently provided an advantage to the defense, Rosecrans used the rise in ground as cover for his maneuvering forces. Following a series of feints toward Bellbuckle and Liberty Gaps, which, had he forced them, would have brought his army up against well-dug-in Rebel soldiers beyond, Rosecrans ordered an attack on Hoover's Gap. The Gap was on the Confederate right, and a force breaking through at that point would outflank the main enemy defensive line and threaten the Southern supply depot at Tullahoma.

Colonel Wilder's brigade, now consisting of the Ninety-eighth and 123rd Illinois and Seventeenth and Seventy-second Indiana Mounted Infantry and

Captain Eli Lilly's Eighteenth Indiana Artillery Battery, was assigned the task of seizing Hoover's Gap. Anticipating fast-moving combat with the mounted infantry, Captain Lilly had acquired two lightweight mountain howitzers to go along with his three-inch Rodman ordnance rifles. Once the Gap was in their control, Wilder and his men were instructed to hold it until infantry reinforcements from Major General George Thomas' XIV Corps arrived to exploit the situation by moving against the flank of Lieutenant General William J. Hardee's Confederate corps.

At 3:00 A.M. on June 24, Wilder's horsemen rode out of their camp three miles north of Murfreesboro and struck out for their objective. Shortly after dawn a steady rain began to fall, which would continue all day and into the night. Around midday the column approached Hoover's Gap, and the colonel ordered his men to advance rapidly

An cavalry soldier armed with a Spencer rifle. (*USAMHI*)

in a "bold dash" that shocked and overwhelmed the Confederate cavalrymen posted to picket the position.

Major James Connolly of the 123rd Illinois wrote that the Rebels were "so much surprised by our sudden appearance that they scattered through the woods and over the hills in every direction, every fellow for himself . . . on foot and every other way, leaving all their tents, wagons, baggage, commissary stores and indeed everything in our hands, but we didn't stop for anything, on we pushed, our boys, with their Spencer rifles, keeping up a continual popping in front."[23]

The unfortunate Southerners were troopers from the hapless First Kentucky Cavalry, Wilder's victims three weeks earlier, under the command of Major J. Q. A. Chenoweth. Chenoweth managed to rally a dozen men to conduct a fighting withdrawal, but lost nine of them in the process. Sergeant Cicero Harris of the First reportedly had his foot "torn to pieces" by a bullet, giving him the dubious distinction of being one of the first men noted as wounded by a Spencer rifle. One fleeing Confederate horseman warned approaching infantry, "Those Yankees have got rifles that won't quit shootin' and we can't load fast enough to keep up."[24]

After rolling through the Gap and seizing the high ground on its southern end, Wilder quickly deployed his brigade in a defensive mode to respond to the inevitable counterattack. He posted the Seventeenth Indiana, 123rd Illinois, and Seventy-second Indiana on high ground to the right of the Manchester Turnpike, with two companies of the Ninety-eighth Illinois holding a hill on the left of the road and the remaining eight companies of that regiment held in reserve to the right. Company E of the Seventy-second had overrun the advance and was isolated across the Garrison Branch of the Duck River to the left of the Pike. Captain Lilly placed his four three-inch rifled guns with the 123rd and his two 12-pound mountain howitzers with the Seventy-second's two-company detachment.[25]

Elements of Major General Alexander P. Stewart's Division of Hardee's Corps rushed to halt the Yankee rampage, with Brigadier General William B. Bate's brigade in the lead. On arrival, Bate decided to assault the Federal position, hoping to drive Wilder back through Hoover's Gap. Bate deployed the Eufala Alabama Artillery with the Fourth Battalion Georgia Sharpshooters in support in the center of his line and secured his right flank with the Fifteenth and Thirty-seventh Tennessee and his left with the Fifty-eighth Alabama as those units arrived later. Bate had but two regiments, the Twentieth Tennessee and Thirty-seventh Georgia, to attack with.

The Confederate commander advanced two companies of Tennesseans as skirmishers to develop the Union position. Lilly had been firing effective counter-battery fire against the Confederate artillery with his accurate rifled cannon. As soon as Rebel infantry came within range, however, he opened up on them. They advanced directly at the Hoosier captain's four rifled guns, one of which became inoperative when a round jammed in its barrel and had to be withdrawn. As they closed on the hill, the Southerners began to fire in the advance, filling the air with bullets. When the Rebels approached the crest, the men of the 123rd Illinois stood up and fired a series of rapid volleys into their faces, staggering them and driving them back. Confederate Lieutenant Tod Carter remembered that "once those blue devils squeezed off the first round, a silence was never heard from their lines."[26]

Major Claybrooke of the Twentieth tried to rally his faltering command by grasping its new colors and waving them aloft. A Spencer bullet cracked the flagstaff, dropping the banner to the ground. The major reached down to grasp it again, but just as he rolled back up into the saddle both he and his horse were riddled by a blizzard of Spencer bullets. As Claybrooke fell, the Tennesseans broke and fell back to rejoin the rest of their advancing regiment. The heavy fire of the Illinois men broke the Twentieth's advance and drove the Rebels back to a fence line, where they continued to engage in a

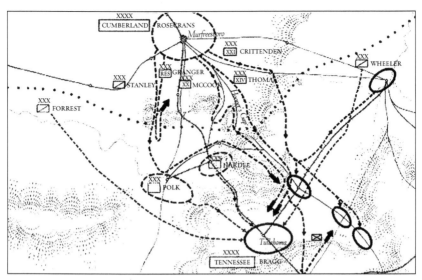

Union and confederate movements during the Middle Tennessee Campaign.
(Adapted from the *West Point Atlas of American Wars*)

firefight with the 123rd. Oddly, the Yankees, originally drilled as rifle musket
armed infantrymen to fight from a stand up line of battle, appear to have not
taken advantage of the more open formation and ability to fire from safer
kneeling and prone positions afforded them by the Spencer breechloader.
This would cost them casualties, as the Confederates kept up a steady, if
slower, fire on the Union line with their muzzleloaders.

Hoping to break the stalemate, Bate ordered the Thirty-seventh Georgia
to try to turn the Union right flank while the Tennesseans kept the 123rd
occupied and his artillery and the Georgia Sharpshooters opened fire along
the rest of the line. The Georgians pushed to within fifty yards of the
Seventeenth Indiana before being checked by the heavy volume of fire the
Yankee Spencers spit out. At that point one of the potential problems envis-
aged by General Ripley in his initial opposition to breechloaders and
repeaters raised its head—the Hoosiers began to run out of ammunition and
fell back down the rear slope of the hill, with the muzzleloader-armed
Georgians in hot pursuit. The Seventeenth's abrupt withdrawal exposed the
flank of the 123rd, already occupied by its duel with the Tennesseans. The
Spencer-armed brigade was on the verge of being driven from its position by
men with muzzleloaders.

Colonel Wilder, a hands-on commander, saw the crisis unfolding, however, and ordered up the eight reserve companies of the Ninety-eighth Illinois
to take over the fight. The Ninety-eighth passed through the Seventeenth
and stormed up the hill shooting, driving the enemy off the crest, down the

other side and past the flank of the Twentieth. The tables were now turned
as the "Suckers" (a nineteenth-century colloquialism for Illinoisians) of the
Ninety-eighth brought their Spencers to bear on the Twentieth Tennessee.
That regiment, now enfiladed, fell back as well.

Bate, desperate to seal the Gap against a major Federal breakthrough,
prepared to launch another attack, this time with the assistance of Brigadier
General Bushrod Johnson's brigade, which arrived to reinforce him. As Bate
conferred with Johnson, Wilder, who had reported to higher headquarters
that Stewart's whole division was moving on him, received an order to withdraw, conveyed from his division commander, Major General Joseph J.
Reynolds via Captain Alexander Rice of Reynolds' staff. The Yankee colonel,
accurately perceiving that his Spencers, coupled with his excellent defensive
position and tactical skills, would enable him to hold on, refused to retreat
and continued to trade fire with the Confederates to his front. Rice then
threatened him with arrest, then rode back to report to Reynolds. Shortly
afterward General Rosecrans, trailed by his chief of staff, Brigadier General
James A. Garfield, arrived along with Thomas and Reynolds. According to
Wilder, Rosecrans turned to Reynolds and said, "Wilder has done right.
Promote him, Promote him," Reynolds agreed. By 7:00 P.M. Union infantry
arrived on the scene, and during the night more and more Federal foot soldiers slogged into Hoover's Gap through the mud and rain. The Gap was
secured. On June 26, Stewart ordered Bate and Johnson to withdraw and
General Thomas pushed his men forward, continuing the flank movement
that would force Bragg to evacuate middle Tennessee and fall back into
Georgia.[27]

Spencer rifles had played a part in Rosecrans' relatively bloodless victory,
but the men behind the guns as well as the proper tactical use made of
repeaters was as important, if not more so, than the actual technology of the
weapons. Colonel Wilder had begun to successfully engage a tactical learning curve, one that many other officers, whatever their opinions on repeaters
or experience with them, never completed or failed to even begin. Colonel
Bate reported that of the 650 men of his brigade actually engaged at
Hoover's Gap, he lost 147 killed and wounded. Of these, the two regiments
most heavily engaged with the Spencer armed Yankees, the Twentieth
Tennessee and Thirty-seventh Georgia, lost ten men killed and thirty-three
wounded and six killed and forty-two wounded, respectively. While these are
not insignificant casualties considering the number of men engaged, they are
not particularly heavy for a Civil War battle. Although the volume of fire generated by the Spencers created a deep impression on Confederate soldiers
like Lieutenant Carter, the technology they represented was not, at this stage
of the game at least, impossible to overcome. In the defense, which also

included the initial offensive thrust through the gap, Colonel Wilder reported his "entire loss in the action of the 24th of June is 1 commissioned officer
killed (J. R. Eddy, chaplain Seventy-second Indiana), 1 commissioned officer
mortally wounded (Lieut. James T. Moreland, Seventeenth Indiana), and 12
enlisted men killed and 47 wounded." And Wilder's brigade was now reborn
as the "Lightning Brigade."[28]

As Grant continued to wrestle with the siege of Vicksburg and Rosecrans
planned his move on Bragg, the Union Army of the Potomac under Major
General Joseph Hooker went down to defeat before General Robert E. Lee's
Army of Northern Virginia at Chancellorsville, Virginia. In the weeks follow-
ing that early May debacle, both armies warily watched each other across the
Rappahannock in the vicinity of Fredericksburg.

In the wake of Chancellorsville, it became clear to the Confederate political and military leadership in Richmond that the next move in the Eastern
Theater of War was up to them. Although several plans were advanced,
including using part of General Lee's army to bolster Confederate forces in
the west that were beleaguered by Rosecrans and Grant, Lee's idea of an
invasion of the North prevailed. Such an incursion would move the seat of
war from ravaged Virginia, allow the Army of Northern Virginia to feed itself
off the enemy's larder, and strengthen the peace movement in the North. A
Southern battlefield victory, which, considering his track record, Lee had
every right to expect, might also gain the Confederacy the international
recognition it needed to survive.

By June 3, many of Lee's veterans were sidling west from the
Rappahannock line toward the Shenandoah Valley, while Lieutenant
General Ambrose P. Hill's corps remained in defensive positions at
Fredericksburg, confronting the puzzled Hooker. Aware the enemy was
moving, but not knowing where, the Federal commander ordered his VI
Corps to conduct a reconnaissance in force across the river, and on June 5,
the corps' Second division secured a bridgehead on the south bank.

General Lee, meanwhile, was on his way to Pennsylvania with the bulk of
his army. On June 9, the Federal cavalry clashed with its Rebel counterpart
at Brandy Station. The ensuing battle, one of the largest mounted encounters of the war, firmly established the improved quality of the Yankee horse
and confirmed the Army of Northern Virginia's shift toward the Shenandoah
Valley invasion route. Ironically, the Spencer-armed Fifth and Sixth
Michigan Cavalry, with the most potential firepower of any mounted units in
either eastern army, remained in garrison in the defenses of Washington as
Brandy Station raged.

By June 13, Confederate Lieutenant General Richard S. Ewell was
advancing his Corps of the Army of Northern Virginia on Winchester,

Virginia, then occupied by forces under the command of Union Major General Robert H. Milroy. Although outnumbered, Milroy decided to stand and fight Ewell, but made the mistake of limiting his defense to the static forts west of the town. Feinting to the south and east, Ewell countermarched north and overwhelmed a Union outpost, then moved to block the road leading north from Winchester. Outmaneuvered, Milroy retreated to Stephenson's Depot, where he was forced to surrender the bulk of his force. Ewell reported a loss of 269 men, while Federal casualties of over 4,400 included over 3,300 men captured. Although some Union troops managed to escape, and many of the prisoners were sick and wounded from other commands hospitalized in Winchester, the disaster did not bode well for the developing campaign.

One aspect of the Winchester debacle of 1863 that is often overlooked is that it provided the Eastern Theater introduction to combat of the Henry rifle. It appears that several of Milroy's regiments were armed in part with Henrys. Colonel J. Warren Keifer of the 110th Ohio, whose command was badly battered at one of Milroy's outposts, reported that he could not "refrain from calling attention to my sharpshooters. Armed with the Henry rifle, in each engagement they fired almost continuous streams into the enemy's ranks, creating great loss of life. They also, under my own eyes, shot down a number of the enemy's officers." Despite Keifer's praise, there is no evidence that the Henrys of the 110th made any significant impression on Ewell's victorious Confederates.[29]

The Twenty-third Illinois, another regiment deployed in western Virginia in the summer of 1863, mustered at least one Henry rifle during the Winchester fight. The Twenty-third, also known as the "Irish Brigade of the West," had begun the war a hard luck outfit. Commanded by Colonel James A. Mulligan of Chicago, the predominantly Irish American regiment was mustered in on June 12, 1861, and moved to Missouri shortly afterward. By September the Twenty-third was in Lexington, where it was part of a 2,700-man force besieged by ten times that number of Confederates. After a nine-day siege the Lexington garrison surrendered and was paroled. The regiment was first mustered out of service, then exchanged, reorganized, and sent to Harper's Ferry, Virginia. It remained in the Eastern Theater for the remainder of the war.

The men of the reorganized Twenty-third were determined to give themselves every advantage should they find themselves in a tight situation again. Lieutenant John Brown, a company commander in the Twenty-third, privately purchased a Henry from a gun dealer named Adams in Wheeling, West Virginia, apparently in the spring of 1863. Brown was so enthused with the rifle that on September 26 he wrote New Haven Arms regarding the purchase of "from fifteen to twenty-five—perhaps thirty—for my company."[30] Soon, a number of soldiers of the Twenty-third would be armed with Henrys.

Although repeaters had begun to appear here and there in the Union armies in the east, until the end of June they were still absent from the Army of the Potomac. As that month passed, Hooker's cavalry, under the command of Brigadier General Alfred Pleasonton, continued to probe the shifting Confederate army, engaging in bitter little cavalry fights with Major General J. E. B. Stuart's Rebel horsemen at places like Aldie and Middleburg. Hooker and Pleasonton called for reinforcements for their stretched and strained mounted units, lobbying for Major General Julius Stahel's division to be added to the Army of the Potomac.

Stahel, a Hungarian-born immigrant who had served heroically in his country's 1848 Revolution against the Hapsburgs, came to America in 1856, where he worked as a journalist in New York and became friendly with German American leaders. Appointed lieutenant colonel of the predominantly German Eighth New York Infantry in 1861, Stahel rose to brigade command in 1862 and temporarily commanded the XI Army Corps in early 1863. In March he was personally assigned by President Lincoln to form the three cavalry brigades in the defenses of Washington into a division and aggressively pursue John Singleton Mosby's partisan rangers, who had been penetrating Union lines at will. Stahel never caught Mosby, but he organized the cavalry, including the Spencer-armed Fifth and Sixth Michigan, and got it into the field in Virginia. Hooker's needs assured that the Wolverines would travel much further afield in the high summer of 1863.

While in Washington the green Fifth and Sixth Michigan cavalry regiments had been brigaded with the Seventh Michigan Cavalry, another new regiment, and all placed under the command of Brigadier General Copeland. In late June the Michigan troopers were attached to the Army of the Potomac and sent north toward Pennsylvania following the Confederates. On the way, they were placed under entirely new division and brigade leadership. Following General Hooker's resignation and Major General George G. Meade's elevation to command of the Army of the Potomac, General Pleasonton cleaned house. At the end of June, both Stahel and Copeland found themselves out of active duty cavalry jobs as Pleasonton took the opportunity to jump several of his favorite young officers into positions of authority.

Stahel's replacement was Brigadier General Judson Kilpatrick, a combative New Jerseyan with a somewhat murky ethical background. Copeland gave way to young George Armstrong Custer, promoted from captain to brigadier general literally overnight. Custer, who had previously unsuccessfully lobbied for a regimental command in the Michigan brigade, now commanded the entire brigade, which was strengthened by the addition of the First Michigan Cavalry, a veteran outfit.

Joining Custer in brigade command under Kilpatrick in what became the Third Division of the Cavalry Corps of the Army of the Potomac was Elon Farnsworth, another young captain advanced to brigadier general. General Pleasonton had little chance to see his favorites perform in their new commands, however, as General Meade, who had assented to the promotions, kept his cavalry commander close to army headquarters, where Pleasonton acted more as a staff officer and advisor than combat commander. The Cavalry Corps' divisions would act as semi-independent entities in the developing campaign.

Each Federal cavalry division was assigned a screening and reconnaissance mission of its own by Meade and Pleasonton, and the Yankee horsemen rode hard, seeking out the enemy and occasionally skirmishing with Stuart's Rebel riders, who were off on a grand raid through Maryland and into Pennsylvania. On June 29, Kilpatrick led his Third Division out of Frederick, Maryland, toward York, Pennsylvania. By the following morning, the division was approaching Hanover, which had recently been occupied by Confederate cavalry, with Custer and his First and Seventh Michigan in the lead.

After gathering intelligence and passing through the town, the Federal rear guard engaged a number of Confederates, initiating a fight in which the Eighteenth Pennsylvania Cavalry was driven into Hanover. A Federal counterattack drove the Rebels back, battering the Second North Carolina Cavalry and capturing its commander, Lieutenant Colonel William Payne, whom a New York trooper helped climb out of a vat of brown dye into which he pitched when his horse was shot.

General Farnsworth's brigade barricaded itself in Hanover and combat soon broke out across the fields around the town, with regiments from both sides fed into the fight piecemeal. By early afternoon, all elements of the Michigan Brigade had returned to the scene and were deployed outside the town to the northwest. As more of Stuart's horsemen arrived, a desultory stalemate punctuated by artillery fire settled in on the battlefield.

In an attempt to break the impasse, General Custer dismounted Colonel George Gray's Sixth Michigan and ordered the Wolverines, armed with a mix of Spencer rifles and Burnside carbines, to move under cover of some trees against one of Stuart's artillery batteries and a cavalry detachment posted to protect it. The Michigan men surprised the Rebels, opening fire on them at a range of between 200 and 300 yards. As Spencer bullets fell in and around the enemy position, the Confederate cavalry took off for the rear. The Yankees advanced but then retreated as Brigadier General Fitzhugh Lee hastened reinforcements to the danger point. The Federals advanced again unsuccessfully and settled down to positions from which they could keep the Rebel line under fire. After dark Stuart disengaged and withdrew. Hanover was the first time Spencer rifles were used by a unit in combat in the Eastern Theater. They would get a more thorough test within days.

On July 1, the Michigan Brigade moved toward East Berlin, Pennsylvania. The troopers could hear the rumble of guns in the distance, as the battle of Gettysburg began, but they did not move to the sound of those guns until Kilpatrick was ordered to bring his division to the battlefield on July 2.

The fight at Gettysburg had been opened by the cavalry division of Brigadier General John Buford, which had held ground west of the town long enough for Federal infantry of the I and XI Corps to arrive on the field. The men of Buford's division were armed with, in addition to sabers and revolvers, Burnside, Gallager, Merrill, Sharps, and Smith single-shot breech-loading carbines. Popular myth has it that Buford's successful delaying action of July 1 was due to the rapid firepower his men put out, with some writers erroneously reporting they wielded Spencer carbines against advancing Confederate infantry. In truth, of course, there were no Spencer carbines then in production, much less in service; the only Spencers in the whole Army of the Potomac were the rifles carried by the Fifth and Sixth Michigan Cavalry, and neither regiment was at Gettysburg on July 1.[31]

The rate of fire of most single-shot breech-loading carbines, with the notable exception of the Sharps, was not dramatically higher than that of muzzle-loading muskets. Rates of fire with the Smith and other single shots were limited by the need to cap before a shot and the need to extract a fired, occasionally jammed, cartridge case with finger power. The true secret of Buford's success that day was that his skirmish line forced the advancing Confederate infantry, who did not know what was behind it, to deploy into line of battle, which took a considerable amount of time.

The early morning hours of July 3 found the Michigan cavalrymen camped at Two Taverns. Roused at 7:00 A.M. by General Kilpatrick after three hours' sleep, the Wolverines prepared to follow their division commander and General Farnsworth's brigade to an assigned position on the Union left flank. An hour later, however, as the Michigan men began to leave camp following Kilpatrick and Farnsworth's departure, a staff officer arrived with a message for Custer from Brigadier General David McMurtrie Gregg, commander of the Second Division of the Cavalry Corps. The general was concerned about the Yankee right flank, and he needed help.

General Gregg was an 1855 West Point graduate and an experienced, astute, and well-liked leader. Late in the day on July 2, his men had fought

Confederate troops at nearby Brinkerhoff's Ridge, successfully diverting the Stonewall Brigade from the main Rebel infantry attack directed toward East Cemetery Ridge. Gregg realized the critical tactical importance of the intersection of the Hanover and Low Dutch roads, key to the Federal right and rear, and asked Custer to temporarily cover the critical crossroads with his brigade.

Gregg left one of his two brigades, under his cousin Colonel John Irvin Gregg, to link up with VI Corps infantrymen in the vicinity of Wolf Hill and led his other brigade, under Colonel John B. McIntosh, to relieve Custer and enable the Michigan brigade to rejoin Kilpatrick. By mid-morning, Gregg's assumption that there might be a Confederate attempt to loop around the Union right flank appeared to be correct. Major General Oliver O. Howard advised Pleasonton that a large Confederate mounted force was heading that way down the York road. Despite this intelligence, the Federal cavalry commander did not countermand Custer's orders to move toward Little Round Top. It was soon abundantly clear to Custer that Confederate cavalry were moving toward the Rummel Farm, to his front.

The mounted force was Stuart's division. The Confederate cavalry commander arrived at the Rummel Farm that morning hoping to take advantage of any opportunity that presented itself to disrupt the Federal right and rear. There is no evidence that there was any coordinated plan for him to attack the Yankee rear in concert with General Longstreet's assault (popularly known as Pickett's Charge) on the Union center, but Stuart was free to do whatever he wished to abet the overall Confederate tactical goal.

Stuart ordered one of his artillery batteries to fire four shells in different directions, most likely in an attempt to discover the Federal positions by provoking a reaction. Eric Wittenberg, author of the most recent and detailed study of the July 3 cavalry fight at Gettysburg, believes the general was indeed looking for a response from the Federals and that he was planning an ambush of Gregg's men. Stuart's subsequent actions appear to confirm this assumption.[32]

The first Confederate units to reach the field were the brigades of Brigadier General Albert G. Jenkins and Colonel John R. Chambliss. Jenkins had been wounded by a shell fragment the day before and was not present. Many of his men had been detailed to guard prisoners but the rest remained with Stuart. The lead unit of Jenkins' brigade and the whole of Stuart's division was Lieutenant Colonel Vincent Witcher's Thirty-fourth Virginia Cavalry Battalion. The twenty-six-year-old Witcher was a tough man from a tough family. Just prior to the war, his father and other relatives had engaged in a gun and knife fight at a local store over depositions filed in a divorce that they believed sullied the honor of a female extended family member. Old man Witcher and his son and son-in-law shot and stabbed the aggrieved husband, James Clement, and his two brothers to death but were acquitted on grounds of self-defense.

Although attached to the Army of Northern Virginia for the Gettysburg campaign, the Thirty-fourth had previously served in an irregular and raiding role in western Virginia and was more accurately classified as a mounted infantry unit than a traditional cavalry outfit. The battalion evolved from an independent company that Witcher raised in 1861, and which eventually grew into a battalion. Witcher's men were initially armed with U.S. Model 1841 Mississippi rifles in .54 caliber. By mid-1863 the unit's armament was more diverse. At Gettysburg they also had some Enfield and Richmond rifle muskets and Richmond Armory short rifle muskets purpose-built for mounted infantry use, all in .577 or .58 caliber, as well as some Austrian rifle muskets, most likely in .54 caliber, in the Thirty-fourth's ranks. These muzzle-loaders fired Minié balls and a sixty-grain charge of powder encased in paper cartridges. In addition, most of the men of the Thirty-fourth carried revolvers.[33]

Stuart ordered Witcher to dismount his battalion and occupy the Rummel Farm, personally posting the Virginians in the barn and along a nearby stone wall. Witcher's men quickly went to work fortifying the barn by cutting loopholes in the walls to poke their muskets through. While they worked, an artillery battery set up and began to fire at Custer's men across the fields to their front. Stuart's other brigades were held in reserve and masked from the Federals by a woodlot, although some of Chambliss' men were apparently in the open.

Custer ordered Lieutenant Alexander C. M. Pennington's Battery M, Second U.S. Artillery, to return fire on the Rebel artillery and dismounted cavalry occupying the farm, and effective Yankee counterbattery fire soon silenced the Confederate guns. As Pennington's gunners opened fire, General Gregg arrived on the field with McIntosh's brigade. McIntosh quickly began to deploy his men to replace the Michigan troopers covering the crossroads, but Gregg, concerned about the potential force to his front, asked Custer to stay on in support. Custer replied that if ordered to do so, he would, and Gregg wasted no time issuing the order.

The Michigan brigade waited in reserve while McIntosh advanced the dismounted First New Jersey Cavalry on the Rebels occupying the Rummel Farm. Reaching a covering stone wall, the Jerseyans unslung their Burnside carbines and began to trade a desultory fire with Witcher's men. The Jersey regiment mustered 199 effectives, but the First's skirmish line was no more than 150 men. Cavalry units reduced their strength by 25 percent when fighting dismounted, since every fourth man was detailed to hold horses.[34]

As the enemy fire intensified, McIntosh sent the 335 troopers of the Third Pennsylvania in to support the Jerseymen. Some of the Pennsylvanians remained mounted in reserve while others dismounted, with horse holders detached, and added their Sharps carbine fire to the fight. While the Yankees engaged the Thirty-fourth, Stuart held the rest of his command, the brigades of Colonel Chambliss and Brigadier Generals Fitzhugh Lee and Wade Hampton, behind and in a nearby woodlot. It appears that he may have used the Thirty-fourth as bait to spring an ambush on Gregg's men, who he hoped would engage and be distracted by the dismounted Rebels, leaving them open to an attack by his mounted brigades. When McIntosh's two regiments ran short of carbine ammunition they withdrew, to be replaced on the skirmish line by Custer's Fifth Michigan and part of the Sixth Michigan, which had moved up in support positions.[35]

As the Jerseyans and Pennsylvanians exchanged places with the Michigan men, the Virginians also ran low on ammunition and fell back to a second line. Relying on a statement in General Stuart's report, many believe that the men of Jenkins' brigade were issued only ten rounds of ammunition each. This was, according to Lieutenant Colonel Witcher, "absolutely untrue." Although the members of the brigade detailed to guard prisoners were limited to ten rounds each, those committed to the battle on Rummel's Farm started out with full cartridge boxes. When several enlisted men sent to bring up more ammunition from the rear failed to return, Witcher himself went to investigate and found one of his men who had been wounded but had acquired a supply of cartridges that he brought back to the firing line.[36]

As the men of the Thirty-fourth refilled their cartridge boxes, they were reinforced by elements of the Fourteenth and Sixteenth Virginia Cavalry. The reinforced line advanced, with, according to Witcher, "all told, 600 men besides officers in line" covering a front of "some 300 or perhaps 400 yards long." It is presumed that this estimate deducts unit horse holders already to the rear. Based on its June 30 strength reports, and deducting losses incurred earlier in the campaign, the Fifth Michigan fielded 646 men, including officers, with, less horse holders, approximately 484 men in a dismounted line of battle.[37]

Witcher's men crossed several stone walls, entered a wheat field, and advanced up to a fence line before they engaged the Michigan regiment. A fierce firefight ensued. Spencer slugs filled the air, and the advancing Virginians were hit by a blizzard of bullets. Captain Edwin Bouldin of the Fourteenth remembered that "the fire was very severe. We were lying down on the ground behind the bottom rails. So deadly was the fire that once, when one of my men was wounded, two others were struck as soon as they rose to bear him from the field." Another officer from the Fourteenth recalled that "our opponents poured a rain of bullets and shells on us, but were forced slowly to fall back. We lost heavily."[38]

The fight went on for some time and it proved too much for the Fourteenth and Sixteenth. Riddled by Spencer fire, both units took off for the rear. Witcher recalled that they "left me and the field," and the Thirty-fourth had to face the Spencers alone. The battalion hung on though, slugging it out. It is unlikely that the Virginians had been fully trained in marksmanship to the military standards of the day, involving range estimation and trajectory compensation. Still, the range of combat on Rummel's Farm was relatively short, and Witcher's men, Mountaineers all, knew well how to draw a bead and smoothly squeeze a trigger. They gave the Wolverines as hot a time as they could handle.

One Michigan veteran remembered "an hour's fighting and we think our line is solid, but 'tis mighty stubborn work. The rebs are solid also in their position. 'Greek has met Greek.'" Major Noah Ferry, commanding the dismounted men of the Fifth, stood up on a tree stump to survey the line of battle, but was pulled down to safety by his men. Ferry, with the fury of the fight upon him, then climbed up on a rock, yelling "Michigan to the res—" as a bullet hit him in the head, killing him instantly. Eventually the Michigan men began to fall back as, similar to the case of the Seventeenth Indiana at Hoover's Gap, they ran out of ammunition.[39]

Seeing the Wolverines move toward the rear, Stuart ordered Colonel Chambliss' brigade to charge. As the Thirty-fourth advanced on foot and Chambliss' horsemen thundered downhill towards the dismounted Yankees, the Seventh Michigan rode to the rescue, clashing with the enemy riders and dismounted riflemen along a fence line. The Seventh's troopers could not get over or through the fence, and began to pile up as their horses shied away from the rails and were shot down. The Thirty-fourth poured a stream of bullets into the Michigan men until they fell back in disorder. Under heavy and effective Federal artillery fire from Pennington's battery and Captain Alanson M. Randol's four gun consolidated Battery E/G, First U. S. Artillery, plus whatever the Seventh could hit them with, Chambliss' brigade fell back as well.

Stuart then launched a second mounted charge, hurling Lee's and Hampton's brigades at the Federals. This time the First Michigan, along with part of the First New Jersey and Third Pennsylvania, charged headlong into the Rebel advance and stopped it cold in a melee of slashing sabers and barking revolvers. While this desperate mounted fight took place, Witcher's men continued to fire into the mounted Yankees from their flanking position. The Thirty-fourth engaged the Fifth Michigan once more, as some men of that regiment, although out of Spencer cartridges, remounted and joined the fight with their revolvers, but were driven back by Virginia musketry.

Stuart's riders retreated beyond the Rummel Farm buildings as the fight abated, and, toward the end of the day the Thirty-fourth fell back as well. The battalion held the farm, however, until the Confederates evacuated the area the following morning. Lieutenant Colonel Witcher's men paid a heavy price for their constancy. Almost twenty-three years later Witcher painfully recalled that he could "never, no never, forget that eventful night when, accompanied by one courier, my adjutant Edwards & sergeant major, both being wounded, I full of grief and Bitterness, rode to the barns in our rear and saw, with tears in my eyes, my brave fellows, from away over the mountains in West Virginia, laid out in windrows, torn and bleeding. I shall never forget that night, or the next morning's parade when I could muster but 96 Enlisted men." The Thirty-fourth, which lost only one man as a prisoner, had a 75 percent casualty rate.[40]

The Fifth Michigan reported fifty-six men killed, wounded, and missing, most of its casualties inflicted by the Thirty-fourth, for an 8.7 percent casualty rate. The Seventh Michigan, which suffered the heaviest losses in the Wolverine brigade, many of them caused by rifles and rifle muskets as the Thirty-fourth fired into the regiment when it piled up at the fence, lost 100 men, for a rate of 26.1 percent. The entire Michigan Brigade, which entered the fight with 1,925 men, lost 257, or 13.3 percent.[41]

Spencer rifles in the hands of the Michigan men proved very effective in a defensive role and inflicted a large number of casualties in the dismounted fight, pouring out bullets and badly shooting up Witcher's command. Spencer fire totally demoralized the two Virginia units that fought alongside Witcher and drove them from the field, but the Wolverines were unable to capitalize on this by advancing to a position that would determine the outcome of the battle. The Thirty-fourth, indeed, held its ground, and, even with terrible casualties, was able to hang on until the Fifth ran out of ammunition and then advance to inflict casualties on the Seventh and First Michigan.

The July 3 cavalry fight at Gettysburg ended in a tactical stalemate. That stalemate prevented Stuart from looping around the Union right, however, and in that sense was favorable to the Federals. Were the Spencer rifles decisive in producing this result, or was the tough horse-to-horse saber and revolver fight that blunted the attack of Hampton and Fitz Lee the decisive

The spirited charge by two companies of the 6th Michigan Cavalry on a Confederate rearguard near Falling Waters, Maryland, as they retreated across the Potomac on July 14. (Illustration by Edwin Forbes, *Library of Congress*)

act of the battle? In the high summer of 1863, although General Custer determined on the spot that the Spencer rifle was the best arm cavalrymen could be issued, the jury was still out. The Michigan Spencers proved that repeating rifles could play a significant tactical role in the war. What that ultimate role would be, and what, if any, kind of tactical doctrine would evolve to make the best use of these new weapons remained unanswered. That repeaters would be used by the Union army in increasing numbers was a given. How they would be employed was still problematic.

SIX

CHICKAMAUGA TO OLUSTEE

B Y THE LATE SUMMER OF 1863, IN THE WAKE OF HOOVER'S GAP AND Gettysburg, the Spencer repeating rifle had acquired an excellent reputation in the field and demand for the guns from Union soldiers and commanders began to escalate. Following General Rosecrans' lead, Major General Stephan A. Hurlbut, commanding the XVI Corps and the city of Memphis, Tennessee, requested Spencer "Navy rifles" to arm two regiments of mounted infantrymen. Hurlbut was bedeviled by Confederate "partisan rangers" sniping at Union shipping on the Mississippi River from the Arkansas side and badly wanted to clean them out. The general had probably seen some of the Navy Spencers shipped west to arm members of the Mississippi Marine Brigade, an Army unit manning converted river steamboats designed to ram enemy craft as well as carry landing parties, and was no doubt eager to get some of these advanced small arms for his Guerrilla hunters.

Chief of Staff Major General Henry Wager Halleck, no friend to innovation, denied Hurlbut's request. The politically connected Hurlbut would not take no for an answer from the likes of Halleck, however, and directly petitioned Abraham Lincoln to grant his request. His curiosity sparked by the general's inquiry, Lincoln requested a Spencer rifle from the Navy to evaluate for himself. Unfortunately, the first gun he received had problems, and so did the second.

The president found that the initial rifle's "[magazine] tube was wound so tight in place that I could not get it out." That was just the beginning. The second rifle had a functioning magazine tube, but when the lever was worked to chamber a cartridge, two jumped forward, jamming the gun so thoroughly that it took fifteen minutes to disassemble and clear it. After the Spencer was reassembled, Lincoln was able to successfully fire a number of shots, but the president was concerned that the two rifles, already inspected

and accepted by the Navy, did not function properly. Based on these misad-
ventures, on August 4, 1863, Lincoln advised Hurlbut that he would not be
getting any Spencers.[1]

Somehow, word of this fiasco reached the indefatigable Warren Fisher,
treasurer of the Spencer Company. In response, Fisher dispatched
Christopher Spencer to Washington in mid-August to stage a personal
demonstration for the president. Spencer brought along a letter of introduction in which Fisher expressed hope that the inventor's "exhibition" would
undo the bad impression created by "the mishaps of our gun at its former trials before you."[2]

Spencer later recalled his visit as "the most gratifying of my war recollections." At Lincoln's request Spencer stripped the rifle down to its component
parts and, the following day, accompanied by the president, Lincoln's son
Robert, and a naval officer, the inventor and the chief executive fired the gun
with satisfactory results at a target painted on a board. Following the shooting session, Spencer recalled that "the navy official cut off the part of the
board that Mr. Lincoln shot at and gave it to me, remarking that it might be
a gratifying souvenir." When they returned to the White House, the president
departed after a "hearty handshake, and good wishes." Lincoln apparently
had another Spencer shooting session with his secretary John Hay the following day. Hay was impressed with the Spencer, recalling that it was "a wonder-
ful gun, loading with absolutely contemptible simplicity and ease with seven
balls and firing the whole readily and deliberately in less than half a minute."[3]

Much folklore has grown around this incident as the decisive point in
assuring substantial additional government orders of Spencer guns. In fact,
as historian Roy Marcot points out, at the time of the inventor's visit to
Lincoln the War Department had already signed a contract for a large number of Spencer carbines and there was a rising tide of requests from the field
which would generate even more orders. Spencer's visit to the White House
simply provided an opportunity to change the poor opinion Lincoln had
developed of the Navy rifle—a bit of marketing insurance, so to speak.[4]

Lincoln's approval aside, by late 1863 the Spencer was well on its way to
becoming a standard Union army firearm. At one point in 1862, Warren
Fisher had proposed carbine sales as a way of salvaging the initial Spencer
contract with the War Department. By June 3, 1863, with the army rifle contract filled and General Ripley apparently not inclined to order any more,
Fisher renewed his offer. A week later, Ripley advised Fisher that "no more
of your rifles are wanted." He did note, however that since "arms of this
description have met with favor from some sources and we are in want of
Cavalry carbines," he would consider a carbine contract, if guns were avail-

able at "reasonable terms." Fisher's price of $25 per carbine proved "reasonable" and resulted in a contract signed on July 17, almost a month before Spencer's demonstration for the president.

Although there was no formal delivery of Spencer carbines to the government before October 1863, there is evidence that a few examples might have been made as early as the spring of that year and distributed, à la Oliver Winchester, to certain officers for field testing and to create a demand in the army for the guns. Captain G. Middleton of the Second Pennsylvania Cavalry wrote the Spencer factory on March 18, 1863, that he had "received the Carbine yesterday" and that "everyone present pronounced it to be the best carbine in use." Colonel T. E. Chickering (perhaps related to the owners of the factory in which the guns were made) of the Forty-first Massachusetts Infantry wrote from Baton Rouge that he and another officer took his carbine out and "fired at target at musket range." Chickering reported that he "hit the target every shot, and put one ball through the very centre of the bulls-eye, beating the whole party. The little gun shoots most admirably, and is all the Rifle Company claim for it."[5]

A few carbine prototypes, or perhaps rare sporting rifles, were in circulation early in 1863 as well. It might have been one of these, or a military carbine taken off the early production line, that Arizona Territorial governor John N. Goodwin purchased from the Spencer Company. Goodwin, whose carbine was "of the large size" (.56-.56 caliber) reported that he carried it "from Leavenworth over the plains to Arizona" in September 1863. The governor enthused that his Spencer "in range and accuracy in firing, simplicity of structure, and the rapidity with which it can be loaded and fired...surpasses any arm I have ever heard of." Goodwin loaned his carbine to King S. Woolsey, who used it on campaign against the Apaches. Woolsey was also full of praise for the gun, and noted that "the fixed ammunition has immense advantage, as soon as it can be easily obtained say at San Francisco even, for it never wastes and can not be injured by transportation."[6]

Ripley had a change of heart in August, no doubt prompted by reports and requests from the field, as well as the prodding of his superiors in the War Department, and asked Fisher if he could supply an additional 2,500 rifles in addition to the 11,000 carbines on order. On August 20 the Spencer treasurer replied that he could deliver rifles at the rate of eighty a day at a price of $35 each beginning in January 1864. If more immediate delivery was desired, Fisher proposed selling the Ordnance Department the rifles being made for the state of Massachusetts, 1,000 of which were already inspected and ready to ship. The Massachusetts order was for 2,000 guns, and Fisher proposed to give the state, which did not have an immediate need, those rifles manufactured in January.[7]

Although he was much more receptive than he had been in previous years, Ripley still stalled field commanders. On September 9, 1863, he replied to Major General Lovell Harrison Rousseau's request for Spencers that "we shall proceed with every effort to obtain them and with every disposition to furnish them as you suggested and desired." Ignoring Fisher's offer of the Massachusetts rifles, however, he advised Rousseau, a division commander in the Army of the Cumberland who was no doubt well acquainted with Spencer performance in the hands of Colonel Wilder's men, that "it is found that none can be made and delivered before next January."[8]

Ripley's reply to Rousseau was one of the last letters he would write as ordnance chief. Ripley, one of the few Civil War leaders born in the prior century (1794), retired on September 15. He had served honorably and honestly, the latter a not insignificant quality in the Civil War era, and had rendered noble service by fending off a host of quacks and charlatans attempting to sell dubious ordnance to the Union in 1861, but his time had passed. Ripley's innate predisposition against innovation had been tempered to a degree by placing him under the watchful eye of Assistant Secretary of War Peter H. Watson in 1862. Watson allied himself with a progressive young ordnance captain named George T. Balch to keep Ripley moving slowly, but surely, in the direction of innovation, and was probably responsible for the ordnance chief's sudden change of heart with Fisher.[9]

Slow but steady was no longer necessary, or acceptable, however, and Ripley was pushed into retirement. Lincoln's choice to succeed the general, whom the New York Times had taken to calling an "old fogy," was Washington Arsenal superintendent Lieutenant Colonel George D. Ramsey, who was not much younger. Although born in 1802, and conservative on a number of ordnance issues, Ramsey was a proponent of breech-loading and repeating rifles and carbines in the service. He was not, however, a favorite of Secretary of War Stanton, or of Watson, who favored advancing the ambitious Balch into the position over the heads of senior officers. In the end, Stanton conceded to Ramsay's promotion and appointment, with the proviso that Balch be his "principal assistant." Within days after Ramsay accepted his new position, Watson ordered him to approve the Massachusetts rifle switch proposed by Fisher. On September 28 Ramsay wrote Fisher requesting that the "two thousand rifles on hand, made for the state of Massachusetts" were "wanted for General Rosecrans and General Burnside, and should be delivered at once."[10]

As the summer of 1863 slipped into autumn, and General Ripley faded into history, the war went on without him. In the wake of Lee's retreat from Gettysburg and the fall of Vicksburg and Port Hudson, the Virginia front evolved into a wary stalemate and the "Father of the Waters flowed unvexed to the sea." The chief arena of conflict shifted to middle Tennessee, where General Rosecrans, after securing Tullahoma, began to advance. This too, would be a campaign of maneuver.

On August 19, General Ambrose Burnside's Army of the Ohio, reinforced by his old command from the east, the IX Army Corps, began to move on Knoxville. Burnside wanted more Spencer rifles, but had to be content with those in the hands of the Eighth Michigan Cavalry. The men of the Eighth had used their Spencers in the pursuit of Confederate raiders in July, and the regiment's Lieutenant Colonel Grover S. Wormer enthusiastically reported that "our arms (the Spencer rifles) proved, as before, a terror to the rebels. They thought us in much stronger force than we were, when each man could pour seven shots into them so rapidly. This is the first instance during the war, I think, where the proportion of killed was greater than the wounded. As far as reports have come in, it is at least 3 killed to 1 wounded, and this fact is owing to the terrible execution of our rifles."[11]

Simultaneous with Burnside's advance, General Rosecrans' army stepped out on the road to Chattanooga. Although nominally an infantry unit in General Thomas' corps, the fast-moving and shooting mounted riflemen of Colonel Wilder's brigade became "Rosey's" spearhead. On August 21, Wilder appeared across the Tennessee River from Chattanooga, and Captain Lilly shelled the town to announce his arrival. Lilly's guns silenced counter-battery fire and sank several boats docked along the riverbank. That night Wilder's men lit a number of fires to deceive the enemy into believing that more than one Union brigade was threatening the city. During the remainder of the month, Rosecrans concentrated the rest of his army near Chattanooga.

As the Yankees began to move, the Confederate high command responded to the threat by reinforcing General Bragg. Troops from the Deep South, including two divisions under the command of Major General John Breckinridge and Major General William Henry Taylor Walker, came up from Mississippi and joined Bragg's army in early September. Although there was talk of another offensive in Virginia, General Lee deferred to General Longstreet's desire to reinforce Bragg with an eye to achieving a significant victory over Rosecrans. In order to insure that, Longstreet and two of his divisions began the trek west.

On September 6, Bragg evacuated Chattanooga, concentrated his forces in the vicinity of Lafayette, Georgia, and hoped the Federals would come after him. In order to close with Bragg, Rosecrans' army would have to divide and march through the passes in Lookout Mountain and Missionary Ridge, subjecting the Yankees to potential defeat in detail. The Unionists came on just as Bragg thought they would, but miscues and poor coordina-

An early production Spencer carbine, left. The carbine had a 22 inch barrel, eight inches shorter than the rifle. Despite the difference in barrel length, both guns were inherently equally accurate. Although most soldiers thought shorter barreled guns were less accurate, and they often were, the fault lay with the shorter distance between front and rear sights, which magnified sighting errors on the part of the shooter. Details, above, of the breech mechanism and magazine. The heavy protection afforded by the stock made many consider the Spencer magazine to be superior to that of the Henry rifle. (*Private collection; photographs by John Hubbard*)

tion among his corps commanders resulted in failure to attack them when they were most vulnerable. As his corps emerged from the critical passes, Rosecrans began to concentrate in preparation for what he believed would be a major battle.

Both armies continued to maneuver carefully into striking distance, skirmishing off and on, and by September 17 were on opposite sides of Chickamauga Creek. That evening Bragg ordered an attack the following day on the Federal left flank, held by Major General Thomas L. Crittenden's XXI Corps. The plan called for Brigadier General Nathan Bedford Forrest's Cavalry Corps and General Bushrod Johnson's infantry division to cross the Chickamauga north of the Union left at Reed's Bridge, which was covered by Union Colonel General Robert H. G. Minty's cavalry brigade. General Walker's corps was ordered to force a crossing further south at the Alexander Bridge, guarded by Colonel Wilder's men. Once across, some 16,000 Rebels would be astride Crittenden's flank.

The Confederates hit Minty early in the morning, and he soon had his hands full. In response to Minty's call for help, Wilder sent a two-gun section of Lilly's battery plus the Seventy-second Indiana and seven companies of the 123rd Illinois to assist the Irishman, who was attempting to hang on to Reed's Bridge against heavy odds.

By noon Rebels were approaching the Lightning Brigade's position, where Wilder had deployed the Seventeenth Indiana and Ninety-eighth Illinois and the remaining four guns of Lilly's battery overlooking the Alexander Bridge. Artillery opened the fight, then General Walker ordered Brigadier General St. John R. Liddell's division to attack. Liddell sent Brigadier General Edwin C. Walthall's brigade forward, but Walthall's Mississippians quickly ran into a storm of Spencer bullets and had to be reinforced by part of Colonel Daniel C. Govan's Arkansas brigade. As Minty fell back from the northern crossing, Wilder, to avoid being trapped, disengaged and retreated as well.

The actual duration of the Alexander Bridge fight is in dispute, with Federal accounts having it last as long as five hours, but General Liddell reporting it as taking "three quarters of an hour." What is not in dispute is that Wilder's men and their Spencers gave a good account of themselves. The Ninety-eighth Illinois lost one man killed, while Liddell had 105 men killed and wounded. Liddell reported that his force had "captured a half dozen or more breech-loading rifles," probably dropped by wounded men. The Confederate commander also stated that he "could only account for this [casualty] disproportion from the efficiency of this new weapon, our attack having been made through thick woods and cedar underbrush, rendering the artillery of the enemy that was used on the occasion comparatively harmless." In the end, General Walker found the bridge of little use. It had been wrecked, forcing him to seek a ford downstream, where his division crossed late that night.[12]

After falling back to the Lafayette road, Wilder established a new line between the Vinyard and Brotherton farmhouses. There he was rejoined by the men he had detached to assist Minty. Minty's horse soldiers formed a dismounted line as well, extending from Wilder's right. Although General Crittenden refused to take Wilder's and Minty's reports of large numbers of Rebels crossing the Chickamauga seriously, they were soon proved correct when the men of an infantry brigade he had ordered forward on a reconnaissance were routed and came streaming back past the Lightning Brigade position.

As the day waned, the enemy, portions of Bushrod Johnson's and Major General John Bell Hood's divisions, the latter just arrived from the Army of Northern Virginia, probed the Federal line and were countered by Spencer fire and musketry from two Federal infantry brigades that joined Minty and Wilder. During the course of the night, Rosecrans redeployed and consolidated his entire line. Wilder's men were relieved at 4:00 A.M. by infantrymen of Major General John McCauley Palmer's division of Crittenden's corps and withdrew to a woodlot about 200 yards behind the Vinyard farm buildings. By dawn Major General George H. Thomas' XIV Corps had moved north to secure the Union far left.

The Lightning Brigade deployed behind a fence line at the edge of the woods, where the brigade's position overlooked an open field crossed by a ravine running parallel to the Lafayette road. In the morning General Thomas pushed out Colonel John T. Croxton's brigade to attack what he believed was an isolated Confederate unit. There were more Rebels out there than Thomas thought, however, and after Croxton made contact, the fight quickly escalated. The battle soon rolled southwest as both armies collided along the line. In mid-afternoon Hood's division, led by Brigadier General Jerome B. Robertson's Texas Brigade, slammed into Brigadier General Jefferson C. Davis' Union division. The Army of Northern Virginia veterans smashed Colonel Hans Heg's brigade, killed him, and rolled up another Federal brigade. They were about to capture the Eighth Wisconsin battery when Wilder ordered his Seventy-second Indiana and 123rd Illinois to hit the swarming Confederates in the flank. Firing as they advanced, Wilder's men, together with men from Davis' division who rallied, closed the breach in the Union line.

No sooner had Davis' attackers been driven back than General Stewart's division began to push hard on the unit to Wilder's left front. In a seesaw fight in thick smoky woods set afire by musketry, the Federals were gradually forced back, with Bate's brigade, the Lightning Brigade's old opponent from Hoover's Gap, the leading Confederate unit in the advance. This time the Ninety-eighth Illinois and Seventeenth Indiana peppered Bate's men with Spencer fire while twenty Union artillery pieces tore the Rebel line apart from the front.

As Bate tumbled back in retreat, Wilder had to save the line on his right once more, when Brigadier Generals John Gregg and Evander McNair's brigades of Johnson's division broke through on that flank. Again elements of the Lightning Brigade struck the Confederate attack in the flank, firing as they advanced and supported by Lilly's artillery. Colonel David Coleman of the Thirty-ninth North Carolina Infantry reported that his regiment and brigade withdrew under Wilder's "fatal flanking fire."[13]

Late in the afternoon Robertson's tough Texans, supported by Brigadier General Henry L. Benning's Georgians, charged the Lightning Brigade's position. The Spencers and Lilly's guns took a heavy toll on the attackers, driving them back into the ditch crossing the Yankee front, which Wilder and Lilly were then able to enfilade. Benning recalled that his "loss was very heavy to my numbers. In the Twentieth [Georgia] Regiment 17 officers out of 23 were killed or wounded. In the other regiments the proportion though not so great was very great. The proportionate loss among the men was but little less." Wilder's fire was steady and effective, with Benning reporting that "toward sunset the enemy's fire from his battery and from his infantry, protected by the wood, became so heavy, and so many of our officers and men had fallen, that we had ourselves to retire a short distance." One of Benning's privates, Theodore T. Fogle of the Second Georgia, was more frank, writing home the following day that "our little regiment has suffered awfully . . . yesterday we lost 88 men and 8 officers killed and wounded. My company has only four men & two officers left." One Texan remembered the scene graphically, recalling that "men were staggering to the rear covered with blood . . . . calling on God to protect them." He felt as if "the world was coming to an end then and there."[14]

Nightfall brought some relief, but soldiers on both sides were shocked by the carnage that continued to assail their senses. They supped on cold bacon and hardtack while listening to the moans of the wounded scattered between battle lines that had shifted back and forth all day. Woods and fields eerily smoldered and burst into occasional open flame and one soldier from the Ninety-eighth Illinois recalled long after the war that "we spent almost as much time fighting fires as we did fighting the enemy."[15]

During the night General Longstreet arrived at Confederate headquarters, bringing with him three more veteran Army of Northern Virginia

brigades. Bragg assigned Longstreet
to command his army's left wing,
while Lieutenant General Leonidas
Polk took charge of the right. The
Confederate commander decided
on launching an *en echelon* attack
rippling from north to south the following day.

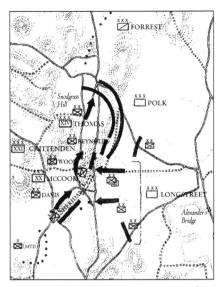

General Breckinridge reopened
the fight at 9:00 A.M. in the morning on September 20, hitting
Thomas' corps. As the battle developed, Thomas called for reinforcements, which were moved from
then quieter areas further south
along the Union position. With no
point where the Federal line was
visible for its entire extent, troops
marching hither and yon, and
Rebels attacking, mistakes were
made. The most grievous, the inad-

Union and confederate movements dur-
ing the Battle of Chickamauga.
(Adapted from the *West Point Atlas of
American Wars*)

vertent removal of Brigadier General Thomas J. Wood's division from the line
of battle, left a gaping hole into which, by a stroke of terribly bad luck for
Rosecrans and good fortune for Bragg, Longstreet launched an assault that
split the Federal army's right wing.

As things began to disintegrate, Major General Alexander M. McCook,
commanding the XX Corps, ordered Wilder to close up on his right, in an
attempt to fill an ever-widening gap in the Union defenses. In response,
Wilder's brigade began to move toward the widow Glenn's house near the Dry
Valley road, about 1,000 yards from its previous position. As Major General
Philip Sheridan's division collapsed and fled the field, abandoning a Missouri
artillery battery to Confederate capture, Wilder ordered a counterattack by
his Ninety-eighth Illinois, which recaptured the guns. At this critical moment,
Wilder was joined by the Thirty-ninth Indiana Mounted Infantry, which had
also been recently rearmed with Spencers. The reinforced brigade provided
an island of controlled firepower in the midst of disaster.[16]

That firepower was soon brought to bear on Brigadier General Arthur M.
Manigault's brigade of Alabama and South Carolina troops. Manigault's
Rebels, charging headlong after fleeing Federals, ran into a Spencer buzz
saw. The Confederate commander reported that his men received a sudden

"heavy enfilade fire from the enemy on their left, which caused a heavy loss." They fell back in some disorder. After repulsing Manigault's brigade, Wilder ordered a counterattack, and pursued the enemy a short distance, capturing a number of prisoners. The Lightning Brigade's fight with Manigault delayed the Confederate attack on the main remaining Federal position on Snodgrass Hill, giving General Thomas time to better prepare his defense.[17]

As the day waned, Colonel Wilder realized that the enemy was in his rear, and prepared to shoot his way through to join General Thomas. Thomas' corps, aided by other Yankees who had not joined General Rosecrans in headlong retreat to Chattanooga, was holding on to its position, preventing a total disaster. Rosecrans' personal bodyguard, Captain Barber's First Battalion, Ohio Sharpshooters, apparently fell back toward Chattanooga with him, depriving the Union line of more than a hundred additional Spencers.

In the event, the Lightning Brigade did not have to fight its way to Thomas. The brigade was ordered to retreat to Chattanooga by Assistant Secretary of War Charles Dana, who came to the field to see a battle, had had quite enough and was looking for an escort out of the combat zone. Wilder provided Dana with a detail to protect him and then made contact with General Sheridan, who advised him to fall back and cover the passes over Lookout Mountain to facilitate the army's retreat. Having done so, the following morning the brigade fell back without molestation. General Bragg, his own army badly damaged by the Chickamauga battle, followed the Army of the Cumberland cautiously, and once the Yankees were back in Chattanooga, occupied the heights around the town, effectively besieging Rosecrans in the Tennessee city.

Although Chickamauga proved a significant Union defeat, Thomas' gutsy defense of Snodgrass Hill allowed much of the Federal army to retreat to Chattanooga. Even though the army to which it belonged was largely routed, Colonel Wilder marched his brigade off the field intact and with a well-earned pride in its performance.

Wilder had displayed great tactical talent in deploying and maneuvering his men and using their Spencer rifles effectively in both defense and counterattack. In light of this, and considering the problems encountered by the Fifth Michigan at Gettysburg, which caused that regiment to retreat after inflicting heavy losses on the enemy, a question arises on ammunition supply and expenditure. How much ammunition did Wilder bring to the battle? He does not, unfortunately, say, but there can be little doubt it was more than the forty to sixty rounds or so that would have been carried by the average infantryman.

Brigadier General James B. Steedman's Reserve Division charges at Snodgrass Hill to support General George H. Thomas' beleaguered forces as they fought to hold back a strong Confederate advance. (Battle sketch by Alfred R. Waud; *Library of Congress*)

Since they were mounted and had pack mules handy, it is likely that Wilder's men had access to an adequate ammunition supply. One unit setting out on a mounted raid in the spring of 1864 carried 250 rounds of Spencer cartridges per man, and we can surmise that the Lightning Brigade was similarly supplied at Chickamauga. In a letter to the Spencer Company, Wilder stated that "the men of my command carry 100 rounds of ammunition in their saddle bags," in addition to the rounds in their cartridge boxes, and, presumably, on pack mules within a short distance. No matter the supply of ammunition, however, such logistical planning would have been wasted without an imposed fire discipline that assured it would not be shot away randomly. Wilder's men were ready to deliver overwhelming firepower when and where it was needed, both to punish the enemy and protect unit integrity. In three days of combat, some of it intense, in one of the bloodiest battles of the Civil War, where many commands on both sides were decimated, the Lightning Brigade suffered the relatively light losses of thirteen men killed, ninety-four wounded, and eighteen missing or captured.[18]

General Thomas was not hesitant about expressing his gratitude to Colonel Wilder nor his belief that the colonel's role in helping him save the Army of the Cumberland to fight another day was vital. According to Thomas: "For his ingenuity and fertility of resource in occupying the attention of an entire corps of the rebel army while our army was getting around its flank, and for his valor and the many qualities of a commander displayed by him in the numerous engagements of his brigade with the enemy before and during the battle of Chickamauga, and for the excellent service rendered by him generally, I would respectfully recommend him [Wilder] to the President of the United States for an appointment as brigadier-general."[19]

There were Henry rifles scattered throughout the Army of the Cumberland on the field at Chickamauga as well, although evidence of their use is harder to uncover. As privately owned arms, Henrys do not appear on unit quarterly ordnance reports, and at this stage of the war, most Henry cartridges were privately purchased as well, so ammunition requisitions provide no clues. One reference to the use of Henrys at the battle is that of Captain John Henry Otto of the Twenty-first Wisconsin, who wrote of the fight on September 20, that "a Regt. of Willichs Brigade Saved us many lives. This Regiment was armed with the Henry breachloader sixteenshooter rifle, that is 16 cartridges could be placed in a groove in the stock and after each discharge a contrivance in the lock loaded the rifle again. The men had bought the rifles themselfes, the Government having promised to pay for the same at discharge." The fact that Otto describes a Henry as loaded through "a groove in the stock" gives pause, but more instructive is that Brigadier General August Willich's brigade included the Thirty-ninth Indiana, which was actually armed with Spencers. Confusing the two arms was not uncommon among those unfamiliar with firearm technology.[20]

Captain J. T. Patton of the Ninety-third Ohio Infantry affords a more significant Henry reference. Almost thirty years after Chickamauga, Patton recalled that after the battle of Murfreesboro, General Rosecrans established elite strike force units in the Army of the Cumberland. According to Patton, "Three privates were selected from each company, three corporals and two sergeants from the regiment and one officer, elected by the officers of the regiment. I was elected from the 93rd. The several companies from the four regiments of the brigade formed a 'light battalion.' We bought Henry rifles and devoted our time to special drill being relieved from all duty except guard at Corps Headquarters. The war department countermanded the order, and we returned to our respective commands. The men of the light battalion [who apparently retained their personally owned Henrys after being returned to their parent units] did valiant service in every battle until the close of the war."[21]

Unlike Captain Otto, Patton was a gun-savvy soldier who was later appointed ordnance officer of his division. His account is further evidence of the innovative tactical views of General Rosecrans, whose General Orders No. 19 commanded the formation of the light battalions on February 14, 1863. Rosecrans considered these men to be "the elite of the army," further stating that "deeds of daring" would be expected of them.

Except for the idea of mounting the units, the concept is remarkably similar to the sharpshooter battalions formed in the Army of Northern Virginia, beginning tentatively in that army in 1862, but maturing in 1864. At Chickamauga, according to Captain Patton, "a number of rebel officers attempted to get a better view of our position, when they were fired upon by our lookouts, composed of the boys who had formerly been of the 'light battalion,' armed with Henry rifles."[22]

According to another account, in the ebb and flow of the battle, a Sergeant C. C. Cowan of the Ninety-sixth Illinois "found himself alone with his Henry rifle, a 16 shooter. He fired away at the advancing rebel line until it was within 15 or 20 yards of him, when he was struck in the shoulder and knocked over. As the rebel line passed him a soldier gave him a drink of water, but took his gun." The rifle, "marked Captured from a Federal Sergeant at the battle of Chickamauga, Sept, 20, 1863," was recovered during the siege of Atlanta.[23]

John H. Ekstrand, ordnance sergeant of the Fifty-first Illinois Infantry, wrote the New Haven Arms Company on November 2, 1863, declaring that he had been a Henry owner for "a long time," adding that "twelve of them have been bought in the regiment and many more would have been bought had I been able to get them in any place." Ekstrand, then besieged in Chattanooga, stated that "we used your rifle in the Battle of Chickamauga with good effect and it is undoubtedly the best gun in the service, far superior to the Spencer rifle and any other rifle." The sergeant wanted to "get as many Henry's Rifles in the Army of the Cumberland so we could drive the Rebs from Chattanooga, so we could get something to eat."[24]

The Rebels overran the Fifty-first, assigned to Sheridan's division, on September 20. Ironically, considering Sergeant Ekstrand's opinion of the Spencer, part of his regiment that rallied with other fragments of Sheridan's command was saved by Colonel Wilder's Spencer-wielding mounted infantrymen, who held the line while the defeated division reorganized and withdrew toward Chattanooga.[25]

A perusal of the Spencer catalog, however, suggests that the good sergeant's assessment of the Spencer as not equal to the Henry might have been colored by a proposition gone wrong. Ekstrand wrote the Spencer Company on September 29, 1863, inquiring about prices, suggesting that his whole regiment was ready to buy Spencers and that "the whole of Sherman's [sic] Division would buy them if we could get them." It is possible that he was fishing for a free rifle or a sales commission, which, considering the fact that virtually all Spencer production was already tied up by government contracts, was not in the offing.

Whatever their prevalence at Chickamauga, privately purchased Henrys were coming into the western Union armies at a steady rate. A reported 2,475 Henrys were made in 1863, in addition to the 1,300 produced in 1862, and it safe to say that most of them ended up in the hands of Union soldiers, primarily west of the Appalachians. Private Lucius L. Longworthy of the Twelfth Illinois Infantry wrote home on November 26, 1863, that "I have got me a sixteen shooter I have got tired of carrying the old musket If I live I calculate to bring it home with me next August It is a bully shooting gun I have been offered forty five dollars in cash several times but I did not buy it to sell If we get into another battle I want some thing I can depend on."[26]

There was even a call for Henrys equipped with extra options. The irrepressible Captain Wilson of the Twelfth Kentucky wrote Winchester in October 1863, requesting that his next Henry be equipped with "a pair [sic] of telescopic sights for target shooting, for I do think, if there is any gun in the world that would take the premium over all other guns, it would be the Henry Rifle if they were made in that style." A month later Oliver Winchester wrote that he intended "to make both globe and telescope sight for our rifles." Whether he ever did is not known. Although New Haven Arms did not manufacture telescopic sights, a surviving early Henry rifle, serial number 731, is mounted with such a sight made by "Malcolm, Syracuse, N.Y." Whether the telescope and special mounts were furnished through New Haven or were an after-market addition is unknown.[27]

Probably the most notable unit associated with the Henry during the war was the Sixty-sixth Illinois Volunteer Infantry, a regiment that began to acquire the rifles in 1863. The Sixty-sixth began life as the Western Sharpshooters as part of Major General John C. Frémont's army at Benton Barracks, Missouri, in the fall of 1861. It was largely recruited in Illinois and Missouri, but had members from states across the Midwest, including Wisconsin, Iowa, Minnesota, Indiana, and Ohio. The unit's first commander was Colonel John W. Birge, which gave rise to its nickname, Birge's Western Sharpshooters.

As sharpshooters, Birge's men were not issued standard infantry weapons. They were originally armed with "the Demmick [sic] American deer and target rifle, but with meagre accoutrements" purchased from Horace E. Dimick, a St. Louis sporting-arms maker and retail dealer. Although Dimick serial numbered and sold these half-stock muzzle-loading sporting rifles to the government, he did not make all of them, purchasing a number for resale from other civilian gun makers. Most appear to have been fitted with rear sights purchased from the Sharps Company. Calibers varied from gun to gun (one surviving rifle is .48 caliber), and each man was supplied with his own bullet mold, serial numbered to his rifle, with which to cast an elongated Minié style Swiss Chasseur bullet. The Chasseur bullet differed from the Minié in having a short post extend rearward from its base cavity.[28]

The Sharpshooters were involved in a number of small actions in Missouri in 1861 and then fought at Forts Henry and Donelson in early 1862. After the battle of Shiloh in April 1862, the regiment acquired a new identity as the Fourteenth Missouri Infantry. As part of the occupation force at Corinth, Mississippi, the sharpshooters participated in a number of counter-Guerrilla raids and patrols through the fall of 1862, and changed identity yet again, to the Sixty-sixth Illinois, in November. The Sixty-sixth remained at Corinth as part of the garrison until November 1863, when it was reassigned to Tennessee, where Union forces in the west were concentrating in the wake of Chickamauga. During this period most of the men took advantage of the bounties being offered by Federal, state, and local governments and reenlisted for another three years.

As early as the spring of 1863 some soldiers from the Sixty-sixth were rearming themselves with privately purchased Henry rifles to provide a firepower advantage in operations against Confederate guerrillas around Corinth. On May 25, the regimental adjutant, Lieutenant William Wilson, noted that "Some of our boys are buying Henry rifles . . . there was 42 that came in today, costing $40 each." Wilson did not mention the origin of the Henry shipment, whether it was ordered from a dealer or directly from the New Haven Arms factory. Wiley Sword speculates that the source of the guns may have been retailer John R. Beard of Pulaski, Tennessee, or wholesaler A. B. Semple & Sons of Louisville, who dealt in Henry sales only by the case. Dimick, who had started off as the regimental gun dealer of sorts, attempted to buy Henrys in quantity for resale in June 1863, but was advised by the company that his request could not be filled due to existing large backorders.[29]

Men from the Sixty-sixth continued to buy Henrys throughout the rest of the year, and those who did were converted into mounted infantry. A picked group of Henry armed soldiers was assigned to special bodyguard duty for Brigadier General Grenville M. Dodge. On September 4, 1863, Lorenzo Barker of Company D recorded in his diary that he "payed $40 for a seventeen shooter." Many men who had not previously been able to afford a Henry were able to in November, when paid their reenlistment bounties. Henrys were still arriving in the Sixty-sixth's camp in January 1864 and at least one arrived in April, just before the Atlanta campaign. Sword estimates that at that date the regiment fielded approximately 250 privately owned Henrys, half the unit's small arms. That month the Federal government began to supply .44 rimfire ammunition for the Henrys.

By the end of 1863, although government contracts still eluded him, Oliver Winchester could sell as many Henrys as he could make to soldiers like the men of the Sixty-sixth. His major problem was that he could not make as many as he could sell. The nineteenth-century gun industry frequently used a system of outside contractors to manufacture a product. Under this method, some or all of the production of a particular gun was, in effect, leased to one or more vendors, who in turn could delegate the work to sub-contractors, with the manufacturer supplying funding, machinery, and production facilities.

In 1859, New Haven Arms Company had entered into a five-year contract with B. Tyler Henry to both superintend the works and manufacture his rifle at the New Haven Arms factory. For some reason, Henry, even when additional machinery was purchased, refused to increase his workforce or production capacity. Herbert G. Houze opines that Henry's reluctance may have been due to his desire to "draw both a straight salary as well as the profits from employing contract employees as long as possible." By December 1863, an increasingly frustrated Oliver Winchester leased a factory in Bridgeport Connecticut, installed gun-making machinery, and contracted with Luke Wheelock to prepare the new facility to expand the manufacture of Henry rifles. The new production facility had to remain idle, however, until Henry's contract ended in May 1864.[30]

While Winchester and Henry squabbled over lack of output in late 1863, the Spencer factory was ramping up its production capacity. The first 1,000 Spencer carbines were delivered to the government on October 3. By November 14, Warren Fisher could advise General Ramsey that "we have delivered at the rate of five hundred carbines for every six working days of ten hours each, less two hundred carbines." In December, Ramsay offered the Spencer Rifle Company a contract for another 34,500 carbines. For some reason, the ordnance chief requested that over 30,000 of these guns be made in .44 caliber, a request no doubt based on a Springfield Armory program to develop a standard .44 carbine cartridge, the caliber that Ramsay preferred. That request was, inexplicably, almost immediately dropped and not reflected in the written contract. Deliveries on the new agreement averaged 2,000 carbines a month, all in the same .56-.56 caliber as the Spencer rifle, throughout the winter of 1863-1864.[31]

Spencer rifles, off the production menu at present, were still very much in demand, however. Major General Quincy Gillmore, commanding the Department of the South at Morris Island outside Charleston Harbor, had made attempts to establish a sharpshooter detachment equipped with Springfield muzzleloaders in August 1863. Gillmore's men had been victim-

ized by short- and long-range sniping from Confederate marksmen armed
with the superbly accurate imported British Whitworth rifle, and he was desperately seeking something to counter them with. By the fall, Gillmore, no
doubt by now familiar with the growing reputation of the repeating rifle, was
requesting Spencers to arm at least some of his sharpshooters. On October
23, 1863, however, General Halleck responded to his request by advising
that "there are not sufficient Spencer rifles manufactured to supply your requisitions, but all that can be obtained will be sent to you in preference to any
one else."[32]

As winter approached, Gillmore's Charleston siege, along with most other
theaters of the conflict, took a back seat to Tennessee. In late September
1863 the most important point on the military map for the Lincoln administration was Chattanooga, where General Bragg's Army of Tennessee had bottled up General Rosecrans' defeated Army of the Cumberland. When
Bragg's army had been threatened by the Union advance that summer, the
Confederate government rushed reinforcements from the Deep South and
Virginia. Similarly, after Chickamauga, the Federal government expedited
assistance to the Army of the Cumberland. General Hooker left Virginia for
Tennessee with three divisions from the Army of the Potomac's XI and XII
Army Corps on September 25, and another 17,000 Union troops from west-
ern Tennessee and Mississippi were on the way as well.

In October, General Bragg, who at first thought Rosecrans would evacuate Chattanooga, began to launch cavalry raids that disrupted, but did not
entirely interdict, his supply lines. The Yankees did feel the pinch, however,
and, as Sergeant Ekstrand, the Henry rifle fan, noted, the primary mission of
the Union soldiers in Chattanooga became getting something to eat.

That same month, Major General Ulysses S. Grant was assigned to lead
a new command, the Military Division of the Mississippi, which included
Chattanooga. Grant moved his headquarters to the city and relieved General
Rosecrans. Rosecrans went on to command the Department of Missouri in
1864 and then sat around "awaiting orders" that never came, until he
resigned his commission in 1867. Grant, who had never liked "Rosey,"
replaced him as commander of the Army of the Cumberland with the reliable and steady George H. Thomas. And so the general who was a master of
large-scale maneuver and possessed the most innovative tactical and technological sense among senior Union field commanders was put out to pasture.

General Grant spent the next month reopening communication lines to
Chattanooga and planning an operation to lift the siege. As part of the movements to restore supply lines to the beleaguered garrison and keep them
open, Union troops were posted along vital routes into the city to fight off

Rebel cavalry raiders and snipers. Among them were Captain Barber's Ohio Sharpshooters. Barber's men finally got a chance to use their Spencers against the enemy, and the captain was delighted with the results, although his range estimation skills might have been more than a little off. On November 8, 1863, Barber wrote of his engagement with some Rebels who were firing at Federal wagon trains that "the river is 500 yards wide, [and] I was ordered to protect the road. The 18th Ky., armed with the Enfield rifle, had been skirmishing with them for two days, and lost three men, and had no effect on the enemy. The first day we opened on them we killed two, wounded several and drove them from every position along the river. We found by actual trial that our guns had longer range and greater accuracy. We seldom missed at 700 yards."[33]

In early November Bragg weakened his force by dispatching General Longstreet in a vain effort to recapture Knoxville, which had fallen to Burnside. At the end of the month Grant ordered a series of attacks at Orchard Knob, Lookout Mountain, and Tunnel Hill by his subordinates Thomas, Hooker, and Sherman. These assaults, which achieved varying degrees of success, were capped by the unexpected surge of the Army of the Cumberland straight up Missionary Ridge, which not only broke the siege but also routed the Army of Tennessee. Like Bragg after Chickamauga, however (and like most Civil War generals), Grant, who quickly dispatched troops to rescue Burnside, was unable to pursue the defeated Rebel army and destroy it.

Grant's failure did not matter, however, as far as Braxton Bragg's career and historical reputation were concerned. In December Bragg was reassigned as military advisor to President Jefferson Davis, and replaced in command of the Army of Tennessee by Lieutenant General William Hardee, who in turn was replaced by Lieutenant General Joseph E. Johnston. Bragg's men, who had lost all confidence in his ability to lead, were glad to see him go. Although a less talented commander than Rosecrans, and an officer to whom history has not been kind, the general had served with the Confederate president in Mexico and was at least spared the indignity of "awaiting orders."

Further east, General Lee, his army weakened by the loan of Longstreet to the Army of Tennessee, had assumed the defensive in Virginia. The departure of the bulk of two Army of the Potomac corps to bail out the Army of the Cumberland, with more Union troops dispatched from Virginia to other theaters, however, reawakened the Army of Northern Virginia commander's aggressive spirit. Lee launched an operation designed to outflank General Meade and interpose his army between Meade's and Washington. The

Federal commander reacted quickly, however, and the resultant hard marching and sharp skirmishing ended with a Confederate defeat in a vicious little
infantry battle at Bristoe Station.

The Rebel mounted arm did better, as J. E. B. Stuart's horsemen successfully routed General Kilpatrick's strung-out division near Buckland Mills in
a fight later referred to by the Confederates as the Buckland Races. Among
Stuart's victims was General Custer, who, although he commanded the
Spencer-armed Fifth and Sixth Michigan Cavalry, had still not figured out
how best to use them in a tactical role. Custer was a good man in a hell-for-
leather charge with smoking revolvers and flashing sabers, but he was, as yet,
no John Wilder when it came to having a true tactical sense of what to do
with Spencer firepower. In the Buckland Mills fight, despite its vastly superior armament, the Fifth Michigan lost seventy-five men as prisoners. Major
John E. Clark of the Fifth ordered the forty-eight men who surrendered
with him to throw their Spencers into the Broad River, "to keep them from
the enemy."[34]

The enemy was getting at least a few Spencers anyway, however. Forrest's
command may have captured some in a skirmish with elements of Wilder's
brigade as early as June 30, 1863. Among the 8,008 rifles "lost and captured"
by the Army of the Cumberland at Chickamauga were seventy Spencers.
Whether or not the Confederates gleaned them all from the field or some
were damaged or destroyed in combat is unknown. No doubt the Rebels
acquired at least some more usable guns than the half dozen or so they
picked up after the September 18 fight at Alexander's Bridge, and Major
General Joseph Wheeler's cavalry reportedly captured a supply wagon
loaded with Spencers in October 1863.[35]

The problem for the Southerners, however, was that such weapons were
useful only as long as there was a supply of captured ammunition. Although
Wheeler's men captured 4,000 Spencer cartridges along with the guns, the
Confederacy had no capability of making that ammunition, or making the
tooling to manufacture the ammunition, and such a capacity was not soon
forthcoming. General Robert E. Lee himself believed it was pretty much a
hopeless case for the South to attempt to compete with the North in
weapons or ammunition technology. Lee is reported to have rationalized his
view of the topic by saying, "we want a rifle the loading of which takes a certain amount of time. That makes the man to value his shot, and not to fire till
he is sure of his aim."[36]

In contrast, not only did the Union have a number of commercial sources
for metallic cartridges, but General Ramsay was initiating plans for government production of such ammunition. Later in the war he wrote that "as far

back as October, 1863, the Subject of making copper cartridges had been considered by this department, and on the 3d of that month Major Laidley, commanding Frankford Arsenal, was instructed to have prepared plans for shops and detached buildings necessary to the manufacture of 250,000,000 percussion-caps, 3,000,000 friction-primers, and 20,000,000 copper cases for cartridges per annum."[37]

Confederate captures of Spencers were more than offset by production over the winter and into the spring of 1864, as an increasing number of repeaters steadily reached the Union armies in the field through both private purchase and government issue. Even Oliver Winchester finally received his longed-for government contract, courtesy of Colonel Lafayette Baker of the First District of Columbia Cavalry. Baker was a shadowy figure, as much a creation of his own imagination as of life experience. Born in New York in 1826, Baker, who claimed descent from Remember Baker, one of Ethan Allen's Green Mountain Boys, lived at a number of locations in the antebellum period, including New York, Philadelphia, and San Francisco. He was apparently involved in the Gold Rush era vigilante movement in California, although there are allegations that he was a "claim jumper" as well.

At the outbreak of the Civil War, Baker approached General Winfield Scott with an offer to provide intelligence about Confederate military activity in Virginia. While his claims of meeting Belle Boyd and Jefferson Davis while posing as an itinerant photographer may be taken with at least a grain of salt, information he provided apparently had some value. A subsequent interview with Abraham Lincoln gained him an eventual colonel's commission and job as "special provost marshal." Heading a staff of detectives and agents, Baker achieved a position of influence in wartime Washington. Toward the end of 1863, he received authorization to raise a four-company cavalry unit of mounted rangers to back up his detective force.

Baker's battalion was ultimately designated as the First District of Columbia (D.C.) Cavalry, with many of its men recruited in Maine. Since the unit was designed to back up secret operations and also serve in a counter-Guerrilla and military police role, Baker wanted the latest in weapons technology. In his ongoing efforts to secure military contracts, Oliver Winchester had previously contacted Baker, whom he knew held the favor of Secretary of War Stanton, and made sure that Baker was present at an 1862 trial of his rifle in Washington. Although communications between Winchester and the shady Baker are lost in the haze of history, the arms maker apparently expected them to result in a government order for 500 Henrys. In the event, the order was for only 240 rifles, a number that was cut in half by General Ripley. Although Winchester was disappointed, his production problems forced him to scramble and canvass his distributors to even get the diminished order to Washington. Eventually, through some fancy footwork, however, Winchester evaded Ripley's restriction and delivered a total of 241 Henrys, some to the Washington Arsenal and others directly to Baker.[38]

As Baker's unit grew, with more companies coming from Maine, the colonel wanted more Henrys. By this time General Ramsay had replaced the recalcitrant Ripley, and the new ordnance chief ordered an additional 800 rifles for the expanded First D.C. The guns were shipped to Washington over the winter, with final deliveries on March 9, 1864. Although Winchester had pushed long and hard for government contracts, one wonders if he was happy with the result. His correspondence seems to indicate otherwise. The ordnance bureaucracy, in the person of a government sub-inspector named Rice, came to New Haven with a vengeance. Rice informed Winchester that each Henry rifle had to be inspected in detail, slowing already sluggish production. He also specified that "a cone wrench and screwdriver, a tompion, a wiper, a spring vice, a tumbler punch or trigger pin, and an extra cone" must accompany each gun accepted. Never mind that the Henry did not use a "cone" or nipple on which to press a percussion cap to fire it; Rice wanted one. After a flurry of letters back and forth, Winchester and Ramsay finally came to a compromise agreement in which New Haven Arms supplied a cleaning rod, screwdriver, and punch with each rifle.[39]

With the Spencer factory turning out carbines as fast as it could, rifle production came to a halt, even though rifles were still in demand. The men of Company K of the Fifty-seventh Massachusetts Veteran Volunteers, a regiment raised over the winter of 1863-1864, were recruited as sharpshooters. The Massachusetts men were promised Spencer rifles, but none were available, so Company K had to borrow muzzleloaders to practice the manual of arms with at Camp John E. Wool outside Worcester, and went off to war without their Spencers.[40]

Although the stubby twenty-two-inch-barreled Spencer cavalry carbines hardly fit the role of sharpshooter weapons, General Gillmore thought they would be fine for arming the special amphibious infantry units he had in mind for operations around Charleston Harbor, and managed to secure some of the earliest carbines delivered. In December 1863 the Seventh Connecticut and Seventh New Hampshire Infantry of his command were issued the short Spencers. Within two months they would be using them in a small but desperate battle in the scrub pines and swamps of northern Florida.

In the modern popular imagination, Florida would no doubt be at or near the top of the list of Civil War backwaters. Although 15,000 Confederate soldiers, most of whom fought elsewhere, were raised in the state, Florida's chief contributions to the Southern war effort were beef cattle and salt production, the latter of great importance to preserve the former in the pre-refrigeration era. As the war progressed, the state's transportation system also served as a source of cannibalized replacement parts for wrecked and deteriorating railroads further north.

Prior to 1864, Union military activity in Florida was limited to coastal raiding and the establishment of strong points on the state's periphery. Fort Pickens in Pensacola and posts in the Keys never left Union hands and Jacksonville was occupied briefly in 1862 and again in 1863. Fernandina and St. Augustine became permanent Federal bases in 1862. In late 1863, General Gillmore proposed an invasion leading to an expanded and more permanent Federal presence in the state. Such an expedition would, according to Gillmore, interdict the shipment north of beef, salt, and other commodities to hard-pressed Confederate armies, as well as provide access to more African American recruits for the Union army. As an added benefit, Union politicians believed there was a significant and growing amount of Unionist sympathy in Florida (as well as a profitable access to cotton) that could be successfully exploited. The possibility of establishing a Unionist state government which could then apply for readmission to the Union under President Lincoln's recently announced reconstruction plan added to the attraction of Gillmore's proposal, and it was quickly approved. Gillmore tapped General Truman Seymour to command the invasion force. Seymour, a Vermonter who had been severely wounded at the storming of Battery Wagner in July 1863, was something of an old Florida hand, since he had served in the last of the state's Seminole Wars in the late 1850s.[41]

Seymour's Division of the X Corps was modified a bit, due to the availability of troops, into a sort of combined arms task force. It included Colonel William B. Barton's brigade, consisting of the Forty-seventh, Forty-eighth, and 115th New York Infantry, Colonel Joseph Hawley's brigade of the Seventh Connecticut and Seventh New Hampshire Infantry and Eighth U.S. Colored Infantry, and Colonel James Montgomery's brigade of the First North Carolina (Colored) Infantry, Fifty-fourth Massachusetts (Colored) Infantry, Fortieth Massachusetts Mounted Infantry, and the Independent Massachusetts Cavalry Battalion. The infantry and cavalry were supported by Batteries B and E, Third U. S. Artillery, Battery M, First U. S. Artillery, Sections C and B of the Third Rhode Island Artillery, and two companies of the First New York Engineers. The Union invasion force totaled around 6,000 men.

General Seymour's little army landed at and captured Jacksonville on February 7, 1864. For the next several days, the Yankees conducted a series of successful raids as far away as Gainesville, while Federal political operatives began to administer loyalty oaths and register voters in the newly occupied territory. Overcoming some initial doubts expressed to Gillmore about the viability of the expedition and Union sentiment in Florida, Seymour shortly began to advance most of his force inland.

There didn't appear to be much to stop him, save 1,500 scratch second-line troops under inexperienced Irish-born Brigadier General Joseph Finegan, a pre-war planter and businessman. Finegan's credentials for command rested almost entirely on his political connections, save for a period as an enlisted man in the pre-war U.S. Army. Naval activity had, however, convinced the Confederate general that something was up on the Union side prior to Seymour's actual landing, leading him to request reinforcements from other areas of Florida and from his superior, General P. G. T. Beauregard, whose area of responsibility was the lower Atlantic Coast. By February 13, Finegan had concentrated around 2,200 men at Olustee, astride the Florida Atlantic and Gulf Railroad and the Lake City and Jacksonville road.

Over the next week and a half Finegan's force grew to around 5,200 men, roughly equal to Seymour's field force. The little Confederate army now included Brigadier General Alfred H. Colquitt's and Colonel George Harrison's brigades of Florida and Georgia infantry and Colonel Caraway Smith's cavalry brigade.

The Union expedition began the campaign with Spencer carbines in the hands of the men of the Seventh Connecticut and the Seventh New Hampshire, two sister regiments that had been so closely identified during their service that they were often collectively referred to as the "Seventy-seventh New England." The reenlisted veterans of the Connecticut unit had returned home on their veteran furloughs, diminishing its strength, but still leaving the regiment with a solid corps of experienced soldiers, even though it had absorbed a number of recent recruits. Instead of the usual ten companies, the Seventh had been temporarily divided into four.

The Seventh New Hampshire, however, had been doubly damaged. An even larger number of its men were recruits, draftees, and substitutes, some of them French Canadians with a poor grasp of English who were relatively untrained and often unenthusiastic soldiers. In addition, shortly after the Jacksonville landing, the regiment had been ordered to exchange half of its Spencers for rifle muskets from the Fortieth Massachusetts Mounted Infantry. The Bay State unit apparently took the opportunity to get rid of its

damaged weapons, some without ramrods or even locks, and with no bayonets, which had been discarded as superfluous by the Fortieth when it was
mounted.[42]

A fifty-man detachment of the Fortieth put its new Spencers to good use
on the Gainesville raid, however, using defensive firepower to hold off a
Confederate cavalry force more than twice as large. One disgruntled Rebel
trooper recalled that the "outcome was anything but creditable to the commander of the Confederate forces."[43]

The morning of February 20, 1864, found Seymour's main force trudging
down the sand road to Lake City while the Fortieth and the Massachusetts
cavalry battalion skirmished with Confederate cavalry to the front. The
Union commander seems to have been unaware of the recent reinforcements Finegan had received and does not seem to have been expecting a
battle. Finegan, for his part, also appears to have had no notion of the size
and disposition of the Federal force advancing on him.

By 1:00 P.M. Union skirmishers reported more Confederates, including
infantry, appearing on their front. The Rebels were Colquitt's Brigade and
part of Harrison's, which Finegan had ordered to advance from the Olustee
field works and engage the Yankees. As it became evident the enemy force
was more than a cavalry screen, Seymour had the presence of mind to order
more of his own infantry forward. Wisely, he assigned the job to the Spencer
armed Seventh Connecticut. The Connecticut men could see Confederate
skirmishers dodging among the pine trees to their front, and one recalled
that "whenever we could get near enough to stand any chance of execution
we would blaze away at them." The Rebels fell back before the Seventh's
advance, but blocked a similar movement by the Fortieth Massachusetts on
the left.[44]

As the Federals pushed the enemy skirmishers in, Captain B. F. Skinner,
commanding the Seventh, encountered the perennial potential Spencer
problem—his "ammunition was very nearly expended." In addition, the
Seventh began to take fire from three sides. Captain Charles C. Mills of the
Seventh afterward reported that his company's "advance was entirely
checked, all the left of the line being thrown into a swamp and exposed to a
galling fire from the enemy's right. From this position the right was advanced
a few rods, the ground being more open and passable, and then ordered to
lie down, maintaining all the while a lively fire. In this position, with an occasional slight advance, our ammunition was nearly all expended, and our line
gradually withdrew, being charged upon by a regiment of the enemy." The
heavy Spencer fire did have an effect, however, on the Sixty-fourth Georgia,
a regiment which had never been in combat. All of the Georgia regiment's

A Kurz & Allen print depicting the Eighth U.S. Colored Infantry under intense fire at the Battle of Olustee. The Eighth had rushed to the front with unloaded muskets, and as the soldiers tried to quickly ram charges down the muzzles of their weapons, they were decimated. (*Library of Congress*)

field officers were killed and wounded and the regiment faltered, but was bucked up by the veteran Twenty-eighth Georgia on its flank.[45]

While the Seventh battled with the Georgians, Seymour began to deploy parts of the rest of his division as they came up. He placed the artillery, which was soon booming through the pines, in the center of his line and ran it forward, then ordered the Seventh New Hampshire and Eighth U.S. Colored to the right and left and in advance of the guns while the Seventh Connecticut withdrew through them. A misunderstood and/or erroneous order from Colonel Hawley to the New Hampshire unit, coupled with the large number of green and unenthusiastic troops and defective weapons in its ranks, soon resulted in a chaotic mess. Only one company of the Seventh New Hampshire actually stood and fought, with the rest, Spencer armed or not, taking off for the rear under heavy Rebel musketry.

The Eighth U.S. Colored, which had never been in action before, was rushed to the front with unloaded muskets, and came within 200 yards of the enemy before attempting to load. As the men of the Eighth, with little prior training in loading and firing their guns, tried to ram charges down the muzzles of their weapons, they were shot to pieces. Lieutenant Oliver Wilcox Norton wrote that "we have had very little practice in firing, and though they could stand and be killed, they could not kill a concealed enemy fast enough to satisfy my feelings." Colonel Charles W. Fribley of the Eighth, who was responsible for his regiment's lack of training, ordered a withdrawal, during which he was mortally wounded.[46]

With infantry support routed, the Union guns became vulnerable to infantry assault, and the Rebels pushed forward firing, taking losses from canister fire yet dropping a number of gunners and battery horses. Rebel reinforcements arrived on the field at around the same time as Barton's brigade of New Yorkers, who took over the position once occupied by the Seventh New Hampshire and were riddled by heavy frontal and flank fire as were their predecessors. Meanwhile, the Seventh Connecticut managed to resupply its ammunition and took a position on the left flank. Estimating the enemy to be around 600 yards away, the Connecticut men set their sights at that distance (a rarity in the Civil War) and fired at the Confederates, halting their advance temporarily. The Seventh then shifted left, reset its sights at 400 yards, and opened fire again.[47]

Just when the New York regiments seemed about to break, the Fifty-fourth Massachusetts and First North Carolina regiments arrived on the field at the double quick, relieving the New Yorkers and halting the Rebel advance in its tracks. While the Confederates recovered from the shock of the two black regiments' vigorous advance, their momentum had been staggered enough to allow a general Federal disengagement. By this time even the Rebels armed with muzzleloaders were running out of ammunition, and a halt to resupply gave the Yankees a further break to facilitate their retreat. Much of the Federal artillery, however, which had been advanced too close to the enemy lines and then silenced by small arms, was left abandoned on the battlefield.

The retreat was initially covered by the Fifty-fourth, which fired twenty thousand cartridges from its Enfields. The regiment then passed through the Union line to the rear and was replaced by the Seventh Connecticut, whose Spencers provided an effective rear guard fire to enable the remains of Seymour's division to escape. Confederate pursuit, for a number of reasons, was tentative and ineffective, a not unusual occurrence in this war. Federal casualties at Olustee were 203 killed, 1,152 wounded, and 506 missing and captured, while the Rebels lost 934 men killed and wounded.

Even though Olustee proved a disaster, and dashed the dream of a Union Florida, Spencer carbines in the hands of the Seventh Connecticut proved effective skirmishing weapons in both the advance and retreat, perhaps even at considerable range. The dual problems of ammunition supply and fire discipline once more raised their heads, however, even in the veteran Seventh Connecticut, which had its advance checked by old-fashioned musketry. In the hands of a portion of the Seventh New Hampshire, moreover, Spencers did not overcome a number of other deficits in discipline, training, armament of the rest of the regiment, or placement on the battlefield. In short,

Spencers could not compensate for bad battle management featuring poor intelligence, faulty tactics, and piecemeal troop commitment.

The Spencer was in the field to stay, however. On January 7, 1864, Colonel John Wilder, the field commander who had the most experience with repeating rifles, provided a glowing endorsement of the gun.

> I could enumerate at least thirty fights in which the "Spencer Rifle" has triumphed over other arms in such apparently overwhelming numbers so as to almost appear incredible. They should be made with a ring on the side of the breech-piece so as to be carried as a carbine. The ammunition being water-proof, is not worn out or destroyed like other kinds.
>
> I believe that if the Government would arm ten thousand mounted infantry with these guns, and put them under a good enterprising officer, they could destroy all principle railroad lines in the South, and do more damage to the rebellion in three months than fifty thousand troops ordinarily armed could in a year.
>
> I wish I could see those having authority in this matter; that I might impress upon them the great importance of using these arms.[48]

When spring came north in 1864, the war entered its fourth and final year. It would be a year in which, despite mixed results at Olustee, the repeater would begin to come of age and be accepted as the best tool for the job at hand by the Union army leadership, even when they did not quite know how to use it properly. There would be plenty of opportunities to learn.

 # SEVEN

THE WILDERNESS TO ATLANTA

O VER THE WINTER OF 1863-1864 THE FEDERAL GOVERNMENT REALIZED
that many of its experienced soldiers who had enlisted in the summer
of 1861 for three years would be discharged in the middle of the 1864 campaign season as their terms of service expired. In order to mitigate this
resource drain, men who were due for discharge the following summer were
offered a $402 bounty to take an immediate discharge and reenlist for three
more years. As additional incentives, a reenlisted veteran earned a thirty-day
furlough to his home state, a special identifying chevron to wear on his
sleeve, and the honorific "Veteran Volunteer."

Many states, counties, and hometown communities, eager to reduce their
assigned troop quotas and reduce the chances of a manpower draft, offered
additional bounties to those who accepted the Federal offer. In New Jersey,
for example, and by implication other venues, a Veteran Volunteer could add
another $200 to $300 in local bounty money to his total. Regiments in which
three-quarters of the men reenlisted became known as Veteran Volunteer
regiments, as were new regiments in which the same percentage of recruits
were discharged veterans with at least nine months of prior service.[1]

After more than two years of hard war, however, for many soldiers no
amount of promised money was attractive enough to induce reenlistment.
One officer in the Third New Jersey Infantry noted that "the company that
I am in don't seem to go in for it [reenlisting] much as yet, but may change
their minds." Despite a lack of enthusiasm among a number of soldiers, high
bounties and a feeling that "the war was nearly at a close" following the
Union victories at Gettysburg, Vicksburg, and Chattanooga motivated many
others to reenlist. Reenlistment was more common in the more confident
western armies than in the long-suffering Army of the Potomac. The men of
the Seventh Kansas Cavalry, for example, "the first regiment in the XVI
Army Corps to veteranize," believed that the war would last less than another year and that the Confederacy was "about *played out*."[2]

Some soldiers who "veteranized" were also eligible for benefits beyond bounties and furloughs. On January 12, 1864, in camp at Scottsboro, Alabama, twenty-five-year-old Colonel Charles C. Walcutt "took pen in hand" to write a memorandum to the officers of his Forty-sixth Ohio Infantry regiment. The colonel informed his subordinates that he had "obtained for your men the 'Spencer Rifle' being in my opinion the most complete arm of the service and one I know your men will feel proud of." Walcutt stressed that the new rifles would be issued to "veterans, *only*" or those soldiers in the regiment who had reenlisted.[3]

Walcutt's regiment was one of many that assembled in the Chattanooga area in the wake of the Chickamauga disaster for Grant's campaign to lift the siege and drive Bragg's army back into Georgia as well as relieve Burnside at Knoxville. Those results achieved, the enhanced force remained at Chattanooga. Grant was promoted in March 1864 to Lieutenant General and assumed command of all Union forces in the field. The new commander moved east to make his headquarters with the Army of the Potomac for the coming campaign season, and Major General Sherman assumed Grant's old command of the Military Division of the Mississippi—in effect, all operations in the West.

As Grant prepared his plans for the coming campaign, Spencers and Henrys continued to roll off the production lines. By the end of April, 13,000 Spencer carbines had been delivered to the Federal government and average production had risen to 2,700 guns a month, virtually all carbines. There was one notable exception in Federal orders. On April 13, General Ramsay offered the Spencer Company a special contract for 100 rifles and cartridge boxes to satisfy the demands of the Fifty-seventh Massachusetts' sharpshooter company. The rifles were delivered within a few weeks, although the regiment did not see them for two months.[4]

A week later Captain Balch informed a no doubt delighted Warren Fisher that "the demand for Spencer carbines and rifles has become so great during the last two months" that the government would take every firearm the company could make. In April the Spencer factory finally finished the Massachusetts rifle and carbine order, and, once again, Governor Andrew allowed Ramsay to take the guns in exchange for a promise to replace them by the end of the year. This act put another 1,868 rifles and 1,176 carbines into Federal hands before the campaign season kicked off.[5]

Oliver Winchester, despite his less than satisfactory relations with the Ordnance Department and his nagging production problems, was still interested in government contracts. In an attempt to answer some of the criticisms of the Henry, including its weight, the power of its cartridges, and the potentially debris-catching slot in the magazine tube, Winchester forwarded a prototype carbine model to the Ordnance Department in January 1864. Unfortunately, the gun, hastily assembled and chambered for a new, longer .44 cartridge with a greater powder capacity, did not prove satisfactory to Major Dyer at Springfield Armory. Dyer reported that the carbine did not ⟨ have a half-cock safety notch, that it was too heavy, and that some cartridges burst on test firing, jamming the mechanism. In addition, he believed that the internal parts were easily "disarranged" and a new style magazine tube was inadequate and could be removed from the gun and lost. Although the latter complaint could also apply to the Spencer, there were just too many potential defects in the Henry for the ordnance men, especially when they had an increasing supply of Spencers flowing off the assembly line. Winchester considered Dyer's report "an injustice" and protested that the failures were easily remedied, but General Ramsay concluded that the Henry in its newest incarnation was "too delicate for service."[6]

If further Henry orders from the War Department did not seem in the cards, the Spencer had not only entered the mainstream of military procurement, but had become a desired arm used to reward proven troops. At Memphis, General Hurlbut, still a strong Spencer proponent, was finally promised some repeaters, although they were carbines, not rifles. In the spring of 1864, Hurlbut was in the process of reorganizing his cavalry after Brigadier General William Sooy Smith's disastrous performance against General Forrest in the Meridian Campaign in February. Many of Hurlbut's most experienced troopers were on reenlistment furloughs, but he ordered that "as soon as the veterans return I wish the best regiments supplied with the Spencer carbine, which has been promised and I suppose will be there."[7]

The Second New Jersey Cavalry, a new regiment raised in the fall of 1863, had more than a few dubious recruits in its ranks and a high initial desertion rate. The regiment was commanded by Colonel Joseph Karge, however, an immigrant Pole and veteran of both the Prussian army and the First New Jersey Cavalry. Karge was a competent and highly regarded officer, whom General Kilpatrick called "one of the best Cav. officers I have ever known," and he whipped his outfit into shape in short order. Although Karge's regiment was specifically requested for duty in the Army of the Potomac, it was assigned to the West. Based no doubt on the colonel's reputation more than its own history, which was yet to unfold, the Second New Jersey was issued Spencer carbines on its way to Tennessee in November 1863.[8]

On April 4, Brigadier General James H. Wilson, who had served on Grant's staff as a lieutenant colonel of Engineers, but was now Chief of the

Cavalry Bureau, reported on the status of the mounted regiments in Sherman's army. Wilson declared that "The general desire of the best regiments is to be armed with the Spencer carbine. By arming one or two regiments in each department with them, their old arms turned in will supply the deficiencies in the other regiments." Among the "best regiments" in the west Wilson noted that the Second and Fourth Michigan Cavalry had already been issued 700 Spencer carbines and the Fourth United States Cavalry 600. Wilson also "proposed to furnish 700 for the Fifth Indiana, and also the Second Iowa, of the Department of the Tennessee."[9]

General Wilson, an 1860 West Point graduate born in Illinois in 1837, rose fast in the army hierarchy through a combination of administrative and tactical ability and a remarkable facility for attracting the attention of and ingratiating himself with important people. Highly regarded by General Grant, Wilson was also a favorite of Assistant Secretary of War Dana. In sharp contrast to Colonel Wilder's brusque dismissal of Dana on the Chickamauga battlefield, Wilson had cultivated the assistant secretary during his visit to the western armies. It was Dana who requested that Grant send Wilson east to take over the Cavalry Bureau, a department in disarray, in January 1864, a suggestion to which the general readily agreed. General Thomas had also asked Grant to assign Wilson to command his Army of the Cumberland cavalry. The high visibility post of Cavalry Bureau Chief in Washington, however, proved a better career move for the ambitious young officer.[10]

As bureau chief, Wilson's most important task was ordering and approving horse purchases, a process that had deteriorated badly over the previous two years and which he thoroughly reformed in short order. Although small arms were funneled to his office through the Ordnance Department, rather than directly contracted for, Wilson became the biggest booster of the Spencer in the service, no small endorsement. Years later, in retrospect, he considered the adoption of the Spencer as the preferred cavalry carbine to be his greatest achievement.[11]

Despite the increases in production and Wilson's enthusiasm, there were more soldiers who wanted Spencers than there were Spencers to supply them with. A number of regiments were promised that if they reenlisted enough men to earn a unit the Veteran Volunteer designation, the veterans would be rearmed with Spencers. In some cases, as in that of Colonel Walcutt's infantrymen, this promise was kept. In others it was not. Toward the end of the war Brigadier General Edward Hatch reported to General Thomas that the Second Iowa Cavalry and Third, Sixth, Seventh, and Ninth Illinois Cavalry had "re-enlisted a year ago as veterans, with the promise if they would re-enlist they should be armed with the Spencer carbine. Of these only the Second Iowa Cavalry and Sixth Illinois Cavalry were armed with the Spencer carbine."[12]

Some commanders requested Spencers for their men because they felt special conditions warranted their issue. In April 1864 Brigadier General Edward W. Hinks, commanding a division of U.S. Colored Infantry in Virginia, noted that his soldiers, who had been threatened with "no quarter" if captured, were armed with rifle muskets. According to Hinks, "these arms will, perhaps, answer for troops who will be well cared for if they fall into his hands, but to troops who cannot afford to be beaten, and will not be taken, the best arm should be given that the country can afford. The retaliation we should at present adopt is to arm our colored troops with Spencer repeating rifles, and I request that my division, or a part of them, may be armed with a repeating or breech-loading fire-arm." As with many repeater petitioners in the spring of 1864, Hinks did not get what he wished.[13]

As winter waned, Federal planning for the campaign of 1864 firmed. Grant resurrected the old strategic idea of a number of simultaneous advances on both eastern and western fronts, denying the Rebels the advantage of interior lines of communication they had used so effectively to reinforce Bragg from the Army of Northern Virginia prior to Chickamauga. General Meade's army, with which Grant made his headquarters, would concentrate on the Army of Northern Virginia and the Confederate capital at Richmond, while Sherman, commanding the composite Armies of the Tennessee, Ohio, and Cumberland, gathered around Chattanooga, was to drive toward Atlanta against General Johnston's Army of Tennessee. These advances, together with ancillary operations, including Major General Franz Sigel's advance up the Shenandoah Valley and Major General Benjamin Butler's Army of the James' advance on Richmond from the Virginia Peninsula, were all scheduled to begin in early May 1864.

In the Army of the Potomac, repeating weapons were confined almost exclusively to the cavalry, where Spencer carbines were being issued as they became available, joining the existing Spencer rifles in the Fifth and Sixth Michigan Cavalry. Cavalry combat preparations were stepped up when General Pleasonton was removed from command of the army's Cavalry Corps in favor of another Grant protégé from the west, Philip Sheridan. Although Sheridan had not distinguished himself in the Chickamauga campaign, he had saved the day earlier at Murfreesboro and caught Grant's attention during the final fight to relieve Chattanooga, when his division scaled Missionary Ridge. The thirty-three-year-old major general, an Ohioan born of Irish immigrant parents, had most recently commanded an infantry division, but had led the Second Michigan cavalry and then a full brigade of horse soldiers in the first year of the war.

General Phil Sheridan and his staff about the time of his cavalry divisions' suc-
cess during the Overland Campaign. Left to right, Maj. Gen. Sheridan, Col.
Joseph Forsythe, Chief of Staff Merritt, Brig. Gen. Thomas C. Devins, and Maj.
Gen. George A. Custer. (*Library of Congress*)

Sheridan arrived in Washington on April 4. Within days yet another significant change occurred in the Army of the Potomac's cavalry chain of command. General Kilpatrick, whose recent raid on Richmond in an attempt to
release Union prisoners of war had ended badly, was relieved of command
of the Third Division of the Cavalry Corps and shipped west to command a
division under Sherman. Kilpatrick's replacement, apparently on Grant's
suggestion, was the by now ubiquitous James Wilson, although Wilson's initial branch of service was the Topographical Engineer Corps and all of his
prior military experience had been as a staff officer. Another, more lament-
ed, change was the replacement of First Division commander John Buford,
a fine soldier who had died of typhoid fever in December, with Brigadier
General A. T. A. Torbert. The rationale for transferring Torbert, who had led
the First New Jersey Infantry Brigade in the VI Corps with competence but
not distinction, to cavalry division command, has puzzled observers, both
then and now. The answer may lie in the fact that Torbert was Sheridan's
West Point classmate.[14]

Despite the fact that some regiments were receiving limited numbers of
Spencer carbines, the overall combat readiness of the Army of the Potomac's
Cavalry Corps was uneven, to say the least. Although many years later
Sheridan recalled that his new command presented a "fine appearance," an
April 17 inspection report on the First and Third Divisions by Captain F. C.
Newhall reveals otherwise. Newhall found many of the two divisions' regi-
ments and brigades "considerably disorganized" with "very large deficiencies
of arms and horses" and with their men often ill uniformed and disheveled.
The captain found even the supposedly crack Spencer-armed Sixth Michigan
in "poor condition."[15]

Although the commander of the Fifth New York Cavalry, a regiment recently issued Spencer carbines, considered them a "capital arm," small arms were a particular problem in the Cavalry Corps. Newhall reported that the First New York Dragoons were "armed with Joslyn carbines, which are unreliable and worthless" and considered the Smith carbines of the First Connecticut Cavalry "entirely unreliable." Some soldiers had no weapons at all, and one brigade was found to have "large deficiencies of carbines and pistols in all the regiments but one."[16]

Meade and Sheridan immediately began to butt heads over the tactical role the cavalry would play in the forthcoming campaign, with the fiery little Irishman insisting that his horsemen be fully supplied and relieved from mundane picket and escort duties. When the fighting began, Sheridan wanted his corps to function as a semi-independent organization engaged in aggressive offensive operations. Meade, on the other hand, foresaw a continuation of the relationship he had with Pleasonton—a cavalry commander who was actually not a field commander, but a member of his staff, with the mounted arm playing a supporting role to infantry operations.

Perhaps because of his connections to the new lieutenant general, Sheridan got much of what he wanted in the short run. Picket duty was reduced and regiments were allowed to rest men and horses. For some there was an improvement in arms as well, and the First New York Dragoons were able to turn in their Joslyns for Spencers. On April 22 Sheridan issued orders for his corps to prepare for battle. Camp baggage and unfit soldiers were sent to the rear, rations were drawn, and 150 rounds of ammunition per man were issued. After midnight on May 4, Wilson's Division began to cross the Rapidan, the Army of the Potomac's Rubicon, at Germanna Ford. The engineer who loved the Spencer was leading that army into the Wilderness. Sheridan's other divisions crossed the river at different points shortly afterward. The campaign was about to begin.

Wilson's initial objective was Wilderness Tavern. Grant intended Meade's army to outflank General Lee's and move beyond the second growth tangle of the Wilderness to fight on open ground, where Union superiority of numbers would, he hoped, prove decisive. The cavalry was assigned to lead the way. Although he was an inexperienced cavalry commander, General Wilson's faith in the Spencer carbine caused him to assign the Fifth New York to spearhead his division's advance. The New York troopers drove Confederate patrols down the Orange Plank Road and then occupied a position beyond Parker's store, where they were soon under attack from Rebel infantry of Longstreet's Corps, who had returned to the Army of Northern Virginia in the nick of time to reinforce Lee.

Although most of Wilson's troopers engaged Confederate cavalry, which attacked vigorously and sent them tumbling to the rear, the men of the Fifth, working their Spencer levers feverishly, held on for some time against growing pressure from Longstreet's infantrymen. The heavy Spencer fire deceived the enemy into thinking they were facing a strong line of Union infantry. Wilson later reported that the Fifth, "with scarcely 500 men, armed with Spencer carbines and fighting on foot, by their gallantry and good management, resisted the rebel infantry in large force for six hours." The regiment's historian recalled that "the Spencer carbines made the dense woods ring, and told with fearful effect upon the enemy. Prisoners . . . swore that a whole brigade must have been in their front."[17]

Stymied in the Wilderness and suffering more than twice the casualties of its opponent in several days of confused fighting, on the night of May 6 the Army of the Potomac, nominally still commanded by Meade but responding to Grant's campaign plan, began to move south once more, toward Spotsylvania. Sheridan's cavalry preceded the main force again, clearing the way, and the Yankee horse soldiers got into a dismounted fight at Todd's Tavern on May 7. Spencers came to the fore again, this time in the hands of the First New York Dragoons, and again played a decisive defensive role in holding off Confederate attacks. The Wilderness terrain forced horse soldiers to fight dismounted, diminishing combat strength by the need to detach horse holders. In addition to weakening the front line by their absence, when the horse holders withdrew from a position they often lost control of the mounts they were leading through dense woods and along narrow dirt roads, creating a chaotic situation. Cavalry units without the extra firepower provided by Spencers that might have gained them a breathing space had a rough time of it in the Wilderness.[18]

As the campaign progressed, relations between Meade and Sheridan rapidly deteriorated, highlighted by the two generals' responses to a massive infantry and cavalry traffic snarl on the road to Spotsylvania, a mess that allowed the Confederates to occupy a vital position before the Federals arrived. In a swearing and shouting match on May 8, Meade called Sheridan incompetent and the Irishman characterized Meade as a meddling bungler. Grant settled the matter by instructing Meade to allow Sheridan to take the bulk of his horsemen off in a massive raid toward Richmond which would draw J. E. B. Stuart's cavalry out in the open for, he hoped, a decisive fight. Other than proceeding "against the enemy's cavalry" and ending up at the Army of the James' main supply depot, Grant's instructions were not specific, granting the cavalry commander wide latitude.[19]

On May 9, in a 10,000-man column thirteen miles long, Sheridan's corps broke away from the Army of the Potomac and started out toward Richmond, marching at a deliberate pace. It didn't take General Stuart long to follow, although he divided his own corps, only taking 5,000 men with him in the pursuit, leaving the remainder with Lee's main army, and split his field force yet again in an attempt to confuse the Yankees.

In its opening days, Sheridan's raid succeeded in defeating Rebel attempts to interdict it, destroyed thousands of rations intended for the Army of Northern Virginia and liberated hundreds of Yankee prisoners heading south. On May 9 General Custer's men torched a railroad depot, over 100 railroad cars, and two engines. On May 11, as the Union horse closed in on Richmond, Stuart, whose efforts so far had failed to have any effect on Sheridan's juggernaut, challenged the Federals to open battle by placing two of his brigades astride their flank at Yellow Tavern. Uncharacteristically, the Confederate cavalry commander then waited for the Yankees to make the next move.

It was not long in coming. Sheridan initially ordered a mounted attack on the Confederate right, in an attempt to flank Stuart's position. When it stalled, he had Brigadier General Wesley Merritt (Torbert was on medical leave for a back problem) order Custer to attack the Rebel left. The Michigan Brigade commander dismounted his Fifth and Sixth regiments and had them advance as skirmishers while ordering the First Michigan and then the Seventh Michigan to make successive saber charges into the enemy's left flank. This combination of Spencer firepower and mounted shock action enabled the Wolverines to overrun a Confederate battery, scatter its cavalry supports and, most important, mortally wound General Stuart. An attack all along the line then drove the Rebels from the field. After brushing against the defenses of Richmond, getting entangled with its defenders and partially surrounded and then shooting their way free, the Union horsemen rode into General Butler's lines on May 13.

Sheridan lent some diversionary support to Butler's Army of the James' attempt to advance on Richmond, then moved north to rejoin the Army of the Potomac, which had fought a series of bloody engagements at Spotsylvania. Once Meade disengaged from the Spotsylvania line, he moved south once more, to the North Anna River, where the cavalry rejoined his army on May 24.

The Army of the Potomac continued to battle its way down the ladder of Virginia rivers that flowed into Chesapeake Bay and the sea, always hopeful of hooking around the Confederate right, yet always frustrated. After his Richmond raid, Sheridan's cavalry resumed its traditional reconnaissance and screening duties, but remained ready to reassume the role of long-range mobile strike force. Following Stuart's death, the Confederate cavalry was divided into three two brigade divisions, under the command of Major Generals Wade Hampton, Fitzhugh Lee and W. H. "Rooney" Lee, all under the direct orders of General Robert E. Lee. This was a rather clumsy command concept that would be largely ignored in future operations. As Grant and Meade closed in on Richmond, and crossed the Pamunkey River, General Lee ordered Hampton to break through the Yankee cavalry and determine the axis of advance of the Federal infantry.

Hampton led his old division and that of Fitzhugh Lee, reinforced by two regiments of Brigadier General Matthew C. Butler's brigade, the Fourth and Fifth South Carolina Cavalry, which had spent the war to date in

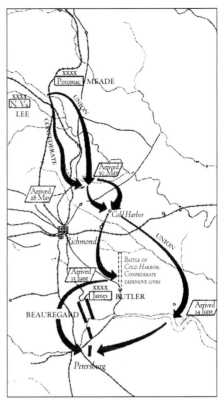

Union and confederate movements during the Grant's Overland Campaign in the spring and summer of 1864. (Adapted from the *West Point Atlas of American Wars*)

their home state. On May 28 Hampton ran into Gregg's division at the little crossroads village of Haw's Shop. Following a meeting engagement in which Confederate horsemen chased the First Pennsylvania through town and then fled themselves in the face of a counterattack, both sides dismounted and began to slug it out from behind improvised breastworks.

Butler's Carolinians, although inexperienced, were particularly fit for the type of fighting that developed that day. They were armed, as were Lieutenant Colonel Witcher's men at Gettysburg, with muzzle-loading rifles. General Butler later recalled that "my brigade . . . was armed with long-range Enfield rifles, and was, in fact, mounted infantry, but for our sabers." His men were the recipients of 18,000 rounds of Spencer ammunition expended by the First Pennsylvania, which failed to move them from their defensive works. Sheridan conceded that the "Carolinians fought very gallantly in this their first fight, judging from the number of their dead and wounded, and prisoners captured." Lieutenant Colonel John W. Kester of the First New Jersey Cavalry, who lost thirteen of his officers killed and wounded, described his regiment's struggle against Butler's men as "the severest cavalry fighting of the war," specifically noting that the Carolinians' Enfields outranged his men's Burnside carbines.[20]

Custer's brigade broke the tactical stalemate at Haw's Shop by again attacking dismounted with Spencers blazing. Since the Confederates had apparently begun to withdraw from the field at the same time, it is difficult to assign the importance of the Spencer fire in hastening their departure, but most of the Rebel casualties in the battle occurred at this point. In the wake of Haw's shop, Lee's headquarters began to take notice of the increased and effective use of Yankee firepower, and its effect on the battlefield.[21]

Although Custer's tactical learning curve had happily continued upward, by Haw's shop most of the Spencer rifles his men shouldered at Gettysburg had been traded in for Spencer carbines, which the troopers believed were not accurate at long range. This assumption is not correct in a theoretical sense, but the diminished sight radius (distance between the rear and front sights) of the shorter-barreled carbines compared to the rifles did magnify sighting errors. The shorter sight radius of the carbine demanded more steadiness and attention from the shooter, and considering the lack of marksmanship training in the Union army, resulted in a consequent decrease in practical combat accuracy. The Spencer was, however (Captain Barber of the Ohio Sharpshooters' protestations to the contrary), with its smaller powder charge and lighter and less ballistically efficient bullet, a shorter-range weapon than the rifle musket. The men of the Ninety-second Illinois Mounted Infantry requested that Spencer ammunition "should be filled with the very best powder—we cannot compete with some of the Rebel guns at long range."[22]

The Union cavalry moved on to Old Church and then Cold Harbor, where Torbert's Division attacked an advance Rebel position. The Rebels gave ground slowly until Custer's Wolverines arrived to tip the fight decisively in favor of the Yankees and then fell back to prepared positions at the Cold Harbor crossroads, which was strongly defended by Brigadier General Thomas L. Clingman's infantry and Fitz Lee's cavalry division. The Federals attacked briskly, and Brigadier General Wesley Merritt's brigade turned the Confederate left flank while Custer ordered a saber charge by the First Michigan as the enemy began to react to Merritt's maneuver. The Rebels quickly withdrew, and the Yankees occupied their abandoned field fortifications.

The following morning 1,500 Confederate infantrymen of Major General Joseph M. Kershaw's division counterattacked Merritt's brigade, which, with horseholders deducted, mustered 600 men of the First and Second U.S., Sixth Pennsylvania, and First New York Dragoons in its firing line. The Dragoons' Spencers, combined with the Sharps carbines of the other regiments, which had a rapid rate of fire in their own right, gave the defenders a great deal of confidence. The cavalrymen expected a severe firefight, however, and even "piled even their pistol cartridges by their sides where they would be handy."[23]

Merritt's horse soldiers held their fire until they could clearly see Kershaw's men coming through the trees to their front, some with rifles fixed with sword bayonets, causing an Irish corporal in the Second U.S.

Private Thomas Hawk of the Ninety-second Illinois Mounted Infantry and his Spencer rifle. (*USAMHI*)

to exclaim "Howly Mother! Here they come wid sabers on fut." The Rebels came on at the double quick, and one soldier remembered that "the rebel yell rang throughout the forest. Then a sheet of flame came from the cavalry line, and for three or four minutes the din was deafening. The repeating carbines raked the flank of the hostile column while the Sharps single-loaders kept up a steady rattle. The whole thing was over in less than five minutes," and Kershaw's shocked infantrymen went tumbling back from whence they came. Shortly afterward Yankee infantry from the VI Corps relieved the horsemen. The ensuing battle of Cold Harbor would not end as advantageously for Union arms as the first encounter, however, and slaughter and stalemate set in upon the campaign yet again.

Stymied at Cold Harbor, Grant and Meade moved south once more, crossing the James River to threaten Richmond and the vital rail center of Petersburg. Once more Sheridan's horsemen were called on to provide a diversion, raiding west to Trevilian Station. The Confederate cavalry divisions of Hampton and Fitz Lee shadowed the raiders and by June 10 Hampton had reached Trevilian ahead of the Yankees. The following day, as Hampton advanced on Sheridan's main force, Custer, detached by Torbert to loop around the enemy's flank, succeeded in totally surprising the Rebels. The Fifth Michigan charged into Hampton's rear and captured 800 prisoners, 1,500 horses, forty ambulances, and fifty wagons. Unfortunately, Colonel Russell A. Alger overextended his regiment and was in turn routed by one of Fitz Lee's units. The Fifth, and part of the Sixth sent to its aid, was scattered across the landscape, losing prisoners and captured baggage, and Alger's troopers never got a chance to bring their Spencers into play.[24]

The rest of the Wolverines were soon in deep trouble as well, as the remainder of Fitz Lee's division and elements of Hampton's attacked the First, Seventh, and the rest of the Sixth Michigan remaining with Custer. Somehow, possibly because of their Spencers, although they were not specifically mentioned, the Michigan men were able to keep from being overrun while the rest of the Federal cavalry tried to break through and save them.

Yet again, Butler's Carolinians and their muzzleloaders played a big part on the Confederate side, holding off the rescuers. One veteran of the First Massachusetts recalled that "Butler's Rebel troopers were armed with 'long toms' which they used with deadly effect, being able to drop our boys before the latter could get within carbine range." He concluded that "one brigade armed with Enfield rifles and posted behind earthworks ought to be a match at any time for more than an entire division of dismounted cavalry."[25]

Despite the Carolinians' fine fighting, Sheridan's men managed to save Custer, and the Rebels withdrew. Although Confederates were later to claim a victory at Trevilian Station, General Butler opined shortly after the fight that the day had "ended disastrously" for the Rebels. The truth was somewhere in the middle. Both forces guardedly watched each other while Sheridan tarried in the area and destroyed several miles of railroad track. Unable to effect a proposed juncture with Federal forces coming east from the Shenandoah Valley, the battered Yankee cavalry began the long march back to the Army of the Potomac, burdened with 377 wounded men and 370 prisoners. On the way, elements of Torbert's division launched a dismounted attack, firing their carbines on Butler's brigade, which was sheltered behind improvised breastworks at Mallory's Crossroads. Butler's riflemen, whom General Torbert mischaracterized as infantry in his report, repulsed the Yankees.[26]

While two of Sheridan's divisions battled Hampton and Lee at Trevilian, the Army of the Potomac, with the assistance of the XVIII Corps of General Butler's Army of the James, which had failed in its own offensive in May, moved on Petersburg. A lack of initiative on the part of Federal commanders, most particularly Major General William F. "Baldy" Smith of the XVIII Corps, coupled with prompt action by Confederate defenders, however, assured yet another deadlock, as veteran Rebel infantrymen reached the Petersburg defenses before the main Union army. This time the impasse settled down to a siege of Richmond and Petersburg that would last until the end of the war, and Army of the Potomac cavalry operations became more limited in scope.

The Petersburg siege featured a succession of attempts to advance Union lines to the south and west of the city and sever road and rail connections between the Cockade City and the rest of the South. The first of these efforts, ordered by Grant in mid-June, involved a raid by Wilson's division, assisted by Brigadier General August Kautz's cavalry division from the Army of the James. Grant ordered Wilson to march on Burkesville and destroy as much of the Southside and Richmond and Danville Railroads as he could.

Wilson's division was worn out from over a month of marching and fighting, and the general thought the Army of the James horsemen would not be much help. Although the German-born Kautz, an experienced West Pointer who had succeeded Wilson at the cavalry bureau, had a good reputation as a military theorist and cavalry officer, equipment in his division was not up to standard, to say the least. The First Massachusetts regiment fielded three types of carbines and, according to Kautz, the Eleventh Pennsylvania Cavalry, armed with Merrills, "started on the 1st of May with 280 carbines; they are now reduced to 117, and this reduction is due almost entirely to defects in the arm itself. The officers report that many burst in the barrel, and other parts give way." Although Kautz's command included the Henry-armed First D.C. Cavalry, Wilson thought it, overall, a "rag, tag and bobtail" outfit. While the men of the First D.C. carried Henrys, many of them were recruits who had been serving as ersatz infantry and had been mounted only days before the raid.[27]

Wilson marched to Burkesville, then to Roanoke Station, destroying the railroad and skirmishing with pursuing Rebels, then attempted to return to the Union lines around Petersburg. He was soon fighting off Rooney Lee's pursuing horsemen as well as local Confederate forces, however, with his column encumbered by a growing number of wounded men and trailed by a small army of escaping slaves. The heat, continual fighting, and increasing chaos caused by night marches, misdirection, and errors of judgment on Wilson's part soon began to tell on the Yankee horse.

Hampton and Fitzhugh Lee, back from the fight with Sheridan, added their forces to the pursuit, joining a number of Confederate infantry units converging on the raiders. Realizing a direct breakthrough to safety at Reams' Station was impossible, Wilson burned his supply trains and retreated, seeking to find another way home. General Kautz, cool under pressure, with "a pocket map of Virginia spread over his knee . . . a mariner's compass . . . and looking at the sun," led a number of men, his own and Wilson's, to safety.[28]

The retreat of Wilson's main force was far more disorderly. His command was attacked while crossing Stony Creek, a situation potentially disastrous to a military force. Fitz Lee's troopers chased down fugitive Yankees caught on the wrong side of the creek and sabered and shot a number of fleeing slaves as well. The survivors staggered into Union lines on July 1. The expedition, in all, suffered 25 percent casualties, including over 1,000 men as prisoners, and Wilson lost all of his baggage and artillery. He seems to have achieved his mission to a degree, however, blocking supplies and reinforcements to the Petersburg/Richmond garrison by railroad from the south for some nine weeks.

As part of the overall campaign in Virginia in the spring of 1864, Grant had ordered Major Generals Franz Sigel and Benjamin Butler to advance up the Shenandoah Valley and the James River, respectively. Sigel, a popular German-American soldier, was more valuable to the Union for his ability to rally his countrymen to the cause than for his military proficiency. That aside, he was given command of the Union effort in the Shenandoah Valley in the spring of 1864 and ordered to move south and rendezvous with a force under the command of Brigadier General George Crook. After the Rebels defeated Sigel's 17,000-man army at New Market on May 15 he was replaced by Major General David Hunter.

Sigel and Hunter's cavalry commander was Brigadier General William W. Averell, a man who was not happy about the state of discipline and leadership in his command in the weeks leading up to the campaign. The cavalry of what was called the Department of West Virginia was divided into two small divisions, Averell's and the other under Brigadier General Stahel.

Averell's divisions were in far worse shape than their Army of the Potomac counterparts. On April 15, 1864, the general requisitioned for the "Fourteenth Pennsylvania Cavalry, 465 Burnside carbines; Twenty-first New York Veteran Cavalry, 566 revolvers, 106 Burnside carbines; Taylor's First New York Veteran Cavalry, 320 revolvers, 750 Spencer carbines; First Virginia Veteran Cavalry, 337 Spencer carbines, 400 revolvers." He also noted that "the First New York Veteran Cavalry, McReynolds, are now making requisitions for 276 revolvers, 484 Burnside carbines, 250 sets horse equipments."[29]

On March 6, 1864, the First New York Veteran Cavalry came out second best in a fight with Lieutenant Colonel John Mosby's guerrillas, at least partially due to poor armament. Captain John J. Carter of the First reported that "22 of my men were assailed (according to the best information) by 32 of the enemy armed with two revolvers and a saber each, while to complete their armament quite a number were armed with good carbines, while my men had but two revolvers in the whole command and without a carbine that was good for anything. To illustrate, in the first volley out of seventeen carbines that there were in line and tried to be fired only four went off, although they were carefully loaded on the ground while awaiting the attack." It appears that Captain Carter's men were armed with Starr carbines, which resembled the Sharps but were not of the same quality and fired a paper cartridge.[30]

Although much of the cavalry operating in the Shenandoah was deployed in counter-Guerrilla operations, Averell's men also filled conventional cavalry roles, including reconnaissance, conducting mounted raids against Confederate lines of communications, and screening infantry movements. When faced by what he believed to be a larger Confederate army at Lynchburg at the end of June, Hunter, taking Averell's horsemen with him, withdrew into West Virginia, removing his whole force temporarily from the war. Although repeating rifles, either issued Spencers or privately owned Henrys, were present in small numbers in Union ranks, they did not play any significant major role in the backwater campaign in Western Virginia in the spring of 1864.

General Butler's operations on the James River line, also scheduled as an abetting operation to the main thrust of Grant and Meade, provided more of a field test for repeaters. Men drawn from the coastal south, including the Spencer carbine-wielding Seventh Connecticut, Fortieth Massachusetts, and Seventh New Hampshire Infantry, reinforced the Army of the James prior to the advent of the campaign.

On May 5 the Army of the James landed on the James River between Petersburg and Richmond. Butler's force totaled around 30,000 men, and his opposition scarcely 5,000, mostly militiamen. A rapid advance on Richmond and/or Petersburg might well have resulted in the capture of one or both of those critical cities. Although a "political" general commissioned because he was a prominent War Democrat, Butler was a good administrator with an interest in military innovation—he had purchased several Gatling guns with his own money—but not an able tactician. His army moved slowly, Confederate reinforcements arrived, and the Yankees ended up bogged down in front of Drewry's Bluff.

In the advance, the Connecticut and New Hampshire infantrymen of the "Seventy-seventh New England" were used extensively as skirmishers, and their firepower also came in handy to squelch enemy counterattacks. On one occasion their brigade commander reported that while under heavy enemy fire, "without flinching, our two regiments as fiercely responded. The enemy began to come over their works to charge, but the fearful fire of our lines (the Spencer carbines here worked to good advantage) staggered and drove him back."[31]

As the army approached Drewry's Bluff the men of the Ninth New Jersey Infantry encountered "a western regiment" they supposed was "armed with sixteen-shooting rifles." On May 13, the regiment moved through the Ninth's skirmish line, "halted, faced to the front, opened its terrible fire for a few minutes and retired," leaving the Jerseymen to continue on with their rifle muskets. The Ninth's historian, J. Madison Drake, remembered that his regiment's skirmishers had a quiet night and believed that "the rapidity of the fire delivered from the Indiana regiment just before we moved into the forest must have frightened the Confederates, as neither they nor ourselves had ever before heard anything like it." What Drake and his friends saw and heard was most likely the Thirteenth Indiana Infantry, which was armed with Spencers, not "sixteen-shooting" Henrys.[32]

Superior firepower to the contrary, Butler's dithering allowed General Beauregard, now in charge of the Richmond defenses, to scour the Carolinas for more men to help defend the capital. On the early morning of May 16 Beauregard attacked the Union forces in front of Drewry's Bluff. General Robert Ransom's four brigades, massed on the Confederate left, advanced out of a fog bank at 5:00 A.M. and overran the Union right. The Rebel attack was successful in penetrating into the Yankee rear, but became disorganized in the fog.

Secondary Confederate assaults on the Union center were repulsed when the attackers became enmeshed in telegraph wire obstructions and then staggered by heavy fire, some of it from the New England regiments' Spencers, especially those of the Seventh Connecticut. According to one report, the Seventh "opened an astonishingly rapid fire, lasting but a minute or two, and ceasing promptly at the bugle-call . . . twice again the enemy made similar attempts, with the same results." The Fortieth Massachusetts, dismounted again, yet still armed with many of the Seventh New Hampshire's Spencer carbines, added its own firepower to the fight.[33]

With his flank compromised and rear threatened, however, General Butler had had enough fighting for the day. He withdrew his army to Half Way House and then to a line of fortifications previously erected at the Bermuda Hundred. Beauregard followed, and in the skirmishing during the withdrawal, the Seventh Connecticut lost a number of men who were cut off and captured, their Spencers passing into Confederate service. Although his men's ammunition ran low at one point, Major Oliver S. Sanford of the Seventh concluded at the end of the operation that "could the right of our lines been held, we could have held our position against any force brought before it, for with the Spencer carbine, plenty of ammunition, and a determined set of men, nothing can stand before them." Although Butler had not

Sharpshooters of the 18th Corps at Petersburg as sketched by Alfred R. Waud in July 1864. (*Library of Congress*)

succeeded, the Spencer in the hands of infantry had received another good review.[34]

The first few Spencer rifles reached the Army of the Potomac's infantry in the Petersburg siege lines in mid-July. The men of the Sixty-third Pennsylvania were "pleased" to exchange their Austrian Lorenz muzzleloaders for Spencers during this period, but not so happy when they began to hear "Spencers to the front" with regularity. The sharpshooters of the Fifty-seventh Massachusetts, promised Spencers back in the depths of winter, finally received them on July 19. Casualties had reduced the original need for 100 rifles to thirty-four, however. One private wrote that the Massachusetts men "tried our rifles out some this forenoon and like them first rate." First Lieutenant John H. Cook, the enthusiastic sharpshooter company commander, took out his men on an expedition between the lines, where they blazed away at the Rebel pickets. Cook recklessly exposed himself while firing, and, as a result, was severely wounded by a Confederate firing a muzzleloader. The Massachusetts men quickly learned that while Spencers provided an edge, they did not make men invulnerable. This was brought home more firmly to the Third Maryland Battalion a few weeks later. The Maryland men were assigned to support the attack on the Confederate lines at Petersburg in the wake of the huge mine explosion of July 30, 1864. Lieutenant colonel Gilbert P. Robinson led fifty-eight Spencer-armed soldiers of the battalion to secure the perimeter of the breach blown in the enemy lines. Robinson noted that "the effectiveness of the Spencer rifle in good hands was abundantly demonstrated during the

day," but his men eventually had to withdraw due to the overall chaos surrounding the failed operation.[35]

Wilson's raid south of Petersburg ended the major cavalry combat of
Grant's overland campaign. Although infantry use of repeaters in the Eastern
armies was minimal in the spring and summer of 1864, for the first time in a
major offensive east of the Appalachians, a significant number of horsemen
had been equipped with repeating carbines. The issue of Spencers to selected regiments in Sheridan's corps, coupled with the corps' tactical employment, had a marked effect on its operations and successes over two months
of sustained combat. The Spencer proved extremely useful in dismounted
combat when a regiment could hold a position even against infantry assault
by virtue of its firepower, as proved by the Fifth New York's fight in the
Wilderness and that of the First New York Dragoons at Cold Harbor. In the
hands of infantrymen from the Seventh Connecticut, the repeating carbine
once again proved a valuable defensive arm against infantry armed with conventional weaponry.

Although the Sharps, taking into consideration its automatic wafer priming system and the time necessary to reload the seven-shot Spencer magazine, had an overall rate of fire not all that inferior to the Spencer, the copper
Spencer cartridges were far more durable than the linen Sharps ammunition.
Prior to the Wilson raid, General Kautz pointed out that the "Sharps carbine
is a favorite arm, but the ammunition in a few days' marching deteriorates so
much as to be a serious objection, as ammunition trains can seldom be taken
on cavalry expeditions, and therefore only a limited supply can be carried by
the men. The same objection exists against all paper cartridges."[36]

In the offense, the Spencer's success was more problematic. At Yellow
Tavern, Custer used his repeaters creatively as a firepower element paired
with the shock action of a mounted saber charge. Firepower alone, however,
was not necessarily decisive. At Haw's Shop the First Pennsylvania's troopers
poured over 18,000 Spencer bullets into the position held by Butler's
Brigade, which held them off with rifle musket fire. Custer's advance, coupled with the Carolinians' withdrawal, which brought them out in the open
and made them vulnerable, was more successful. In short, it is evident that
then, as now, small arms firepower alone was not sufficient to decide an
offensive action against a well-drilled unit fighting from behind good cover.
A combination of good maneuvering skills coupled with Spencer firepower,
however, showed exceptional tactical promise. In the Seventh Connecticut,
at least, the threat of men losing control and shooting away all their ammunition was lessened by the institution of fire discipline through use of the
bugle, the traditional communication method of rifle regiments.

Although Sheridan's campaign revealed that the Spencer was not the answer to all the Union's problems, it also became clear that the repeating rifle was no longer an experimental or unneeded luxury for the average soldier, but a necessity. General Kautz said it best before the campaign began: "The best carbines for cavalry are breech-loading repeaters, with metallic percussion cartridges. Of this kind Spencer's carbine is preferred, next the Henry rifle or carbine." There was no argument with that premise anywhere in the Union army anymore, least of all in the west, where the Spencer and the Henry both increased their reputations in the spring and summer of 1864.[37]

As Grant and Meade closed in on Richmond, General Sherman pressed General Joseph Johnston's Confederate Army of Tennessee back on Atlanta. Sherman's consolidated forces included the Army of the Cumberland (IV, XIV, and XX Corps) under Major General George Thomas, the Army of the Tennessee, commanded by Major General James B. McPherson (XV, XVI, and XVII Corps), and Major General John M. Schofield's Army of the Ohio (XXIII Corps). These infantry forces, including infantry, cavalry, artillery, and support troops, totaled over 100,000 men.

Repeating rifles were scattered throughout Sherman's army, with a number of privately owned Henrys in such units as the Seventh, Sixty-fourth, Sixty-sixth, and Eighty-sixth Illinois. In May 1864 the unit with the most Henrys was no doubt the Sixty-sixth, but as the campaign wore on, deliveries directly to the front continued unabated. A July 29, 1864, letter from a soldier in the Seventh Illinois, for example, noted that "Captain Smith got through with our 16 shooters day before yesterday." The unit's historian recorded that by September "the regiment is now armed with the Henry repeating rifle, which was obtained by the men at their own expense." In July a man in the Sixty-fourth Illinois reported to his hometown newspaper that "the Henry's repeating rifles…are a breech loader, and a more efficient weapon, as a man can load and fire 16 loads in the same length of time it would take to load and fire one shot with a muzzle loader. They have a metalic cartridge and do not need caps. A part of the regiment are armed with these guns and all of the boys will be if the guns can be obtained. We have to pay for our own guns." None of these units was, despite popular impression, entirely armed with Henrys. At the end of the third quarter of 1864, for example, the Seventh Illinois still carried 337 rifle muskets on its ordnance reports, and the Sixty-fourth, 424. One Henry owner in the latter regiment wrote that "the rest of the regiment have Whitney or Windsor rifles and the Springfield rifle. These latter are good guns but not half so good as the Henry rifle."[38]

Spencers, issued by the government rather than privately purchased, were, of course, more common. A few infantry regiments, including Colonel Walcutt's Forty-sixth Ohio boys, were armed with the Spencer rifle. Five companies of the 102nd Illinois were mounted in August 1863 and provided with Spencers. The regiment was dismounted before the Atlanta campaign, but still counted 173 Spencer rifles, in addition to fifty-three Springfield and 284 Enfield rifle muskets on its ordnance report for the second quarter of 1864. The men of the Fourteenth Michigan, also mounted and issued Spencers around the same time, retained their repeaters when returned to the ranks as foot soldiers as well. Like Henrys, Spencers continued to arrive during the course of the campaign. When the men of the Second Michigan Cavalry returned from their veteran reenlistment furlough, they were rewarded with Spencer carbines, which they considered "the newest and most effective weapon in the service." The Fourth Iowa Cavalry was issued Spencer carbines at Memphis on July 4, and the men of the Third Ohio Cavalry exchanged their Sharps and Burnside carbines for Spencers on August 13.[39]

Brigadier General Kenner Garrard's Second Division of the Army of the Cumberland's Cavalry Corps fielded the largest concentration of Spencers in Sherman's army. Garrard's division included the Lightning Brigade mounted infantry and Colonel Minty's crack cavalry brigade. Although recruits had augmented the Lightning Brigade's manpower, the new men were armed with "old Burnside carbines—no better for actual service . . . than potatoe pop guns." More important, although Wilder, returned from sick leave, retained command, his and Rosecrans' tactical vision of a mounted infantry spearhead had been abandoned. More telling, Rosecrans' and Thomas' recommendations for Wilder's promotion went unfulfilled. On the positive side, Minty's three veteran regiments, the Fourth Michigan, Seventh Pennsylvania, and Fourth U.S. Cavalry, best known for their fine and aggressive work with the saber, were issued Spencer carbines in April 1864, making them the most versatile and well-armed cavalry brigade in the western armies. This combination, to which was added Colonel Eli Long's disciplined Ohio cavalry brigade, gave Garrard perhaps the best mounted division in the Union army.[40]

Sherman initiated his campaign in conjunction with that of the eastern armies, advancing on the Confederate Army of Tennessee, concentrated around Dalton, Georgia, on May 6. The Rebel commander, General Joseph Johnston, mustered around 55,000 men, with reinforcements on the way. The two armies first made contact at Rocky Face Ridge, where Sherman had McPherson and Schofield threaten the Confederate flanks while Thomas advanced on the enemy center. During some locally heavy skirmishing, Colonel Franklin Smith of the 102nd Illinois employed his Spencer-armed companies as skirmishers. The colonel believed that he had "evidence that the enemy suffered severely from the fire of my skirmishers, especially from the fire of the Spencer rifle." His position compromised by Federal forces on his flank, Johnston retreated to Resaca and entrenched.[41]

Federal attacks against the Resaca defenses on May 14 met with limited success, but a turning movement threatening the Army of Tennessee's rear, in which a Federal division across the Oostenaula River to the southwest of Resaca, caused Johnston to fall back once more. Henry rifles came to the notice of Brigadier General Grenville M. Dodge in a fight on May 15. The general noted that the Sixty-sixth Illinois, "in part armed with the Henry rifle (seventeen-shooters), by a stubborn resistance, and a steady, cool fire, checked the enemy's advance, and gave me time to throw forward to its support . . . the balance the of Second Brigade and part of the Third Brigade. The Sixty-sixth Illinois then fell back gradually to its supports." After skirmishing at Cassville on May 18, Johnston, advised by John Bell Hood (now a lieutenant general) and Leonidas Polk that their positions could be enfiladed, again withdrew to Altoona Pass. Following severe fighting at New Hope Church, Pickett's Mill, and Dallas on May 25, 27, and 28, Sherman once more maneuvered to threaten Johnston's lines of communication while returning to the railroad to ensure his own supplies, and Johnston responded by withdrawing once more.[42]

Part of the Federal line at Dallas was held by Colonel Walcutt's brigade, which repulsed an attack by Hood's corps. The Spencers wielded by Walcutt's old outfit, the Forty-sixth Ohio, allowed the regiment to deliver an intensive fire in the face of Rebel attack and also permitted Walcutt to cover a longer defensive line than he would have had his men been solely armed with muzzleloaders. The colonel reported after an attack by Hood's men that "244 dead and wounded rebels were found in my front." His Spencers had done their deadly work well. According to one veteran of the Forty-sixth they were also used with good effect shortly afterward. Walcutt's men gave a yell in conjunction with a bugle blast and the Rebels, anticipating an attack, manned the firing steps of their trenches with their heads exposed, only to be greeted by "seven volleys" from the regiment's "seven shooters."[43]

Johnston established a new line at Brush, Pine, and Lost Mountains. The Confederate position was a strong one, and it seemed unlikely that it could be easily penetrated. On June 5 Sherman's army arrived at Big Shanty. For two weeks the Union commander probed the enemy defenses and reorganized his forces while both sides skirmished and tested each other. On one occasion, Major General Daniel Butterfield reported to XX Corps commander Joe Hooker that a "force advanced to drive in our pickets on the right front, saying: 'Let's drive in the damned Yanks, and not let them fortify to-night.' The Spencer rifle sharpshooters of Seventy-ninth Ohio, one company, opened briskly on them and checked their advance."[44]

Fearing a flanking movement, a nervous Johnston abandoned the Brush, Pine, and Lost Mountain line and fell back to a new line based on Kennesaw Mountain. Uncharacteristically, considering his actions in the campaign to date, Sherman decided to make a frontal assault on the Confederate position at Kennesaw. His rationale appears to have been that after the series of flanking movements, Johnston would not expect a direct attack. The Yankee commander calculated it had a good chance of success, even though two solid weeks of rain had turned the red Georgia clay fields and hills his men would charge across and up into a morass of muck.

The Federal commander ordered an attack for June 27, assigning the divisions of Brigadier Generals Morgan L. Smith, John Newton, and Jefferson C. Davis to the task. The result was a bloody repulse by the Confederate divisions of Major Generals Patrick Cleburne and Benjamin F. Cheatham and Brigadier General Winfield S. Featherston. Brigadier General Dan McCook of Davis' division led his brigade right up to the Rebel line, and touched the enemy berm before being mortally wounded at point-blank range. Pinned down, many Federals dug in within yards of the Confederates.

The Eighty-sixth Illinois attacked the portion of the line known as the "Dead Angle" defended by Cleburne's and Cheatham's men. Sergeant John H. Brubacker of the Eighty-sixth recalled that he fell along with "seven shot dead and 14 wounded who lay in a heap around me." The regiment's Lieutenant Colonel Allen L. Fahnestock owned a Henry rifle, and thirty-six-year-old Principal Musician Alason P. Webber, whose usual position was behind the lines, asked to borrow it and go into combat that day. When the Eighty-sixth was pinned down in front of the Dead Angle, Webber advanced with Fahnestock's Henry and 120 rounds of ammunition. He made it to a tree "within twenty-seven feet of the Rebel line of battle," where he sniped at the enemy for hours to allow his comrades a chance to carry off their wounded. Webber won a Medal of Honor for his actions and was able to withdraw with his Henry to safety, but such was not the case with every Henry-armed soldier at Kennesaw. During a truce called to bury bodies two days after the fight, Confederate Captain Robert D. Smith, a member of General Cleburne's staff, "succeeded in getting 90 rifles from the field, 7 of them were Henry's patent, 16 shooters."[45]

Further to the left, Walcutt's brigade and two others made a diversionary attack on Little Kennesaw Mountain. Slipping and sliding on greasy mud and crawling through brush, pelted with bullets and even rocks rolled down the hillside, these Yankees were pinned down like their comrades attacking the Dead Angle. Fortunately for the rest of Walcutt's men, the Forty-sixth Ohio, which had used the shock action provided by its rapid-fire rifles to capture 120 Rebel skirmishers in the first rush, was able to provide a blistering covering fire so the rest of the brigade could

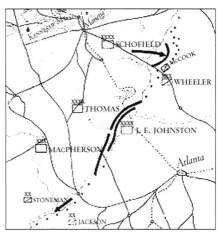

Union and confederate movements during the battles for Atlanta. (Adapted from the *West Point Atlas of American Wars*)

withdraw. All in all, the Kennesaw attack was a disaster for Sherman's army. The Federals lost 1,999 men killed and wounded and 52 missing, and the Confederates reported 270 killed and wounded and 172 missing, most of the latter scooped up by the Forty-sixth.[46]

Although Kennesaw was a Union defeat, Johnston retreated again in the face of Sherman's post-battle maneuvering, and attempted yet another stand along the Chattahoochee River line. The Lightning Brigade was ordered to cross the river in the face of Confederate pickets in rifle pits on the other side. Colonel Abraham Miller, who had replaced Colonel Wilder after Wilder had left the field and the brigade once more due to illness, ordered four companies of the Seventy-second Indiana to dismount and wade to the other side. The Hoosiers plunged into the water and immediately began to draw scattered fire. Because of their waterproof Spencer ammunition, they were able to load and fire back with impunity, sometimes even ducking beneath the water to lever another round in. One soldier heard a Rebel cry out, "Look at them Yankee sons of bitches, loading their guns under water." With their firepower supplemented by artillery and the rest of the brigade firing over their heads, the Indiana boys secured a bridgehead with no casualties.[47]

Multiple crossings by Union forces using fords and pontoon bridges all along the line on July 8 once more made Johnston's position untenable. The following night the Confederate commander slipped away to the outskirts of Atlanta, establishing a new line across Peach Tree Creek. Sherman's horsemen led the pursuit, and on July 14, the lead elements of Garrard's division, under Colonel Jonathan Biggs of the Lightning Brigade's 123rd Illinois, encountered a Rebel cavalry rear guard at Cross Keys. Biggs dismounted his ad hoc task force, which included the Seventy-second Indiana and Minty's Seventh Pennsylvania, and moved it forward in a loose skirmish formation. The three regiments fought a Tennessee cavalry brigade for several hours with inconclusive results before pulling back when Biggs thought his flank threatened. His total casualty list was one man wounded.[48]

President Jefferson Davis, in a Richmond threatened itself by relentless Union forces in midsummer, did not take Johnston's continual retrograde movements lightly. As Sherman closed in on Atlanta, the Confederate president relieved the Army of Tennessee's commander and replaced him on July 17 with General Hood, who, albeit with a reputation for tactical aggressiveness, had never held independent command before. The new commander was not long in fulfilling his stereotype and attacked Thomas' Army of the Cumberland after it crossed Peach Tree Creek three days later. During the attack, the colonel of the Spencer-armed 102nd Illinois later reported, "there being no enemy in our immediate front we changed our position by wheeling slightly toward the left and opened upon the advancing column an enfilading fire, pouring volley after volley in quick succession, such as the Spencer rifle alone can give, until we had the proud satisfaction of seeing the enemy vanquished and seeking safety in flight." Repulsed with heavy losses, Hood withdrew into the extensive prepared defenses surrounding Atlanta.[49]

Two days later Hood attacked again, sending Hardee's corps against the left flank and rear of McPherson's Army of the Tennessee while General Frank Cheatham hit it in front. The Rebel attack temporarily succeeded in surprising and driving back McPherson's force and killing him. As the Confederates swarmed toward the Yankee rear, they confronted Grenville Dodge's XVI Corps, which included the Sixty-sixth Illinois. In a standup firefight across an open field, the Sixty-sixth, which probably mustered more Henrys than any other unit in Sherman's army, formed a line of battle and blazed away. Private Prosper Bowe of the Sixty-sixth remembered that once "we started our sixteen shooters to work. The first column in front of us nearly all fell at the first two or three volleys." Bowe fired "ninety rounds without stoping." The Rebels were stopped cold by the torrent of fire, and, although they stood their ground for a while, fell back, fortunately for the Yankees, when Bowe and his comrades had just about shot up all their ammunition. After an ammunition resupply, the Sixty-sixth trotted two miles to the right and helped recover two Federal batteries that had been lost at the beginning of the attack. As initial advantage turned into defeat, Hood retreated, having

lost twice as many men as the
Yankees.[50]

Over the next two weeks
Sherman gradually tightened his
grip on Atlanta. On July 26, he
ordered Major General Oliver O.
Howard, now leading the Army of
the Tennessee, to move to the right
of the Army of the Cumberland. As
Howard approached Ezra Church
on July 28, skirmish firing steadily
increased. Although Sherman did
not expect another Confederate
attack, Stephen D. Lee, new to
corps command, launched a rash

Sherman's troops fought through the
tough mountainous landscape of northern Georgia as captured by Alfred R.
Waud in this watercolor. (*Library of
Congress*)

attack when he unexpectedly encountered Federal troops near Ezra Church
on the Lick Skillet Road. Lee's troops, joined in piecemeal attacks by elements of Stewart's corps, were easily repulsed by Maj. Gen. John Logan's XV
Corps. During the course of one of these desperate fights, Colonel John
Oliver, commanding the Third Brigade of the XV Corps' Fourth Division,
reported: "A part of the [Forty-eighth Illinois], armed with Smith and
Wesson rifles, running out of ammunition, had to withdraw." At a terrible
cost, the Rebels temporarily halted Logan's advance, but did not defeat
him.[51]

What Colonel Oliver meant by the "Smith and Wesson rifles" used by
men of the Forty-eighth is open to question. It is possible that he was referring to the Henry, with its strong resemblance to the prewar Volcanic rifle
and its association with Smith and Wesson, in an effort to identify the regiment's weapons. More likely, however, he meant the Frank Wesson (brother
of Edwin) single-shot .44 rimfire caliber military carbine. In late 1863 the
federal government bought 151 of these guns from B. Kittredge and
Company, a Cincinnati firearms distributor. Kittredge also sold Wessons to
the states of Indiana, Kansas, Kentucky, Missouri, and Ohio and no doubt
individual soldiers. Ammunition returns for Sherman's army reveal that it
consumed 80,000 rounds of "Smith and Wesson carbine cartridges" during
the Atlanta campaign.[52]

Unlike General Grant, who dispatched Sheridan on a massive raid with
his whole corps early in the campaign against Lee, during most of the Atlanta
campaign Sherman used his horsemen sparingly and in traditional roles. The
nominal commander of the Army of the Cumberland's Cavalry Corps,

Brigadier General Washington L. Elliott, for example, seldom left headquarters, much like General Pleasonton in Meade's Army of the Potomac. One of Elliott's division commanders stated he never saw him in the field.

In conjunction with his infantry moves around Atlanta, Sherman ordered his mounted divisions to raid and destroy the railroad running from the besieged city south to Macon. Brigadier General George Stoneman was instructed to take his division and Garrard's and head for Macon and Brigadier General Edwin M. McCook to lead his own and Brigadier General Lovell Rousseau's small divisions and strike the railroad at Lovejoy.

The Federal cavalry raids ended disastrously. On leaving the Union lines on July 27, Stoneman had taken his secondary mission, freeing Union prisoners at Andersonville, as a primary one. Unaccountably, he detached Garrard's large division, bristling with firepower, on a decoy course across the countryside, while he and 2,200 men headed for the prison camp. Blocked by Georgia militia and Major General Joseph Wheeler's cavalry, the inept Stoneman ended up surrendering with 700 of his men. McCook's raid was marginally more successful, and resulted in at least some damage to the railroad, but his force barely escaped as well, losing 500 men as prisoners. Garrard's division, in contrast, which had not been used to its full potential, ranged through Georgia without any serious resistance, and came into Union lines after having suffered few casualties with 172 prisoners, 100 liberated "contrabands," and a large number of captured horses and mules in tow.[53]

In early August, Sherman sidled once more to the right with his XXII and XIV Corps. By this point, however, he had stretched his lines so thin that he had to order Minty's and Miller's brigades of Garrard's division into the trenches to replace the infantrymen lengthening the siege lines. The Yankee horse soldiers, a little over 2,000 strong, replaced 11,000 infantrymen, but the fact that they were armed with Spencer rifles and carbines equalized the defensive firepower of the absent foot soldiers and made the substitution possible.

Sherman's infantry move west to Utoy Creek ended in stalemate. When Joe Wheeler's cavalry subsequently raided the Union lines of communication, Sherman responded by sending Kilpatrick's division, reinforced by Garrard's, on a raid toward Jonesboro. On August 20, at Lovejoy's Station, two of Minty's regiments dismounted to fight on foot and got caught by a small Rebel infantry brigade advancing at an oblique angle to their line. A volley of rifle musket fire at 150 yards followed by a bayonet charge routed the Spencer-armed Federals, many of them caught while trying to reload their carbines, with follower spring tubes out and shaky fingers dropping rounds down the buttstock magazine tubes. Minty's men ran until they reached Eli Long's brigade of Ohioans and an artillery battery and then made a stand, shooting it out at close range. Although the ever-effusive J. O. Buckeridge wrote that "more than 2,000 rebel infantry" were involved in "this rare victory of the muzzleloader over the repeater," a more scholarly account suggests that there were only about 300 Southern foot soldiers present on the field. Their advantage accrued from their tactical disposition. The Confederate infantry ran low on ammunition and withdrew but enemy cavalry then beset Kilpatrick's force. The Jersey general finally shot his way out of the situation, but did not accomplish his mission of destroying the railroad between Jonesboro and Griffin.[54]

Following Kilpatrick's failure, Sherman moved all of his infantry east and south toward the railroad once more. On August 31 his advance units cut the line into Atlanta in two places, triggering a reaction from Hood, who unleashed an attack by Hardee's and Lee's corps at Jonesboro. During the fight, Kilpatrick, who was screening the Union right, dismounted five of his cavalry regiments to fire into the flank of Cleburne's division. The cavalry was gradually pushed back by Confederate infantry, with the Spencer-armed Ninety-second Illinois Mounted Infantry covering its withdrawal, but the Confederates were unable to secure any advantage and withdrew to their own field works. Late on September 1 the Federals counterattacked the thinly manned Rebel lines and the XIV Corps broke through. Hardee retreated into the night, joining the rest of Hood's army, which then evacuated Atlanta. On September 2, the XX Corps, with flags flying and bands playing, marched into the city and occupied the old Rebel defensive positions. Atlanta was, as Sherman wrote, his, and "fairly won."[55]

The Atlanta campaign provided a good opportunity to field test both Henrys and Spencers in significant numbers. Much praise, and no serious complaints, attended the use of both guns under demanding combat conditions beset by dust, mud, rain, and excessive heat. Although units, either regiments within brigades or companies within regiments, armed with repeaters were likely to find themselves on the skirmish line more often than not, there was no concerted effort on the part of army or corps commanders to develop a tactical doctrine for the use of repeating rifles. Additionally, there was not, at any level of command, a significant effort to concentrate units armed with repeaters and use them as an offensive spearhead. The potential of the repeater in the offense may have begun to dawn on commanders at the end of the campaign, however. In the wake of Ezra Church, General Howard remarked that a cavalry attack "of two regiments, armed with Spencer rifles . . . rushed for the river-bank, and fired so fast that the rebels could with difficulty reply."[56]

Lower-level commanders realized that repeaters were a good thing to have available on the skirmish line and in the trenches, and no doubt some tactical thought went into the use of Garrard's division to replace a much larger number of infantrymen in the trenches at Atlanta. During the campaign the most notable and effective use of repeaters, including the Sixty-sixth Illinois' rescue of the XVI Corps baggage trains during the Battle of Atlanta, or the Forty-sixth Ohio's providing covering fire for a withdrawal at Kennesaw Mountain, was in a defensive role. An offensive doctrine was yet to evolve.

While it is impossible to determine the actual number of Henry rifles in use by Sherman's men, ammunition expenditure provides a few hints. A total of 21,340,222 Springfield and Enfield rifle musket cartridges were expended by his three armies, compared to 127,204 Henry rounds. If the expenditure tables are any indication, most of the Henrys were in General McPherson's (later Howard's) Army of the Tennessee, which consumed 93,655 of the .44 rimfire rounds, with 10,249 used by the Army of the Cumberland and 23,300 by the Army of the Ohio. According to Wiley Sword, there were about 250 Henrys in the ranks of the Sixty-sixth Illinois, or enough to arm around half of its men, in January 1864. Sword's analysis of the regiment, its arms, and its ammunition suggests that the Sixty-sixth expended approximately 83,500 rounds of .44 rimfire ammunition, or 89.2 percent of that used by the Army of the Tennessee, in the Atlanta campaign. Of course ammunition expenditure does not necessarily correlate with actual ammunition fired at the enemy. Included in these tables are cartridges that were lost or destroyed, the latter being a problem with paper or linen rounds which were subject to deterioration from weather and handling. Rimfire metallic cartridges were far more durable, however, and it is probably that most of the number noted was actually fired. By way of comparison, Sherman's armies also expended 390,322 Spencer carbine and rifle cartridges.[57]

During his long push south, Sherman was concerned about his rear areas and his long lines of communications, as well he should have been. Nathan Bedford Forrest was a particular annoyance to Sherman. The Confederate cavalryman, perhaps the best commander of horsemen on either side in the conflict, specialized in deep and successful raids, and bested a whole series of Union officers sent against him. On June 1, 1864, in conjunction with the Atlanta campaign, Brigadier General Samuel D. Sturgis was ordered to lead a column from Memphis against Forrest, who at that time was concentrating a large force at Tupelo, Mississippi, prior to attacking Sherman's supply lines. Sturgis' force of 3,300 cavalrymen and 5,000 infantry included the Spencer-armed Second New Jersey Cavalry.

Although a side raid to Rienzi by the Second was successful, Sturgis' main column staggered and straggled down bad roads into Mississippi. On June 10, a day the temperature rose to 107 degrees Fahrenheit, the Yankee cavalry, under Brigadier General Benjamin Grierson, ran into Forrest's horsemen at Brice's Crossroads. The outnumbered Rebels fell back slowly, managing to bluff the Yankees until Forrest's main force arrived. When the Confederates attacked a section of the line held by the Second New Jersey, the only unit in the whole force armed with Spencers, they came under heavy fire. One Tennessean recalled that "the fence and abatis were ablaze with the fire of the enemy's breech loaders, and the men began to fall thickly on the field." In order to counter the rapid volume of fire, Forrest's men began blazing away with their revolvers. Under pressure at another point, however, Colonel George E. Waring, the Jerseyans' brigade commander, pulled the regiment out of the firing line, which led to a Rebel breakthrough. Exhaustion, poor coordination, tactical miscues on the part of Sturgis, and Forrest's aggressive brilliance and personal charisma led to a subsequent Federal rout.[58]

The following day Sturgis assigned the Second New Jersey, which was still well organized, to rear guard duty. The Jerseymen pumped their Spencer levers for all they were worth, and managed to hold off the pursuing enemy until Sturgis and the remains of his force made good their retreat. Although the Second prevented what was already a disaster from turning into a catastrophe, it lost over fifty men when a company took a wrong turn in the dark and was captured.

The Jersey Spencers thus acquired went into Confederate service as their former owners were marched off to prison camps. By late 1864, the number of repeaters in use in Rebel ranks was increasing. Private William A. Fletcher of the Eighth Texas Cavalry was captured near Rome, Georgia that summer when his carbine malfunctioned, which puzzled him as it had never done so before and it "was loaded and had magazine full." Fletcher's recollection, some forty years later, may have been hazy, but the mention of a "magazine" denotes that he may well have been carrying a captured Spencer or Henry. In November 1864, one of Forrest's brigades reported seventy-three Spencers in use. An inspection report of Wade Hampton's Cavalry Division in the Army of Northern Virginia the same month revealed that four out of five brigades had some Spencers in service.[59]

A memoir account alleging that the servants of some of Forrest's men were armed with Spencers as early as Chickamauga, is, however, no doubt in error. While they may have been armed, at that date the only Spencers they could possibly have obtained were in the hands of Wilder's men, who lost their first half dozen or so in the fight for Alexander Bridge, when Confederate General Walker remarked on their novelty. In addition, if a few Spencers were indeed in Confederate possession it is unlikely that they would have been in the hands of rear area nominal non-combatants. By September 1864, though, numerous Spencers, principally carbines, had indeed fallen into Confederate hands. One account states that of the 2,001 Spencer carbines with which Minty's brigade began the Atlanta campaign, 1,000 were no longer on the brigade's reports by September. Many, if not most, of these guns were no doubt destroyed in combat or turned in to the Ordnance Department after soldiers were mustered out, wounded, or sent back to remount camp. It may safely be assumed, however, that some were likely in the possession of Joe Wheeler's cavalrymen by the fall of 1864.[60]

As autumn approached, the repeating rifle and carbine were finally firmly established as an important and appreciated military asset. The summer campaigns of 1864 proved to even the most skeptical and conservative Union commanders that the repeaters were the best fighting tools available, certainly for cavalry and probably for much of the infantry as well. Some of those commanders even began to consider ways to effectively use the increased firepower they once feared would be wasteful. Likewise, savvy Confederate officers like Nathan Bedford Forrest and John Mosby began to acquire as many Spencers and as much captured ammunition for their own men as they could. The final seven months of the war would witness the rapid escalation of all of these trends.

EIGHT

SHENANDOAH TO APPOMATTOX

IN THE SUMMER OF 1864, THE CITIZENS AND POLITICAL DENIZENS OF Washington came closer to the war than they ever had before. General Lee, locked in a life-and-death struggle with Grant and Meade at Petersburg, had been keeping track of Union General Hunter's movements up the Shenandoah Valley. Lee saw in the Shenandoah an opportunity to relieve pressure on his own front and create problems for his enemy at the same time. In June the Confederate commander sent Major General Jubal Early and his Second Corps of the Army of Northern Virginia to the valley. Early was ordered to defeat Hunter and then exploit the situation as he saw fit. Lee believed that a move down the valley toward Maryland and the District of Columbia would, as in previous years, shift the emphasis of the Army of the Potomac closer to home and perhaps reduce some of the attention on him. Since Grant had stripped the District of most of its defensive garrison for field service, the capital was more vulnerable than it had been at any time since the summer of 1861.[1]

Arriving in Lynchburg with 10,000 troops, Early picked up the local garrison and began to move north. Offering no resistance, Hunter retreated. Nervous about Guerrilla action against his long supply lines, the Federal general incredibly headed in the wrong direction, taking himself and his troops into the West Virginia wilderness and exposing Maryland and the capital. The other Federal commander in the Valley, Franz Sigel, who had been repulsed prior to Hunter's effort, holed up on Maryland Heights, across from Harper's Ferry, and allowed Early to bypass him. While this series of events transpired, Grant and Meade did nothing, unaccountably unaware, through a complete breakdown in intelligence, that Stonewall Jackson's old corps was heading toward Washington.

Although Early left Lee's army in the middle of June, Grant did not discover his whereabouts until July 5, when "Old Jubilee" crossed the Potomac. The way before him clear of serious potential opposition, Early mused on capturing Washington and liberating the Confederate prisoners of war at

Point Lookout on the Chesapeake. Armed with weapons from Washington's arsenals (including a growing trove of Spencer carbines) the freed prisoners would double his force.

Finally aroused to the danger, Grant detached the Third Division of the VI Corps and sent it to defend the capital. The division marched from the Petersburg lines in the early morning of July 6, boarded transports headed north, and eventually joined an ad hoc force of militia commanded by Major General Lew Wallace along the Monocacy River near Frederick, Maryland. On July 9, Wallace's force was attacked and defeated by Early's veterans. Wallace did, however, manage to hold up the Confederate advance long enough for the remaining two divisions of the VI Corps to reach Washington. Confronted by a strong force of seasoned Army of the Potomac veterans, Early withdrew from the capital suburbs and retired back into the Shenandoah Valley.

The Confederates remained a threat to the capital, as well as to Yankee resources in Maryland and Pennsylvania, however, and Grant assigned General Sheridan the dual task of destroying Early's army and the valley itself, long a source of Confederate supplies. Sheridan's new Army of the Shenandoah included a cavalry arm under General Torbert, consisting of Torbert's old division under General Custer and General Merritt's division, both from the Army of the Potomac, as well as General Averell's small cavalry division from Hunter's army. His infantry force included Major General Horatio G. Wright's VI Corps, Brigadier General William H. Emory's two XIX Corps infantry divisions recently arrived from Louisiana, and the two divisions of the VIII Corps, Hunter's former Army of West Virginia command now led by Brigadier General George Crook. Over the next month and a half the Army of the Shenandoah marched up and down the Valley, shadowed by Early's Rebels, as both commanders maneuvered for position.

Sheridan had a considerable edge on Early in both manpower and firepower. When the campaign began, the Irishman mustered a total of around 48,000 men, while Early's strength, which waxed and waned as reinforcements came and went, never exceeded 23,000. Most of Sheridan's available Spencers were the carbines his cavalry regiments brought with them from the Army of the Potomac, but some of his infantrymen were carrying repeaters as well, including a number of privately owned Henrys in the VIII Corps' Twenty-third Illinois. By mid-summer of 1864 there was a new, albeit limited, source of Spencer rifles for Union infantry use. The rifles became available when the Fifth and Sixth Michigan Cavalry exchanged their remaining rifles for carbines and the new Massachusetts contract was co-opted by the Federal government. While passing through Washington on July 14, the VI Corps' Thirty-seventh Massachusetts Infantry was issued Spencer rifles. Some men in other regiments armed themselves with breechloaders through their own actions. An ordnance inventory of the Fifteenth New Jersey Infantry taken on August 19 revealed that while most of the regiment was equipped with standard Springfield rifle muskets, two Jerseymen were carrying Sharps carbines and one a Spencer carbine. When these "unauthorized" weapons were turned in on August 30, the First Brigade of the VI Corps' First Division, the Fifteenth's parent unit, was issued sixteen Spencer rifles to arm a sharpshooter detachment command-ed from brigade headquarters. Six of the guns went to men from the Fifteenth.[2]

Spencers were much in demand among Sheridan's foot soldiers. On July 18, 1864, Colonel Elisha Hunt Rhodes of the Second Rhode Island Infantry borrowed forty of the Thirty-seventh Massachusetts' rifles to surprise some Rebel pickets who were sniping at his regiment. Armed with the Spencers, the Rhode Island men delivered a volley, and "the Rebels supposing we had the muzzle loading muskets would leave their shelter as soon as we fired and shout some insulting message. But they soon found out that the fire was kept up, my forty men doing the work of perhaps five times as many. One Rebel called out 'I say, Yankees, what kind of guns have you got?' Our reply was another volley."[3]

In September, Sheridan turned on Early, attacking his army at Winchester in an attempt to catch the Rebel leader with his forces divided. Although Federal cavalry rapidly crossed the Opequon River and dispersed light opposition, a traffic jam that developed in the Union army's passage through the Berryville canyon allowed the Confederates to concentrate in front of Winchester, just in time to reinforce Major General Stephen D. Ramseur's hard-pressed men. Major General John B. Gordon's division delivered a smashing counterattack against the Union right, stopping the XIX Corps cold, while Major General Robert E. Rodes' division moved up to cover Gordon's right.

The VI Corps continued to advance on Ramseur when the XIX stopped, opening up a gap that provided a golden opportunity to Brigadier General Cullen A. Battle's Alabamans, who charged through the gap in Sheridan's line. The First New Jersey Brigade, under Lieutenant Colonel Edward L. Campbell, plugged the gap temporarily, giving division commander Brigadier General David A. Russell time to arrange an impromptu defense. One important cog in that defense was the Thirty-seventh Massachusetts. As the Jerseymen fell back, the Bay State boys advanced through them and laid down a blizzard of bullets to halt the enemy advance.[4]

As a stalemate developed along the line of battle, the Thirty-seventh ran short of ammunition. Colonel Rhodes of the Second Rhode Island was ordered by his brigade commander to "help out" the Massachusetts men, who were now in front of the main Union line lying down in front of a redoubt. Rhodes, who accounted the Thirty-seventh "one of the best regiments I ever saw," ordered his own regiment to move along the line of battle under fire to a position in the rear of the Thirty-seventh. Fortunately, the army's wagons were just behind the Second's position and Rhodes "saw the ammunition train and on one wagon in large letters '37th MASS,'" indicating that regiment's backup supply of cartridges. His men ran to the wagon, broke open ammunition crates, filled their pockets with pasteboard boxes of .56-.56 rounds, and carried them across the field to the Thirty-seventh, which had indeed shot away its ammunition and was lying helpless under fire. Resupplied, the Bay State men resumed firing, pinning down the Rebels to the front in their redoubt. Colonel Oliver Edwards, commanding the Thirty-seventh's brigade, did not report the ammunition resupply, but noted that the regiment "lost over one-third its number, nothing but their . . . Spencer rifles" enabling the Massachusetts men to hold on. Rhodes, a gun buff who served as president of the Officer's Rifle Association of Rhode Island in the 1890s, was impressed enough with the Spencer to carry a carbine as his personal weapon in the closing months of the war.[5]

After General Crook moved his VIII Corps to the XIX's right and managed to lap around the Confederate left flank, the whole Yankee line began to advance. As the enemy infantrymen started to give way, a massive mounted attack from the Union cavalry smashed the Rebel horse and completely penetrated the Confederate left flank. Early's routed army, its commander cursing his cavalrymen, fled south down the Valley Pike, but rallied and established a new line atop Fisher's Hill. Three days later Crook's VIII Corps once more outflanked the Rebels and in combination with another frontal assault, routed them. Following his victory at Fisher's Hill, Sheridan began to ravage the Shenandoah Valley, and his men lived high on confiscated livestock and produce.

As Sheridan despoiled his way back down the valley, his army was shadowed by Confederates, particularly General Thomas L. Rosser's "Laurel Brigade" of Virginia cavalry, which harassed the Yankee rear guard. Dubbed "the Savior of the Valley," Rosser could do little against the heavily armed Yankee horse, but he was an annoyance to Sheridan, who told Torbert, his erratic chief of cavalry, to either whip Rosser or get whipped himself.

On October 9, Torbert turned on his pursuers and launched the divisions of Custer and Merritt at Rosser's force. The Rebels got whipped. At a cost of fifty-six casualties, the Federal horsemen inflicted 400, capturing nearly all of Rosser's wagons and eleven of his twelve artillery pieces in an affair which became known as the Battle of Tom's Brook, but was popularly called the "Woodstock Races." Ironically, Rosser's defeat was a result of a mounted fight, the type of combat that had been the forte of the Confederates three years earlier. Spencer firepower played no significant part in the affair. There were some Henrys captured from the First D.C. Cavalry near Petersburg in use in the Laurel Brigade, including a dozen in the Eleventh Virginia Cavalry, but they had no noticeable role in the action either.[6]

Pure saber- and revolver-wielding Confederate cavalry, except for Guerrilla raiders who fairly bristled with handguns and specialized in hit-and-run operations, was decidedly in the eclipse in 1864. On the other hand, muzzle-loading rifle musket or rifle-armed Rebel horsemen like those commanded by Lieutenant Colonel Witcher or General Butler were still a significant battlefield presence wherever they appeared. That fall a Yankee trooper in the Shenandoah confided to Captain John W. DeForest of the Twelfth Connecticut Infantry that "at close range we can whip [Brigadier General Lunsford L.] Lomax's [cavalry]men; they have no sabres and generally no revolvers. But at long range we are rather afraid of them; they carry Enfields which shoot farther than our carbines."[7]

With Jubal Early apparently soundly beaten after Fisher's Hill, the valley campaign seemed over, and the VI Corps men prepared to return to the trenches at Petersburg. There was one more card in the Rebel leader's hand, however, and he chose to play it on October 19, launching a pre-dawn surprise attack on the Army of the Shenandoah's camp at Cedar Creek while General Sheridan, returning from a visit to Washington, slept soundly at Winchester. The Rebels overran and routed the VIII Corps, badly battered the XIX Corps, and then swarmed toward the VI Corps camps. The VI Corps, which had warning enough to form into line of battle, managed to stage a fighting withdrawal to a position overlooking its old camps. It is perhaps an indication of how badly Sheridan believed Early had been beaten that prior to the attack he had detached the Thirty-seventh Massachusetts and its Spencers from the army to serve as the garrison of Winchester, miles away.

While the successful Confederate attack degenerated into an exercise in camp looting, Sheridan arrived on the battlefield and rallied other troops to join the VI Corps and his cavalry in launching a counterattack, which swept Early's disorganized army from the field. The Union victory at Cedar Creek ended major fighting in the Shenandoah Valley, allowing the VI Corps to return to the Petersburg lines in December.

Although repeating rifles did not play a significant part in the overall Shenandoah campaign, they were featured in a side struggle. In August, frustrated by the Guerrilla operations of John S. Mosby's Partisan Rangers and others, who would hit his supply lines and then disperse, Sheridan turned to General Crook, his old West Point roommate, for advice. Crook, who spent much of the war in West Virginia, had formed a special unit dubbed the Legion of Honor to scout and suppress guerrillas in his area of operations, and offered his Legion to Sheridan to hunt down Mosby's Forty-third Virginia Partisan Ranger Battalion. Commanded by West Virginia-born Captain Richard Blazer of the Ninety-first Ohio, the 100-man detachment, now dubbed Blazer's Scouts, soon began to pursue Confederate irregulars in the Shenandoah. Although Blazer's prime target was Mosby, he also stalked any Rebel Guerrilla targets of opportunity who crossed his men's path.[8]

Convinced by his spring campaign of the efficacy of the Spencer carbine, Sheridan wrote Major General Christopher C. Augur, commanding the Department of Washington: "I have 100 men who will take the contract to clean out Mosby's gang. I want 100 Spencer rifles for them. Send them to me if they can be found in Washington." The Union commander no doubt knew the difference between rifles and carbines, and his specific request for the harder to acquire rifles may have come from a perceived accuracy and range advantage of the latter. Whether or not rifles or carbines were delivered is unclear, as a Confederate newspaper account has Blazer's men armed with Spencer carbines.[9]

Throughout late summer and into the fall, Blazer's men picked off Mosby's troopers and guerrillas from other commands and then surprised and routed one of Mosby's companies at Myers' Ford. Although Blazer claimed "the seven shooters proved too much for them," his success at Myers' Ford was determined as much by his swift movements and mastery of surprise than his men's Spencers. Mosby's men certainly weren't afraid of Spencers. Several days prior to the Myers' Ford affair, the Partisan Rangers wrecked a detachment of the Spencer carbine-armed Sixth New York Cavalry under Major William E. Beardsley. Beardsley deployed some of his men as dismounted skirmishers, and kept others on horseback as a reserve, a standard tactical disposition. Confederate Captain Samuel Chapman split his two-company force and hit the Yankees in a mounted rush from different directions. With revolvers blazing, his men overran the Federal skirmishers and slammed into the Sixth's reserve force, routing it.[10]

As major battles raged and then abated in the valley, Blazer's counterinsurgency campaign continued apace. Despite a number of small successes, the Yankee captain was not able to seriously degrade Mosby's battalion, which, at that time, numbered "between 600 and 700 men." Blazer proved a serious annoyance to the Rebel partisan ranger leader, however—so much so that Mosby specifically instructed one of his most trusted subordinates, Captain Dolly Richardson, to "wipe Blazer out." The captain, a talented tactician, took his instructions seriously.[11]

Richardson's force, numbering around 100 men, encountered Blazer's Scouts, at that time sixty-two strong, at Kabletown on November 17. While one company engaged Blazer's men and then pulled back in the face of Spencer fire from dismounted skirmishers, another company waited, mount-

Harper's Weekly artist Alfred R. Wauld's sketch of Sheridan's march through the Shenandoah Valley after his army's victory at Fisher's Hill. (*Library of Congress*)

ed, in concealment. As the Yankees pursued Richardson's withdrawing company, it suddenly turned and attacked, reserving revolver fire until close range. Simultaneously, the men of the concealed company hit Blazer in the flank, rapidly firing their handguns as well. Outnumbered and outgunned, the Scouts collapsed and fled, closely pursued by the guerrillas, who carried as many as four revolvers each. Blazer briefly rallied some of his men in Myerstown, but was overrun by charging Rangers. In the end, the Federal counterinsurgency force was effectively destroyed, with sixteen men killed and between eleven and thirty, including Blazer himself, captured. In the wake of Kabletown, Sheridan abandoned the idea of special operations to combat guerrillas, and looked to increasing his ravaging of the insurgents' civilian base to solve the problem. It never did.[12]

While Sheridan's army was securing the safety of the military and civilian bureaucracy in Washington, technical change marched on. Although General Ramsay had enthusiastically supported the introduction of breech-loading and even repeating rifles in the army, he had not lived up to the hopes of ordnance progressives in other areas and had become involved in a political dispute concerning suppliers of the Absterdam artillery shell. As a result Ramsay was relieved of command on September 12, 1864, and replaced by Major Alexander Dyer, who was elevated to brigadier general over many officers his senior.

Although superintendent of Springfield Armory, and thus tasked with producing muzzleloaders, Dyer, the first officer to test the Spencer, was accounted one of the most progressive ordnance men in the army, and not hesitant in predicting that breech-loading arms were the future, and that the future had arrived. Shortly after his appointment, Dyer, citing foreign developments, proposed that, although "the use of breech-loading arms has, with few exceptions, been confined to mounted troops," that experience "indicates the advisability of extending this armament to our infantry also." He also recommended that, for the sake of quality control and design, any new breechloaders be manufactured by the government, not "private armories."[13]

As part of his emphasis on modernizing the army's small arms and giving the government a controlling interest in this effort, the new ordnance chief launched a Springfield Armory program to develop a .50 caliber self-contained rimfire round for which all private carbine contractors would be expected to chamber their arms. The armory had, under Ramsay's instructions, been working on a .44 caliber cartridge during most of 1864, but that project was discarded in favor of what came to be called the .50 caliber Springfield carbine cartridge. Later known commercially as the .56-.50 Spencer, the round had a slightly tapered cartridge case with a 350-grain bullet loaded ahead of forty-five grains of black powder, producing a muzzle velocity of 1,200 feet per second. The Crittenden and Tibbals .56-.56 round, by way of contrast, launched a 350-grain nominally .54 diameter bullet at around 900 feet per second. Not only was the .50 caliber cartridge flatter shooting and thus more tolerant of range estimation errors, but the lubrication grooves of its bullet were contained within the copper case, protecting the lubricant from drying out or collecting foreign matter that might damage the gun's bore on firing. The fact that the bullet was more deeply seated in the case also made the new ammunition more sturdy overall. The .50 carbine cartridge could be chambered and fired in the older Model 1860 .56-.56 Spencers (although the cartridge case would split), but the reverse was not true.[14]

Along with chambering its guns for the .50 caliber round, Dyer requested the Spencer Company to make some physical changes to the Model 1860 carbine, including shortening its barrel from twenty-two to twenty inches. This and other minor manufacturing modifications led to a weight reduction from nine pounds two ounces to eight pounds five ounces for the new "Model 1865" carbine. The Burnside Rifle Company of Providence, Rhode

Island, also manufactured the 1865 carbine. On applying for a new contract for their single-shot breechloader in May 1864, Burnside executives had been advised that the price paid for their gun would be reduced, as it was not as desirable as it had once been. General Ramsay wrote that "repeating arms are the greatest favorites with the army and should be supplied in quantities," and the Burnside Company took his words to heart, subsequently signing a contract to make repeaters under license from Spencer along with their own carbines. The Burnside contract, originally for Model 1860 Spencers, was subsequently changed to require Model 1865 carbines fitted with the "Stabler magazine cut-off," a device invented by Edward Stabler. When in use, the cut-off blocked the magazine, allowing the gun to be single loaded with seven shots held in reserve until needed. Model 1865 carbines of both Spencer and Burnside manufacture were not delivered to the government until April 1865, too late for use in the war, and most of them were not fitted with the Stabler cut-off.[15]

Alexander Byrdie Dyer (1815 –1874), was chief of Stephen W. Kearny's ordnance during the War with Mexico and, although a native Virginian, remained with the Union at the start of the Civil War. He continued in his capacity as an expert of ordnance and was in charge of the Springfield Armory until finally assuming the mantle of Chief of Ordnance of the U.S. Army in 1864. (*Arlington Cemetery*)

While Oliver Winchester was still angling for government contracts in the late fall of 1864, he was not about to submit a bid to manufacture Spencers. When B. Tyler Henry's contract to produce the gun that bore his name expired in late spring, C. M. Manning replaced the inventor as superintendent at Winchester's New Haven factory. The new factory at Bridgeport, operated by Allen Bowe for Winchester, was now able to produce Henrys as well. Within a month after Henry left the New Haven plant its staff almost doubled, from thirty-three to sixty-five workers, and by September there were 100 employees working at Bridgeport, thirty-seven of them women making .44 cartridges.[16]

With higher potential production in the offing, Winchester tried again to interest the army in his carbine variant of the Henry, which featured a more powerful .44 caliber cartridge. Winchester himself attended the tests this time, conducted by Lieutenant H. Stockton at the Washington, D.C.,

Arsenal on August 26, 1864. Again there were problems, including no half-cock or safety notch on the hammer, the failure of some of the ammunition to fire and excessive fouling that hampered operation of the gun. In the end, General Dyer's unfavorable assessment of the carbine in April remained unchanged. And since Dyer was now ordnance chief, there was no likelihood of orders for the new Henry.

Winchester was interested in product improvement that might eventually change the government's mind, though, and employed a full-time designer, George W. Briggs, to, among other things, make the Henry's feeding system less vulnerable to mud and rust. Briggs set about modifying the collar that fit over the magazine tube and barrel at the muzzle and was twisted to open the magazine for loading. New Haven Arms tried out one of Briggs' fixes, a locking sliding cover for the collar that protected it somewhat from the elements, on a government contract, but the order was not from the U.S. government. Winchester sought government work elsewhere, and the Briggs modification was applied to 500 rifles made for "Mad King Ludwig" of Bavaria in late 1864. In January 1865, Winchester and his chief financial partner, John M. Davies, ostensibly retired and turned rifle manufacturing over to their sons. Winchester then departed for Europe. Although his junket was no doubt planned as a much-needed vacation, he appears to have also used the opportunity as a sales trip and continued to pursue his interest in alternative magazines for the Henry. In the spring of 1865, Winchester had Swiss gun maker Weber Ruesch make him a rifle and shotgun based on the Henry action with a removable magazine spring and follower.[17]

Individual sales of Henry rifles continued apace throughout 1864, and not all of them to soldiers. Although the U.S. Navy had been the earliest contractor for Spencer rifles, and Navy Secretary Welles averred that "the Spencer rifle was much sought after and that officers once having it in use prefer it to any other," privately purchased Henrys saw maritime service as well. John S. Tennyson, who served as a pilot on several Mississippi River Squadron vessels, wrote New Haven Arms several times following his 1863 purchase of a Henry rifle. Tennyson, who piloted the *Black Hawk* on Major General Nathaniel P. Banks' ill-fated 1864 Red River expedition, stated that his "Henry rifle figured largely" in the campaign, but unfortunately neglected to elaborate. An avid target shooter, the pilot bragged that he had vanquished shooters of both Sharps and "Smith & Wesson" (most likely Wesson) rifles in matches fired at 400 and 500 yards. On June 23, 1864, Tennyson claimed he had fired over 2,000 rounds from his Henry to date and that although it had been hit twice by enemy fire, it was "in no way disabled."[18]

One infantry unit was actually issued Henry rifles by the War Department in late 1864 as well. The four-company Seventh West Virginia

Infantry Battalion, serving in the Petersburg lines with the II Army Corps, was issued Henrys, probably from the overage of the First D.C. Cavalry order, as an "acknowledgement of the superior qualities of the battalion." As the siege of Petersburg dragged on into the fall and winter, Union commanders began to realize the value of repeating rifles in the close-range sniping and picket fighting that developed as the armies skirmished with each other daily between sporadic line-lengthening battles. In September 1864, II Corps commander Major General Winfield Scott Hancock requested enough Spencers to arm six of his regiments. He received enough to arm "three small regiments" and picked one in each of his divisions, the First Delaware and the 105th and 148th Pennsylvania Infantry. Several regiments in the Army of the James, including the Tenth New Hampshire and 118th New York Infantry, were also issued Spencers. In October, the Third New Hampshire Infantry used its Spencer carbines to delay an enemy advance along the New Market Road. In his report of the affair, Lieutenant Colonel James Randlett remarked that he hoped "the importance of the repeating rifle or carbine for skirmishing will be fully appreciated, as . . . the same number of men armed with any other piece would not have held the enemy in check for a moment." Of a detachment of 2,650 men from the Army of the James sent to New York City in November to guarantee order during the elections, 500 were armed with either Spencer carbines or rifles.[19]

The Rebels were acquiring more repeaters as well. During a raid to capture a herd of 3,000 cattle at a Union supply depot at Coggins Point on September 16, Wade Hampton's cavalry encountered a herd guard of 250 men from the First D.C. and 150 from the Thirteenth Pennsylvania Cavalry at Sycamore Church. The Seventh Virginia Cavalry attacked dismounted, while other regiments enveloped the Federals. In the end, vastly outnumbered by the two brigades Hampton sent against them, the First D.C. troopers found that their Henrys did little good, as they were routed, with most ending up as prisoners. The Confederate army got a much needed supply of beef, several regiments of Rosser's Laurel Brigade captured the repeaters they would later bring with them to the Shenandoah—and Wade Hampton acquired his own personal Henry.

The seeming sudden desire to arm Army of the Potomac infantrymen at Petersburg with repeating rifles coincided with the continued development of dedicated division sharpshooter detachments. This later development might seem ironic, considering that the official sharpshooter regiments of the army, the First and Second U.S. (Berdan's) Sharpshooters were mustered out of service over the winter of 1864-1865 and their reenlisted veterans and recruits who still had time to serve were reassigned to regiments from their native states.

The Yankees were far behind their opponents in the Army of Northern Virginia in the creation of special sharpshooter units as integral segments of larger formations. Fred Ray's comprehensive study of the sharpshooter battalions of Lee's army traces their origins to a May 1862 act of the Confederate Congress. The law authorized "a battalion of sharp-shooters for each brigade, consisting of not less than three nor more than six companies, to be composed of men selected from the brigade, or otherwise, and armed with long range muskets or rifles." At the time, most Confederate units bearing the honorific title of "sharpshooters" did not fulfill the role, and initial attempts to create the companies and battalions specified by the legislation failed to mature.[20]

Ray dates the earliest formation of a true brigade sharpshooter battalion to December 1862, when Brigadier General Richard Rodes "felt the absolute need of trained skirmishers always ready to go to the front." Rather than trusting to random assignment of soldiers to the duty, Rodes assigned Major Eugene Blackford of the Fifth Alabama Infantry to create an elite "Corps of Sharpshooters" in his brigade. Each regiment supplied a company, selecting individual men judged on their "soldiering, marksmanship and 'fidelity to the Southern cause.'" Blackford, a crack shot who carried a Sharps breechloader himself, drilled his men in range estimation and how to properly adjust the sights of their Enfields. He also trained them constantly in open formation skirmishing tactics and in how to respond to bugle calls, the traditional method of controlling riflemen's movements on the skirmish line.[21]

Progress in establishing sharpshooter battalions throughout the Army of Northern Virginia was sporadic; some brigades created units and disbanded • them after the campaign season ended, others maintained them year round, and still others neglected to form them at all. Over the winter of 1863-1864, however, the battalions were established on a permanent basis. They were composed of three or four sixty-man companies each and were to assume all skirmishing, scouting, and picket duties for their parent units when the army was in contact with the enemy.

Individual soldiers assigned to the battalions were picked applying the same criteria Blackford used for his 1862 unit and were trained in the same manner, using the tactical concepts laid out in Confederate Brigadier General Cadmus Wilcox's translation of a French manual on shooting and skirmishing. The sharpshooters were armed with muzzleloaders, preferring the shorter-barreled Enfield rifle used by the British army's rifle regiments. They were not "snipers" in the modern sense, although some units were issued limited numbers of long-range British Whitworth or Kerr rifles, some with telescopic sights. The sharpshooters more closely resembled World War

A squad from the Second US Sharpshooters photographed in early 1862, when they were still armed with Colt Revolving rifles. (*USAMHI*)

I German storm troopers, and Ray's use of the term "shock troops" to describe them is entirely appropriate. The fact that the aggressive sharp-shooters were the spearhead of the advance and the rearmost element of the rear guard of the Army of Northern Virginia in the summer and fall of 1864 contributed mightily to that army's resilience and survival.[22]

It is difficult to assess if the division sharpshooters that began to appear in the Union armies in 1864 were selected as rigorously as their Confederate counterparts, but they must have been subject to some selection process. There is evidence of men being detailed, at least temporarily, as "brigade sharpshooters" in the Army of the Potomac as early as the spring of 1863, when Colonel Roy Stone of the 149th Pennsylvania reported that his brigade sharpshooters captured twenty-four Confederates at Chancellorsville. At the same battle, Colonel Byron R. Pierce of the Third Michigan reported that designated "sharpshooters" covered his brigade's front. Colonel William Smyth of the Thirty-first Iowa notes that his unit was screened by the "divi-sion sharpshooters" at one point during the Atlanta campaign and seems to differentiate between them and the usual skirmish line, but does not elabo-rate. What criteria were used to select these men and how permanent their organization was is unknown, and there is no indication of any special efforts to supply them with advanced arms.[23]

In April 1864, the Fifteenth New Jersey, and by implication other Union units, selected a regimental sharpshooter detachment based on scores in a target shooting match held at 300 yards as well as the men's "coolness under fire and undaunted courage." What tasks these soldiers were assigned in the Overland Campaign is, considering the available sources, impossible to determine, as the otherwise detailed diary of the Fifteenth's adjutant, Lieutenant Edmund Halsey, is silent on the matter.[24]

By the end of 1864, however, division sharpshooters are regularly mentioned in reports of the XVIII Army Corps and General Getty's division of the VI Corps. In the wake of the Crater battle, Lieutenant Colonel Robinson of the Spencer-armed Third Maryland Battalion of the IX Corps suggested that the actions of his men, who "did great execution upon the enemy" in an ultimately losing cause, "demonstrated the advantages of an organized corps of sharpshooters." The obvious implication to be drawn from Robinson's conclusion is that those sharpshooters should be armed with Spencers.[25]

As fall deepened and visions of a grim winter began to set in upon the Petersburg siege lines, armies were on the move to the south and west. Following the fall of Atlanta, General Hood withdrew to Lovejoy and then to Palmetto, where he resupplied and reorganized his diminished army. Forrest and Wheeler remained a threat to the long Federal line of communications, and Sherman detached the reliable General Thomas to take charge of it and the Union defenses of Chattanooga and Nashville. In October Hood began to move his army, three corps commanded by Generals Cheatham, Lee, and Stewart, north. Stewart's corps, aided by Rebel cavalry, began to wreck Sherman's lifeline to Tennessee, the Western and Atlantic railroad, scooping up small Yankee garrisons deployed to protect the tracks at Big Shanty, Moon's Station, and Acworth. Hood directed Stewart to order General French to take his division to Allatoona pass and block the railroad at that narrow gap in the mountains. French arrived at Allatoona, a major Federal supply depot north of Kennesaw Mountain, early on the morning of October 5.[26]

Sherman had reinforced the Allatoona garrison just in time, and, as luck would have it, one of the regiments that reached the pass before the Rebels was the Seventh Illinois, a regiment with a number of Henrys in the ranks. The Seventh, along with the Thirty-ninth Iowa and the Ninety-third Illinois, a total of 904 men, were deployed in some field works in front of one of several redoubts thrown up to protect the railroad and supply dump.

French ordered two of his brigades, totaling 1,350 men, to assault the position held by the three regiments. The Seventh and Thirty-ninth took the brunt of the attack. The attacking Rebels ran into heavy fire from front and flank, however, as other Federals fired into them as well. The historian of the Seventh recalled that "the sixteen shooters are doing their work; the very air seems to go faint as it breathes their lurid flame." Despite the fire, French's men managed to cut their way though a tangled abatis and overrun the Yankee position, inflicting heavy losses on the Seventh and Thirty-ninth. All three regiments fell back to the redoubt, where they remained pinned down

The men of the color guard of the Seventh Illinois Infantry, a unit with a significant number of Henrys in its ranks, pose with their flag at the end of the war.
The Seventh's toughest fight was at Allatoona. (*Library of Congress*)

by withering Rebel musketry. Although French's assault was initially successful, in the end it proved a bloody stalemate. The Federals hung on in the
redoubt, the Confederates ran low on ammunition, and French, wary of
Sherman advancing to the rescue, abandoned his attack.[27]

Although there is no doubt that the Seventh Illinois had some Henrys at
Allatoona, how many they had and how decisive they were in helping the
garrison hold on is inconclusive, despite the regimental historian's florid
1868 rhetoric that "their sixteen shooters are performing a terrible work of
death." There is no mention of the efficacy of the repeaters in any of the
Federal after-action reports, and a review of the Seventh's Quarterly
Ordnance report for the fourth quarter of 1864 reveals that the regiment still
carried 274 rifle muskets. According to reliable accounts, the Seventh only
took nine of its ten companies, totaling 291 men, into the battle, losing forty-
eight of them killed or mortally wounded in the fight. There is evidence of
Henrys received by some men of the regiment at the end of July 1864.
Although the postwar Illinois Adjutant General's report and the famous pic-
ture of the unit's Henry armed color guard taken at the close of the war suggest that the regiment was largely armed with the rifles from 1864 on, the
actual number of Henrys in the ranks that October is unknown. An educated guess would involve figuring the Seventh's total strength, including the
missing company, at approximately 320, thus accounting for approximately
forty-six Henrys. A fair amount of firepower, to be sure, but not enough to
prevent the regiment from being overrun by French's men.[28]

With a garrison of Union troops still in Atlanta, Sherman's field army occupied a position near Rome. Hood planned to move further north into Tennessee, drawing Sherman with him, but the Federal commander made other plans—to sever his lines of communication entirely and strike out for the coast. In late October, leaving the IV and XXIII Corps and most of his cavalry with Thomas, Sherman returned to Atlanta, and on November 15, after destroying everything that might be of military value in the city, struck out on his *chevauchée* to Savannah. Sherman's army, around 62,000 men strong, included a two-brigade cavalry division under Judson Kilpatrick and the XIV, XV, XVII, and XX Corps, and was divided into two wings led by Major Generals Howard and Henry W. Slocum.

Kilpatrick had one regiment armed with Spencer rifles in each of his brigades; the Eighth Indiana Cavalry, which as the Thirty-ninth Indiana Mounted Infantry had fought alongside the Lightning Brigade at Chickamauga, served in Colonel Eli H. Murray's First Brigade. Colonel Smith D. Atkins' Second Brigade included the Ninety-second Illinois Mounted Infantry. Although not formally part of Kilpatrick's division, the Ninth Illinois Mounted Infantry added another 170 Spencer rifles to the army's horseback firepower base. Repeating rifles were scattered throughout the ranks of the army's infantry, including the Spencers of the Forty-sixth Ohio and the Henrys of the Sixty-sixth Illinois. Opposing this Yankee juggernaut was a force of around 13,000 men, divided between Georgia militia and Wheeler's cavalry, under the overall command of General Hardee.[29]

There was little serious fighting in the March to the Sea. Sherman's men were largely unopposed, and when they were, the opposition was usually futile. One such fight took place at Griswoldville, site of Samuel Griswold's revolver factory. During the Civil War, feeble attempts at domestic arms production contributed little to the Southern war effort, but Griswold did better than most manufacturers. Ironically, the Rebel gun maker was a Connecticut Yankee who had, prior to the war, built several mills and factories to make soap, candles, and cotton gins at Griswoldville in partnership with Daniel Pratt of New Hampshire. The little town that resulted from the partners' industrial efforts, also known as Griswold Station, grew up along the Central Railroad of Georgia near Macon.[30]

In 1862 Griswold converted his cotton gin factory to the production of pikes, long obsolete weapons promoted by Georgia governor Joseph Brown, perhaps emulating the late but unrelated John Brown, as good home-guard arms. Later that year Griswold partnered with a Mr. Gunnison to produce more realistic armament, copies of the .36 caliber Model 1851 Navy Colt revolver. Short of steel, Griswold used bronze for his revolver frames and iron for other parts and managed, with a workforce of twenty-four, twenty-two of whom were slaves, to turn out an average of five handguns a day through November 22, 1864, when Colonel Murray's cavalry came a-knocking.[31]

After an initial skirmish with Wheeler's Rebel horsemen, backed up by Georgia militia infantry, Murray was reinforced by General Walcutt's foot soldiers. The Yankees drove Wheeler back on his supports, then Walcutt's brigade hastily erected field fortifications and awaited a counterattack. The Georgia militia assaulted the Yankee position several times, advancing into Spencer-based Federal fire so heavy that Confederate General Gustavus W. Smith, commanding the attackers, thought he was facing an entire division. Although Walcutt himself was wounded in the leg, his opponents suffered 523 casualties, many of them no doubt falling to the Spencer bullets of the Forty-sixth Ohio. The defeated Confederates withdrew and the Federals burned Griswold's gun factory to the ground. In his brief career as an arms maker, the Connecticut Confederate had managed to turn out approximately 3,700 revolvers, more than any other Southern handgun contractor.[32]

After skirmishing with Wheeler's horsemen on an almost daily basis, and being bested by them on several occasions, Kilpatrick came upon the Rebel cavalry, dismounted and behind heavy cover, near Waynesboro in early December. After one unsuccessful attempt to drive the enemy from their field fortifications, the Jersey general launched a coordinated attack, with the men of the Ninety-second Illinois dismounted and advancing on the Rebel center, rapidly firing their Spencers while mounted units struck the Confederate flanks. Wheeler quickly fell back to a second line closer to the town. Kilpatrick repeated his tactic, this time using the Spencers of the Eighth Indiana for suppressive fire. Wheeler's men broke and ran, and over 200 of them were cut down by saber-wielding Yankees of the Second, Third, and Fifth Kentucky and Ninth Pennsylvania Cavalry.[33]

Sherman's army reached Savannah on December 10, and began to invest the city, which was garrisoned by 10,000 men under General Hardee. A supply-laden Federal fleet awaited Sherman offshore, and the Yankee general quickly began to maneuver his army into position to make contact with the Navy prior to attacking the city. General Kilpatrick may have realized he was on to something big with the tactic of using Spencer firepower as suppressive fire to facilitate an assault, which he had first witnessed at Yellow Tavern and successfully used at Waynesboro. On approaching Fort McAllister on the Great Ogeechee River, the Jerseyman advised Sherman that he had "old infantry regiments, armed with Spencer rifles, who could work their way up to within easy range and force every man to keep his head beneath the parapet, and, finally, force my way into the fort."[34]

Sherman, who seems to have had no great interest in new small arms technology, and a deep suspicion of the usefulness of any mounted troops, cavalry or infantry, declined Kilpatrick's offer and ordered one of his infantry brigades to storm the fort and its 200-man garrison on December 13. The Federal foot soldiers took their objective, but at a loss of twenty-four men killed and 110 wounded, many of them lost to land mines or "torpedoes." Hardee, seeing the handwriting on the wall with Sherman now in contact with the Union fleet and ordering siege guns disembarked, evacuated Savannah on December 21. The Union general had his Christmas present.[35]

As Sherman moved east, his former rival General Hood continued his northward march. Hood's army arrived in Decatur on October 26, then moved to Tuscumbia, Alabama, to await supplies and a linkup with General Forrest, an event that occurred on November 17. As Hood reorganized, so did General Thomas, concentrating his field force under Major General John M. General Schofield at Pulaski, Tennessee. Schofield commanded the IV and his own XXIII Corps, about 25,000 men, and also had about 5,000 cavalrymen at his disposal. Another 40,000 Union troops of varying quality were scattered around central Tennessee. Hood's army, with Forrest's force attached, mustered around 40,000 men.

The Confederate commander began moving north again on November 19, attempting to outflank Schofield's position at Pulaski. To avoid being trapped, the Federal general marched north two days later, heading for the Duck River crossing at Columbia. Over the next ten days Schofield raced Hood north, slipping out of several enveloping maneuvers, particularly at Spring Hill, and arrived at Franklin, Tennessee, on November 30, with the Rebels a day behind in hot pursuit. Franklin nestles in a bend in the Harpeth River, and while Schofield's engineers repaired the bridges across the Harpeth, he had his men prepare a series of defensive lines, improving some old earthworks, astride the Columbia Pike just south of the town. Two Federal brigades were stationed in a tripwire position across the Pike a half mile in advance of the main Federal line.

By late afternoon the bridges were repaired and Schofield's supply trains had successfully crossed the Harpeth. At around 4:00 P.M., his men were shocked to see, a mile away, a gray tide heading their way. Schofield had been apprehensive that the Confederates would cross the Harpeth on his flank while his men repaired the bridges, but he need not have worried. Hood was unhappy about the way his troops had performed in the race to Franklin and, despite misgivings expressed by his commanders, ordered a massive frontal assault on Schofield's lines in hopes of catching the Federal commander in the act of crossing the river. With Cheatham's corps on the west of the Columbia Pike and Stewart's on the right, seven divisions of Rebel infantry, more than 20,000 men, advanced with flags flying. Behind them massed bands played the finest song of the war, perhaps the finest military song of the nineteenth century, the "Bonnie Blue Flag," along with "Dixie" and "The Girl I Left Behind Me," to inspire the last great Confederate charge of the Civil War.

As Schofield's army watched agape, the two Yankee tripwire brigades, which should have retreated as soon as the Rebels came into view, stood their ground and began to fire at the approaching tide. A brief distant sputter of musketry died as the attack swarmed over, around, and through the position. Within minutes, those Yankees not captured or shot streamed toward the main Federal line in a disorganized mob, forcing Schofield's men to hold fire for fear of hitting their comrades. The hesitation was almost fatal. The Federals opened up at the last moment, even at the risk of hitting some of their own men as the horde of fugitives, with Rebel infantry hot on their heels, poured over into the defenses. As the Union center cracked, Yankee reserves rushed forward and sealed the breach in a bloody hand-to-hand melee with the attackers. Some Confederates made temporary lodgments in other sections of the line, but a wall of musketry, combined with flank fire from Union artillery batteries across the Harpeth, stopped most of them cold.

Part of that wall of defensive fire was from Henry rifles in the hands of the men of Company A of the Sixty-fifth Indiana Infantry. As the Rebels advanced, the Sixty-fifth's brigade commander, Colonel John S. Casement, had told his men to "whip hell out of" the "damned Rebel sons of bitches." They did. Casement's men had woven and staked an abatis of Osage Orange branches in front of their position, and as the gray-clad infantry hacked away at the obstacle, the Indiana boys poured fire into them. Further down the line the men of the Twelfth Kentucky added to the carnage with their Colt revolving rifles. A Rebel enlisted man remembered that the rain of bullets from the Sixty-fifth's Henrys was so heavy that men "pulled their hats over their faces as if to shield them from a storm of hail." One soldier in Casement's Sixty-fifth Illinois thought it a wonder "that any of them escaped death or capture." Major General Walthall, commanding the division of Stewart's corps that hit Casement's portion of the line, recalled that the Yankee line spit out "a continuous living fringe of flame." Walthall thought it "the most deadly fire of both small arms and artillery that I have ever seen troops subjected to." When the attack wound down around 9:00 P.M., the ground in front of the Sixty-fifth Indiana was strewn with Rebel bodies, while the regiment lost one man killed and five wounded. That night Schofield withdrew across the Harpeth and continued north to Nashville.[36]

The Battle of Franklin proved, in retrospect, the Army of the Tennessee's Waterloo. While inflicting 2,500 casualties on Schofield's army, Hood suffered 7,000, including 1,750 officers and men killed and mortally wounded. Of the twenty-eight Confederate generals who entered the fight at Franklin, fifteen became casualties. Among the dead was General Patrick Cleburne, accounted by many as the best division commander in the Confederate army.

At the time, however, Hood considered Franklin a victory and pursued Schofield all the way to Nashville. In truth, he did not have many options. What awaited him at Nashville was not a pleasant surprise, however. General Thomas had been concentrating all the available troops he could gather, ranging from 12,000 tough veterans under Major General Andrew J. Smith to a hastily organized emergency battalion of Quartermaster Department civilian employees. Also present in Nashville was the by now ubiquitous Brigadier General Wilson, who returned to the west in October to assume the position of Chief of Cavalry of the Military Division of the Mississippi. Wilson was busily engaged in reorganizing and re-equipping the horsemen of his new command, in the beginning stages of creating what would become a virtual cavalry army by the spring. His horsemen, some armed with Spencers, had screened Schofield's retreat from Pulaski, but had not been heavily engaged.

Schofield arrived at Nashville on December 1, and Hood, minus some troops under Major General Bate detached to attack Murfreesboro, the following day. In increasingly bad weather over the next two weeks Hood's battered 23,000-man army established a line four miles long outside the Union defenses to the south of the city. Although Hood would later maintain that he was waiting for reinforcements from across the Mississippi, there is no evidence that was in his mind at the time or that anyone thought it likely. His only hope, it seemed, was to bait the Yankees into an attack that would, if he was lucky, fail disastrously. While the Confederates suffered from the elements, waiting for something to happen, more Federal troops entered Nashville, increasing Thomas' available force to around 50,000 men.

Hoping to draw some of Thomas' strength away down, Hood increased his Murfreesboro task force by sending Forrest with two divisions of cavalry to assist Bate. While Thomas waited patiently until all prospects for success were in place before attacking, General Grant became impatient and apprehensive at what he perceived as dithering, deciding at one point to relieve the Union commander, but then thought better of it.

Thomas began to move Wilson's cavalry across the Cumberland River in the middle of an ice storm on December 12. Three days later, after a warm rain that melted the icy slopes the Yankees would have to transverse to attack

Continuing his policy of the offensive at any cost, Gen. John B. Hood brought his reduced army before the defenses of Nashville, where it was overthrown by Gen. George H. Thomas on December 15-16. If the date borne on this photograph by George N. Barnard is correct, December 16, it was taken in the course of the battle. (*Library of Congress*)

Hood's position, Thomas feinted at the Confederate right and launched an infantry attack on Stewart's corps, holding the Rebel left. The Federal assault on Hood's right was repulsed. The Rebel left initially resisted stubbornly, then collapsed, although Stewart managed to hold on until dark, when the Yankee attack stalled. Wilson's dismounted horsemen, attacking with Spencers blazing, were a significant factor in the operation. The Yankee general reported that he had "seen columns of infantry hesitate to attack positions not half so strong, but [Colonel Datus E.] Coon's brigade, armed with the Spencer carbine and in a strong line of skirmishers, at the command of General Hatch, advanced at the charge. In spite of the steep acclivity and withering fire of artillery and musketry from the rebel parapet, the redoubt was carried, with the battery of 4 guns and 250 prisoners."[37]

The following afternoon another attack on the Rebel right failed, but Wilson's horsemen pushed the undermanned Confederate cavalry aside and a 4:00 P.M. assault by Union infantry broke through on the left flank, leading to a disintegration of Hood's army, which streamed south. Hood lost around 6,000 men, almost 4,500 as prisoners, while the Federals lost less than half that number. The whole army collapsed and fled to the south back through Franklin and to Bainbridge, Alabama, where, on Christmas Day, 1864, it crossed the Tennessee River, never to return.

As the new year of 1865 arrived, it was clear to anyone with an interest in the subject that the day of the muzzleloader was as done as the Army of

Tennessee. On December 5, 1864, General Dyer informed Secretary of War Stanton that "the experience of the war has shown that breech-loading arms are greatly superior to muzzle-loaders for infantry as well as for cavalry." He went on to say that "measures should immediately be taken to substitute a suitable breech-loading musket in place of the rifle musket which is now manufactured at the National Armory and by private contractors for this department." In order to find a suitable design, Dyer requested that a board "composed of ordnance, cavalry, and infantry officers, be constituted to meet at Springfield Armory, and at such other place or places as the president or senior officer of the Board may direct, to examine, test, and recommend for adoption a suitable breech-loader for muskets and carbines, and a suitable repeater or magazine carbine, and that the arms recommended by the Board may, if approved by the War Department, be exclusively adopted for the military service."[38]

It is interesting to note that Dyer wanted the board to approve a "suitable repeater or magazine carbine" for the cavalry, but his only specification for the infantry arm was that it be a "suitable breechloader." The ordnance chief was not interested in a repeater for infantry use because of the power and range limitations of the cartridges that repeaters used. This fact, along with cost, had long mitigated against breechloaders in general in military service.

The breech-loading Dreyse needle gun was first used in combat in the Prussian War against Denmark in 1864 and then again against Austria in 1866, both victorious campaigns for the Prussians. Still, some Prussian officers were concerned that their breechloaders were wasteful of ammunition and concerned that they did not have the range of muzzleloaders. An assessment of needle gun deployment in battle was inconclusive. Although some attributed the Prussian victory in 1866 to the breechloaders, other analysts differed. To this school of tactical thought, the Austrians' densely packed formations provided excellent targets for any firearm. This, coupled with their officers' "incapability . . . to make efficient use of their excellent Lorenz rifles, which had a far greater range and higher accuracy than the Prussian needle rifles," were more instrumental in the Austrian defeat than the Prussian needle gun.[39]

The needle gun did lack range, and was limited by its unique ammunition, a problem whose resolution awaited the introduction of the metallic cartridge pioneered by Flobert and Smith & Wesson. The difficult task of infantry rifle developers was to develop a sturdy cartridge as powerful and effective at long range as the ammunition used in muzzle-loading infantry rifles. In 1855, Sylvestr Krnka, a Czech, designed a large-bore rimfire cartridge based on the Frenchman Pottet's shotgun cartridge, with a metal base and cardboard body, which had durability limitations. Krnka would not produce a true metallic cartridge until 1868.

In the summer of 1864 the British established a committee to address the same concerns Dyer expressed regarding a new breech-loading infantry arm. To reduce costs, the committee established several conditions. The new weapon must be a conversion of the existing Enfield muzzleloader, be as accurate as that gun, and cost less than one pound sterling to produce. By the fall the committee was reviewing and inspecting conversion plans submitted by forty-five British gun makers. Six makers were selected to convert several Enfields and return them with 1,000 rounds of ammunition for more thorough testing. Only one of the finalists, Snider, provided a gun chambered for self-contained ammunition; the others submitted capping breechloaders. The Snider conversion, which involved milling out a portion of the gun's breech and installing a breech block that swiveled to the side for loading, was eventually accepted in 1866. The centerfire .577 cartridge was difficult to produce and somewhat delicate, involving a metal base, paper lining, and foil case. Tests revealed, however, that it actually produced comparable range and better accuracy than its muzzle-loading predecessor did and had a rate of fire of fifteen rounds a minute.[40]

No doubt cognizant of the work going on in Britain, Dyer formally appointed a board of officers under Major Theodore T. S. Laidley to convene at Springfield Armory in January 1865. Laidley was instructed to assess submitted breechloaders and test them in "all that relates to range, durability and arrangements of parts" as well as "adaptability for service in the hands of foot troops" and "manipulations on horseback" for cavalrymen. The board eventually tested sixty-five rifles and carbines, including the Henry rifle and the Spencer carbine and rifle. The Spencer Company submitted two standard thirty-inch-barrel rifles, one equipped with the Stabler cut-off and one carbine in the now standard .50 caliber cartridge. Another Spencer submission was a unique .50 caliber rifle with a rifle-musket-length thirty-nine-inch barrel categorized as a "single loader with magazine cut-off." One of the standard rifles was described as "single loader and repeater with magazine cut off." The details of the longer barreled gun are unfortunately lost to history. In April 1865 the board concluded that the Spencer carbine was the best cavalry arm, and the Peabody single-shot rifle best suited for infantry use. Neither conclusion was sustained in the postwar period.[41]

While Laidley and his board formed, deliberated, and tested, the war went on. In the last major operation of 1864, General Butler led an expeditionary force from his Army of the James that attempted to close the last open Confederate port, Wilmington, North Carolina, by capturing Fort

Fisher, a forty-seven-gun sand redoubt sited on a peninsula between the Atlantic Ocean and the Cape Fear River. When intelligence of the move reached General Lee, he detached troops from the Army of Northern Virginia to check Butler's effort. Although Federal troops actually landed and advanced on the Rebel defenses, bad weather, the failure of an exploding ship scheme, and the approach of Major General Robert F. Hoke's troops from Virginia caused Butler, on the recommendation of his subordinate, Major General Godfrey Weitzel, to withdraw.

General Grant was unhappy with Butler's effort, and the Massachusetts general was replaced as commander of the Army of the James by Major General Otho C. Ord. A new effort against Fort Fisher, commanded by Brigadier General Alfred H. Terry, who had gained experience in amphibious operations at Charleston earlier in the war, was initiated in January 1865. Terry's landing force, dubbed Terry's Provisional Corps, included infantry elements from the XXIV and XXV Corps, as well as heavy mortar and siege gun detachments from the Petersburg/Richmond front. Among the infantry regiments assigned to the expedition were the Seventh Connecticut, and its sister unit, the Seventh New Hampshire, recovered from their Olustee debacle and armed with Spencer carbines. Another Spencer carbine-armed regiment from the Army of the James, the Thirteenth Indiana, also joined the expedition. The invasion flotilla, sixty transport and war ships, appeared off Fort Fisher on January 12, causing local Confederate commanders to reinforce the fort's 1,200 man garrison with an additional 600 soldiers. Hoke's 6,000 man division, which had remained in the area after Butler's December attack, established a defensive position on the peninsula north of the fort.

After a point-blank naval bombardment of the fort on January 15, Terry's infantry established a beachhead blocking Hoke's position. Under the cover of naval fire, a sixty-man detachment from the Thirteenth Indiana armed with Spencer carbines, supplemented by forty volunteers carrying rifle muskets and shovels from Colonel N. Martin Curtis' brigade of New York troops, rushed to within 175 yards of the fort. The task force dug in immediately and opened a suppressive small arms fire on the parapets. This was an increasingly common offensive tactic using repeating rifles, as evidenced from Kilpatrick's proposal to Sherman at Fort McAllister.

Under the resulting covering fire, Curtis moved his whole brigade up to a position fifty yards behind the Hoosiers. Colonels Galusha Pennypacker and Louis Bell displaced forward as the New Yorkers advanced. At around 3:30, Curtis assaulted the section of the fort's parapet directly to his front, while Pennypacker assaulted to his right and Bell to Pennypacker's right. The enemy line broke, but the garrison did not surrender until after several

An artist's rendition of the assault on Fort Fisher. The illustration features the fort's famous rifled Armstrong gun. This English-made artillery piece hurled a 150-pound shell up to five miles. The photograph on the right taken after the action shows the same gun as captured by Union forces. The furious close-in action of the assault on Fort Fisher, the largest joint amphibious operation in U.S. history until the Normandy invasion, played to the strengths of the Spencer, both its quick firing and ease of reloading while prone. (*Library of Congress*)

hours of desperate hand-to-hand combat. A volunteer column of sailors and marines, the former armed with cutlasses and revolvers, reached the fort at another location, but was routed by heavy musketry from the defenders. Although a Navy veteran recalled the repulse of the sailors and leathernecks as "mortifying," they did distract some defenders from opposing the army's successful attack. It would be specious to claim that the Thirteenth Indiana's fire was responsible for the victory at Fort Fisher, but there is no doubt that it helped. More tactically significant was the conscious deployment of the Spencer-armed Hoosiers in a dedicated offensive role recognizing and taking advantage of their repeaters.[42]

Grant was able to detach a division-size task force to capture Fort Fisher because by January 1865 all was quiet along the Shenandoah and Petersburg fronts. In the wake of Cedar Creek, Jubal Early ceased to be a threat to Washington, and Sheridan released the VI Corps to return to the Army of the Potomac. Additional troops from the Army of the Shenandoah's VIII Corps, including the Twenty-third Illinois, were reassigned to the Army of the James.

Grant continued to lengthen the lines of the Armies of the Potomac and James through the winter, advancing the II and V Corps to Dabney's Mills and Hatcher's Run in early February. Although attacked by the Confederates, the Union troops held on to their gains, tightening the noose on Petersburg yet a bit more. Throughout the winter Grant's armies received new regiments and new recruits for their old regiments, and the general lull in combat gave them time to integrate and train these reinforcements. Federal cavalry regiments continued to be rearmed with Spencer carbines as the new guns became available. The men of the Third New Jersey Cavalry were issued some Spencers at the end of 1864, and the First New Jersey Cavalry exchanged its Burnsides for Spencers in January 1865. By that date most soldiers wanted repeaters if they could get them. Winfield Scott Hancock's First Veteran Corps, raised among discharged veterans in early 1865, used breechloaders, including Sharps rifles and repeating Henrys, as incentives for reenlistment.[43]

Privately purchased Henrys continued to appear in the ranks, especially in the western armies, in the final months of the war. Seeking replacements to fill the ranks of his Thirty-fifth New Jersey Infantry, which fought in the Atlanta campaign, the March to the Sea, and the final campaign in the Carolinas, Colonel John J. Cladek visited the offices of the Trenton (New Jersey) State Gazette with Henry rifle in hand. The impressed editor reported: "We have been shown, by Colonel Cladek, of the 35th New Jersey Regiment, a new rifle (Henry's Patent) which he has received authority to purchase for the use of his command." The colonel advised that a recruit could pay for his Henry with $50 out of his $250 enlistment bounty. Considering that the price of a Henry was $42, it appears the colonel (later dismissed for other financial chicanery) was not above making a buck on the deal. How many, if any, Jerseymen actually bought Henrys from Cladek is unknown. In February, 1865, Lieutenant Colonel Samuel Simison, commanding the Twenty-third Illinois, who had purchased "some fifty stand of Henry's repeating rifles" for his unit over the winter of 1863-1864, wrote Oliver Winchester that he was now interested in arming his "entire battalion" with them.[44]

Although Spencer rifles were relatively uncommon compared to carbines, those available were sent where they could do the most good, the trench lines around Petersburg where picket skirmishing and trench raids were more or less constant. Private William L. Phillips of the VI Army Corps' Fifth Wisconsin Infantry noted in December 1864 that "A and B Companys are going to draw Sharps [sic] 6 Shooters they are skirmishers. They need good rifles." The rifles were most likely Spencers. In mid-March 1865, Phillips reported that he went on a patrol between the Petersburg lines with another soldier, and "it would have taken several rebs to have taken us for the other felow had A dispencer 7 Shooter rifle and I had musket and A six shooter revolver."[45]

As winter waned, so did the prospects of the Southern Confederacy. Following the capture of Savannah, Sherman began to make his way north

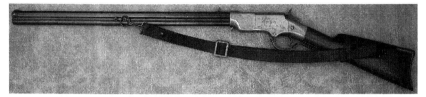

An 1864 Henry rifle owned and inscribed by Michael G. Buzard of the First Missouri Engineers, an outfit responsible for building pontoon bridges during Sherman's "March to the Sea." The rifle retains its original sling swivels with leather sling. (*Rob Kassab, RareWinchesters.com*)

through the Carolinas, with the goal of eventually knocking on Richmond's back door. General Lee, promoted to overall command of Southern forces in February, looked south and did not like what he saw. In an effort to hold Sherman, he replaced General Beauregard, commanding Confederate troops in the Carolinas, with a rehabilitated General Johnston, and made plans to launch an attack at Petersburg in hope of forcing Grant to contract his lines, freeing some Rebel defenders to march south.

As Lee planned what would be his final moves at Petersburg, there was more trouble in the offing. In late February 1865, General Sheridan left Winchester, Virginia, with two cavalry divisions and marched south up the Shenandoah Valley in an effort to destroy the remains of Jubal Early's army. Although much of the remnant of Early's force had returned to Petersburg, the Confederate commander still held Waynesborough with less than 1,000 men when Sheridan moved against him. On March 2, 1865, Custer attacked Early, using the now tried-and-true cavalry offensive tactics against fixed positions. He dismounted the Third New Jersey, Seventh Ohio, and First Connecticut Cavalry, advanced them through some woods to within 100 yards of the Rebel line and ordered a charge. The dismounted troopers rushed the Southerners with Spencer carbines firing while the remainder of Custer's men pounded down on them with a mounted saber charge. Early's force was destroyed and he barely escaped himself.[46]

Early disposed of, Sheridan marched on to Charlottesville then on to Petersburg, destroying public property and railroad tracks on the way. Sheridan arrived at the Petersburg lines on March 26, eager to deliver a deathblow to Lee's tottering army. With Sheridan's arrival and the continuing deterioration of the Confederate cause in the Carolinas, Lee's plan to make Grant shorten his lines took on a new desperation. General Gordon, entrusted with the actual implementation of the plan, sought to stage a breakthrough at Fort Stedman, only 150 yards from the Rebel front line, leading, he hoped, to the capture of the huge Yankee supply dump at City Point.

Led by the crack Rebel sharpshooter battalions, still a force to be reck-
oned with, Gordon's pre-dawn attack on March 25 captured Fort Stedman,
pushed out into open territory, but became unhinged when the forward
assault elements could not find their objectives and resistance stiffened. A
massive Federal counterattack drove the enemy forward elements back
toward Fort Stedman, where artillery and small arms crossfire pinned down
almost 2,000 Rebels, who surrendered. Total Confederate casualties were
around 4,000—men Lee could not replace.

In response to the assault on Fort Stedman, Meade ordered the VI and
II Corps to attack and capture the Confederate picket line on their fronts.
While the II Corps failed to accomplish its mission, the VI was successful.
Private Phillips of the Fifth Wisconsin noted that "the shells and balls came
in in perfect showers but most of them went over our heads the rebs tried to
flank us but the 37 Masachusets deployed as skirmishers with their 7 shooters and kept the rebs back." The seizure of the picket line set the stage for
the end of the Petersburg siege a week later.[47]

On March 29 Major General Ord led three divisions of the Army of the
James down to reinforce the Army of the Potomac for what would prove the
final Petersburg attack. That same day Sheridan marched his Cavalry Corps,
supported by the V Corps, toward Dinwiddie Court House and the
Southside Railroad, the last intact rail line into Petersburg. Sheridan pitched
into Rebel cavalry at Five Forks, and then ran into two Confederate infantry
divisions under Major General George Pickett, who Lee had sent to the
assistance of his hard-pressed horsemen. Sheridan wanted the VI Corps
infantrymen, favorites of his since the Shenandoah, as reinforcements, but
they were too far away and the roads were turning into bottomless mud, so
the V Corps was assigned to the operation.

In a confused series of attacks and counterattacks on March 31 and April
1, Federal and Confederate dismounted cavalry and infantry surged back
and forth, with Spencer carbine-armed Yankee horsemen holding their own
against Confederate cavalry and infantry in impromptu defensive positions.
At the end of the second day, despite suffering heavier casualties, the
Federals had severed the White Oak Road, isolating Pickett from Lee. After
he finally got his force in hand, Sheridan launched an attack, including dismounted cavalrymen firing Spencers as they advanced, that wrecked the
whole Confederate force and captured Five Forks, in a victory reminiscent
of his triumphs in the Shenandoah Valley.

With Sheridan on the rampage, the rest of the Union army prepared to
break the Rebel main line. At 4:30 A.M. on April 2, 1865, the Army of the
Potomac began the last full-scale assault of its history. At dawn the IX Corps

moved on the Jerusalem Plank
Road line but its offensive
stalled. The VI Corps swarmed
forward with three divisions
abreast from the picket lines it
captured the week before. The
Corps' commander, Major
General Horatio G. Wright,
ordered that his three division
commanders see that the "division sharpshooters will be so disposed as to be rendered most
effective."[48]

The First Division's sharpshooter battalion, commanded
by Captain James T. Stewart of

A damaged but historically interesting photograph of Confederate prisoners captured
at Five Forks by Sheridan's troops. (*Library
of Congress*)

the Forty-ninth Pennsylvania, had some men armed with Spencer rifles and
others with muzzle-loading target rifles. Stewart reported that he "was
ordered to form those of my men who were armed with Spencer rifles as a
skirmish line . . . the men armed with the telescope and globe [aperture
sight] rifles were ordered to remain in Fort Fisher." Once the division
secured the Confederate works, the sharpshooters with the heavy rifles
leapfrogged forward to engage targets in forts not yet captured, specifically
artillerymen.[49]

The First Division's Third Brigade, commanded by the Thirty-seventh
Massachusetts' Colonel Edwards, deployed a volunteer shock troop detachment of seventy-five men armed with Spencer rifles and "twenty axemen
selected from the pioneer corps" to hack and shoot their way through the
Confederate abatis and defenders on their front. With the Thirty-seventh
and the Fifth Wisconsin in the first line augmenting the skirmish line's
Spencers, the brigade broke into the enemy works like a firestorm. Edwards
immediately deployed his Spencer shooters left and right and had them
direct a stream of fire to help clear the trenches in front of the division's First
and Second Brigades.[50]

The VI Corps scored a decisive breakthrough, and moved southwest
toward Hatcher's Run, driving the enemy before it. The II Corps also broke
through the Petersburg defenses and drove toward Sutherland Station. The
Federals halted to consolidate late in the day, and that night the Army of
Northern Virginia evacuated not only Petersburg, but the Bermuda
Hundred and Richmond lines as well. Lee intended to unite and reorganize

these forces at Amelia Courthouse, where he expected to find rations and supplies, and then move south to link up with Johnston's army in North Carolina.

Grant launched a relentless pursuit to block Lee's escape, which led to a series of rear guard actions beginning on April 3. The most significant fight of the retreat occurred on April 6, when the II and VI Corps caught up with General Ewell's catchall command. Ewell's troops included the remnants of a number of infantry units, Confederate marines and sailors, heavy artillerymen from the Richmond defenses, and even the first (and last) company of African American Confederates, who had enlisted in Richmond in March. Ewell deployed his eclectic force on Little Sayler's Creek, where elements of the VI Corps attacked him. The Rebels repulsed the initial Yankee assault, but were then enveloped by more VI Corps infantrymen and Sheridan's cavalry. Although some vicious hand-to-hand fighting ensued, most of Ewell's men, including the general himself, were captured. Further north along Sayler's Creek the II Corps battered General Gordon's division. Estimates of Confederate casualties for the day run to around 8,000, eight times those lost by the Federals. Repeating rifles proved crucial during one phase of the Sayler's Creek fight. The Thirty-seventh Massachusetts was flanked, but maneuvered so that "the enemy were finally forced back and they taken in flank; their line being swept by the fire of the Spencers they surrendered."[51]

Trapped by his pursuers at Appomattox Courthouse on April 8, General Lee surrendered the remains of the Army of Northern Virginia the following day. The only hope left for the survival of the Southern Confederacy was the increasingly beleaguered remains of the Army of Tennessee commanded by General Johnston, then backpedaling before Sherman in North Carolina. It was a dim hope.

Part of the rationale for attacking Fort Fisher in December and January was to capture Wilmington and provide a port in North Carolina through which Sherman could conveniently receive supplies and reinforcements as he moved north. Terrible winter weather conditions delayed Sherman's advance until February 1, 1865, but supporting operations proceeded apace. General Schofield and his XXIII Corps were transferred from the West and forced Hoke to abandon Wilmington. Combining with troops already present in the coastal south, Schofield began to move inland at the end of February. Other Federals advanced into North Carolina from New Bern, which had been held by the Union since 1862. These forces totaled around 30,000 men.

There was little to stop Sherman and his 60,000-man army. After evacuating Savannah, General Hardee had a field force of around 25,000 troops

composed of Wheeler's cavalry, assorted Georgia militiamen, the former
Savannah garrison, fragments of other commands, and General Butler's
tough South Carolina mounted infantrymen, recently returned from the
Army of Northern Virginia. Leadership changes in February placed General
Beauregard in overall command, with the talented and newly promoted
Lieutenant General Wade Hampton in charge of Beauregard's mounted
men. Beauregard ordered a withdrawal and consolidation of Confederate
forces in the interior of South Carolina.

Sherman's greatest opponent proved to be the weather. Beset by heavy
late winter rains, the Yankee column was slowed by the need to ford over-
flowing rivers and fell trees to corduroy roads for supply wagons. As they
advanced, the Yankees also destroyed enemy railroads and rolling stock and
burned cotton and military supplies. Vandalism against private property also
ran high in South Carolina, the state most Federal soldiers held most responsible for the war. Retaliation from Southern horsemen (often not above vandalism themselves) shadowing the army was often swift and ruthless. Yankee
scouts or foragers carrying a Spencer or Henry were far more able to defend
themselves than those with muskets or single-shot breechloaders. Half the
Seventh Illinois infantry, now largely armed with Henrys, were mounted and
used for scouting and foraging duties, while the dismounted portion of the
regiment remained with its infantry brigade.

Columbia, South Carolina, fell to the Federals on February 17, and the
state capital went up in flames shortly afterward, with both sides accusing
each other of the arson. Shortly afterward, General Lee, for the first time in
command of all Confederate armies, replaced Beauregard with General
Johnston. Johnston took over a scattered command attempting to concentrate, as per his predecessor's orders, at Cheraw, South Carolina. The new
Confederate commander, appraising Sherman's advance, redirected the concentration to Fayetteville, North Carolina. Meanwhile Schofield was driving
in from the coast, pushing the Rebels on his front west. Sherman planned to
link up with him at Goldsboro.

Sherman's army continued to march in two columns, the left wing under
Slocum and the wing under Howard. Johnston, who had a force of about
21,000 men, decided to attack Slocum's wing, composed of the XIV and XX
Corps, at Bentonville to even the odds a bit. On March 16, in the opening
phases of the battle, Federal infantry attacked Hampton's cavalry and were
driven back by a Rebel infantry counterattack. Slocum consolidated his force
and held fast under several assaults on his position. Unable to defeat Slocum,
Johnston withdrew and assumed a defensive position of his own, while
Sherman reinforced Slocum. By March 20, Sherman had concentrated his

whole army and attacked Johnston, attempting to pin him in place and also cut off his route of retreat. The attack was not successful, and that night Colonel Frederick J. Hurlbut ordered Major Edward S. Johnston, commanding the dismounted section of the Seventh Illinois, to take his "seventy men, mainly armed with Henry rifles," to secure the brigade picket line and take the enemy's should the opportunity arrive. One soldier from the Fifty-seventh Illinois, supporting the Seventh, observed that the Henry-armed soldiers were "as usual having lots of fun with their sixteen shooters." More and more commanders were realizing the value of repeaters and using them in a tactically appropriate manner. A brigade commander slept better at night with Henrys on the picket line.[52]

During the night Johnston disengaged and withdrew. Sherman continued his march the next day, arriving at Goldsboro on March 23. United with the Federals driving in from the coast, Sherman mustered 80,000 men. Johnston, at Smithfield, reorganized his little army into three corps, under Generals Stewart, Hardee, and S. D. Lee. He soon realized that the Army of Northern Virginia was no longer on the way and, recognizing the utter hopelessness of his position, called for an armistice on April 13 and surrendered on April 26.

Although there was still one big Yankee strike into the heart of Alabama to come, the Civil War was almost at an end. And the Spencer and Henry played their part in this, General Sherman's last major campaign. Ordnance records indicate that Sherman's army in the Carolinas expended 213,448 rounds of Spencer rifle and carbine ammunition and 38,654 Henry cartridges between January 1 and April 26, 1865. By way of comparison, Sherman's men consumed 1,233,636 Springfield and Enfield cartridges along with 112,000 Sharps cartridges. As we noted regarding the records of ammunition usage of Sherman's armies during the Atlanta campaign, it is safe to assume that the Henry and Spencer cartridges were, for the most part, fired, whereas bad weather or the simple wear and tear of carrying them often destroyed many of the paper musket cartridges and linen Sharps rounds.

Although all was quiet in Virginia, several campaigns were still under way to the west, including the most massive mounted operation of the war, in which the Spencer carbine would earn its greatest reputation as a cavalry weapon.[53]

 # NINE

Selma and Beyond

HE MAN WHO LOVED SPENCERS WAS NOW KING OF THE WESTERN
cavalry. Major General James Harrison Wilson, the Topographical
Engineer officer who started his accelerated climb up the career ladder on
General Grant's staff, had learned the cavalry trade on the job as chief of the
Cavalry Bureau in Washington and a division commander under Sheridan in
the Virginia campaign of 1864. In October, he returned to the western theater as Chief of Cavalry for the Military Division of the Mississippi, a position equivalent to the one Sheridan held in the east that spring.

Wilson, an efficient administrator, whipped the neglected western horse
into fair shape and led it reasonably well during the Franklin and Nashville
campaigns. In the wake of the Army of the Tennessee's disaster, and with
Confederate attention drawn to Sherman's march north through the
Carolinas, Alabama appeared open to Federal exploitation via a raid to
Selma, an important military and industrial center, and Wilson was tapped
for the job.

The general held the complete confidence of both Grant and Thomas
and had a free hand in the reorganization and concentration of his scattered
horsemen. His goal was to create an even better armed and organized cavalry corps than the one in which he had served the previous spring. Wilson's
initially high opinion of Spencer carbines had, if anything, increased in the
interim, and his correspondence with ordnance officials and commanders
requesting them is reminiscent of Rosecrans' 1863 petitions for repeaters.
The cavalry chief wrote unabashedly on December 30, 1864, that the
"Spencer carbine is undoubtedly the best fire-arm ever put into the hands of
the soldier." He requested that Spencers be "supplied for the entire command" and dismissed all other carbines as "bad by comparison," concluding
that "troops armed with the Spencer carbine, or rifle, consume less ammunition than any other, and are more effective." Although his ammunition

consumption conclusion seems arguable, it no doubt counted fragile paper and linen cartridges destroyed in normal day-to-day activity. Whatever his rationale, Wilson's overwhelming enthusiasm for the Spencer was apparent.[1]

General Wilson harassed the War Department on a regular basis for the 10,000 Spencers he thought he needed. On February 17, 1865, he presented a detailed rearmament request "for Spencer carbines and Blakely [sic] patent cartridge-boxes. I wish the First Division supplied first, and in the following order: Eighth Iowa, First Wisconsin, Fourth Kentucky (mounted) Infantry, Fourth Kentucky Cavalry, Sixth Kentucky Cavalry, Fourth Indiana, Second Michigan, Seventh Kentucky, Second Indiana. Next, the Fifth Division in the following order: Third Illinois, Seventh Illinois, Twelfth Missouri, Twelfth Tennessee, and Eleventh Indiana Cavalry."[2]

On March 8, Wilson informed his inspector of cavalry that "1,000 Spencer carbines have been ordered here for [Brigadier General Edward] Hatch. I hope others will follow soon..." The flow of carbines from Boston was not sufficient to supply all of the regiments Wilson wanted to rearm, however, and the Burnside company was yet to deliver its first Spencers. As an ad hoc remedy, he decided to shift Spencer carbines from those regiments not part of his field force to those who were.[3]

Wilson ordered General Hatch and Colonel Coon to hand over "the Spencer carbines belonging to the troops of the Fifth Division . . . to be delivered to Brigadier-General Croxton, commanding First Division, Cavalry Corps, together with the ammunition for the same." The soldiers giving up their Spencers received "a corresponding number of such arms, with ammunition, as are possessed by that portion of General Croxton's command with which the exchange is made." Included among that hodgepodge of exchanged guns were obsolete Halls.[4]

By grabbing any new Spencers he could and cannibalizing the arms of garrison units, Wilson ended up with three divisions armed almost exclusively with repeaters by the time he was ready to set off on his raid. He reported that the troopers of his "First, Second, and Fourth Divisions, with the exception of a few hundred, were armed with the Spencer carbine, and all had arms using cartridges with metallic cases."[5]

Along with Spencer carbines, Wilson requested Blakeslee cartridge boxes, noting, "in regard to the Blakely [sic] cartridge box. Please do what you can to have them furnished. It is with this box as it is with the Spencer carbine, all bad by comparison." One inherent problem with the Spencer was that reloading its magazine significantly reduced the gun's overall rate of fire. To reload, a soldier removed the Spencer's follower and spring tube from the buttstock magazine well, dropped seven individual rounds into the

well, and then replaced the spring and follower assembly in the stock. Spencer cartridges were carried in conventional cartridge boxes, with the cavalry box containing a block of wood drilled to accept twenty rounds, and the infantry box fitted with
tin trays to hold six cardboard packages of
seven Spencer cartridges each.[6]

Colonel Erastus Blakeslee, the commander of the First Connecticut Cavalry,
had a better idea. Blakeslee designed and
patented a cartridge box with a wooden
insert drilled to hold six metal tubes, each
of which held a complete seven cartridge
reload. To use the Blakeslee box, a trooper
withdrew the magazine follower and spring
tube from the gun and a loading tube from
the box, inserted the tip of the loading tube
in the magazine well, let all seven rounds
slide in, and then replaced the follower
tube. Although some writers have assumed
that the Blakeslee box was issued with
Spencer carbines and rifles from 1863 on,
this was not the case. The colonel applied
for a patent on his invention in September
1864 and it was granted in December.[7]

General Dyer ordered 500 Blakeslee
boxes for field trials in September, and these
were issued to the First New York
Dragoons, a regiment equipped with
Spencer carbines since the spring of 1864.

James Harrison Wilson (1837
–1925), a strong proponent of
the Spencer carbine, served as
head of the cavalry bureau, a
cavalry division commander in
the Army of the Potomac, and
Chief of Cavalry in the west. His
raid into Alabama in early 1865
succeeded in penetrating the
dying Confederacy to its heart,
and led to the capture of
Jefferson Davis. Wilson resigned
from the army in 1870 to
become a civilian engineer, but
returned to duty in the Spanish
American war, retiring in 1901
as a brigadier general. When he
died at his home in Delaware in
1925, he was one of the last surviving Union generals. (*Library
of Congress*)

On February 15, 1865, Major Rufus Scott of
the First reported that he thought the Blakeslee boxes "unsuitable" for several reasons, chief among them that the wooden block drilled to hold the
reloading tubes swelled in wet weather, making it "impossible to draw them
from the wood" and that the "battering" of the bullet by the "constant jolting"
of riding with the box slung over a soldier's shoulder tended to cause explosions of "the lower cartridges." Scott reported "a number of accidents" from
such explosions. He also noted, however, that his men "even with these
defects . . . prefer the 'Blakeslee Cartridge Box' to any other in use."[8]

In his response to Scott's critique, Blakeslee explained that the wood blocks in the hastily manufactured boxes had swollen because they had not been properly kiln dried and that the explosion problem could be "reduced by packing the bottom of each tube with rubber." In November and December 1864, even before Scott's evaluation was complete, however, General Dyer ordered 12,000 six-tube Blakeslee boxes (without any rubber packing) from Emerson Gaylord of Chicopee, Massachusetts, a well-known military leather accoutrement maker, in an order that may well have been the result of Wilson's lobbying. Dyer also ordered ten-tube Blakeslee boxes for infantry use in December and again in March 1865.[9]

There is some debate and little source material on whether or not any Blakeslee boxes were actually issued beyond the initial test run. General Wilson, however, usually got what he ordered if it was available. An enigmatic report from Dr. F. Salter, his medical director on the Selma raid, suggests that at least some Blakeslee boxes did see service on the operation:

> Two accidents arose from the magazines of the Spencer carbine exploding from being half filled while on "hot march" by concussion. *In one instance the magazine was in the pouch*, [author's italics] in the other in the stock of the carbine. The tin tubes, or magazines which contain the fixed ammunition, metallic cartridges, should be therefore kept filled. Four inches of play on a hot day may explode them, as evidenced in these two cases. The greatest energy and assiduity on the part of all the medical officers was observable throughout the campaign.
>
> F. Salter, Surg., U. S. Vols., Med. Director, Cav. Corps, Military Division of the Mississippi.[10]

It is unlikely that the heat of an Alabama March or April had anything to do with exploding the cartridges in question, but no doubt that concussion was the cause. A rimfire round is primed by mechanically "spinning" the fulminate priming compound into the cartridge case's outside hollow rim. Should any of the compound remain in the middle of the case, where the bullet nose of the cartridge behind it can impact it, an explosion may well result when the nose hits the priming with any force.

Although some may have seen service in the last days of the Petersburg siege, there is no evidence that the Blakeslee infantry boxes were ever issued, and all types of Blakeslee boxes are very rare today. According to a European source, many cavalry and infantry boxes were sent to France with Spencers purchased by the French government in 1870 during the Franco-Prussian War.[11]

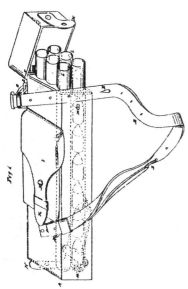

The Spencer cartridge box designed and patented by Erastus Blakeslee had a wooden insert drilled to hold six metal tubes, each of which held a complete seven cartridge reload. A trooper withdrew the magazine follower and spring tube from the gun and a loading tube from the box, inserted the tip of the loading tube in the magazine well, let all seven rounds slide in, and then replaced the follower tube. A reproduction, above, and the patent drawing, left. (*Phil Siess, S&S Firearms*)

With his force carrying as many Spencers as he could gather, Wilson led the divisions of Brigadier Generals Edward M. McCook, Eli Long, and Emory Upton, the latter best known as an innovative infantry tactician, from their base in northern Alabama toward Selma on March 22, 1865. Brushing aside minor resistance, the Yankee column encountered some Rebels near Tuscaloosa but met its first serious opposition, under the redoubtable Nathan Bedford Forrest, near Montevallo. Forrest's depleted command was no longer the almost mystically unbeatable force it had been in earlier years, and on March 31, Wilson's Spencer-wielding troopers brushed it aside. Forrest, not one to give up easily, fought Wilson again at Plantersville, then fell back on Selma.

Although Selma was protected by extensive defensive works, Forrest had but 2,500 of his own troops and a like number of local militia to man them. It was a hopeless defense. On April 2, the same day the Petersburg line cracked, Long's and Upton's divisions assaulted the Selma defenses, routing the defenders. Long reported that "we moved forward steadily until within short range, when a rapid fire was opened by our Spencers, and with a cheer the men started for the works on a run, sweeping forward in solid line over fences and ravine, scaling the stockade and on the works with resistless force."[12]

Under heavy pressure, Forrest, aided by the firepower of his own Spencer-armed bodyguard detachment, disengaged and withdrew the remains of his force to join Lieutenant General Richard Taylor's command, which surrendered a month later. Wilson's men spread out across Alabama and Georgia, and captured fleeing Confederate President Jefferson Davis at Irwinsville, Georgia, on May 10. Although scattered skirmishing would continue on into June, General Wilson had effectively applied the *coup de grâce* to the Confederacy at Selma.

Even as they went down to defeat, some Southerners were better armed than they had ever been before. Through the final days of the conflict, the number of Spencers in Confederate custody continued to increase. In February 1865, Colonel Minty assigned one of his scouts to discover the whereabouts of enemy guerrillas in the vicinity of Gravelly Springs, Alabama. The scout reported that "he met twenty of them and learned that there are about seventy between here and Waynesborough. Their chief haunt is a cypress swamp about fourteen miles out. The twenty he met were chiefly armed with Spencers, only two having shotguns, and one a long rifle." Later that month General Kilpatrick complained to Confederate General Wheeler that Rebels from a Texas unit under Wheeler's command armed with Spencers had killed several Union prisoners, and on March 27 a Federal scout detachment in Florida captured five Rebels and three Spencer carbines. Confederate sharpshooter Berry Benson began a picket line fight at Petersburg on March 31, 1865, carrying a Spencer rifle that his brother, also a sharpshooter, had captured. Benson recalled that he "fired so fast that once I had to stop to let my gun cool." He only had forty rounds of rimfire ammunition, however, and swapped his empty Spencer for a muzzle-loading Enfield the following day. Although they were generally not for sale on the civilian market, Spencers were apparently readily available through other channels by 1865. John Wilkes Booth managed to acquire two Spencer carbines to abet his escape after the assassination of Abraham Lincoln.[13]

Some Henry rifles were in Confederate service as well, of course, and had been since 1862, but were generally available to the public in the north. This fact frightened Governor John Brough of Ohio, who, in 1864, fantasized an uprising by thousands of Henry-armed pro-Southern draft dodgers. Brough frantically telegraphed Secretary of War Stanton with a request to stop sales of the Henry in Ohio for ninety days. According to the governor, "over fifty [Henrys] have been sold here in the last forty-eight hours to go into one copperhead county." Stanton replied that the government had no jurisdiction because the Henry was not a contract arm at that time, but the Henry salesman, who protested he sold only to loyal men, agreed to store his unsold weapons in an armory. In late January 1865, Provost Marshal Captain Benjamin Thomas apprehended a deserter, smuggler, and all-around thug named Dustin in a raid on his paramour's house in Arkansas. Thomas found Dustin hiding "under the floor with his Henry rifle."[14]

Although Nathan Bedford Forrest seems to have had no problem capturing enough Spencer ammunition to feed his captured carbines, other
Confederate forces were constrained in their use of repeaters, as was Berry
Benson at Petersburg, by a shortage of ammunition. On December 8, 1864,
a *Richmond Sentinel* editorialist wrote, "the captures which we have made
from the enemy embrace a large number of these Spencer Rifles. It would
be eminently desirable to arm our cavalry with them, and *thus remove that
inequality between the opposing lines which told so heavily against us in the
cavalry encounters of the past campaign*" (original italics). The writer did,
however, acknowledge a critical problem with such a policy: "The Spencer
Rifle cannot be used with any cartridge yet furnished to our soldiers." As a
solution, he proposed that "the thing needed is the manufacture of cartridges for the Spencer Rifle. It surely cannot be long before they will be
made, and in abundance." It never happened. The South simply did not have
the technical capacity to produce rimfire cartridges.[15]

Despite the lack of metallic cartridges, the Confederates managed to
hold their own for some time, both with captured Spencers and without.
Confederate General Basil Duke considered the "Spencer rifle . . . an excellent weapon for a weak line to hold works with, where the men were accus-
tomed to note the ground accurately, and would, therefore, be apt to aim
low, and it is desirable to pour in a rapid, continuous fire to stagger an attacking line." His ultimate conclusion, however, was that it "would be very convenient to attribute every whipping we ever got to the use of breach-loading
rifles by our antagonists, but . . . very wide of the truth." Lieutenant Colonel
Witcher and General Butler would no doubt have agreed with Duke, but
what the result of another year of war and steadily improving Yankee firepower and improved tactics would have been was yet another question. That
possibility was on the mind of Confederate chaplain Charles T. Quintard,
who opined to one of Wilson's staff officers on May 26, 1865, that Rebel
efforts to stop the Yankee juggernaut during the Selma campaign were
"absurd." Quintard believed that "our men using muskets neither new in pattern nor effective in execution and the federals armed with the Spencer rifle
which discharges seven loads in as many seconds" determined the outcome
of the campaign at its outset.[16]

Some historians have alleged that the use of repeating rifles in the Civil
War caused a revolution in tactics, but there is no solid evidence to buttress
that assertion. Civil War "tactics" manuals were essentially drill manuals.
One printed Spencer manual written for use with the infantry rifle by
Captain Barber of the Ohio Sharpshooters, which appears to have been
copied by Colonel Walcutt of the Forty-sixth Illinois, simply provides

instruction in the manual of arms. Interestingly, the extant copy reproduced in Roy Marcot's book is not a government publication, but privately published by the Spencer Company. One movement Barber and Walcutt describe, if followed to the letter, which is doubtful in battle, instructs soldiers to return to the ready position with the rifle held at waist level horizontal to the ground after firing a shot before levering in another cartridge and cocking the gun. This may well have been an attempt to reduce or control the Spencer's rate of fire and limit ammunition wastage. There is, to date, no evidence of a similar manual for cavalry usage.[17]

Most repeating rifle tactics used in the Civil War appear to have been improvised by field commanders and apparently became fairly well known as unofficial doctrine, but were never committed to paper. General Rosecrans and Colonel Wilder had a vision of spearhead columns of highly mobile infantrymen riding to battle, seizing key terrain, dismounting, and fighting with force-multiplying rapid-fire rifles to hold it against counterattack until their comrades on foot arrived. This scenario was played out precisely at Hoover's Gap. The defensive lessons Wilder learned in holding the gap were subsequently expanded and put to good use at Chickamauga, where the colonel made a number of astute tactical moves to plug holes in the Yankee line, rake the flanks of advancing enemy columns, and stave off total disaster. Were Wilder's actions instrumental in saving Rosecrans' army from total defeat that day? Although it is impossible to say with certainty, they rendered vital aid to General Thomas' stand, by Thomas' own generous admission.

General Custer's use of Spencer rifles in the hands of his Fifth Michigan Cavalry, a unit originally intended by Colonel Copeland to serve the same tactical function as Wilder's brigade, did not prove so decisive. General Custer used the Fifth's firepower to decimate the Thirty-fourth Virginia battalion, but the rugged Rebels held their position with muzzle-loading rifles and rifle muskets. In addition, the Fifth shot away its ammunition, fulfilling the assessment detractors had envisioned for the repeater in combat. It can be safely said that the Spencers at Gettysburg did not influence the final outcome of the Rummel's Farm fight or the battle in general, although the fact that their use could result in considerable casualties was certainly proved.

Some commanders of Spencer-armed troops, like Colonel Wilder, appear to have quickly learned to exercise considerable fire control while at the same time applying their available firepower at the proper tactical moment. Colonel Walcutt, who had time before the Atlanta campaign to contemplate what he would do with his Spencers, appears to have thought along the same lines as Wilder. Neither Wilder nor Walcutt spent much time instructing their men in target practice, however, a common failing throughout both armies during the Civil War. Although Captain Barber of the Ohio Sharpshooters probably did conduct some marksmanship training, his assessment that his men could hit Confederate soldiers at the distance of 700 yards with regularity using Spencers seems to be fantasy.[18]

Not every commander had the luxury of time to introduce his men to their new wonder weapons. The men of Colonel Oliver Edwards' Thirty-seventh Massachusetts were issued Spencer rifles while marching through Washington in the late summer of 1864, but received absolutely no formal training in their use and were in combat shortly afterward. At Winchester the Bay State boys ran out of ammunition and had to be resupplied by another regiment. Sharpshooters lucky enough to be issued Spencers at Petersburg, where relatively short-range encounters were the rule, used them effectively on the picket lines. Their firepower, added to that of the Thirty-seventh, was instrumental in the VI Corps' April 2, 1865, breakthrough against a severely degraded Rebel army. Had that attack taken place on the Army of Northern Virginia in its prime, even with Spencers, the results may well have been different, however.

During the course of the war's final year, ad hoc Spencer tactics evolved significantly as soldiers armed with the repeaters were assigned to missions beyond simply holding or advancing a skirmish line. At Kennesaw, Walcutt's Ohioans dispersed enemy skirmishers with offensive firepower, then held a defensive position and provided covering fire for a withdrawal. During the siege of Atlanta in August, 2,000 Spencer-armed horsemen were deployed in the trenches to replace 11,000 infantrymen, in what was considered a fairly equal firepower swap, freeing the infantry for offensive operations. By the end of the Atlanta and Savannah campaigns and at Fort Fisher, Petersburg, and Selma, Spencers were increasingly used to provide heavy suppressive covering fire for assaults. The issue of available Spencer rifles to specific regiments and detachments in the Army of the Potomac in the late summer of 1864, one regiment per division in the II Corps, reveals that the usefulness of the rapid-fire rifles for various tactical tasks was beginning to be appreciated by higher commanders.

With the possible exception of Chickamauga, however, there were never enough Spencer infantry rifles available to unequivocally state that they seriously influenced the outcome of a major battle. Ironically, some of the infantry exploits of the Spencer, at Olustee, Drewry's Bluff, and Fort Fisher, were actually attributable to cavalry carbines in the hands of foot soldiers, and the Spencer did indeed gain its greatest reputation as a cavalry arm. The tactics Spencer carbine armed cavalrymen used so effectively in 1864 and 1865 had their origins in pre-repeater days, however. Dismounting a portion

of a regiment with carbines and advancing them as skirmishers while holding a mounted reserve ready to dash in with the conventional cavalry arms of
handgun and saber at the critical moment was not a new idea. It became a
much more effective tactic with repeaters, as evidenced by Custer's attack at
Yellow Tavern and the final fate of Jubal Early's diminished force in the
spring of 1865. Sometimes, though, it failed in the face of an aggressive
mounted attack, as occurred when Captain Chapman of Mosby's command
rode down the Sixth New York Cavalry in the Shenandoah in the fall of 1864.

Despite the claims of some foreign observers at the time like Colonel
François de Chenal and Major General Sir Henry Havelock, as well as future
historians, the Union cavalry did not evolve into mounted infantry over the
course of the war. The traditional saber charge was alive and well throughout the conflict. On June 27, 1863, a hell-for-leather cavalry charge by
Minty's brigade of Yankee horsemen thoroughly trounced Joe Wheeler's
Rebel cavalry near Shelbyville, Tennessee, and the classic cavalry battle of
Brandy Station was mostly fought on horseback. The massive saber charges
at Winchester and Tom's Brook in the Shenandoah Valley in 1864 provide
ample evidence of the continuing value of the saber to the Union horse,
although it was used in conjunction with the repeating carbine. A perusal of
Stephen Z. Starr's definitive three-volume study, *The Union Cavalry in the
Civil War*, reveals forty-six separate saber charges. The vast majority of
these, however, were on the squadron, battalion, or regimental level.[19]

In the waning days of the war, there is evidence of more open assault formations involving Spencer-armed troops. Rapid-fire repeaters lessened the
need to mass firepower by concentrating human bodies, which also provided an opportunity for commanders to deploy their men so as to provide more
difficult targets, although this could exacerbate control problems. Colonel
Coon launched a full-scale attack at Nashville with a Spencer-armed heavy
skirmish line, as did Eli Long at Selma. In both instances the more open sin-
gle-line formation overran prepared Southern defensive positions using
assault fire of the type that failed the Thirty-seventh Massachusetts at
Winchester, but served the same regiment well at Petersburg. It should be
noted, however, that all of these attacks broke undermanned lines held by
outnumbered troops and, in the case of Selma, local militia, not Hood's,
Lee's, or Forrest's men at the height of their capabilities.

The evolution of tactical practices by soldiers carrying the Henry rifle is
harder to follow than those of men shouldering Spencers. Few regiments
were ever completely armed with the Henry, and the actual number of
Henrys in the ranks of any given unit is a matter of guesswork, since the
guns, for the most part privately owned, are not noted on official Quarterly

Ordnance Reports. Interpolations can be made comparing regimental ordnance reports and pay muster rolls revealing unit strength, as well as ammunition requisitions, but the results are murky. References to units being "entirely" armed with Henry rifles are often problematic and vaguely referenced, with possibly self-serving postwar memoir accounts somewhat dubious sources. The misidentification of Spencers and Henrys evidenced in the stories of non-gunwise veteran memoirists from other regiments adds to the problem.

Having said that, it is safe to assume that the Henry was, by and large, tactically treated the same as the Spencer, especially in the early days when both guns were relatively rare in the ranks. "Spencers to the front" or "Henrys to the front" sums up the usual commander's initial approach to repeaters—as effective weapons on the skirmish line in the offense or defense. Like that of Spencers, the use of Henrys diversified as time went on. Henrys in the hands of the Sixty-sixth Illinois, deployed in conventional line of battle, certainly played a significant role in saving the Union rear area from being overrun at Atlanta, possibly determining the outcome of that battle. Their record at Allatoona is less clear, although it is possible that the Seventh Illinois' Henrys, of indeterminate number, did help slow General French's attack until Union reinforcements approached, prompting a Confederate withdrawal.

With notable exceptions, ammunition wastage became less of a problem with repeaters as the war progressed. Providing plenty of ammunition in close proximity to the front solved part of the problem. A readily available ammunition wagon full of Spencer cartridges clearly marked with regimental designation facilitated the Second Rhode Island's resupplying of the Thirty-seventh Massachusetts at Winchester. In December 1864, in preparation for the Carolina campaign, the XV Army Corps's adjutant general ordered that "for each regiment armed with Henry rifles one wagon-load of that kind of ammunition will be taken." Ammunition, even for privately owned firearms, was apparently abundant in the Union supply chain, and by 1864 ammunition shortfalls do not seem any more common in units armed with repeaters than in units armed with muzzleloaders.[20]

Fire discipline was apparently enforced as well. In Wilson's raid in the final weeks of the war, troopers were issued 100 rounds each, with another eighty-five per man in reserve. Considering that a Spencer magazine can (conservatively) be emptied in under ten seconds and reloaded in the same amount of time from a Blakeslee box or under a minute from a conventional cartridge box, Wilson's horsemen could have, in theory, shot away their whole ammunition supply in half an hour. Yet a veteran commander considered 185 rounds enough for an entire campaign, and in the event it proved sufficient. By 1865 Union commanders had seamlessly integrated repeating rifles into the Federal army's overall war effort.

Did lever-action breech-loading repeating rifles win the Civil War for the Union? In a word, no. Would the Union have won the war without them? In a word, yes. Did they help end the war sooner and make the Union army, especially its cavalry, a more tactically formidable force than it otherwise would have been? Again, yes. Were they the wave of the military small arms future? Although at first glance it seems certain they would be, they were not. They served as prefigurations of a military future they would largely not participate in.

Even as lever-action repeating rifles seemed to seize the imagination of soldiers and civilians alike, they were slipping into military obsolescence. Although Laidley's board had recommended the Spencer above all other carbines while endorsing the single-shot Peabody breechloader for infantry use, General Dyer informed both the Spencer and Burnside Companies in July 1865 that the government would need no more repeating carbines or rifles. Guns already contracted for with Spencer, but not Burnside, were accepted through January 1866. The Spencer Company would survive the advent of peace, at least temporarily, but Burnside would not.

A second board assigned to consider small arms for use in United States service, headed by Major General Winfield Scott Hancock, was convened in early 1866. Despite a communication to General Dyer from a major in the Fourth U.S. Cavalry who classified the Spencer carbine as "good" but thought the Sharps "the best cavalry arm," the board again endorsed the repeater. Its report of June 4, 1866, concluded, after exhaustive testing, that the "Spencer magazine carbine is the best service gun of this kind yet offered."[21]

Despite the double endorsement, the repeater was on its way out of service. The Spencer rifle was never really in contention for adoption as an infantry arm, although the men of the Third U.S. Infantry carried Spencer rifles as late as 1867. The worldwide trend in military arms selection, as evidenced by the British ordnance committee of 1864, was toward a breech-loading infantry arm that provided the same power, range, and accuracy as the rifle musket it was replacing. That requirement necessitated a gun that could fire a metallic cartridge holding a powder charge of at least seventy grains loaded behind a bullet of at least 400 grains. In order to accommodate those criteria, the case for such a cartridge had to be at least two inches long. Neither the Spencer nor Henry action could feed a round meeting those specifications from its magazine, putting both guns out of the running as potential new infantry arms.[22]

Even before the end of the
war, Springfield was making
some single-shot breechloaders
for field trials. From January
through March 1865, working
with breech actions supplied by
the Joslyn Firearms Company, a
manufacturer of single-shot carbines, Springfield built a number of rifles chambered for the
.50-60-450 rimfire cartridge.
The new .50 caliber round was
manufactured at Frankford
Arsenal and loaded with sixty
grains of musket powder and a
450-grain bullet. An odd-looking
action with its breech directly in

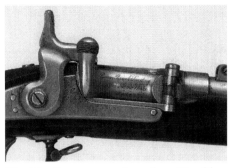

The Needham conversion of a .58 caliber
rifle musket to breech loading configuration. The Needham conversion was one of
many potential breech loading conversions
of muzzle loading arms offered at the end of
the Civil War, but not adopted by the US or
any other major power. (*Private collection;
photograph by John Hubbard*)

front of the shooter's eye when firing, the Joslyn was probably a sturdy
enough arm, but its appearance did not inspire confidence. A number of
these guns were issued to a Veteran Volunteer regiment stationed in the
Shenandoah Valley toward the end of the war. One soldier in the Sixth U.S.
Veteran Volunteers wrote, "the Joslyn rifles [are] a sort of a double-back
action concern, warranted to kill the man who fires it." The Joslyn cartridge,
while more powerful than either the Henry or Spencer rounds, did not meet
the increasingly narrow power parameters for infantry rifles, and the project
was dropped.[23]

The boards of 1865 and 1866 recommended the Peabody and Berdan
breeching systems for infantry adoption, but the Allin flip up "trapdoor" system, invented by Springfield Armory's Erskine A. Allin, won out in the end.
Allin's proprietary breech design was actually an improvement on the prewar
experimental conversion action of William Mont Storm. In 1858, Mont
Storm sold the government the right to convert 2,000 muzzleloaders to his
system at Harper's Ferry Armory. How many Mont Storm conversions were
completed is unknown, but one estimate is around 400. Most, like the innovative Morse conversion, were apparently destroyed in the Harper's Ferry
fire of 1861. The original Mont Storm system used a paper cartridge and
leaked gas, but Allin's improvement, chambered for a .58 caliber rimfire
round, provided a simple and effective method to convert existing stocks of
muzzle-loading Springfield rifle muskets. Dyer authorized Springfield to
produce Allin conversions in .58 caliber rimfire in October 1865, and pro-

duction began at the armory in early 1866. By July, however, the chambering of the new Springfield breech-loading rifle was changed to the .50-70-450 caliber centerfire cartridge, a refinement of the Joslyn ammunition that, with priming in the center of the base of the cartridge case, rather than around its rim, created a stronger and more reliable round. Old musket barrels were relined to meet the bore dimensions of the new, smaller caliber.[24]

While modern conventional wisdom might consider the decision to adopt a single-shot breechloader rather than a repeating rifle a mistake, it did not appear that way to the American professional soldiers of the time. They were aware of progressive European military thought on the matter, as well as the difficulty troopers armed with the Spencer carbine, or for that matter rifle, encountered when they fought Confederate mounted infantrymen armed with muzzle-loading rifles or rifle muskets capable of longer-range accuracy. The Spencer reigned supreme at close range, but the performance of Witcher's battalion at Gettysburg and Butler's Carolinians at Haw's Shop are instructive, as is a cavalryman's 1864 admission to Captain DeForest that "at long range we are rather afraid of them; they carry Enfields which shoot farther than our carbines."

Despite its range limitations, the Model 1865 Spencer remained the principal cavalry carbine through 1873, although some units on the frontier were armed with obsolete Starr and Maynard carbines as late as 1867. As backup and an option to the Spencers, in late 1867 the Ordnance Department contracted with the Sharps Company to convert a number of Sharps percussion ignition carbines to the .50-70 infantry round. By 1869 Sharps had re-chambered more than 30,000 carbines for the new rifle cartridge.[25]

In the early postwar period, however, outnumbered frontier commanders petitioned for as many Spencer carbines as they could get. They did not always get enough. The fact that twenty-seven of his men carried Spencer carbines and two attached civilians were armed with Henrys failed to save Captain William J. Fetterman's eighty-man force, wiped out by the Sioux near Fort Phil Kearny on December 21, 1866. In truth, Fetterman's tactical blunders were probably more responsible for the fate of his command than its arms. Model 1865 carbines in the hands of his fifty civilian scouts, most of them Union and Confederate veterans, were, however, along with a solid defensive position, responsible for Colonel George A. Forsyth's successful fight at Beecher's Island in the Republican River against the Cheyenne in September 1868. General George Custer, downgraded to the rank of lieutenant-colonel in the new smaller army, revealed he had learned something during the war by drilling his Seventh U.S. Cavalry in marksmanship with their Spencers at ranges of 100, 200, and 300 yards prior to the winter campaign of 1868. Custer's men were able to hold off large numbers of Indians with their rapid Spencer fire at the Battle of the Washita in a successful disengagement.[26]

Still, despite its continuing popularity among some soldiers, the Spencer was losing adherents as the decade elapsed. An ordnance report from 1869 revealed that although "the Spencer carbine at the end of the war was generally regarded with favor . . . the altered Sharps carbine gives great satisfaction, and is preferred by some of the cavalry regiments to the Spencer." The report concluded that the Sharps, "particularly in the ammunition," was "decidedly superior to the Spencer carbine." An ordnance board of 1870 actively sought a replacement for the Spencer, testing several types of single-shot carbines, including one based on the Springfield Allin action, which was judged the best.[27]

Both the 1865 and 1866 ordnance boards had recommended a .45 caliber cartridge with seventy-grain powder charge and a bullet of around 400 grains as an ideal infantry rifle cartridge. The ultimate adoption of the Model 1873 Springfield Allin trapdoor action single-shot series of rifles and carbines, which were new guns and not converted muskets, finally achieved that goal. As a bonus, although carbine and rifle rounds were loaded with different powder charges, the new ammunition was interchangeable in a pinch. The .45-55-405 carbine cartridge could be fired in the rifle and the .45-70-405 rifle cartridge in the carbine, although the rifle cartridge produced fairly heavy recoil in the lighter carbine.

The Spencer carbine was phased out of frontline service as Model 1873 carbines were issued, and the endorsement of the Spencer as the ideal cavalry carbine by two ordnance boards did not benefit the company any save as potential advertising copy. By the end of 1865, the United States government had more than enough Spencers in storage to meet all foreseeable future requirements, and Dyer's contract cancellation order remained in place in the years following the war. On the surface it appeared that New Haven Arms was in a similar situation, as the government had decided against buying any more Henrys for military use, and the company's private sales, most of them to soldiers, took a dip with the advent of peace. Oliver Winchester sold 4,000 Henrys in 1864, including the Bavarian contract, and 3,000 in 1865, but only 308 in the first six months of 1866. Both companies had to scramble for overseas military contracts and look to exploiting whatever American civilian market existed to continue in business.[28]

The end of the Civil War brought Oliver Winchester out of semi-retirement. The ousted B. Tyler Henry provided an incentive when he and some disaffected shareholders attempted a takeover of New Haven Arms in the spring of 1865. In response, Winchester, still a significant stockholder in New Haven, returned from Europe and, along with his son William and business partner John M. Davies, incorporated the Winchester Arms Company on July 1, 1865. One of the first efforts of the new company was to improve the Henry design to compete successfully with New Haven Arms, in which Winchester still held a significant interest. He tasked his new plant superintendent at Bridgeport, Nelson King, with the job of furthering some design ideas developed by assistant superintendent James D. Smith and others. Their goal, which Winchester had calculated as the most important improvement the Henry needed, was to fashion an effective system to load the rifle through a port in the breech action or rear of the magazine tube, removing once and for all its troublesome magazine slot. By January 1866, despite a lawsuit filed by Henry, Winchester succeeded in merging New Haven Arms with his own new company. New Haven closed its books in July 1866 and both companies merged into the Winchester Repeating Arms Company shortly afterward.[29]

King continued his work on the Henry through 1866, and came up with a perfected system in July. The first of the new pattern rifles, Model 1866 Winchesters, chambered for the same .44 rimfire cartridge as their predecessors and often called "Improved Henrys" by the public, were shipped in September. Orders poured in. Winchester, following the lead of Sam Colt, had made valuable personal contacts during his 1864-1865 sojourn in Europe, including Baron Von Nolken, his subsequent German agent, Weber Ruesch of Switzerland, and François de Suzanne, a large French gun dealer. In November 1865, Suzanne brokered a deal to send 1,000 rifles to the French forces in Mexico serving Emperor Maximilian. He requested that the guns be shipped from New York via Cuba, probably to evade undue scrutiny from U.S. government officials concerned about French violations of the Monroe Doctrine in Mexico. The rifles supplied to fulfill the contract appear to have been an interim unofficial model between the Henry and the true Winchester Model 1866 with King's patent loading port. In a subsequent display of nonpartisanship, Winchester sold 1,000 Model 1866 guns to Mexican Revolutionary Benito Juárez a year later.[30]

Winchester, a ruthless competitor and aggressive marketer, actively submitted arms to foreign trials and placed articles extolling his product in a number of publications. His French agent Suzanne, who received an early Model 1866 in October of that year, reported that he "shot it in the woods this morning and it functioned superbly." Suzanne demonstrated the gun for Marshal Canrobert, who was impressed enough to request further samples for formal testing as cavalry arms. In a British trial of 1868, a Winchester pro-

The Winchester Model 1866, the "improved Henry." The most notable changes included a loading gate in the right side of the receiver, a completely enclosed magazine tube, and a wooden forearm. (*Rob Kassab, RareWinchesters.com*)

totype musket, firing a centerfire .44 caliber cartridge loaded with a 326-grain bullet, beat out the repeating rifle competition offered by Spencer and Ball & Lamson. Winchester also submitted rifles to the Swiss army trials held in 1865 and 1866, where his sample gun proved more accurate than any other entries. The Swiss government selected the home-grown Vetterli bolt-action repeater (with a tubular magazine using a King-style loading gate) for infantry service, but made a deal with the American arms maker in which he supplied 200 Model 1866 breech actions to be barreled and stocked in Switzerland for sharpshooter use. Chile purchased 1,000 Model 1866 rifles in 1867, and used them to help win the War of the Pacific in 1879.[31]

The biggest Winchester contract in the decade following the Civil War was brokered with the Turkish government by Aristakes Azarian, an Armenian gun dealer with offices in Boston and Constantinople. In the immediate postwar period, Azarian also represented the Spencer, but when both that rifle and the Henry were demonstrated for Ottoman governor Mithat Pasha, the Turkish notable preferred the Henry by far. Further trials and demonstrations resulted in an 1870 order for 15,000 Model 1866 muskets and 5,000 carbines. The Winchester factory worked two ten-hour shifts a day to fulfill the Turkish contract, and an Ottoman order for 30,000 more guns was filled the following year.[32]

Although the Turks, following the modern military practice of the day, armed their infantry with Peabody Martini single-shot rifles chambered for a long-range cartridge, they issued Winchesters to their artillery, cavalry, and irregular Bashi-Bazouk horsemen. The Ottomans were still using the Model 1866 when they went to war with Russia in 1877. The Turks lost the war, but inflicted enormous casualties on their opponents, most notably at the siege of Plevna, Bulgaria, where the Russians attacked General Osman Pasha's well-prepared defensive positions in mass formations. Many casualties were due to long-range rapid fire from Peabody single shots, but in close the Model 66 took a heavy toll, which was noted by foreign observers. One British officer recalled that "the Winchester was made use of with deadly effect by the Turkish troops." During Osman Pasha's failed attempt to break out of Plevna in December 1877, Winchesters were issued to all officers.[33]

In contrast to the energetic Oliver Winchester, who spent the immediate postwar years reorganizing his business, improving his product, and finding new markets by personally hustling it worldwide, the Spencer management, perhaps grown fat by a seemingly endless supply of government contracts, was soon in economic trouble. Winchester, whose Henry production never met consumer demand during the war, did not suffer inordinately from a temporary postwar drop in demand and in short order had the luxury of actually expanding production to meet new demand, actively expanded that demand, and had, by late 1866, something new to sell. Warren Fisher and his associates, in contrast, faced exactly the opposite problem, finding markets to dispose of an obsolescent, unimproved arm that seems to have passed its peak of popularity in a historical eye blink.

Winchester had a winner to begin with. The old Volcanic/Henry design was always a more streamlined firearm than the Spencer and could deliver more rapid fire due to its higher capacity magazine and the fact that it was unnecessary to manually cock its hammer. Winchester's new 1866 repeating rifle and carbine was a significant improvement on the Henry and filled a vital niche in the American civilian arms market below the powerful new single-shot Sharps and Remington cartridge guns designed for infantry military use, long-range target shooting, and buffalo hunting. The Winchester's magazine capacity and breech-loading port increased the rapid-fire advantage of the Henry-style gun over the Spencer. The gun appealed to foreign governments for some military and police uses, and proved a favorite with hunters and explorers worldwide. The Winchester/Henry rimfire cartridge was of adequate power for many short-range hunting applications and entirely adequate for self-defense purposes. In addition, Winchester's product improvement program was actively working on a more powerful centerfire replacement round for the .44 rimfire.

Due to the occurrence of uneven priming compound distribution, early rimfire ammunition was often subject to ignition problems, one reason for the Henry double-pronged firing pin designed to strike a cartridge rim in two places. Unfortunately, poor quality lots of ammunition, which apparently deteriorated with age, did little to enhance the Spencer's reputation with the military or public in the postwar period. Cartridges in both .56-.56 and .56-50 calibers made by Jacob Goldmark, a cartridge maker located in Brooklyn who became the army's chief postwar supplier of .56-50 ammunition, had a high failure rate—so high in fact that "thousands of cases" of this ammunition had to be destroyed between 1866 and 1869. In addition to priming failures, the soft copper used in early self-contained cartridges was susceptible to occasional overexpansion on firing if quality control failed. During the Modoc War of 1872-1873, Spencer cartridge failures in one cavalry unit "almost caused a panic."[34]

There were rumors of ammunition problems early on. In late 1865 the English company of Greenwood & Batley offered James H. Burton a job. Burton, former acting master armorer of the Harper's Ferry arsenal, chief engineer of the Royal Small Arms Factory at Enfield, and Superintendent of Confederate Armories had been unemployed since the disintegration of the Confederacy. He had worked for Greenwood and Batley, a manufacturer of machinery and armaments, for a brief period in 1860 and was glad for the work. Burton's British employers were considering signing on as European agents for the Spencer and wanted him to check out the gun, which they had heard was "the very perfection of a Military weapon," by stopping to see the Cheney brothers and Warren Fisher in Boston on his way to Leeds.[35] Subsequent correspondence indicates that the Englishmen were having second thoughts about the Spencer. They asked Burton to "Get to know if you can in Military Quarters if there is any objection to the Spencer owing to the bursting of the guns or cartridges. An impression exists here in some quarters that the Spencer is unsafe on these grounds, but we don't see why it should be unsafe." In the event, Burton did not visit the Spencer factory, he was not courted by Warren Fisher as one might expect, and Greenwood and Batley did not become distributors for the Spencer.[36]

Winchester appears to have largely solved ammunition problems by manufacturing his own, a practice that inspired disfavor from General Ripley in 1861, but proved an asset when quality control became important and provided another profitable postwar product line. Although famed British missionary and explorer Dr. David Livingstone complained in 1873 that his Henry "fifteen shooter cartridges" had proved "not satisfactory" in the torrid African climate, such complaints seem few and far between. Centerfire priming and brass rather than copper cartridge cases perfected the self-contained cartridge within a decade after the end of the Civil War. Unfortunately, the Spencer did not survive to benefit.[37]

Despite ammunition woes, Spencer still developed a few markets in the immediate postwar period. In 1866, the Canadians purchased 300 Model 1865 rifles in .56-50 caliber to use against the "Fenians," a group of Irish American revolutionary activists, many of them Civil War veterans, determined to "twist the lion's tail" and win freedom for their native land by invading Canada. The Irish faced the Canadian militia at Ridgeway, Ontario, in a brief battle in which the militiamen shot away all their Spencer ammunition and retreated, leaving the field to the Irishmen, who were largely armed with surplus muzzleloaders and some single-shot breechloaders. Fortunately for the Canadian government, poor Fenian leadership and overall planning led to an Irish withdrawal to the United States side of the border. In the wake of the Fenian incursion, the Canadians bought another 4,000 Spencers, mostly intended for cavalry use. By 1872, however, the Canadian Spencers were replaced in service by Snider single-shot breechloaders.[38]

The Canadian sales and the fact that retail gun dealers carried new Spencer carbines and sporting rifles in their inventories alongside Henrys and Winchesters in the late 1860s failed to generate enough income to save the Spencer Company. Roy Marcot has disposed of the popular myth that the Spencer's chief problem was competition from its own rifles dumped on the market as war surplus. As Marcot points out, large-scale government sales of stored Spencers did not occur until 1870. Most of those guns actually ended up overseas. The Spencers appearing in the west after the war were from new retail sales plus those distributed by the Federal government to local militiamen and government workers at military posts, as well as individual government sales to discharged Civil War veterans, the latter totaling 2,844 rifles and 8,289 carbines.[39]

The only significant "new" Spencer product the company offered to the postwar public was the .56-46 cartridge chambering. Rather than a Spencer innovation, however, this caliber appears to be the .44 caliber round General Ramsay had Springfield Armory develop in 1864. While interesting, and more powerful than the .44 Henry, the .56-46 was too little too late to save the Spencer Firearms Company. By three years after Appomattox, the company had failed to generate a significant new military or civilian market overseas or in the United States and was on the verge of bankruptcy. In December 1868 the Fogarty Repeating Rifle Company purchased Spencer's assets. Valentine Fogarty, who had his own gun design, was more interested in the company's machinery than in continuing the manufacture of its firearms. Fogarty changed the merged company's name to the American Repeating Rifle Company the following year, but failed in his efforts to produce a successful new rifle. In April 1869 Oliver Winchester solidified his position atop the repeating rifle world by purchasing Fogarty's firm and all its assets. In short order he sold off the company's machinery and tooling at auction but kept the thousands of Spencer rifles and carbines that were part of the deal. Ironically, through this purchase, overnight Winchester became the largest Spencer dealer in the world. The year 1870, a big money year for Winchester due to rising domestic sales and the Turkish and other foreign orders, provided an unexpected bonus in coupling the acquisition of the

Spencers and Napoleon III's defeat and capture by the Prussians in the Franco-Prussian War.[40]

Following the French emperor's September 1, 1870, disaster at Sedan, a new government arose determined to continue the war. The French were desperate for arms and bought them from a number of sources, including dealers in the United States. Remington Arms Company, acting as a French agent, brokered a deal in which Winchester sold his entire supply of surplus Spencers, plus a significant number of new Model 1866 rifles, to France. Never one to let favorable publicity slip by unnoticed, Oliver Winchester later wrote the *Army and Navy Journal* that Model 1866 rifles in the hands of "a battalion of four hundred Garibaldians," destroyed the Sixty-first Prussian Infantry regiment at Dijon on January 23, 1871.[41]

The Garibaldians, a mixed force of Italian and French irregular volunteers under the command of renowned Italian commander Giuseppe Garibaldi, were among the few French troops to get to use their repeaters on the Prussians before the end of the war. In all, the French government purchased 500,000 weapons from various countries, including 391,110 from American arms merchants, 44,772 Spencer rifles and carbines and 4,406 Model 1866 Winchester muskets and rifles among them, all arriving in France between September and December 1870. The Spencers, which came from Winchester and other dealers, including Schuyler, Hartley, and Graham of New York, included both Model 1860 and 1865 guns and ammunition, and problems arose when non-English-speaking officers distributed .56-.56 ammunition with .56-.50 caliber guns.[42]

Not all the Spencers saw action in France. By January 23, five days before the war ended, 3,063 rifles had been issued to regular army troops and 15,400 carbines put in the hands of *franc tireurs*, irregulars who fought hit-and-run actions against Prussian patrols. French officers thought the Spencers "difficult to maintain" because the gun was "too good, too delicate" to entrust to raw recruits. They thought it an "excellent arm for an elite troop, but not for a raw troop." One noted that "It is so fragile that the soldier must take care not to put the buttstock on the ground but on his foot, otherwise sand or earth can get inside the magazine tube and block the mechanism." Initially, French officers considered the 1866 a purely short-range weapon, but their tests, as with the Swiss trials, revealed the gun to have surprisingly good accuracy up to 300 yards.[43]

Oddly enough, in a strange footnote to the Spencer story, and probably because of the familiarity the Spencer gained in Europe from the large French purchase of 1870, a Belgian manufacturer, Falisse & Trappman, produced a run of Spencer carbine clones in 1873. Roy Marcot estimates the company's production at less than a thousand guns, but what market they were intended to fulfill remains a mystery. After the war, the French Spencers were kept in reserve until 1876, as "potentially usable arms," then apparently downgraded to emergency use status until they were finally sold at public auctions as surplus arms in 1900, at eighteen francs each.[44]

In the end, Oliver Winchester's business skills and marketing abilities made his name a synonym for "rifle" around the world, while the Spencer was largely forgotten. By the late nineteenth century, aside from the notable Turkish contract, though, Winchester's 1860s lever-action rifles and their descendants were not primarily known as military weapons. Despite this, design aspects of the Civil War-era lever-action repeaters lingered for a generation in military repeating rifles. The basic buttstock and under-barrel tubular magazine concepts introduced by the Spencer and Henry endured in the Vetterli, Hotchkiss, Kropatscheck, and Mauser Model 1884 repeaters, all bolt-action guns chambered for the large black powder military cartridges of the day.

Winchester actually manufactured the buttstock magazine Hotchkiss, the company's first bolt-action rifle. The U.S. Army purchased several thousand Hotchkiss actions from Winchester to build .45-70 carbines and rifles on at Springfield, as well as some complete guns for field trials, although the army never formally adopted the design. Winchester made more than 84,000 Hotchkiss rifles, muskets, and carbines between 1879 and 1899. Assistant Surgeon (later general) Leonard Wood carried one during the Apache campaign of 1886. Wood recalled that Geronimo was quite taken with the Hotchkiss after his surrender, and asked to borrow it and take a few shots. According to Wood, the chief "fired at a mark, just missing one of his own men who was passing. This he regarded as a great joke, rolling on the ground and laughing heartily and shouting, 'Good gun.'"[45]

The under-barrel tubular magazine pioneered in the Henry even survived into the early days of the small-bore smokeless powder era, as the feeding system of the 8-millimeter Model 1886 French Lebel rifle. That same year the Winchester Company produced its first lever-action gun able to chamber, feed, and fire the .45-70 military cartridge. It was clear by then, however, that the military rifle's future was with the smaller yet more powerful high-velocity smokeless powder cartridges and bolt-action rifles in these calibers with clip-fed box magazines directly under the action like the Mannlicher, Lee, and Mauser.

The John Browning-designed Winchester Model 1895, with its box magazine and chambered for modern cartridges, was the last lever action with any traction in the military market. The United States government ordered

The Winchester Model 1895, a strongly built rifle designed by firearms genius John Browning, was a significant departure for Winchester, as it featured a box magazine under the action, rather than the usual tubular magazine under the barrel. While this limited magazine capacity to five shots, it also allowed the use of the high powered long-range cartridges with pointed bullets used in the bolt action military rifles of the day, and was able to be quickly reloaded using five shot disposable clips of ammunition. The 1895 was chambered for a number of popular military calibers. The United States bought a number during the Spanish American War in .30-40 caliber, but they saw minimal use and were sold off as surplus shortly after the war. The Model 1895 was a popular big game hunting rifle, however, and one of President Theodore Roosevelt's favorite guns. (*Rob Kassab, RareWinchesters.com*)

10,000 Model 1895 muskets in 1898 in the same .30-40 caliber as the army's Krag Jorgensen bolt-action rifle to offset a Spanish-American War production shortfall of that arm. In the end, a mere 100 were issued in the Philippines in 1899, but played no significant part in the war effort and were sold to a civilian gun dealer shortly afterward. The remaining 9,900 muskets were purchased by a New York arms merchant who disposed of them in Cuba.[46]

The Model 1895, however, does have the distinction of being the last lever-action rifle used in large-scale combat. In late 1914 the Russian government, after suffering catastrophic losses of troops and arms in the opening battles of World War I, ordered 100,000 Model 1895s in 7.62-millimeter caliber. These guns were fitted with a slot atop the action to facilitate loading with the same pre-packaged five-shot stripper clips used with the Russian issue Moisin-Nagant bolt-action rifle. By 1917, Winchester had delivered over a quarter of a million Model 1895s to the tsar's government, when the Russian Revolution abruptly terminated the contract. Ironically, some Model 1895s ended up in the hands of Soviet soldiers who used them against United States troops sent to northern Russia to protect Western interests at the end of World War I.[47]

The Model 1895 ended the interrupted story of the lever-action repeating rifle in warfare begun by the Spencer and Henry almost sixty years before. In truth, the self-contained metallic cartridges the lever-action repeaters were chambered for and that made them and future repeaters technically possible provided the real revolution in arms technology, more so than the arms they were chambered in. Once reliable repeating actions were matched with more powerful self-contained cartridges, all the world's armies adopted them. The use of breech-loading rifles and then repeating arms made possible by the metallic cartridge forced a significant change in tactics, making dispersion of troops a necessity, continuing a trend that had its origins in the closing days of the Civil War. Mass formations became suicide formations.

Although successive generations of lever-action Winchester sporting rifles have been sold down to the present day, the last Henry rifle was made in the early autumn of 1866, and the last Spencer probably rolled off the assembly line sometime in 1868. Both guns remained in civilian service for several generations, however. While rimfire ammunition for both guns (and in the case of the .44 for the Winchester Model 1866 as well) was produced up to the end of World War I, existing stocks were consumed or deteriorated into uselessness over the next several decades. By the mid-twentieth century, the absence of commercial ammunition, coupled with the development of more powerful modern arms, relegated the Spencer and the Henry to the category of curios and collectibles.

It seemed like the end for the formerly famous lever actions, and yet it was not. The intense interest in the Civil War reawakened during the conflict's centennial in 1965 did not diminish. The North-South Skirmish Association, which promotes target shooting with Civil War-era rifles, muskets, revolvers, and cannon, as well as reenactment units dedicated to the recreation of Civil War battles and public presentations of "living history" demonstrations of Civil War soldier life, flourished in the wake of the centennial celebrations up to the present. These groups provided a growing market for reproduction firearms as original guns became rarer and escalated in value on the antique collectible market. The arrival of "cowboy action shooting" as a sport, coupled with the popularity of films like *Dances with Wolves* and *Lonesome Dove,* expanded the potential market for newly made Henry rifles.

Italian gun maker Aldo Uberti, who specialized in replicating classic nineteenth-century American arms, reintroduced the Henry rifle in the 1970s. One run of Henrys in the original .44 rimfire caliber, along with original-style rimfire ammunition, was produced for collectors through the auspices of the Navy Arms Company of Ridgefield, New Jersey, a large wholesale and retail firearms dealer. Most modern Henry rifles are, however, chambered for the .44-.40 or .45 Colt cartridges, developed in 1873 yet still in use. The fired cases of centerfire ignition cartridges, unlike rimfire rounds, can be reloaded with new powder and bullets after they are fired.

For a long time it seemed the Spencer would not have a similar renaissance, but ultimately its moment came. In the 1980s, antique arms parts dealer S&S Firearms of Glendale, New York, began to offer a replacement breech block to convert original guns to fire custom made .56-.56 or .56-.50 cartridges. Ironically, the S&S modification, allowing a more reliable centerfire cartridge to be used in the Spencer, might have provided a significant and inexpensive modernization of the gun back in 1866, when the company was starved for new ideas to stimulate sales.

Russian World War I soldiers armed with model 1895 Winchesters, the last significant use of the lever action rifle as a military arm. These rifles remained in Russian service even after the war. (*Private Collection*)

In the 1990s, increasing hobbyist and reenactor interest in Spencer shooting led to the creation of handmade reproductions of the Spencer Model 1860 rifle and carbine by custom rifle maker Larry Romano of Pennellville, New York. For the convenience of shooters, Romano chambers his Model 1860s in a centerfire version of the original Model 1865's .56-50 caliber. At the end of the 1990s, Taylor's & Company of Winchester, Virginia, an importer of nineteenth-century reproduction firearms, began to offer Spencer Model 1865 carbines made in Italy and chambered for the .45 Schofield and .44 Russian pistol cartridges as well as the .56-.50 centerfire rifle caliber, for which cartridge cases are now commercially available.

The future renaissance of obsolete guns among historical hobbyists was far from the mind of Oliver Winchester as he continued to modernize and expand his product line through the 1870s. In 1880, long before his Model 1866 rifle went out of production, Winchester, at the top of his financial, industrial, and marketing game, died. His consumptive son and heir William passed away the following year. The company Winchester founded endured, however, through good years and bad, under new and varied ownership and management, producing numerous new sporting gun models and fulfilling huge government arms and ammunition contracts during World Wars I and II and down to the present day. Except for lending his name to the revolutionary gun he developed, B. Tyler Henry faded into oblivion after 1865.

Christopher Spencer, never a principal of the company that bore his name, moved on to other things in 1866. He collaborated with fellow arms inventor Sylvester H. Roper of Amherst, Massachusetts, in developing Roper's idea of a repeating shotgun with a revolving magazine, a concept he later expanded to rifles. The company failed, largely due to the high cost of its products, after several years of limited production. By 1872 the Roper Sporting Arms Company had become Billings and Spencer, a company offering Roper guns yet primarily occupied with commercial drop forgings and sewing machine shuttles.

Christopher Spencer maintained his interest in guns. In 1872 he patented a single-shot rifle capable of chambering and firing the same large military and hunting cartridges as the Springfield, Sharps, and Remington rifles, but it never went into production. Spencer and Roper invented the first pump-action shotgun in the early 1880s, a novel arm that also eventually failed commercially. Spencer's later firearms inventions never caught the public imagination like his famous Civil War repeater, but his fortune was secured with his greatest invention, the automatic screw machine he patented in 1873. One of the most significant inventions in industrial history, the screw machine made Christopher Spencer a wealthy man, with time to spare for his hobbies of hunting, fishing, boating, playing with his children, and fiddling with mechanical things that captured his fancy. His interest in innovation was unflagging and included building a steam-powered automobile which he drove from Hartford to New York in 1901. In 1920 Spencer proved he was a man of the twentieth century as well as the nineteenth by taking several short trips in an airplane. This most unusual Yankee, who was tutored in the gunsmith's art by a Revolutionary War veteran, shot targets with the most significant president of the nineteenth century and played perhaps as influential a role in industrial history as any single American, passed away on at his home in Windsor, Connecticut, on January 14, 1922.

Oliver Winchester and Christopher Spencer provide graphic examples of the transformation wrought by industrialization in America. They were new men spawned by an earlier, almost medieval, world. Raised in an era when citizens who saw George Washington still walked the earth, both were driven by a modernization ethos born of the American Industrial Revolution. Winchester became the new American businessman. No gentleman merchant, he was conversant with fiscal and corporate maneuvering, industrial and technical manufacturing techniques, and was a master of product and self-promotion with a tad of flimflam thrown in, building on the prototype created by his predecessors Eli Whitney and Sam Colt. Christopher Spencer, on the other hand, was the type of man whose inventiveness made it possible for the Oliver Winchesters of the world to pursue their own obsessions. He was the quintessential American folkloric Tom Swiftian inventor, mechanic, tinkerer, and fixer with little formal education, a genius in greasy clothes, an archetype of Edison and Ford.

Nineteenth-century men like Winchester and Spencer gave birth to modern America. Almost unintentionally (no abolitionists they), pursuing goals of their own, they abetted the destruction of an anachronistic agricultural world built on a culture of human slavery. That older world had to disappear as part of the creation of the modern, which in turn raised its own new set of problems of industrial and social justice. In the good and the bad, for better or worse, we who live in the world they helped create are all their heirs.

NOTES

CHAPTER ONE: PAST IS PROLOGUE

[1] Thomas W. Hyde, *Following the Greek Cross or, Memories of the Sixth Army Corps* (Boston: Houghton Mifflin, 1895), p. 205.

[2] Charles C. Trench, *A History of Marksmanship* (Chicago: Follett, 1972), p. 9.

[3] Ibid., p. 10; W. W. Greener, *The Gun and Its Development,* 9th ed. (Birmingham: Greener, 1910), p. 1; John J. Hennessy, *Return to Bull Run: The Campaign and Battle of Second Manassas* (New York: Simon & Schuster, 1993), p. 357.

[4] Edward A. Dieckmann, Sr., "Stone Age Guided Missiles," *Gun Digest*, 1966.

[5] H. J. Soushanany, untitled handwritten history of shooting manuscript, dated 1864, French Army Archives, Vincennes.

[6] Dieckmann, "Stone Age Guided Missiles."

[7] Ibid.

[8] Trench, *Marksmanship*, pp. 19-20.

[9] Dieckmann, "Stone Age Guided Missles."

[10] Ibid.

[11] Robert Hardy, *Longbow: A Social and Military History*, 3rd ed. (London: Bois D'Arc Press, 1992), p. 5.

[12] Trench, *Marksmanship*, p. 35.

[13] Ibid., pp. 32-33.

[14] Hardy, *Longbow*, pp. 25-26.

[15] Ibid., pp. 28-30; Hugh D. Soar, *The Crooked Stick: A History of the Longbow* (Yardley, Pa.: Westholme, 2004), p. 17.

[16] Hardy, *Longbow*, pp. 34-36.

[17] Ibid., p. 29.

[18] Ibid., p. 68.

[19] Soushanany mss; Hardy, *Longbow*, pp. 122-125.

[20] Hardy, *Longbow*, p. 130.

[21] Ibid., pp. 131-132.

[22] Robert M. Hyatt, "Crossbows," *Gun Digest*, 1965.

[23] Ibid.; Soar, *Crooked Stick*, p. 45.

[24] Ibid., pp. 27-30.

[25] Gustav Freytag, "The Citizen and His Shooting Festivals," *Gun Collector*, 37 [n.d.].

[26] Soushanany mss.

[27] Soushanany mss.; Hardy, *Longbow*, p. 129.

[28] Jaroslav Lugs, *Firearms Past and Present: A Complete Review of Firearm Systems and Their Histories,* vol. 1 (London: Grenville, 1975), p. 12; Albert Manucy, *Artillery Through the Ages: A Short History of Cannon, Emphasizing Types Used in America* (Washington, D.C.: United States Government Printing Office, 1949), pp. 3-4; Trench, *Marksmanship*, p. 105.

[29] Lugs, *Firearms Past and Present*, pp. 13-14.

[30] Michael A. Bellesiles, *Arming America: The Origins of a National Gun Culture* (New York: Knopf, 2000), pp. 22-25; P. Valentine Harris, "The Decline of the Longbow," *Journal of the Society of Archer-Antiquaries,* 19, 1976; William Aldis Wright, ed., *English Works of Roger Ascham* (Cambridge: University Press, 1904), pp. 3-119. Cover blurbs from scholars for *Arming America* describe it as "astonishingly original and innovative," "splendidly subversive,"

"meticulously, even extravagantly researched," and "stunning history." The book, which is rife with technical as well as interpretive errors, received totally uncritical and even gushing praise from Garry Wills, who has no demonstrated expertise in the subject at all but apparently fit the political mold desired, in a front-page review in the *New York Times Book Review*. Wills and others greeted the exposition of potential fraud in Bellesisles' research, resulting in the revocation of his Bancroft Prize and loss of tenure at Emory University, with an equally "stunning" silence. To be fair, *Arming America* does have an excellent bibliography.

[31] Freytag, *Shooting Festivals*; Soushanany mss.

[32] Harold L. Peterson, *Arms and Armor in Colonial America* (New York: Company of Military Historians, 1956), pp. 12-16.

[33] Howard L. Blackmore, *British Military Firearms, 1650-1850* (London: Herbert Jenkins, 1961), p. 6.

[34] D. F. Harding, *Smallarms of the East India Company, 1600-1856, Vol. 4, The Users and Their Smallarms* (London: Foresight, 1999), pp. 288-289.

[35] Richard Akehurst, *Sporting Guns* (London: Octopus Books, 1968), p. 4.

[36] Peterson, *Arms and Armor*, pp. 20-21.

[37] Greener, *The Gun*, pp. 65-66; Lugs, *Firearms Past and Present*, p. 19.

[38] Akehurst, *Sporting Guns*, p. 8.

[39] Peterson, *Arms and Armor*, p. 25.

[40] Blackmore, *British Military Firearms*, pp. 21-22.

[41] Ibid.; Lugs, *Firearms Past and Present*, p. 26.

[42] Peterson, *Arms and Armor*, pp. 29-32.

[43] Ibid., pp. 32-33; Major Noel Cory, "The Miquelet Lock," *Gun Digest*, 1985.

[44] G. A. Hayes-McCoy, *Irish Battles: A Military History of Ireland* (London: Longmans, Green, 1969), pp. 220-221.

[45] Ibid.; Francis Grose, *Military Antiquities*, 2 vols. (London, 1786-1788), vol. 1, p. 177, cited in Brent Nosworthy's unpublished manuscript "The Anatomy of a Victory."

[46] Blackmore, *British Military Firearms*, p. 39.

[47] Akehurst, *Sporting Guns*, p. 12.

[48] Peterson, *Arms and Armor*, p. 9.

[49] Ibid., pp. 12-15.

[50] Ibid., p. 23.

[51] Henry J. Kauffman, *The Pennsylvania-Kentucky Rifle* (New York: Bonanza Books, 1960), pp. 8-17; Joseph Ruckman, *Recreating the American Longhunter, 1740-1790* (Excelsior Springs, Mo.: Fine Arts Press, 2000), p. 9.

[52] Bob Bell, "The Most Important Shot Ever Fired?" *Gun Digest*, 1998; Joseph G. Bilby, "A Soldier of Military Distinction and Honor: The Story of Pattie Ferguson and His Rifle," *Dixie Gun Works Black Powder Annual*, 2004.

[53] Blackmore, *British Military Firearms*, pp. 67-68.

[54] D. F. Harding, *Smallarms of the East India Company, 1600-1856, Vol. 3, Ammunition and Performance* (London: Foresight Books, 1999), pp. 218-219, 224.

[55] F. Myatt, *The Illustrated Encyclopedia of 19th Century Firearms* (New York: Crescent Books, 1994), pp. 18-19.

[56] Ibid.

[57] Ibid., p. 20.

[58] Samuel Baker, *Wild Beasts and Their Ways: Reminiscences of Europe, Asia, Africa and America* (New York: Macmillan, 1890), p. 2.

[59] Ned H. Roberts, *The Muzzle Loading Caplock Rifle* (Harrisburg, Pa.: Stackpole, 1952), pp. 166-171.

[60] Soushanany mss.

[61] Myatt, *The Illustrated Encyclopedia of 19th Century Firearms*, p. 52.

[62] Ibid., pp. 62-64.

63 Major Calhoun Benham, *A System for Conducting Musketry Instruction Prepared and Printed by Order of General Bragg for the army of Tennessee,* with introduction by Joseph G. Bilby (1863; reprint, Auburn, Va.: J. W. Henry Publishing, 1998); Joseph G. Bilby, ed., *A System of Target Practice For the Use of Troops When Armed with the Musket, Rifle Musket, Rifle or Carbine, Prepared Principally from the French* (1862; reprint, Auburn, Va.: J. W. Henry Publishing, 1998).

CHAPTER TWO: BREECHLOADER TO REPEATER

1 Manucy, *Artillery Through the Ages,* p. 6.

2 Greener, *The Gun and Its Development,* pp. 104–106; Trench, *History of Marksmanship,* p. 109; Manucy, *Artillery Through the Ages,* p. 6.

3 Lugs, *Firearms Past and Present,* pp. 19, 21.

4 Greener, pp. 104-105.

5 Lugs, *Firearms Past and Present,* p. 45; Greener, *The Gun and Its Development,* p. 105.

6 Blackmore, *British Military Firearms,* p. 82.

7 Ibid., p. 71.

8 Ibid., p. 83.

9 Ibid., p. 84.

10 Bilby, "A Soldier of Military Distinction and Honor."

11 Ibid.

12 Blackmore, *British Military Firearms,* p. 85.

13 Harding, *Smallarms of the East India Company, 1600-1856,* vol. IV, pp. 124, 197-200.

14 Blackmore, *British Military Firearms,* pp. 86-87.

15 Lugs, *Firearms Past and Present,* p. 46.

16 Ibid.

17 Myatt, *The Illustrated Encyclopedia of 19th Century Firearms,* p. 71.

18 Lugs, *Firearms Past and Present,* p. 45.

19 Ibid., pp. 49-50.

20 Merritt Roe Smith, *Harper's Ferry Armory and the New Technology* (Ithaca: Cornell University Press, 1977), p. 185.

21 Ibid., p. 186.

22 Philip B. Sharpe, *The Rifle in America* (New York: Funk & Wagnalls, 1953), p. 13; Smith, *Harper's Ferry,* pp. 186-188; John D. McAulay, *Civil War Breechloading Rifles: A Survey of the Innovative Infantry Arms of the American Civil War* (Lincoln, R.I.: Andrew Mowbray, 1991), p. 31.

23 Smith, *Harper's Ferry,* pp. 188-189.

24 Ibid., p. 189.

25 R. T. Huntington, *Hall's Breechloaders* (York, Pa.: Shumway, 1972), p. 11.

26 Louis A. Garavaglia and Charles G. Worman, *Firearms of the American West, 1803-1865* (Albuquerque: University of New Mexico Press, 1984), p. 118.

27 Huntington, *Hall's Breechloaders,* p. 169.

28 McAulay, *Civil War Breechloading Rifles,* p. 33.

29 Garavaglia and Worman, *Firearms of the American West,* p. 119.

30 Lugs, *Firearms Past and Present,* pp. 59, 68.

31 Garavaglia and Worman, *Firearms of the American West,* pp. 126-128; A modern test of a Hall rifle in good condition revealed, according to the author, that the gun was a "sound and serviceable, if somewhat complicated rifle." Dennis Bruns, "Shooting the Hall Breechloader," *Gun Digest,* 1997.

32 Samuel E. Chamberlain (Roger Hunterfield, ed.), *My Confession* (New York: Harper & Brothers, 1956), pp. 58, 188-191; In his modern test, Dennis Bruns used the Hall breech as a pistol successfully, although accuracy was nil beyond point blank range. Bruns, "Hall Breechloader."

[33] John D. McAulay, *Civil War Carbines*, Vol. II: *The Early Years* (Lincoln, R.I.: Andrew Mowbray, 1991), pp. 46-47.

[34] Garavaglia and Worman, *Firearms of the American West*, pp. 129-130; McAulay, *Civil War Carbines*, pp. 47-49.

[35] Earl J. Coates and John D. McAulay, *Civil War Sharps Carbines and Rifles* (Gettysburg, Pa.: Thomas, 1996), pp. 3-4.

[36] Garavaglia and Worman, *Firearms of the American West*, p. 138.

[37] John D. McAulay, *Carbines of the Civil War, 1861-1865* (Union City, Tenn.: Pioneer Press, 1981), p. 38.

[38] Garavaglia and Worman, *Firearms of the American West*, p. 188.

[39] Quoted in Michael McIntosh, *Shotguns and Shooting* (Camden, Me.: Countrysport Press, 1995), p. 137.

[40] Lugs, *Firearms Past and Present*, p. 133.

[41] Blackmore, *British Military Firearms*, pp. 235-240.

[42] Lugs, *Firearms Past and Present*, p. 151.

[43] Ibid., pp. 151-152.

[44] Blackmore, *British Military Firearms*, pp. 92-93.

[45] Ibid., p. 251.

[46] Ibid.

[47] Herbert C. Houze, *Colt Rifles and Muskets from 1847 to 1870* (Iola, Wisc.: Krause, 1996), p. 7.

[48] Ibid., pp. 10-11.

[49] Ibid., p. 12.

[50] Ibid., pp. 26-41.

[51] Garavaglia and Worman, *Firearms of the American West*, pp. 280-283.

[52] McLaughlin's report specifically notes that multiple discharges were traceable to problems with percussion caps, but many modern gun writers and historians have assumed that such accidents were the result of flame cross-ignition from the front of the cylinder. Although this is possible with ill-fitting bullets, it is very rare, and impossible with bullets that fit the gun properly, effectively sealing the chamber. Houze, *Colt Rifles and Muskets*, p. 12.

[53] Houze, *Colt Rifles and Muskets*, pp. 71-79.

[54] "Colt's Revolving Rifle," *Military Gazette*, 3, no. 18, Sept. 15, 1860, p. 276.

[55] McAulay, *Civil War Breechloading Rifles*, p. 14.

[56] Charles A. Stevens, *Berdan's United States Sharpshooters in the Army of the Potomac: 1861-1865* (reprint, Dayton, Ohio: Morningside Books, 1984), p. 27.

[57] McAulay, *Civil War Breechloading Rifles*, p. 17.

[58] Ken Baumann, *Arming the Suckers, 1861-1865: A Compilation of Illinois Civil War Weapons* (Dayton, Ohio: Morningside, 1989), p. 115; for a list of these regiments, see McAulay, *Civil War Breechloading Rifles*, p. 18.

[59] Frederick P. Todd, *American Military Equipage, 1851-1871,* vol. II, *State Forces* (New York: Chatham Square Press, 1983), pp. 943, 1195, 1217. Model 1855 carbines were available in .36, .44, and .56 calibers.

[60] Bauman, *Arming the Suckers*, p. 53; McAulay, *Civil War Breechloading Rifles*, p. 18.

[61] William B. Edwards, *Civil War Guns* (Harrisburg, Pa.: Stackpole, 1988), p. 321.

[62] John E. Parsons, *The First Winchester* (New York: Winchester Press, 1969), p. 35.

CHAPTER THREE: THE SEARCH FOR THE PERFECT CARTRIDGE

[1] Donald Dallas, *Purdey Gun and Rifle Makers: The Definitive History* (London: Quiller Press, 2000), p. 48; Lugs, *Firearms Past and Present*, p. 76; Pauly patent papers, French National Archives, Paris.

[2] Lugs, *Firearms Past and Present*, p. 77.

[3] Ibid.

[4] Ibid.

[5] *Army & Navy Journal*, vol. 2, 1864, p. 278.

[6] Lugs, *Firearms Past and Present*, p. 70.

[7] Ibid., pp. 71-72.

[8] Ibid., p. 72.

[9] Blackmore, *British Military Firearms*, p. 227.

[10] Ibid.

[11] Lugs, *Firearms Past and Present*, pp. 75-76.

[12] Myatt, *Illustrated Encyclopedia of 19th Century Firearms*, pp. 88-90.

[13] Dallas, *Purdey*, p. 49.

[14] George Madis, *The Winchester Book* (Brownsville, Tex.: Art & Reference House, 1961), p. 13.

[15] Ibid., p. 14.

[16] Ibid., p. 15; Norm Flayderman, *Flayderman's Guide to Antique American Firearms and Their Values*, 7th ed. (Iola, Wisc.: Krause, 1998), p. 260; Roy G. Jinks, *History of Smith & Wesson*, revised 10th ed. (N. Hollywood, Calif.: Beinfield Publishing, 1991), p. 16.

[17] Flayderman, *Guide*, p. 261; Jinks, *Smith & Wesson*, pp. 18-19.

[18] Flayderman, *Guide*, pp. 261-262; Madis, *Winchester*, pp. 15-16; Garavaglia and Worman, *Firearms of the American West*, p. 260.

[19] Frank C. Barnes, *Cartridges of the World* (Chicago: Follett, 1965), p. 271; Lugs, *Firearms Past and Present*, p. 78; Raymond Caranta, "Louis Nicolas Auguste Flobert; His Rimfire Rifles and Cartridges," *Gun Digest, 1974* (Northfield, Ill.: Digest Books, 1973), pp. 122-123.

[20] Caranta, "Flobert," p. 125.

[21] Jinks, *Smith & Wesson*, p. 20.

[22] Ibid., pp. 20-21.

[23] Ibid., pp. 22-23.

[24] Garavaglia and Worman, *Firearms of the American West*, p. 323.

[25] William Hosley, *Colt: The Making of an American Legend* (Amherst: University of Massachusetts Press, 1996), p. 39.

[26] David Freeman Hawke, *Nuts and Bolts of the Past: A History of American Technology, 1776-1860* (New York: Harper & Row, 1988), pp. 97-102.

[27] Smith, *Harper's Ferry Armory*, pp. 197-198.

[28] Hawke, *Nuts and Bolts*, pp. 105-108.

[29] James E. Hicks, *U.S. Military Firearms, 1776-1956* (Alhambra, Calif.: Borden Publishing, 1962), pp. 85-86; Flayderman, *Guide*, pp. 463-464, 530; McAulay, *Civil War Breechloading Rifles*, pp. 120-124.

[30] John E. Parsons, *The First Winchester* (New York: Winchester Press, 1955), pp. 5-7; Herbert G. Houze, *Winchester Repeating Arms Company: Its History and Development from 1865 to 1981* (Iola, Wisc.: Krause, 1994), pp. 8-9, 14.

[31] Parsons, *First Winchester*, pp. 8-9.

[32] Ibid., p. 9.

[33] Wiley Sword, *The Historic Henry Rifle* (Lincoln, R.I.: Andrew Mowbray, 2002), p. 9; Houze, *Winchester Repeating Arms*, pp. 13-14.

[34] Sword, *Historic Henry Rifle*, p. 9.

[35] Parsons, *First Winchester*, pp. 3-4.

[36] Ibid., p. 7; Houze, *Winchester Repeating Arms*, p. 9.

[37] "Firearms and Rifle Breechloaders," *Scientific American*, 4, no. 4, New Series, January 26, 1861.

38 Parsons, *First Winchester*, p. 10.

39 McAulay, *Civil War Breechloading Rifles*, p. 41.

40 Houze, *Winchester Repeating Arms*, p. 16; Houze, *Colt Rifles and Muskets*, pp. 44-60.

41 Robert V. Bruce, *Lincoln and the Tools of War* (Urbana: University of Illinois Press, 1989), p. 99; Houze, *Winchester Repeating Arms*, p. 16. In his memoir, Stoddard, a prototype of Zelig or Forrest Gump if all his stories are to be believed, probably confused this alleged incident with the actual test of a Spencer rifle by Lincoln the following year.

CHAPTER FOUR: CHRISTOPHER SPENCER INVENTS A GUN

1 Tyler Bennett, ed., *Lincoln and the Civil War in the Diaries and Letters of John Hay* (New York: Dodd, Mead, 1939), p. 82; Bruce, *Lincoln and the Tools of War*, pp. 113-114.

2 Roy M. Marcot, *Spencer Repeating Firearms* (Rochester, N.Y.: Rowe, 1990), pp. 12-13.

3 Hawke, *Nuts and Bolts*, pp. 109-110.

4 Marcot, *Spencer*, p. 13.

5 Spencer U.S. patent 27,393, March 6, 1860, quoted in McAulay, *Breechloading Rifles*, p. 93; Marcot, *Spencer*, pp. 15-16.

6 Marcot, *Spencer*, p. 189.

7 Ibid., p. 207.

8 Ibid., pp. 25-26; Edwards, *Civil War Guns*, p. 146.

9 Christopher Spencer to James H. Kennedy, March 26, 1912, C. M. Spencer Papers, Windsor (Conn.) Historical Society; Welles to Dahlgren, June 4, 1861, Andrew F. Lustyik collection, quoted in Marcot, *Spencer*, p. 28.

10 Dahlgren to Captain Andrew A. Harwood, June 8, 1861, USNA, quoted in Marcot, *Spencer*, p. 28; Christopher Spencer to James H. Kennedy, March 26, 1912, C. M. Spencer Papers.

11 L. D. Satterlee, comp., *Ten Old Gun Catalogs: Spencer Catalog 1866* (Chicago: Gun Digest Company, 1957), p. 4.

12 Marcot, *Spencer*, p. 29.

13 U.S. Government, *The War of the Rebellion: A Compilation of the Official Records of the Union and Confederate Armies* (Washington, D.C.: Government Printing Office, 1880-1901), Ser. I, Vol. V, p. 30. Hereafter cited as *O.R.*

14 Kingsbury to Brig. Gen Maxey, November 4, 1861, quoted in Marcot, *Spencer*, p. 29.

15 Satterlee, *Spencer Catalog*, p. 4; Carl L. Davis, *Arming the Union: Small Arms in the Union Army* (Port Washington, N.Y.: Kennikat Press, 1973), p. 136.

16 Quoted in Marcot, *Spencer*, p. 52.

17 Bruce, *Lincoln and the Tools of War*, p. 203; Christopher Spencer to James H. Kennedy, March 26, 1912, C. M. Spencer Papers. Blaine was also, at the time, a Maine legislator. He was elected to Congress in 1863, and became Speaker of the House in 1869. He later twice served as Secretary of State and ran unsuccessfully for president in 1884.

18 James W. Ripley to Simon Cameron, December 11, 1861, Senate Executive Document 72, 37th Congress, 2nd Session, Quoted in Marcot, *Spencer*, p. 35.

19 Warren Fisher, Jr., to Simon Cameron, December 18, 1861, Stuart C. Mowbray and Jennifer Heroux, eds., *Civil War Arms Makers and Their Contracts: A Facsimile Reprint of the Report by the Commission on Ordnance and Ordnance Stores, 1862* (Lincoln, R.I.: Andrew Mowbray, 1998), p. 422.

20 Marcot, *Spencer*, p. 34.

21 Quoted in Edwards, *Civil War Guns*, p. 146.

22 Marcot, *Spencer*, p. 37.

23 Mowbray and Heroux, *Civil War Arms Makers*, p. iii.

24 Ibid., p. 424.

25 Ibid.

26 Marcot, *Spencer*, p. 37.

27 Mowbray and Heroux, *Civil War Arms Makers*, p. 427.

28 Ibid.

29 Ibid., pp. 419-422.

30 Ibid., pp. 427-428.

31 Marcot, *Spencer*, pp. 30-33; Mowbray and Heroux, *Civil War Arms Makers*, p. 421.

32 Wiley Sword, "Those Damned Michigan Spencers," *Man at Arms Magazine*, 19, no. 5, October 1997.

33 Ezra J. Warner, *Generals in Blue: Lives of the Union Commanders* (Baton Rouge: LSU Press, 1992), p. 92; Sword, "Those Damned Michigan Spencers."

34 Sword, "Those Damned Michigan Spencers."

35 Ibid.

36 Ibid.

37 Ibid.

38 Chrisopher M. Spencer, "Address to the Southern Society," C. M. Spencer Papers; Sword, "Those Damned Michigan Spencers."

39 Quoted in Sword, "Those Damned Michigan Spencers."

40 Marcot, *Spencer*, p. 42.

41 L. D. Satterlee, comp., *Ten Old Gun Catalogs: New Haven Arms Catalog*, p. 21; Marcot, *Spencer*, p. 43.

42 Sword, "Those Damned Michigan Spencers."

43 Crisfield Johnson, comp., *History of Cuyahoga County, Ohio, in Three Parts* (Cleveland: D. W. Ensign & Company, 1879).

44 Satterlee, *Spencer Catalog*, p. 7; Marcot, *Spencer*, p. 53.

45 The famous Pullman sleeping car, invented by George Pullman, did not make its appearance until 1865; Spencer, "Address to the Southern Society."

46 Warner, *Generals in Blue*, p. 410.

47 *O.R.*, Ser. I, Vol. XVII, Pt. 2, p. 19.

48 Stephen Z. Starr, *The Union Cavalry in the Civil War, Vol. III: The War in the West, 1861-1865* (Baton Rouge: LSU Press, 1985), p. 24.

49 *O.R.*, Ser. I, Vol. XVII, Pt. 2, pp. 105, 154, 281; Brent Nosworthy, *The Bloody Crucible of Courage: Fighting Methods and Combat Experience of the Civil War* (New York: Carroll & Graf, 2003), p. 618.

50 *Official Records*, Ser. I, Vol. XX, Pt. 2, pp. 57-58; Nosworthy, *Bloody Crucible*, p. 482.

51 Glenn W. Sunderland, *Wilder's Lightning Brigade—and Its Spencer Repeaters* (Washington, Ill.: BookWorks, 1984), pp. 19-24.

52 Satterlee, *New Haven Arms Catalog*, p. 16.

53 Sword, *Historic Henry*, p. 24.

54 Sunderland, *Wilder's Lightning Brigade, p. 19.*

55 Christopher Spencer to James H. Kennedy, March 26, 1912, C. M. Spencer Papers.

56 *Cincinnati Gazette*, March 11, 1863, quoted in John W. Rowell, *Yankee Artillerymen: Through the Civil War with Eli Lilly's Indiana Battery* (Knoxville: University of Tennessee Press, 1975), p. 65.

57 Ken Baumann, *Arming the Suckers, 1861-1865* (Dayton, Ohio: Morningside Press, 1989), p. 214.

CHAPTER FIVE: LOUISVILLE TO GETTYSBURG

1 Houze, *Winchester Repeating Arms*, p. 16.

2 Sword, *Historic Henry Rifle*, pp. 10, 15.

3 Ibid., p. 10; Satterlee, *New Haven Arms Catalog*, pp. 38-39.

4 Sword, *Historic Henry Rifle*, p. 10.

5 Ibid., p. 11.

[6] *O.R.,* Ser I, Vol. XVI, Pt. 1, p. 864.

[7] Sword, *Historic Henry Rifle,* p. 11; Wayne B. Austerman, "Von Borcke's Volcanic—or Did Heros Have a Henry?" *Dixie Gun Works Black Powder Annual,* 2003.

[8] Austerman, "Von Borcke's Volcanic."

[9] Sword, *Historic Henry Rifle,* p. 12.

[10] Satterlee, *New Haven Arms Catalog,* pp. 34-35; Parsons, *First Winchester,* p. 17.

[11] Sword, *Historic Henry Rifle,* pp. 16-18.

[12] Parsons, *First Winchester,* p. 17; *O.R.,* Ser. I, Vol. XXIII, Pt. 1, p. 302.

[13] *O.R.,* Ser. I, Vol. XXII, Pt. 2., p. 49; Sword, *Historic Henry Rifle,* p. 78. The unit designation should read "1st Indian Regt."

[14] Marcot, *Spencer Repeating Firearms,* p. 50.

[15] Ibid.

[16] Sword, *Historic Henry Rifle,* p. 18

[17] Ibid.

[18] Ibid., p. 19.

[19] Ibid., pp. 20-22.

[20] Sunderland, *Lightning Brigade,* p. 33; Baumann, *Arming the Suckers,* p. 187; Joseph G. Bilby, *Civil War Firearms* (Conshohocken, Pa.: Combined Books, 1996), pp. 79-84.

[21] Satterlee, *Spencer Catalog,* p. 10.

[22] Ibid., p. 11.

[23] James Connolly (Paul M. Angle ed.), *Three Years in the Army of the Cumberland: The Letters and Diary of Major James A. Connolly* (Bloomington: Indiana University Press, 1987), p. 90.

[24] Sunderland, *Lightning Brigade,* p. 39; *Chattanooga Daily Rebel,* July [?], 1863.

[25] Sunderland, *Lightning Brigade,* p. 38.

[26] *Chattanooga Daily Rebel,* July [?]. 1863.

[27] John T. Wilder, "The Battle of Hoover's Gap," Ohio MOLLUS *Sketches of War History,* 6, p. 172.

[28] *O.R.,* Ser. I, Vol. XXIII, Pt. 1, pp. 613-614, 459.

[29] Edwin B. Coddington, *The Gettysburg Campaign: A Study in Command* (New York: Charles Scribner's Sons, 1968), p. 254; *O.R.,* Ser. I, Vol. XXVII, Pt. 2, p. 63.

[30] Satterlee, *New Haven Arms Catalog,* p. 19.

[31] J. O. Buckeridge, *Lincoln's Choice* (Harrisburg, Pa.: Stackpole, 1956), pp. 55-56; Shelby Foote, *The Civil War, A Narrative: Fredericksburg to Meridian* (New York: Random House, 1963), p. 465; William H. Hallahan, *Misfire: The History of How America's Small Arms Have Failed Our Military* (New York: Charles Scribner's Sons, 1994), pp. 176-177. The latter is a particularly shallow treatment of small arms history and the author seems to have depended on Buckeridge for most of his information on the Spencer.

[32] Eric J. Wittenberg, *Protecting the Flank: The Battles of Brinkerhoff's Ridge and East Cavalry Field* (Celina, Ohio: Ironclad Publishing, 2002), pp. 57-59.

[33] Bill Adams, "Weapons of the 34th," www.34thvacav.org/weapons.html.

[34] John W. Busey and David G. Martin, *Regimental Strengths and Losses at Gettysburg* (Hightstown, N.J.: Longstreet House, 1994), p. 104.

[35] Ibid.

[36] Vincent Witcher to "Hon. Jno. Daniels," January 26, 1906; Vincent Witcher to General Lunsford Lomax, August 30, 1908, copies courtesy Bill Adams.

[37] Vincent Witcher to "My Dear Gen.," April 6, 1886, courtesy Bill Adams; Busey and Martin, *Regimental Strengths,* p. 108.

[38] Robert J. Driver, *14th Virginia Cavalry* (Lynchburg, Va.: Howard Publications, 1988), p. 23.

[39] Richard A. Sauers, ed., *Fighting Them Over: How the Veterans Remembered Gettysburg in the Pages of The National Tribune* (Baltimore: Butternut and Blue, 1998), pp. 466-467.

[40] Vincent Witcher to "My Dear Gen.," April 6, 1886.

[41] Busey and Martin, *Regimental Strengths*, p. 259.

CHAPTER SIX: CHICKAMAUGA TO OLUSTEE

[1] Marcot, *Spencer Repeating Firearms*, p. 56.

[2] Ibid., p. 57.

[3] Christopher Spencer to James H. Kennedy, March 26, 1912, Spencer address to "Mr. President and Gentlemen of the Southern Society." C. M. Spencer papers. For the full recollection, see Marcot, *Spencer Repeating Firearms*, p. 57; Dennett, ed., *Lincoln and the Civil War*, p. 82.

[4] Marcot, *Spencer Repeating Firearms*, p. 59. In 1930, a King Features Syndicate "Here's How" cartoon reproduced in Marcot's book featured a craggy Abraham Lincoln inspecting a crudely drawn and unidentifiable rifle in the hands of a Bela Lugosi looking individual representing Christopher Spencer, the "young Connecticut inventor [who] revolutionized warfare . . . and helped win the Civil War." According to the cartoonist, Lincoln was so impressed by Spencer's "automatic rifle" that he "ordered 100,000 for immediate delivery" and the gun became "one of the chief factors in the Union's triumph."

In 1956 Lincoln's shooting session even provided a title for an entertaining but unfortunately often erroneous and fanciful account of the Spencer rifle and carbine's role in the Civil War, J. O. Buckeridge's *Lincoln's Choice*. The book advanced the mistaken theory that Spencer's demonstration so impressed Lincoln that the president took a personal interest in ordering the rifle. Buckeridge's story has been passed down as gospel by many, however, even historians with pretense to expertise in the subject. Among Michael Bellesiles' factual errors and failures to evaluate sources across the historical spectrum in his work *Arming America* was using Buckeridge as his main source on the Spencer when Roy Marcot's work was available. Bellesiles, *Arming America*, p. 422.

[5] Satterlee, *Spencer Catalog*, pp. 12, 11.

[6] Ibid., p. 18; Marcot, *Spencer Repeating Firearms*, p. 77.

[7] Ibid., p. 65.

[8] Ibid.

[9] Bruce, *Lincoln and the Tools of War*, p. 260.

[10] Ibid., pp. 265-267; Marcot, *Spencer Repeating Firearms*, p. 65.

[11] O.R., Ser. I, Vol. XXIII, Pt. 1, p. 666.

[12] O.R., Ser. I, Vol. XXX, pp. 447, 251.

[13] Ibid., p. 500.

[14] Ibid., p. 518; quoted in Richard A. Baumgartner and Larry M. Strayer, *Echoes of Battle: The Struggle for Chattanooga* (Huntington, W.Va.: Blue Acorn Press, 1996), pp. 106, 95.

[15] Quoted in Sunderland, *Wilder's Lightning Brigade*, p. 82.

[16] The Lightning Brigade's Chickamauga monument is located at this final position on the field.

[17] O.R., Ser. I, Vol. XXX, Pt. 1, p. 342.

[18] Satterlee, *Spencer Catalog*, p. 13.

[19] O.R. Ser. I, Vol. XXXII, Pt. 2, p. 276.

[20] David Gould and James B. Kennedy, eds., *Memoirs of a Dutch Mudsill: The "War Memories" of John Henry Otto, Captain, Company D, 21st Regiment Wisconsin Volunteer Infantry* (Kent, Ohio: Kent State University Press, 2004), p. 173.

[21] J. T. Patton, "Personal Recollections of Four Years in Dixie," War Paper 20, Michigan Commandery, MOLLUS, 1892, p. 10.

[22] Nosworthy, *The Bloody Crucible of Courage*, p. 620; Patton, "Personal Recollections of Four Years in Dixie," p. 15.

[23] *National Tribune*, October 7, 1885, p. 52.

[24] Satterlee, *New Haven Arms Catalog*, pp. 25-26.

[25] O.R., Ser. I, Vol. XXX, Pt. 1, p. 598.

26 Sword, *Historic Henry Rifle,* pp. 71-72; Robert Batten, "L. L.'s Henry Repeating Rifle," San Diego Civil War Round Table Skirmish Line, May 19, 2004.

27 Satterlee, *New Haven Arms Catalog,* p. 26; Madis, *The Winchester Book,* p. 41.

28 Dan P. Fagan, "The Dimick Rifles of the 66th Illinois Infantry," *Gun Report,* March 1989.

29 Sword, *Historic Henry Rifle,* p. 62.

30 Houze, *Winchester Repeating Arms,* pp. 18-19.

31 Marcot, *Spencer Repeating Firearms,* pp. 66-67.

32 *O.R.,* Ser. I, Vol. XXVIII, Pt. 2, p. 112.

33 Satterlee, *Spencer Catalog,* p. 14.

34 Sword, "Those Damned Michigan Spencers."

35 *O.R.,* Ser. I, Vol. XXX, Pt. 1, p. 233; Larry J. Daniel, *Soldiering in the Army of Tennessee: A Portrait of Life in a Confederate Army* (Chapel Hill: University of North Carolina Press, 1991), p. 46; Wayne R. Austerman, "Bedford Forrest's Booty Spencers," *Dixie Gun Works Black Powder Annual,* 2004.

36 Thomas M. Maguire, *The Campaign in Virginia, May and June, 1864* (London, 1908), p. 32.

37 *O.R.,* Ser. III, Vol. V, Pt. 4, p. 594.

38 Sword, *Historic Henry Rifle,* pp. 44-46.

39 Ibid., pp. 48-50.

40 Warren Wilkinson, *Mother, May You Never See the Sights I Have Seen: The Fifty-seventh Massachusetts Veteran Volunteers in the Last Year of the Civil War* (New York: Harper & Row, 1990), p. 15.

41 One of the best sources of information on the subsequent battle of Olustee and the events leading up to it, including extensive primary sources, is the Battle of Olustee website at http://extlab1.entnem.ufl.edu/olustee/index.html. For a comprehensive and detailed account of Florida in the Confederacy, as well as the political machinations leading up to the battle of Olustee and the course of the battle itself, see William H. Nulty, *Confederate Florida: The Road to Olustee* (Tuscaloosa: University of Alabama Press, 1990).

42 *Boston Herald,* March 2, 1864.

43 Nulty, *Confederate Florida,* p. 110.

44 Ibid., pp. 134-135.

45 *O.R.,* Ser. I, Vol. XXXV, Pt. 1, pp. 308, 310.

46 Oliver Norton to sister, February 29, 1864, posted on Olustee website.

47 Nulty, *Confederate Florida,* pp. 152, 158.

48 *Scientific American,* New Series, 10, no. 11, March 12, 1864, p. 170.

CHAPTER SEVEN: THE WILDERNESS TO ATLANTA

1 Joseph G. Bilby and William C. Goble, *Remember You Are Jerseymen: A Military History of New Jersey's Troops in the Civil War* (Hightstown, N.J.: Longstreet House, 1998), p. 82. Although newly recruited over the winter of 1863-1864, the Fifty-seventh Massachusetts Infantry, for example, was denominated a Veteran Volunteer regiment due to the number of prior service recruits in its ranks.

2 Oscar Westlake to mother, January 6, 1864, Westlake Letters, John Kuhl Collection; Josiah Brown, "Record of My Experience During the Civil War from October 1, 1861 to July, 1865," typescript, New Jersey Historical Society; Stephen Z. Starr, *The Union Cavalry in the Civil War,* Vol. III, *The War in the West, 1861-1865* (Baton Rouge: LSU Press, 1985), p. 376.

3 John C. McQueen, *Spencer: The First Effective and Widely Used Repeating Rifle and Its Use in the Western Theater of the Civil War* (Columbus, Ga.: Communicorp, 1989), pp. 28-29.

4 Marcot, *Spencer Repeating Firearms,* p. 70.

5 Ibid., p. 71.

6 Sword, *Henry Rifle,* pp. 53-54.

7 *O.R.,* Ser. I, Vol. XXXII, Pt. 3, p. 546.

[8] Bilby and Goble, *Jerseymen,* p. 465.

[9] *O.R.,* Ser. I, Vol. XXXII, Pt. 3,, p. 257.

[10] Stephen Z. Starr, *The Union Cavalry in the Civil War,* Vol. II: *The War in the East from Gettysburg to Appomattox, 1863-1865* (Baton Rouge: LSU Press, 1981), pp. 68-69.

[11] Starr, *Union Cavalry,* Vol. II, pp. 68-69.

[12] *O.R.,* Ser. I, Vol. XLIX, Pt. 2, p. 39.

[13] *O.R.,* Ser. I, Vol. XXXIII, p. 1021.

[14] Starr, *Union Cavalry,* Vol. II, pp. 75-76.

[15] Philip Sheridan, *Personal Memoirs of P. H. Sheridan* (New York: Charles L. Webster, 1888), p. 353; *O.R.,* Ser. I, Vol. XXXIII, pp. 891-892.

[16] *O.R.,* Ser. I, Vol. XXXIII, pp. 891-892.

[17] *O.R.,* Ser. I, Vol. XXXVI, Pt. 1, p. 876; Louis N. Boudrye, *Historic Records of the Fifth New York Cavalry* (Albany, N.Y., 1865), p. 122.

[18] Edward G. Longacre, *Lincoln's Cavalrymen: A History of the Mounted Forces of the Army of the Potomac* (Mechanicsburg, Pa.: Stackpole, 2000), p. 260; Starr, *Union Cavalry,* Vol. II, pp. 90-91.

[19] Longacre, *Lincoln's Cavalrymen,* p. 263.

[20] *O.R.,* Ser. I, Vol. XXXVI, pt. 1, pp. 793, 861; M. C. Butler, "The Cavalry Fight at Trevillian Station," in Clarence Clough Buel and Robert Underwood Johnson, eds., *Battles and Leaders of the Civil War,* Vol. IV (New York: Century Company, 1884-1887), p. 237; Longacre, *Lincoln's Cavalrymen,* p. 274.

[21] Longacre, *Lincoln's Cavalrymen,* p. 274; Sword, "Those Damned Michigan Spencers"; Douglas Southall Freeman, *R. E. Lee: A Biography* (New York: Charles Scribner's Sons, 1934), pp. 365-366.

[22] Baumann, *Arming the Suckers,* p. 179.

[23] Theodore F. Rodenbaugh, "Sheridan's Richmond Raid," in *Battles and Leaders,* Vol. IV, p. 193.

[24] Starr, *Union Cavalry,* Vol. II, pp. 139-140.

[25] Stanton P. Allen, *Down in Dixie: Life in a Cavalry Regiment in the War Days from Wilderness to Appomattox* (Boston: D. Lothrop, 1893), p. 366.

[26] Starr, *Union Cavalry,* Vol. II, pp. 141-143.

[27] *O.R.,* Ser. I, Vol. XL, Pt. 3, pp. 245, 250.

[28] Starr, *Union Cavalry,* Vol. II, p. 201.

[29] *O.R.,* Ser. I, Vol. XXXIII, p. 235.

[30] Ibid.

[31] *O.R.,* Ser. I, Vol. XXXVI, Pt. 2, p. 52.

[32] J. Madison Drake, *The History of the Ninth New Jersey Veteran Volunteers* (Elizabeth, N.J.: Journal Printing House, 1889), p. 184.

[33] *O.R.,* Ser. I, Vol. XXXVI, Pt. 2, p. 53.

[34] Ibid., p. 63.

[35] Gilbert A. Hays, comp., *Under the Red Patch: Story of the Sixty-Third Regiment Pennsylvania Volunteers, 1861-1865* (Pittsburgh, 1908), pp. 67-68; Wilkinson, *Mother, May You Never See the Sights I Have Seen,* pp. 222-223; *O.R.,* Ser. I, Vol. XL, Pt. 1, pp. 114, 542.

[36] *O.R.,* Ser. I, Vol. XL, Pt. 3, p. 250.

[37] Ibid.

[38] Baumann, *Arming the Suckers,* pp. 70-71, 150, 151.

[39] Ibid., pp. 192-193; Frederick H. Dyer, *A Compendium of the War of the Rebellion, Vol. III* (reprint, Dayton, Ohio: National Historical Society, 1979), p. 1287; Bruce, *Lincoln and the Tools of War,* p. 287; Marshall P. Thatcher, *A Hundred Battles in the West: St. Louis to Atlanta, 1861-1865* (Detroit, 1884), p. 181; David Evans, *Sherman's Horsemen: Union Cavalry Operations in the Atlanta Campaign* (Bloomington: Indiana University Press, 1996), p. 393.

[40] Baumann, *Arming the Suckers*, p. 179; Samuel P. Bates, *History of Pennsylvania Volunteers, 1861-1865* (Harrisburg: B. Singerly, 1869), Vol. II, p. 1119.

[41] *O.R.*, Ser. I, Vol. XXXVIII, Pt. 2, p.352.

[42] *O.R.*, Ser. I, Vol. XXXVIII, Pt. 3, p. 378.

[43] Ibid., p. 317; Larry M. Strayer and Richard Baumgartner, eds., *Echoes of Battle: The Atlanta Campaign* (Huntington, W.Va.: Blue Acorn Press, 1991), p. 126.

[44] *O.R.*, Ser. I, Vol. XXXVIII, Pt. 4, p. 526.

[45] Strayer and Baumgartner, *The Atlanta Campaign*, pp. 178-179, 174; W. F. Beyer and O. F. Keydel, *Deeds of Valor: How America's Civil War Heroes Won the Congressional Medal of Honor* (reprint, Stamford, Conn.: Longmeadow Press, 1992), p. 372. This writer observed Fahnestock's engraved Henry on display at an Allentown, Pennsylvania, antique gun show several years before publication of this volume.

[46] *O.R.*, Ser. I, Vol. XXXVIII, Pt. 3, p. 337.

[47] Evans, *Sherman's Horsemen*, pp. 22-24.

[48] Ibid., p. 75.

[49] *O.R.*, Ser. I, Vol. XXXVIII, Pt. 2, p. 356.

[50] Prosper Bowe to sister, July 28, 1864, in Richard A. Baumgartner and Larry M. Strayer, "A Brief History of the 66th Illinois Infantry, 1861-1865," in reprint of Lorenzo A. Barker, *With the Western Sharpshooters, Michigan Boys of Company D, 66th Illinois* (Huntington, W.Va.: Blue Acorn Press, 1994), p. 175.

[51] *O.R.*, Ser. I, Vol. XXXVIII, Pt. 3, p. 344.

[52] *O.R.*, Ser. I, Vol. XXXVIII Pt. 1, p. 126; Robert M. Reilly, *United States Military Small Arms, 1816-1865* (Baton Rouge, La.: Eagle Press, 1970), p. 169.

[53] Evans, *Sherman's Horsemen*, p. 194.

[54] Ibid., pp. 438-444; Buckeridge, *Lincoln's Choice*, p. 184.

[55] *O.R.*, Ser. I, *Vol. XXXVIII, Pt.* 5, p. 777.

[56] *O.R.*, Ser. I, *Vol. XXXVIII, Pt.* 3, p. 44.

[57] *O.R.*, Ser. I, *Vol. XXXVIII*, Pt. 1, p. 126; Sword, *Historic Henry Rifle*, pp. 65-70.

[58] Edward C. Bearss, *Forrest at Brice's Crossroads* (Dayton, Ohio: Morningside, 1994), pp. 74-78.

[59] William A. Fletcher, *Rebel Private, Front and Rear: Memoirs of a Confederate Soldier* (reprint, New York: Meridian, 1995), p. 139; Earl J. Coates and John D. McAulay, *Civil War Sharps Carbines and Rifles* (Gettysburg, Pa.: Thomas Publications, 1996), p. 24.

[60] Wayne R. Austerman, "Bedford Forrest's Booty Spencers," *Dixie Gun Works Blackpowder Annual*, 2004.

CHAPTER EIGHT: SHENANDOAH TO APPOMATTOX

[1] Directions in the Shenandoah Valley are classified as "up" or "down" due to the course of the Shenandoah River, which flows north to join the Potomac.

[2] Satterlee, *Spencer Catalog*, p. 24; Edmund Halsey Diary, August 19, 30, 1864, *U.S. Army Military History Institute*, Carlisle, Pa.

[3] Robert Hunt Rhodes, ed., *All for the Union: The Civil War Diary and Letters of Elisha Hunt Rhodes* (Lincoln, R.I.: A. Mowbray, 1985), p. 173.

[4] Joseph G. Bilby, *"Three Rousing Cheers": A History of the Fifteenth New Jersey from Flemington to Appomattox* (Hightstown, N.J.: Longstreet House, 2001), p. 185.

[5] Rhodes, ed., *All for the Union*, p. 184; *O.R.*, Ser. I, Vol. XLIII, Pt. 1, p. 185.

[6] Richard L. Armstrong, *The Seventh Virginia Cavalry* (Lynchburg, Va.: H. E. Howard, 1992), p. 97.

[7] John William DeForest, *A Volunteer's Adventures: A Union Captain's Record of the Civil War* (New Haven, Conn.: Yale University Press, 1946), p. 196.

[8] Jeffrey D. Wert, *Mosby's Rangers* (New York: Simon and Shuster, 1990), pp. 202-203.

[9] *O.R.*, Ser. I, Vol. XLIII, Pt. 1, p. 860; *O.R.*, Ser. II, Vol. VII, p. 1270.

[10] Wert, *Mosby's Rangers*, pp. 204-205.

[11] Ibid., pp. 250-252.

[12] Ibid., pp. 253-258.

[13] Marcot, *Spencer Firearms*, p. 74.

[14] Ibid., pp. 205, 189.

[15] Ibid., pp. 80-98.

[16] Houze, *Winchester Repeating Arms*, pp. 19-20.

[17] Ibid., pp. 21-23.

[18] Satterlee, *New Haven Arms Catalog*, pp. 21-23.

[19] William F. Fox, *Regimental Losses in the American Civil War, 1861-1865* (Albany, N.Y.: Brandow, 1898), p. 310, 302; Satterlee, *Spencer Catalog*, p. 20; *O.R.*, Ser. I, Vol. XLII, Pt. 1, p. 798; Vol. XLIII, Pt. 1, p. 559; Vol. XLII, Pt. 1, p. 721.

[20] Fred L. Ray, "Shock Troops of the Confederacy: The Sharpshooter Battalions of the Army of Northern Virginia," p. 19, unpublished manuscript, courtesy Fred L. Ray.

[21] Ibid., pp. 27-28.

[22] Bilby, *Civil War Firearms*, pp. 117-120.

[23] *O.R.*, Ser. I, Vol. XXV, Pt. 1, pp. 297, 436; Vol. XXXVIII, Pt. 3, p. 160; Vol. XXXIX, Pt. 1, p. 777; Fox, *Regimental Losses*, p. 28.

[24] Bilby, *Three Rousing Cheers*, p. 114.

[25] *OR*, Ser. I, Vol. XL, Pt. 1, p. 495; XLII, Pt. 1, pp. 802, 814; Vol. XLII, Pt. 2, p. 290; Vol. XLII, Pt. 3, p. 168; Vol. XLIII, Pt. 1, p. 193; Vol. XL, Pt. 1, p. 541.

[26] Sam Davis Elliott, *Soldier of Tennessee: General Alexander P. Stewart and the Civil War in the West* (Baton Rouge: LSU Press, 1999), p. 219; Samuel G. French, *Two Wars, an Autobiography* (Nashville: Confederate Veteran, 1901), p. 249.

[27] D. Leib Ambrose, *From Shiloh to Savannah: The Seventh Illinois Infantry in the Civil War* (1868; reprint, DeKalb: Northern Illinois University Press, 2003), p. 179; French, *Two Wars*, p. 251.

[28] Ambrose, *Shiloh to Savannah*, p. 181; Baumann, *Arming the Suckers*, pp. 71-72.

[29] Starr, *Union Cavalry*, Vol. III, p. 569; Baumann, *Arming the Suckers*, p. 75.

[30] William A. Albaugh III, Hugh Benet, Jr., and Edward N. Simmmons, *Confederate Handguns* (New York: Bonanza Books, 1963), p. 23.

[31] Ibid., pp. 24-30.

[32] Flayderman, *Guide*, p. 521.

[33] Starr, *Union Cavalry*, Vol. III, pp. 572-573.

[34] *O.R.*, Vol. XLIV, Ser. I, p. 698.

[35] Ibid., pp. 110-111.

[36] James Lee McDonough and Thomas Connelly, *Five Tragic Hours: The Battle of Franklin* (Knoxville: University of Tennessee Press, 1983), pp. 119-125; *O.R.*, Ser. I, Vol. XLV, Pt. 1, p. 425; Wiley Sword, *Embrace an Angry Wind: The Confederacy's Last Hurrah, Spring Hill, Franklin and Nashville* (New York: HarperCollins, 1992), pp. 216, 219.

[37] *O.R.*, Ser. I, Vol. XLV, Pt. 1, p. 563.

[38] *O.R.*, Ser. III, Vol. IV, pp. 971-972.

[39] Lugs, *Firearms Past and Present*, Vol. 1, pp. 74-75.

[40] Myatt, *19th Century Firearms*, pp. 76-79; T. F. Fremantle, *The Book of the Rifle* (London: Longmans, Green, 1901), pp. 66-68.

[41] Marcot, *Spencer Firearms*, pp. 100-104.

[42] Buel and Johnson, eds., *Battles and Leaders*, Vol. IV, pp. 660-661.

[43] Bilby and Goble, *Jerseymen*, pp. 653-654, 459.

[44] *Trenton* (N.J.) *State Gazette*, September 19, 1864; Satterlee, *Henry Catalog*, p. 26.

[45] William L. Phillips to father and mother, December 26, 1864, March 17, 1865, William Phillips collection, Mss. 142S, Wisconsin Historical Society.

46 *O.R.*, Ser. I, Vol. XLVI, Pt. 1, p. 502.

47 Phillips to father and mother, March 26, 1865, WHS.

48 *O.R.*, Ser. I, Vol. XLVI, Pt. 1, p. 902.

49 Ibid., p. 940.

50 Ibid., p. 941.

51 Ibid., p. 942.

52 *O.R.*, Ser. I, Vol. XLVII, Pt. 1, p. 366; Mark L. Bradley, *Last Stand in the Carolinas: The Battle of Bentonville* (Campbell, Calif.: Savas Woodbury, 1996), p. 364.

53 *O.R.*, Ser. I, Vol. XLVII, Pt. 1, p. 184.

CHAPTER NINE: SELMA AND BEYOND

1 *O.R.*, Ser. I, Vol. XLV, Pt. 2, p. 429.

2 *O.R.*, Ser. I, Vol. XLIX, Pt. 1, p. 737.

3 Ibid., p. 826.

4 Ibid., pp. 825-826.

5 Ibid., p. 356.

6 Ibid., p. 737; Marcot, *Spencer Repeating Firearms*, pp. 175-177.

7 Marcot, *Spencer Firearms*, pp. 168-169.

8 Ibid., p. 174.

9 Ibid., p. 170.

10 *O.R.*, Ser. I, Vol. XLIX, Pt. 1, p. 409.

11 Lugs, *Firearms Past and Present*, p. 138.

12 *O.R.*, Ser. I, Vol. XLIX, Pt. 1, p. 438.

13 Ibid., p. 744; Vol. XLVII, Pt. 1, pp. 860, 166; Susan W. Benson, ed., *Berry Benson's Civil War Book: Memoirs of a Confederate Scout and Sharpshooter* (Athens: University of Georgia Press, 1992), p. 183.

14 *O.R.*, Ser. III, Vol. IV, pp. 598, 606-607; Ser. I, Vol. XLVIII, Pt. 1, p. 73.

15 Austerman, "Bedford Forrest's Booty Spencers"; Satterlee, *Spencer Catalog*, p. 23.

16 Basil W. Duke (James A. Ramage, ed.), *The Civil War Reminiscences of General Basil W. Duke, C.S.A.* (reprint, New York: Cooper Square Publishers, 2001), pp. 178-179; Sam Davis Elliott, ed., *Doctor Quintard, Chaplain C.S.A. and Second Bishop of Tennessee: The Memoir and Civil War Diary of Charles Todd Quintard* (Baton Rouge: LSU Press, 2003), p. 261.

17 Marcot, *Spencer Firearms*, pp. 162-164; McQueen, *Spencer*, pp. 33-42.

18 Griffith, *Battle Tactics of the Civil War*, pp. 86-90.

19 Jay Luvaas, *The Military Legacy of the Civil War: The European Inheritance* (Lawrence: University Press of Kansas, 1988), pp. 95, 109-110; Bilby, *Civil War Firearms*, p. 166.

20 *O.R.*, Ser. I, Vol. XLIV, p. 650.

21 Marcot, *Spencer Firearms*, pp. 105-109.

22 Frederick P. Todd, et al. *American Military Equipage: 1851-1872*, Vol. II (Providence, R.I.: Company of Military Historians, 1977), p. 386.

23 Flayderman, *Guide*, pp. 465-466; William B. Styple, ed., *Writing and Fighting the Civil War: Soldier Correspondence to the New York Sunday Mercury* (Kearny, N.J.: Belle Grove, 2000), p. 357.

24 Flayderman, *Guide*, p. 464; Hicks, *U.S. Military Firearms*, pp. 90-91; McAulay, *Civil War Breechloading Rifles*, pp. 119-120.

25 Louis A. Garavaglia and Charles G. Worman, *Firearms in the American West 1866-1894* (Albuquerque: University of New Mexico Press, 1985), p. 21.

26 Robert M. Utley, *Frontier Regulars: The United States Army and the Indian, 1866-1890* (New York: Macmillan, 1973), pp. 147-149, 104; Garavaglia and Worman, *Firearms in the American West, 1866-1890*, p. 23.

Notes 251

27 Garavaglia and Worman, *Firearms in the American West, 1866-1890*, pp. 23-26.

28 Parsons, *First Winchester*, p. 48.

29 Houze, *Winchester Repeating Arms*, pp. 29-42.

30 Ibid., p. 59.

31 Ibid., pp. 47, 45-63, 59; James E. Hicks, *Notes on U. S. Ordnance,* Vol. II, *1776-1942* (New York: W. W. Norton, 1941), p. 79.

32 Parsons, *First Winchester*, pp. 87-88; Houze, *Winchester Repeating Arms*, pp. 71-73.

33 Parsons, *First Winchester,* pp. 88-90; Frederick William von Herbert, *The Defence of Plevna, 1877* (1911; reprint, Istanbul: Turkish Ministry of Culture, 1990), pp. 4, 298.

34 Marcot, *Spencer Firearms*, p. 200.

35 Thomas K. Tate, *From Under Iron Eyelids: The Biography of James Henry Burton, Armorer to Three Nations* (Bloomington, Ind.: Authorhouse, 2005), p. 305.

36 Ibid., pp. 306-307.

37 Parsons, *First Winchester*, p. 98.

38 Marcot, *Spencer Repeating Firearms*, p. 126.

39 Ibid., p. 89.

40 Ibid., pp. 153-155.

41 William B. Edwards, *Civil War Guns* (Harrisburg, Pa.: Stackpole, 1962), pp. 405-412; Parsons, *First Winchester*, p. 85.

42 Email from Alex Scheer, May 21, 2005, based upon Scheer's translations from Pierre Lorain and Jean Boudriot, *Les Armes Américaines de la Défense Nationale* (Paris: Lorain and Boudriot, 1970), and "La Guerre Franco-Allemande, 1870-1871," *Gazette des Armes Magazine*, No. 11, 2001; Herbert C. Houze, "Schulyer, Hartley & Graham's Military Sales to France During the Franco Prussian War, 1870-1871," *Gun Report*, June 1993. Edwards, in *Civil War Guns*, provides the most comprehensive account of the dubious dealing and political machinations of American arms dealers in the French sales of 1870.

43 Ibid.

44 Marcot, *Spencer Repeating Firearms*, pp. 153-154, 205, 155-156; Scheer email.

45 Flayderman, *Guide*, pp. 274-275; "Old Apache Chief Geronimo Is Dead," *New York Times*, February 18, 1909.

46 Madis, *Winchester Book*, p. 481.

47 Houze, *Winchester Repeating Arms*, p. 181.

BIBLIOGRAPHY

BOOKS

Akehurst, Richard. *Sporting Guns*. London: Octopus Books, 1968.

Albaugh, William A. III, Hugh Benet, Jr., and Edward N. Simmons. *Confederate Handguns*. New York: Bonanza Books, 1963.

Allen, Stanton P. *Down in Dixie: Life in a Cavalry Regiment in the War Days from Wilderness to Appomattox*. Boston: D. Lothrop, 1893.

Ambrose, D. Leib. *From Shiloh to Savannah: The Seventh Illinois Infantry in the Civil War*. DeKalb: Northern Illinois University Press, 2003 (reprint of 1868 edition).

Anderson, Edward J., et al. *The Military Arms of Canada*. Bloomfield, Ontario: Upper Canada Historical Arms Society, 1963.

Armstrong, Richard L. *The Seventh Virginia Cavalry*. Lynchburg, Va.: H. E. Howard, 1992.

Bailey, DeWitt. *British Military Longarms, 1715-1865*. London: Arms and Armour Press, 1986.

Baker, Samuel. *Wild Beasts and Their Ways: Reminiscences of Europe, Asia, Africa and America*. New York: Macmillan, 1890.

Barker, Lorenzo A. *With the Western Sharpshooters: Michigan Boys of Company D, 66th Illinois, 1861-1865*. Huntington W.Va.: Blue Acorn Press, 1994 (reprint of 1905 edition).

Barnes, Frank C. *Cartridges of the World*. Chicago: Gun Digest, 1965.

Bates, Samuel P. *History of Pennsylvania Volunteers, 1861-1865*. 5 vols. Harrisburg: B. Singerly, 1869.

Baumann, Ken. *Arming the Suckers, 1861-1865*. Dayton, Ohio: Morningside, 1989.

Baumgartner, Richard A., and Larry M. Strayer. *Echoes of Battle: The Struggle for Chattanooga*. Huntington, W.Va.: Blue Acorn Press, 1996.

Bearss, Edwin C. *Forrest at Brice's Crossroads*. Dayton, Ohio: Morningside, 1994.

Benham, Major Calhoun. *A System for Conducting Musketry Instruction Prepared and Printed by Order of General Bragg for the army of Tennessee*. Richmond, Va., 1863. (Reprint, Auburn, Va.: R. W. Henry Publishing, 1998, with introduction by Joseph G. Bilby)

Bennett, Tyler, ed. *Lincoln and the Civil War in the Diaries and Letters of John Hay*. New York: Dodd, Mead, 1939.

Benson, Susan W., ed. *Berry Benson's Civil War Book: Memoirs of a Confederate Scout and Sharpshooter*. Athens: University of Georgia Press, 1992.

Belleiles, Michael A. *Arming America: The Origins of a National Gun Culture*. New York: Knopf, 2000.

Beyer, W. F., and O. F. Keydel. *Deeds of Valor: How America's Civil War Heroes Won the Congressional Medal of Honor*. Stamford, Conn.: Longmeadow Press reprint, 1992.

Bilby, Joseph G. *Three Rousing Cheers: A History of the Fifteenth New Jersey from Flemington to Appomattox*. Hightstown, N.J.: Longstreet House, 1993.

——. *Civil War Firearms: Their Historical Background, Tactical Use and Modern Collecting and Shooting*. Conshohocken, Pa.: Combined Books, 1996.

Bilby, Joseph G., ed. *A System of Target Practice For the Use of Troops When Armed with the Musket, Rifle Musket, Rifle or Carbine, Prepared Principally from the French*. Washington, 1862. 1998 reprint Auburn, Va.: J. W. Henry Publishing, 1998).

Bilby, Joseph G., and William C. Goble. *Remember You Are Jerseymen: A Military History of New Jersey in the Civil War*. Hightstown, N.J.: Longstreet House, 1998.

Blackmore, Howard L. *British Military Firearms, 1650-1850*. London: Herbert Jenkins, 1961.

Boatner, Mark M., III. *The Civil War Dictionary*. New York: Vintage Books, 1987.

Boudrye, Louis N. *Historic Records of the Fifth New York Cavalry*. Albany, N.Y., 1865.

Bowen, James L. *History of the Thirty-Seventh Regiment, Mass. Volunteers in the Civil War of 1861-1865*. Holyoke, Mass.: Clark W. Bryan & Company, 1884.

Bradley, Mark L. *Last Stand in the Carolinas: The Battle of Bentonville*. Campbell, Calif.: Savas Woodbury, 1996.

Brown, Dee. *Morgan's Raiders*. New York: Konecky & Konecky, 1995 reprint.

Bruce, Robert V. *Lincoln and the Tools of War*. Indianapolis: Bobbs-Merrill, 1956.

Buckeridge, J. O. *Lincoln's Choice*. Harrisburg, Pa.: Stackpole, 1956.

Buel, Clarence Clough, and Robert Underwood Johnson, ed. *Battles and Leaders of the Civil War*. 4 vols. New York: Century Company, 1884-1887.

Burton, E. Milby. *The Siege of Charleston: 1861-1865*. Columbia: University of South Carolina Press, 1970.

Busey, John W., and David G. Martin. *Regimental Strengths and Losses at Gettysburg*. 4th edition. Hightstown, N.J.: Longstreet House, 2005.

Carr, Caleb. *The Devil Soldier*. New York: Random House, 1992.

Castel, Albert. *Decision in the West: The Atlanta Campaign of 1864*. Lawrence: University Press of Kansas, 1992.

Chamberlain, Samuel E. (Roger Hunterfield, ed.). *My Confession*. New York: Harper & Brothers, 1956.

Chant, Christopher, ed. *How Weapons Work*. London: Cavendish, 1980.

Chapman, John R. *Instructions to Young Marksmen—The Improved American Rifle*. (reprint) Beinfield Publishing, 1976.

Cleveland, H. W. S. Practical Directions for the Use of the Rifle. Salem, Mass.: Gazette and Mercury, 1861.

Cline, Walter M. *The Muzzle Loading Rifle—Then and Now*. Huntington, W.Va.: Standard Printing and Publishing, 1942.

Coates, Earl J. and Dean S. Thomas. *An Introduction to Civil War Small Arms*. Gettysburg, Pa.: Thomas, 1990.

Coates, Earl J., and John D. McAulay. *Civil War Sharps Carbines and Rifles*. Gettysburg, Pa.: Thomas, 1996.

Coddington, Edwin B. *The Gettysburg Campaign: A Study in Command*. New York: Charles Scribner's Sons, 1968.

Connolly, James A. (Paul M. Angle, ed.). *Three Years in the Army of the Cumberland*. Bloomington: Indiana University Press, 1959.

Cozzens, Peter. *The Shipwreck of Their Hopes: The Battles for Chattanooga*. Urbana: University of Illinois Press, 1994.

Dallas, Donald. *Purdey Gun and Rifle Makers: The Definitive History*. London: Quiller Press, 2000.

Daniel, Larry J. *Soldiering in the Army of Tennessee: A Portrait of Life in a Confederate Army*. Chapel Hill: University of North Carolina Press, 1991.

Davies, Paul J. *C. S. Armory Richmond: A History of the Confederate States Armory, Richmond, Virginia and the Stock Shop at the C. S. Armory, Macon, Georgia*. Carlisle, PA: Author, 2000.

Davis, Burke. *Sherman's March*. New York: Random House, 1980.

Davis, Carl L. *Arming the Union: Small Arms in the Union Army*. Port Washington, N.Y.: Kennikat Press, 1973.

DeForest, John William. *A Volunteer's Adventures: A Union Captain's Record of the Civil War*. New Haven, Conn.: Yale University Press, 1946.

Drake, J. Madison. *The History of the Ninth New Jersey Veteran Volunteers*. Elizabeth, N.J.: Journal Printing House, 1889.

Driver, Robert J. *14th Virginia Cavalry*. Lynchburg, Va.: Howard Publications, 1988.

Duke, Basil W. (James A. Ramage, ed.). *The Civil War Reminiscences of General Basil W. Duke, C.S.A.* New York: Cooper Square Publishers, 2001 (reprint).

Dupont, Henry A. *The Campaign of 1864 in the Valley of Virginia and the Expedition to Lynchburg*. New York: National Americana Society, 1925.

Dyer, Frederick H. *A Compendium of the War of the Rebellion*. 3 vols. Dayton, Ohio: National Historical Society reprint, 1979.

Edwards, William B. *Civil War Guns*. Harrisburg, Pa.: Stackpole, 1962.

Elliott, Sam Davis. *Soldier of Tennessee: General Alexander P. Stewart and the Civil War in the West*. Baton Rouge: LSU Press, 1999.

Elliott, Sam Davis, ed. *Doctor Quintard, Chaplain C.S.A. and Second Bishop of Tennessee: The Memoir and Civil War Diary of Charles Todd Quintard*. Baton Rouge: LSU Press, 2003).

Evans, David. *Sherman's Horsemen: Union Cavalry Operations in the Atlanta Campaign*. Bloomington: Indiana University Press, 1996.

Flayderman, Norm. *Flayderman's Guide to Antique American Firearms and Their Values*. 7th ed. Iola, Wisc.: Krause, 1998.

Fletcher, William A. *Rebel Private: Front and Rear—Memoirs of a Confederate Soldier*. New York: Penguin reprint, 1995.

Foote, Shelby. *The Civil War, a Narrative: Fredericksburg to Meridian*. New York: Random House, 1963.

———. *The Civil War, a Narrative: Red River to Appomattox*. New York: Random House, 1974.

Fox, William F. *Regimental Losses in the American Civil War, 1861-1865*. Albany, N.Y.: Brandow, 1898.

Freeman, Douglas Southall. *R. E. Lee, A Biography*. New York: Charles Scribner's Sons, 1934.

Fremantle, T. F. *The Book of the Rifle*. London: Longmans, Green, 1901.

French, Samuel G. *Two Wars, An Autobiography*. Nashville: Confederate Veteran, 1901.

Garavaglia, Louis A., and Charles G. Worman. *Firearms of the American West 1803-1865*. Albuquerque: University of New Mexico Press, 1984.

———. *Firearms of the American West, 1865-1894*. Albuquerque: University of New Mexico Press, 1985.

Glathaar, Joseph T. *The March to the Sea and Beyond: Sherman's Troops in the Savannah and Carolinas Campaigns*. New York: New York University Press, 1985.

Gould, David, and James B. Kennedy, eds. *Memoirs of a Dutch Mudsill; The "War Memories" of John Henry Otto, Captain, Company D, 21st Regiment Wisconsin Volunteer Infantry*. Kent, Ohio: Kent State University Press, 2004.

Greener, W. W. *The Gun and Its Development*. 9th edition. Birmingham: Greener, 1910.

Griffith, Paddy. *Battle Tactics of the Civil War*. New Haven, Conn.: Yale University Press, 1989.

Hagerman, Edward. *The American Civil War and the Origins of Modern Warfare: Ideas, Organization and Field Command*. Bloomington: Indiana University Press, 1988.

Hallahan, William H. *Misfire: The History of How America's Small Arms Have Failed Our Military*. New York: Charles Scribner's Sons, 1994.

Harding, David F. *Smallarms of the East India Company, 1600-1856, Vol. III, Ammunition and Performance*. London: Foresight, 1999.

———. *Smallarms of the East India Company, 1600-1856, Vol. IV, The Users and Their Smallarms*. London: Foresight, 1999.

Hardy, Robert. *Longbow: A Social and Military History*. 3rd edition. London: Bois D'Arc Press, 1992.

Hartzler, Daniel D., Larry W. Yantz, and James B. Whisker. *The U.S. Model 1861 Springfield Rifle-Musket*. Bedford, Pa.: Tom Rowe Publications, 2000.

Hawke, David Freeman. *Nuts and Bolts of the Past: A History of American Technology, 1776-1860*. New York: Harper & Row, 1998.

Hays, Gilbert A. (comp.). *Under the Red Patch: Story of the Sixty Third Regiment Pennsylvania Volunteers, 1861-1865*. Pittsburgh, 1908.

Hayes-McCoy, G. A. *Irish Battles: A Military History of Ireland*. London: Longmans, Green, 1969.

Hennessy, John J. *Return to Bull Run: The Campaign and Battle of Second Manassas*. New York: Simon & Schuster, 1993.

Herbert, Frederick William von. *The Defence of Plevna, 1877*. Istanbul: Turkish Ministry of Culture, 1990 (reprint of 1911 edition).

Hicks, James E. *Notes on U.S. Ordnance, Vol. II, 1776-1942*. New York: W. W. Norton, 1941.

———. *U.S. Military Firearms, 1776-1956*. Alhambra, Calif.: Borden, 1962.

Houze, Herbert G. *Colt Rifles and Muskets From 1847 to 1870*. Iola, Wisc.: Krause, 1996.

———. *Winchester Repeating Arms Company: Its History and Development from 1865 to 1981*. Iola, Wisc.: Krause, 2004.

Hughes, Major General B. P. *Firepower: Weapons Effectiveness on the Battlefield, 1630-1850*. London: Sarpedon, 1997.

Huntington, R. T. *Hall's Breechloaders*. York, Pa.: Shumway, 1972.

Jinks, Roy G. *History of Smith & Wesson*. Revised 10th ed. N. Hollywood, Calif.: Beinfield Publishing, 1991.

Johnson, Crisfield, comp. *History of Cuyahoga County, Ohio, in Three Parts*. Cleveland: D. W. Ensign & Company, 1879.

Johnson, Paul D. *Civil War Cartridge Boxes of the Union Infantryman*. Lincoln, R.I.: Andrew Mowbray, 1998.

Kauffman, Henry J. *The Pennsylvania-Kentucky Rifle*. New York: Bonanza Books, 1960.

Kelly, Dennis. *Kennesaw Mountain and the Atlanta Campaign: A Tour Guide*. Atlanta: Kennesaw Mountain Historical Association, 1990.

Kidd, James H. *Personal Recollections of a Cavalryman*. Ionia, Mich.: Sentinel, 1908.

Kimball, W. W. *The Small Arms of European Armies, 1889*. London: Research Press, 2000 (reprint of 1889 edition).

Ladd, David L., and Audrey Ladd, eds. *The Bachelder Papers: Gettysburg in Their Own Words, 3 vols*. Dayton, Ohio: Morningside, 1994.

Lewis, Berkeley R. *Small Arms and Ammunition in the United States Service*. Washington, D.C.: Smithsonian Institution, 1956.

———. *Notes on Cavalry Weapons of the American Civil War*. Washington, D.C.: American Ordnance Association, 1961.

Longacre, Edward G. *Jersey Cavaliers: A History of the First New Jersey Volunteer Cavalry, 1861-1865*. Hightstown, N.J.: Longstreet House, 1992.

———. *The Cavalry at Gettysburg: A Tactical Study of Mounted Operations During the Civil War's Pivotal Campaign, 9 June-14 July, 1863*. Lincoln: University of Nebraska Press, 1993.

———. *Lincoln's Cavalrymen: A History of the Mounted Forces of the Army of the Potomac*. Mechanicsburg, Pa.: Stackpole, 2000.

Lorain, Pierre, and Jean Boudriot. *Les Armes Américaines de la Défense Nationale*. Paris: Lorain and Boudriot, 1970.

Lugs, Jaroslav. *Firearms Past and Present: A Complete Review of Firearm Systems and Their Histories*. 2 vols. London: Grenville, 1975.

Luvaas, Jay. *The Military Legacy of the Civil War: The European Inheritance*. Lawrence: University Press of Kansas, 1988.

Madis, George. *The Winchester Book*. Brownsboro, Tex.: Art and Reference House, 1979.

Maguire, Thomas M. *The Campaign in Virginia, May and June, 1864*. London, 1908.

Manucy, Albert. *Artillery Through the Ages: A Short History of Cannon, Emphasizing Types Used in America*. Washington, D.C.: U.S. Government Printing Office, 1949.

Marcot, Roy M. Spencer *Repeating Firearms*. Rochester, N.Y.: Rowe, 1990.

McAulay, John D. *Carbines of the Civil War, 1861-1865*. Union City, Tenn.: Pioneer Press, 1981.

———. *Civil War Breechloading Rifles: A Survey of the Innovative Infantry Arms of the American Civil War*. Lincoln, R.I.: Andrew Mowbray, 1991.

———. *Civil War Carbines, Vol. II: The Early Years*. Lincoln, R.I.: Andrew Mowbray, 1991.

McDonough, James L., and Thomas L. Connelly. *Five Tragic Hours: The Battle of Franklin*. Knoxville: University of Tennessee Press, 1983.

McIntosh, Michael. *Shotguns and Shooting*. Camden, Me.: Countrysport Press, 1995.

McPherson, James M. *Battle Cry of Freedom: The Civil War Era*. New York: Oxford University Press, 1988.

McQueen, John C. *Spencer: The First Effective and Widely Used Repeating Rifle and Its Use in the Western Theater of the Civil War*. Columbus, Ga.: Communicorp, 1989.

Moore, Warren. *Weapons and Accoutrements of the American Revolution*. New York: Promontory, 1967.

Mordecai, Alfred. *Military Commission to Europe in 1855 and 1856, Report of Major Alfred Mordecai of the Ordnance Department*. Washington, D.C.: U.S. House of Representatives, 1861.

Mowbray, Stuart C., and Jennifer Heroux, eds. *Civil War Arms Makers and their Contracts: A Facsimile Reprint of the Report by the Commission on Ordnance and Ordnance Stores, 1862*. Lincoln, R.I.: Andrew Mowbray, 1998.

Myatt, F. *The Illustrated Encyclopedia of 19th Century Firearms*. New York: Crescent, 1994.

Nosworthy, Brent. *The Bloody Crucible of Courage: Fighting Methods and Combat Experience of the Civil War*. New York: Carroll & Graf, 2003.

Nulty, William H. *Confederate Florida: The Road to Olustee*. Tuscaloosa: University of Alabama Press, 1990.

Parsons, John E. *The First Winchester: The Story of the 1866 Repeating Rifle*. New York: Winchester Press, 1969.

Power, J. Tracy. *Lee's Miserables: Life in the Army of Northern Virginia from the Wilderness to Appomattox*. Chapel Hill: University of North Carolina Press, 1998.

Pyne, Henry R. (Earl Schenck Miers, ed.). *Ride to War: The History of the First New Jersey Cavalry*. New Brunswick, N.J.: Rutgers University Press, 1961. (Reprint of 1871 edition).

Reilly, Robert M. *United States Military Small Arms, 1816-1865*. Baton Rouge: La.: Eagle Press, 1970.

Rhodes, Robert Hunt, ed. *All for the Union: The Civil War Diary and Letters of Elisha Hunt Rhodes*. Lincoln, R.I.: A. Mowbray, 1985.

Roads, C. H. *The British Soldier's Firearm From Smoothbore to Smallbore, 1850-1864*. Livonia, N.Y.: R&R Books, 1994.

Rowell, John M. *Yankee Artillerymen: Through the Civil War with Eli Lilly's Indiana Battery*. Knoxville: University of Tennessee Press, 1975.

Ruckman, Joseph. *Recreating the American Longhunter, 1740-1790*. Excelsior Springs, Mo.: Fine Arts Press, 2000.

Satterlee, L. S., comp. *Ten Old Gun Catalogs*. Chicago: Gun Digest Company, 1957.

Sauers, Richard A., ed. *Fighting Them Over: How the Veterans Remembered Gettysburg in the Pages of The National Tribune*. Baltimore: Butternut and Blue, 1998.

Sharpe, Philip B. *The Rifle in America*. New York: Funk & Wagnalls, 1953.

Sheridan, Philip. *Personal Memoirs of P. H. Sheridan*. New York: Charles L. Webster & Company, 1888.

Smith, Merritt Roe. *Harper's Ferry Armory and the New Technology*. Ithaca, N.Y.: Cornell University Press, 1977.

Soar, Hugh D. H. *The Crooked Stick: A History of the Longbow*. Yardley, Pa.: Westholme, 2004.

Starr, Stephen Z. *The Union Cavalry in the Civil War, Vol. II: The War in the East from Gettysburg to Appomattox, 1863-1865*. Baton Rouge: LSU Press, 1981.

———. *The Union Cavalry in the Civil War, Vol. III: The War in the West, 1861-1865*. Baton Rouge: LSU Press, 1985.

Stephenson, Darl L. *Headquarters in the Brush, Blazer's Independent Union Scouts*. Athens: Ohio University Press, 2001.

Strayer, Larry M., and Richard Baumgartner, eds. *Echoes of Battle: The Atlanta Campaign*. Huntington, W.Va.: Blue Acorn Press, 1991.

Styple, William B., ed. *Writing and Fighting the Civil War: Soldier Correspondence to the New York Sunday Mercury*. Kearny, N.J.: Belle Grove, 2000.

Sunderland, Glenn W. *Wilder's Lightning Brigade and Its Spencer Repeaters*. Washington, Ill.: BookWorks, 1984.

Sword, Wiley. *Sharpshooter: Hiram Berdan, His Famous Sharpshooters and Their Sharps Rifles*. Lincoln, R.I.: Andrew Mowbray, 1988.

———. *The Confederacy's Last Hurrah: Spring Hill, Franklin and Nashville*. Lawrence: University Press of Kansas, 1992.

———. *The Historic Henry Rifle*. Lincoln, R.I.: Andrew Mowbray, 2002.

Tate, Thomas K. *From Under Iron Eyelids: The Biography of James Henry Burton, Armorer to Three Nations*. Bloomington, Ind.: Authorhouse, 2005.

Thatcher, Marshall P. *A Hundred Battles in the West: St. Louis to Atlanta, 1861-1865*. Detroit, 1884.

Thomas, Dean S. *Round Ball to Rimfire: A History of Civil War Small Arms Ammunition, Part One*. Gettysburg, Pa.: Thomas Publications, 1997.

Tobie, Edward P. *History of the First Maine Cavalry, 1861-1865*. Boston: Emery, 1887.

Trench, Charles C. *A History of Marksmanship*. Chicago: Follett, 1972.

Todd, Frederick P., George Woodbridge, Lee A. Wallace, and Michael J. McAfee. *American Military Equipage: 1851-1872*. Providence, R.I.: Company of Military Historians, Vol. II, 1977.

Trudeau, Noah A. *Bloody Roads South: The Wilderness to Cold Harbor, May-June, 1864*. New York: Fawcett, 1989.

United States Government. *The War of the Rebellion: A Compilation of the Official Records of the Union and Confederate Armies*. Washington, D.C., 1880-1901.

Utley, Robert M. *Frontier Regulars: The United States Army and the Indian, 1866-1890*. New York: Macmillan, 1973.

Warner, Ezra J. *Generals in Blue: Lives of the Union Commanders*. Baton Rouge: LSU Press, 1992.

Wert, Jeffrey D. *From Winchester to Cedar Creek: The Shenandoah Campaign of 1864*. Carlisle, Pa.: South Mountain Press, 1987.

———. *Mosby's Rangers*. New York, Simon & Shuster, 1990.

Wilkinson, Warren. *Mother, May You Never See the Sights I Have Seen: The Fifty-Seventh Massachusetts Veteran Volunteers in the Last Year of the Civil War*. New York: Harper & Row, 1990.

Wittenberg, Eric. *Protecting the Flank: The Battle for Brinkerhoff's Ridge and East Cavalry Field*. Celina, Ohio: Ironclad, 2002.

Wright, William Aldis, ed. *English Works of Roger Ascham*. Cambridge: University Press, 1904.

ARTICLES

Austerman, Wayne B. "Von Borcke's Volcanic—or Did Heros Have a Henry?" *Dixie Gun Works Blackpowder Annual*, 2003.

——. "Bedford Forrest's Booty Spencers." *Dixie Gun Works Blackpowder Annual*, 2004.

Batten, Robert. "L.L.'s Henry Repeating Rifle." *San Diego Civil War Round Table Skirmish Line*, May 19, 2004.

Beck, Tony. "An Introduction to Civil War Breechloaders." *Dixie Gun Works Blackpowder Annual*, 1993.

Bell, Bob. "The Most Important Shot Ever Fired?" *Gun Digest*, 1998.

Bilby, Joseph G. "Lava Bed War: The U.S. Army and the Modocs." *Dixie Gun Works Blackpowder Annual*, 1993.

——. "The Battle of Hubbardton." *Dixie Gun Works Blackpowder Annual*, 1998.

——. "Aladdin's on the Hudson: The Story of Bannerman's." *Dixie Gun Works Blackpowder Annual*, 2002.

——. "A History of Firearms from Rock to Wheel Lock." *Dixie Gun Works Blackpowder Annual*, 2003.

——. "A Soldier of Military Distinction and Honor: The Story of Pattie Ferguson and His Rifle." *Dixie Gun Works Blackpowder Annual*, 2004.

Blancard, Stephen F. "Christopher Spencer's Horizontal Shot Tower." *Black Powder Report*, September 1985.

Boltz, Martha. "Train of Wounded Troops Pulled by Black Soldiers: The Battle of Olustee." *Washington Times*, February 3, 2001.

"Breech Loading Rifles." *Scientific American*, New Series, 10, no. 11, March 12, 1864.

Bruns, Dennis. "Shooting the Hall Breechloader." *Gun Digest*, 1997.

Caranta, Raymond. "Louis Nicolas Auguste Flobert; His Rimfire Rifles and Cartridges." *Gun Digest*, 1974.

Carlile, Richard. "The 1st District of Columbia Cavalry." *Military Images Magazine*, September-October 1986.

"Colt's Revolving Rifle." *Military Gazette*, 3, no. 18, September 15, 1860.

Cory, Major Noel. "The Miquelet Lock." *Gun Digest*, 1985.

Dieckmann, Edward A., Sr. "Stone Age Guided Missiles." *Gun Digest*, 1966.

Fagan, Dan P. "The Dimick Rifles of the 66th Illinois Infantry." *Gun Report*, March 1989.

"Firearms and Rifle Breechloaders." *Scientific American*, 4, no. 4, New Series, January 26, 1861.

Freytag, Gustav. "The Citizen and His Shooting Festivals." *Gun Collector*, 37 [n.d.].

Hall, Thomas E. "Forerunners of the First Winchester--Part 1." *Gun Digest*, 1957.

——. "Forerunners of the First Winchester--Part 2." *Gun Digest*, 1958.

——. "Forerunners of the First Winchester--Part 3." *Gun Digest*, 1959.

Harris, P. Valentine. "The Decline of the Longbow." *Journal of the Society of Archer-Antiquaries*, 19, 1976.

Houze, Herbert C. "Schuyler, Hartley & Graham's Military Sales to France During the Franco Prussian War, 1870-1871." *Gun Report*, June 1993.

Hyatt, Robert M. "Crossbows." *Gun Digest*, 1965.

"La Guerre Franco-Allemande, 1870-1871." *Gazette des Armes Magazine*, 2001, Hors Série No. 11.

Luvaas, Jay. "Bentonville--Johnston's Last Stand." *North Carolina Historical Review*, 33, no. 3, July 1956.

"Old Apache Chief Geronimo Is Dead." *New York Times*, February 18, 1909.

Patton, J. T. "Personal Recollections of Four Years in Dixie." War Paper 20, Michigan

Commandery, MOLLUS, 1892.

Roberts, John B. "The Sam Colt of Denmark." *Guns*, May 1989.

Spangenberger, Phil. "Uberti, King of the Replicas." *Dixie Gun Works Blackpowder Annual*, 1989.

Sword, Wiley. "Those Damned Michigan Spencers: Colonel Copeland's 5th Michigan Cavalry and Their Spencer Rifles." *Man at Arms*, 19, no. 5, October 1997.

Warren, Stan. "The Battle of Plevna." *Dixie Gun Works Annual*, 2002.

Weller, Jac. "Breechloaders in the Revolution." *Gun Digest*, 1959.

Wilder, John T. "The Battle of Hoover's Gap." Ohio MOLLUS Sketches of War History, Vol. 6.

Wilson, R. L. "Genesis of the Winchester." *American Rifleman*, June 1991.

Wiltsey, Norman B. "Spencer's Great 7-Shooter." *Gun Digest*, 1962.

MANUSCRIPTS, PRIMARY AND SECONDARY
William Adams Collection

Vincent Witcher to "Hon. Jno. Daniels, January 26, 1906 (copy of typescript).

Vincent Witcher to General Lunsford Lomax, August 30, 1908, Vincent Witcher to "My Dear Gen." April 6, 1886 (copy of typescript).

John Kuhl collection

Oscar Westlake Papers

National Archives of France

Samuel Pauly Brevet d'Invention, 1812

Houllier Brevet d'Invention, 1844

New Jersey Historical Society

Josiah Brown, "Record of My Experience During the Civil War from October, 1, 1861 to July, 1865." Original typescript.

Fred L. Ray, "Shock Troops of the Confederacy: The Sharpshooter Battalions of the Army of Northern Virginia," unpublished manuscript.

United States Army Military History Institute, Carlisle, Pa.

Edmund Halsey Diary

Windsor (Conn.) Historical Society

Christopher M. Spencer Papers.

Wisconsin Historical Society, Madison, Wisc.

William Phillips letter collection, Mss. #142S

PERIODICALS
Army and Navy Journal
Boston Herald
Military Gazette
National Tribune
New York Times
Scientific American
Trenton (N.J.) Gazette and Republican

INTERNET SOURCES
Adams, Bill. "Weapons of the 34th," http://www.34thvacav.org/weapons.html

Olustee Battle Website, http://extlab1.entnem.ufl.edu/olustee/index.html

Perkins, Robert, "Atlatl Bob," Precision Atlatl and Dart Systems, BPS Engineering, http://www.atlatl.com

INDEX

ACKNOWLEDGMENTS

I WOULD LIKE TO THANK SEVERAL PEOPLE WHO I HAVE NEVER MET personally, but whose work made this book possible. Herbert G. Houze, Roy Marcot, and Wiley Sword did all the primary source research in company and archival records on the Henry and Spencer, making it possible for me to synthesize their work to support my own. Their books, cited in the notes and bibliography, are essential to a complete understanding of the technical and business history surrounding both rifles and their inventors and manufacturers, and should be on the shelf of every historian, collector, and general reader with an interest in the subject. Likewise, I would like to thank Louis A. Garavaglia and Charles G. Worman, whose pioneering work on firearms on the American frontier established a "holistic" school of firearms history, elevating it from an antiquarian exercise to a scholarly discipline.

A number of other people contributed directly to the completion of this work and made it a better book. Brent Nosworthy supplied valuable primary source material and a whole new perspective on Civil War tactics and their relationship to military thought in the rest of the world. Bill Adams and Tony Beck read chapter drafts, corrected me when I was wrong, and corroborated me when I was right. I am especially grateful to Bill for sharing his extensive sources on the Thirty-fourth Virginia Cavalry battalion. Cavalry scholar Eric Wittenberg also supplied important Gettysburg material, and he and Bill both offered helpful advice on the Gettysburg chapter in particular. Sam Elliott, Army of Tennessee biographer par excellence, provided guidance and corrections on the western theater of operations as well as on-the-ground reconnaissance and photography of crucial terrain.

My "French Connections" provided invaluable material as well. Dr. Helen D. Lepine of Neuilly Plaisance arranged a research trip to the French military Archives at Vincennes and dug up nineteenth-century French firearms patents in the National Archives in Paris. She and her husband Phillipe generously provided room and board for myself and my family during a research trip to Paris, and Dr. Lepine, in conjunction with Dr. Jan Hamier of Montreal, translated the Soushanany manuscript. Alex Scheer of Courbevoie shared his knowledge of and enthusiasm for the study of nineteenth-century American and French arms and history, as well as translations and summaries of several French scholarly sources.

I would also like to thank all the members of the email Civil War Discussion Group and the Forlorn Hope email discussion group and others for support and research leads. Bob Batten, Wayne Bengston, Martha Boltz, Kay Brockman, Earl J. Coates, Paul J. Davies, Bob Huddleston, J. David Petruzzi, Teej Smith, Paul Speck, Tom Teagle, Dave Tooley, Jeff Williams, and Lee White provided valuable tips and encouragement, and their responses to various portions of the manuscript let me know I was on the right track. Thanks, too, to John W. Kuhl for allowing his collection to be part of this book, John Hubbard for his excellent photographs, and Rob Kassab of RareWinchesters.com, Stephan Juan of AntiqueFirearms.com, and the Sharpsburg Arsenal for providing images from their collections.

Last, but by no means least, I'd like to thank my publisher Bruce Franklin for granting me a deadline extension after knee surgery put a crimp in my writing schedule, and my wife Patricia, daughters Kate and Meg, son John and future son-in-law Second Lieutenant Jarrett Feldman, U.S. Army, for their support and for putting up with my monopoly of the computer at all hours of the day and night.